*Everyman, I will go with thee,*
*and be thy guide*

## THE EVERYMAN
### LIBRARY

*The Everyman Library was founded by J. M. Dent
in 1906. He chose the name Everyman because he wanted
to make available the best books ever written in every
field to the greatest number of people at the cheapest
possible price. He began with Boswell's* Life of Johnson;
*his one thousandth title was Aristotle's* Metaphysics,
*by which time sales exceeded forty million.*

*Today Everyman paperbacks remain true to
J. M. Dent's aims and high standards, with a wide range
of titles at affordable prices in editions which address
the needs of today's readers. Each new text is reset to give
a clear, elegant page and to incorporate the latest thinking
and scholarship. Each book carries the pilgrim logo,
the character in* Everyman, *a medieval mystery play,
a proud link between Everyman
past and present.*

# Samuel Taylor Coleridge

# POEMS

*Edited by*
**JOHN BEER**
*Peterhouse, Cambridge*

**EVERYMAN**
J. M. DENT · LONDON
CHARLES E. TUTTLE
VERMONT

Selection and textual editing © J. M. Dent 1993
Introduction © David Campbell Publishers Ltd

First included in Everyman's Library 1963
Reprinted, with new appendices, 1986
Last reprinted 1990
Reissued 1991
This new edition first published by J. M. Dent in an Everyman
paperback 1993

All rights reserved

Typeset at The Spartan Press Ltd,
Lymington, Hants
Printed in Great Britain by
The Guernsey Press Co. Ltd,
Guernsey, C.I.
for
J. M. Dent
Orion Publishing Group
Orion House
5 Upper St Martin's Lane, London WC2H 9EA
and
Charles E. Tuttle Co., Inc.
28 South Main Street, Rutland, Vermont
05701, USA

This book if bound as a paperback is subject to the condition
that it may not be issued on loan or otherwise except in its
original binding.

British Library Cataloguing in Publication Data is available
upon request.

ISBN 0 460 87316 4

# CONTENTS

# NOTE ON THE AUTHOR AND EDITOR

Samuel Taylor Coleridge was born on 21 October 1772 at Ottery St Mary in Devon. After being educated at Christ's Hospital in London and Jesus College, Cambridge, he worked as an independent writer, speaker and thinker, producing his first collection of poems in 1796 and enlarging it in 1797. Close collaboration with Wordsworth in north Somerset resulted in joint production of the volume *Lyrical Ballads* in 1798 and stimulated his poetic powers more generally: this period saw poems as diverse as *Frost at Midnight*, *Kubla Khan* and the unfinished *Christabel*. After wintering in Germany in 1798-9 he settled, like Wordsworth, in the Lake District, where he wrote *Dejection: An Ode* (1802), a fruit of his hopeless love for Wordsworth's sister-in-law Sara Hutchinson and the growing unhappiness of his marriage. The poem also signalled fears about the continuance of his creativity, but although he now turned increasingly to prose, writing on politics (*Essays on his Own Times* and *Lay Sermons*), criticism (Lectures on Shakespeare and *Biographia Literaria* (1817)), and religion (*Aids to Reflection* (1825) and *On the Constitution of the Church and State* (1829)), and planning a great new philosophical work, poetry continued to flow. After going to live with the Gillmans at Highgate in 1816, he published *Sibylline Leaves* (1817)), containing revisions of his earlier poems and new ones such as 'Limbo' and 'Ne Plus Ultra'. Further such collections followed and new poems (some looking back wistfully to his early life) continued to appear in most years until his death on 25 July 1834.

John Beer's work on Coleridge includes two books, *Coleridge the Visionary* and *Coleridge's Poetic Intelligence*, the editing of a collection of bicentenary essays, *Coleridge's Variety*, and his edition of *Aids to Reflection* for the *Collected Coleridge*. He is also general editor of the series *Coleridge's Writings* and has written on a variety of other authors, including books on Blake, Wordsworth and E. M. Forster. He is Professor of English Literature in the University of Cambridge.

# CHRONOLOGY OF COLERIDGE'S LIFE

---

| Year | Age | Life |
|------|-----|------|
| 1770 | | |
| 1771 | | |
| 1772 | | Born 21 October at Ottery St Mary, Devonshire, to the Revd John and Ann (Bowden) Coleridge, youngest of their ten children |
| 1774 | | |
| 1775 | | |
| 1776 | 4 | |
| 1778 | 6 | Attends Ottery Grammar School |
| 1779 | | |
| 1780 | | |
| 1781 | 9 | Death (6 October) of Coleridge's father |
| 1782 | 10 | Attends Christ's Hospital, London (September, to 1791); to meet Charles Lamb |
| 1783 | 11 | |
| 1784 | 12 | |
| 1785 | 13 | |
| 1787 | 15 | |
| 1788 | 16 | Elected Grecian (early summer); meets Evans family |

# CHRONOLOGY OF HIS TIMES

| Year | Literary Context | Historical Events |
|------|------------------|-------------------|
| 1770 | Wordsworth born | |
| 1771 | Scott born | |
| 1772 | | |
| 1774 | Southey born | Priestley discovers oxygen |
| 1775 | Lamb born | |
| 1776 | Adam Smith, *Wealth of Nations* Gibbon, *Decline and Fall* (to 1788) | US Declaration of Independence (4 July) |
| 1778 | Hazlitt born Rousseau and Voltaire die | |
| 1779 | Johnson, *Lives of the Poets* (to 1781) | |
| 1780 | | The Gordon Riots |
| 1781 | Lessing dies Kant, *Critik der reinen Vernunft* Schiller, *Die Räuber* Rousseau, *Confessions* (to 1788) | |
| 1782 | | |
| 1783 | Blake, *Poetical Sketches* | Treaty of Versailles. Pitt's first ministry |
| 1784 | Samuel Johnson dies | |
| 1785 | De Quincey born Cowper, *The Task* and *John Gilpin* | |
| 1787 | Thomas Taylor, *Concerning the Beautiful* (Plotinus) | |
| 1788 | Byron born Crowe, *Lewesdon Hill* | |

| Year | Age | Life |
|------|-----|------|
| 1789 | 17 | |
| 1790 | 18 | |
| 1791 | 19 | Jesus College, Cambridge (October), Exhibitioner, Sizar, Rustat Scholar; to meet W. Frend, S. Butler, Porson, C. Wordsworth, Wrangham |
| 1792 | 20 | Wins Browne medal with Greek Sapphic *Ode on the Slave Trade* |
| 1793 | 21 | Attends Cambridge trial of William Frend. Enlists in 15th Light Dragoons as Silas Tomkyn Comberbache (2 December) |
| 1794 | 22 | Meets Robert Southey in Oxford and plans pantisocracy; Welsh tour. *Religious Musings* begun (24 December) |
| 1795 | 23 | Political Lectures begin. Marriage (4 October) to Sara Fricker |
| 1796 | 24 | Meets Erasmus Darwin, Joseph Wright (painter). *The Watchman* and *Poems on Various Subjects*. Hartley Coleridge born; move to Stowey |

| Year | Literary Context | Historical Events |
|------|------------------|-------------------|
| 1789 | Blake, *Songs of Innocence* <br> Erasmus Darwin, *The Botanic Garden* (to 1792) | Fall of Bastille (14 July) <br> French Revolution |
| 1790 | Burke, *Reflections on the Revolution in France* | |
| 1791 | Paine, *Rights of Man* <br> Boswell, *Life of Johnson* | Anti-Jacobin riots at Birmingham (July); Priestley's house attacked |
| 1792 | Rogers, *Pleasures of Memory* <br> Wollstonecraft, *Rights of Woman* | |
| 1793 | Godwin, *Political Justice* <br> Wordsworth, *An Evening Walk* and *Descriptive Sketches* | Louis XVI executed (January); France declares war on England and Holland (February); Reign of Terror begins (June); Marie Antoinette executed (October) |
| 1794 | Paine, *Age of Reason* <br> Paley, *Evidences of Christianity* <br> Radcliffe, *Mysteries of Udolpho* <br> Blake, *Songs of Experience, Europe, Book of Urizen* <br> E. Darwin, *Zoonomia* (to 1796) | Robespierre executed (July); end of Terror. State Trials (October–December): Hardy, Tooke and Thelwall acquitted |
| 1795 | Keats born (31 October) <br> Carlyle born (4 December) <br> M. G. Lewis, *Ambrosio, or the Monk* <br> Goethe, *Wilhelm Meister* | |
| 1796 | Robert Burns dies (July) <br> Mary Lamb's violent illness (September) | Threats of invasion of England. Jenner performs first smallpox vaccination |

| Year | Age | Life |
|------|-----|------|
| 1797 | 25 | At Racedown (June). The Wordsworths to Alfoxden House. *Poems*, (July–September). *Kubla Khan* composed ('Fall of the year'). Walk with Wordsworths to Lynton (13–16 November); *Ancient Mariner* begun. Poetry in *Morning Post* (December), including *Visions of the Maid of Orleans* |
| 1798 | 26 | Wedgwood £150 annuity accepted. *Frost at Midnight* (February). *The Recantation* (later *France: An Ode*; March); *Fears in Solitude*. *Lyrical Ballads* published (September); the Wordsworths, Chester and Coleridge to Hamburg (19 September) |
| 1799 | 27 | Death of Berkeley Coleridge (February); news reaches Coleridge *c.* 6 April. Coleridge to University of Göttingen (12 February). Ascent of Brocken (May). Meets Sara Hutchinson at Sockburn (26 October) |
| 1800 | 28 | *Morning Post* reporter and leader-writer (January–6 April); translating *Wallenstein* at Lamb's |
| 1801 | 29 | *Lyrical Ballads* (1800) published (January); prolonged illnesses. |
| 1802 | 30 | First version (4 April) of *Dejection* as '*A Letter to* — [Sara Hutchinson]'. *Dejection* ode in *Morning Post* (4 October). Sara Coleridge born. |
| 1803 | 31 | Scottish tour with Wordsworths |
| 1804 | 32 | Under-secretary (July) to Alexander Ball, British High Commissioner at Malta. |
| 1805 | 33 | Appointed Acting Public Secretary in Malta |
| 1806 | 34 | In Rome (January), meets W. van Humboldt, L. Tieck and Washington Allston. Lands in England (17 August) |
| 1807 | 35 | Hears Wordsworth read *Prelude*, writes *To W. Wordsworth* (late January) |

| Year | Literary Context | Historical Events |
|---|---|---|
| 1797 | *Anti-Jacobin, or Weekly Examiner* begins (20 November) Radcliffe, *The Italian* | Pitt proposes to finance the war against France by increasing taxes. Mutinies in British navy (April–June). Burke dies |
| 1798 | Lloyd, *Edmund Oliver* Malthus, *Essay on the Principles of Population* | Swiss cantons suppressed (spring). Bonaparte invades Egypt (July); Battle of the Nile (1–2 August) |
| 1799 | Schiller, *Piccolomini* and *Wallensteins Tod* published | Bonaparte first consul under new constitution (9 November). Royal Institution founded |
| 1800 | | Fox returns to Parliament (February); Bill for Union passed (February) |
| 1801 | | Battle of Copenhagen (2 April); Austria makes peace; French gains in Germany |
| 1802 | Paley, *Natural Theology* Scott, *Minstrelsy of the Scottish Border* begun | Peace of Amiens |
| 1803 | Malthus, *Essay on . . . Population* (2nd edn) Priestley dies (6 February) | War declared against France |
| 1804 | | Bonaparte becomes emperor (May) |
| 1805 | T. Wedgwood dies (10 July) Scott, *Lay of the Last Minstrel* (May) | Bonaparte becomes king of Italy; Bonaparte's victory at Ulm (October); Trafalgar and Austerlitz |
| 1806 | | Pitt dies (January); 'Ministry of All the Talents' |
| 1807 | Crabbe, *The Parish Register* Byron, *Hours of Idleness* | Bonaparte attacks Russia (February). Abolition of slave trade. Peninsular War begins |

| Year | Age | Life |
|------|-----|------|
| 1808 | 36 | Lectures at Royal Institution on Poetry and Principles of Taste |
| 1809 | 37 | *The Friend* (1 June–15 March 1810) |
| 1810 | 38 | Sara Hutchinson leaves Grasmere for Wales (March). *The Friend* last number. Montagu precipitates Wordsworth-Coleridge quarrel |
| 1811 | 39 | Lectures (18 November–27 January 1812) on Shakespeare and Milton at Scot's Corporation Hall, attended by Collier, Byron, Rogers, Crabb Robinson |
| 1812 | 40 | Lamb and Crabb Robinson patch quarrel with Wordsworth (May). Belles Lettres lectures in Surrey Institution (3 November–26 January 1813). Lectures in Bristol. Illness and spiritual crisis at Bath and Bristol (winter) |
| 1813 | 41 | |
| 1814 | 42 | *Remorse* performed in Bristol (1 August). Moves with Morgans to Calne, Wiltshire |
| 1815 | 43 | Printing (August–September) of *Sibylline Leaves* begins at Bristol |
| 1816 | 44 | Accepted (15 April) as patient and house-mate by James Gillman, Surgeon, Highgate. *Christabel, Kubla Khan* and *The Pains of Sleep* (25 May). *Statesman's Manual* published |
| 1817 | 45 | Second *Lay Sermon, Biographia Literaria, Sibylline Leaves, Zapolya* |

| Year | Literary Context | Historical Events |
|------|------------------|-------------------|
| 1808 | John and Leigh Hunt begin *Examiner* <br> Goethe, *Faust*, Part I | Convention of Cintra (30 August); Bonaparte invades Spain (December) |
| 1809 | Byron, *English Bards and Scotch Reviewers* (9 March) <br> Wordsworth, *Convention of Cintra* pamphlet | Bonaparte captures Vienna |
| 1810 | Scott, *Lady of the Lake* <br> Southey, *Curse of Kehama* <br> Crabbe, *The Borough* | George III generally recognized as insane |
| 1811 | Shelley, *Necessity of Atheism* <br> Jane Austen, *Sense and Sensibility* | Prince of Wales made regent. Luddite uprisings begin |
| 1812 | Coombe, *Tour of Dr Syntax in Search of the Picturesque* <br> Byron, *Childe Harold*, Cantos I and II | Spencer Perceval assassinated. Bonaparte enters Russia; retreat from Moscow |
| 1813 | Jane Austen, *Pride and Prejudice* <br> Shelley, *Queen Mab* | Wellington enters France |
| 1814 | Wordsworth, *Excursion* <br> Scott, *Waverley* <br> Cary's *Dante* completed | Bonaparte abdicates, exiled to Elba; restoration of the Bourbons |
| 1815 | Wordsworth, *Poems* of 1815; *The White Doe of Rylestone* | Bonaparte escapes from Elba; the Hundred Days (March–June); Waterloo (18 June) |
| 1816 | Shelley, *Alastor and Other Poems* <br> Peacock, *Headlong Hall* | Byron's departure from England (24 April). Spa Fields riot (2 December) |
| 1817 | *Blackwood's Magazine* founded (April) <br> 'Immortal evening' (28 December) at Haydon's <br> Keats, *Poems* | Elgin Marbles purchased for British Museum |

| Year | Age | Life |
|------|-----|------|
| 1818 | 46 | 'Treatise on Method' (January) published in *Encyclopaedia Metropolitana*. *The Friend*, 3-vol. edition. Lectures: on History of Philosophy, on Shakespeare, on Milton, Dante, Spenser, Cervantes |
| 1819 | 47 | Meets Keats (11 April) in Millfield Lane; Hartley Coleridge elected Probationary Fellow of Oriel (14) |
| 1820 | 48 | Renewed plans (March) for Great Work; Hartley Coleridge refused renewal of fellowship at Oriel |
| 1821 | 49 | |
| 1822 | 50 | First record (29 December) of table talk made by H. N. Coleridge |
| 1823 | 51 | Gillmans move to 3 The Grove; Coleridge's attic study |
| 1824 | 52 | Carlyle calls at Highgate |
| 1825 | 53 | 'On the *Prometheus* of Aeschylus' delivered before Royal Society of Literature (18 May). *Aids to Reflection* published |
| 1827 | 55 | Derwent Coleridge marries Mary Pridham |
| 1828 | 56 | Netherlands and Rhine Tour with Dora and William Wordsworth. *Poetical Works*, 3 vols. (June–July). |
| 1829 | 57 | *Poetical Works*, 2nd edn (May); Sara Coleridge marries her cousin H. N. Coleridge (3 September); *On the Constitution of the Church and State* |

| Year | Literary Context | Historical Events |
|---|---|---|
| 1818 | Keats, *Endymion*<br>Hazlitt, *Lectures on the English Poets*<br>Peacock, *Nightmare Abbey*<br>Mary Shelley, *Frankenstein* | |
| 1819 | Wordsworth, *Peter Bell* and *The Waggoner*<br>Byron, *Don Juan* (to 1824)<br>Shelley, *Masque of Anarchy* | Peterloo massacre (16 August) |
| 1820 | Keats, *Lamia . . . and Other Poems*<br>Lamb, *Essays of Elia* in *London Magazine*<br>Shelley, *Prometheus Unbound* etc. | George III dies |
| 1821 | Keats dies (23 February) in Rome<br>De Quincey, *Confessions of an Opium Eater*<br>Southey, *A Vision of Judgment* | |
| 1822 | Shelley dies (8 July)<br>Byron, *The Vision of Judgment*<br>Shelley, *Hellas* | Congress of Verona |
| 1823 | Hazlitt, *Liber Amoris* | War between France and Spain |
| 1824 | Landor, *Imaginary Conversations* | Byron dies (19 April) aiding Greek Independence |
| 1825 | Hazlitt, *The Spirit of the Age* | Stockton to Darlington railway opened |
| 1827 | Blake dies | |
| 1828 | Hazlitt, *Life of Napoleon* (to 1830) | |
| 1829 | Sir Humphry Davy dies (29 May) | Catholic Relief Bill passed |

| Year | Age | Life |
|------|-----|------|
| 1830 | 58 | *The Devil's Walk* reissued as by Coleridge and Southey |
| 1832 | 60 | |
| 1833 | 61 | At Cambridge (24–9 June) for meetings of British Association; Emerson calls (5 August) |
| 1834 | | *Poetical Works*, 3rd edn (March–August). Dies at Highgate, 25 July |

| Year | Literary Context | Historical Events |
|------|------------------|-------------------|
| 1830 | Lyell, *Principles of Geology*<br>Tennyson, *Poems, chiefly Lyrical*<br>Hazlitt dies (18 September) | Death of George IV |
| 1832 | Crabbe dies (3 February)<br>Goethe dies (22 March)<br>Bentham dies (6 June)<br>Scott dies (21 September) | Reform Bill becomes law |
| 1833 | Carlyle, *Sartor Resartus*<br>Lamb, *Last Essays of Elia*<br>Browning, *Pauline* | Keble's sermon (14 July);<br>'Hadleigh Conference'<br>(25–9 July) at H. J. Rose's<br>Rectory; Oxford Movement<br>initiated |
| 1834 | Lamb dies (27 December) | New Poor Law (February)<br>Tolpuddle Martyrs |

# INTRODUCTION

## Two Major Themes

With the growth of scientific attitudes in the seventeenth and eighteenth centuries, intelligent poets came slowly to realize that their status was being eroded. In ancient times a poet might have thought of himself simply as his society's bardic representative, giving back to his fellows a heightened version of their own beliefs and aspirations, an 'ancestral voice' to warn them of dangers, and prophesy concerning right courses of action. The development of society towards a community based upon technological achievement offered less scope for such a rôle. In a society where mathematical thinking was the dominant intellectual mode the poet would find their public utterance circumscribed, their task being more often to express private disquiets and an individual vision.

It was not surprising, then, if they looked for ways of enhancing their vocation. During the eighteenth century, for example, when rational modes were particularly dominant, they came to concern themselves with the theme of nature, and particularly with those aspects of nature which transcended or escaped the ordered patternings of mathematical form. Just as contemporary gardeners had come to appreciate that the geometrically shaped flower-bed and the straight path were not always the best model for a garden, and that a particular locality might have its own 'genius of place', which a knowing gardener could understand and propitiate, so poets also turned to the wayward side of nature for inspiration. In addition, they became interested in certain aspects of human behaviour which eluded control by the rational powers — as, for example, when some spontaneous power within seemed to rise up and initiate new creative action. The evidence of such powers among mankind generally seemed to give a wider significance to old concepts such as those of 'inspiration' and 'genius'. Similar interests encouraged the growth of what is sometimes called the 'cult of sensibility'.

There were occasions, it seemed, when the strictly prudential behaviour to which rational appraisal of a particular situation might direct a human being was abandoned in favour of a free flow of tenderness and compassion, springing directly from the heart – and the possibility of this could be regarded as one of humanity's greatest assets, guarding it against the sterile individualism which might otherwise throttle social life.

As a young man of wide-ranging intelligence, growing up in a London where various strands of intellectual speculation crossed and recrossed, Coleridge was naturally attracted by these elements in the sub-culture of his day, some of which fuelled his already kindled enthusiasm for romantic literature. From the time when, as a child, he had pored with almost morbid fascination over *The Arabian Nights*, he had developed an omnivorous taste for romances of all kinds. This taste continued: indeed, phrases and incidents from the romances sometimes start up with astonishing directness in his later work. When, for example, we open James Ridley's *Tales of the Genii* to find there the tale of the Merchant Abudah, who was shown a vision of a dome, made entirely of precious stones and metals, which seemed to cover a whole plain and reach to the clouds, and who voyaged along a meandering river by woods of spices, we begin to recognize the landscape of *Kubla Khan* – a recognition which is supported by the merchant's subsequent adventure, in which, after the temple collapses around him, falling in 'huge fragments', he is forced to crawl through the 'dungeon of lust', but finally comes out on a high mountain, where to his surprise ten thousand voices acclaim him emperor. Another adventure, in which two lovers, finding themselves in a sensuously beautiful landscape, seek to embrace one another only to find themselves separated by a dismal chasm, while warlike music floats up from a dark abyss, again suggests that the corresponding elements in Coleridge's poem are rooted deep in recollected reading of Eastern romance.

The taste that had fed on romances led Coleridge to travel-books of all kinds, from which he culled raw materials for many of the vivid details in *The Ancient Mariner*; it also continued to haunt him throughout his life. When he wrote *The Garden of Boccaccio* in 1828, he was still dwelling on the extraordinary power of a romance to induce in the reader a willing suspension of disbelief and an entry into its own world.

Coleridge was also sufficiently a child of his time to be attracted by the cult of 'sensibility' which had been initiated by Rousseau, Sterne and others. In his *Letter to Sara Hutchinson* he was to describe how, trapped in the severe surroundings of a city school, he had been attracted by the great appearances of the sky, and by the ways in which certain of these seemed to foster links of sympathy in the human beings that saw them. The resemblance of the evening star to the lovelight in a girl's eye, for example, had seized on him as the emblem of a love which he himself might one day enjoy.

It may be that these enthusiasms would not have gained so tenacious a hold on Coleridge's mind had it not been for his discovery, whilst still at school, of Boehme's *Aurora*, a strange and attractive work of German mysticism over which, he later said, he 'conjured'. Boehme's work gave new depth to a taste for romance and the cultivation of sensibility by its assertion that there existed in the universe a threefold correspondence between nature, the human heart and the divine. In Boehme's work the human heart is akin to God. Sometimes it is pictured as a sun, sometimes as a fountain, sometimes as both at the same time, but the import is always the same – that if we study the points of correspondence between the human heart and certain elements in nature, we shall find there a key to the nature of God himself:

> When the flash is caught in the fountain of the Heart, then the Holy Ghost riseth up in the seven qualifying or fountain spirits, into the Brain like the Daybreak, Dawning of the Day, or Morning Redness . . .

The Fall of Man, likewise, is a fall from enlightenment, which has deprived man of a paradise that formerly existed within him. Boehme also pictures this as the fall from a nature which was sensuously delightful. To express his idea he uses the image of the light from a wax candle or of an air which is a 'lovely, pleasant, still breath or voice, blowing or moving . . . ' or of a water which he can liken only to 'the sap or *juice* in an apple, but very bright and lightsome, like heaven, which is the spirit of all powers'. In the same way he likens the angels to 'little children who walk in the field in *May* among the *flowers*, and pluck them, and make dainty garlands and posies, carrying them in their hands rejoicing . . . '

Some of these images, particularly those of the sun and the fountain, are also to be found in the writings of the Neoplatonist philosophers; indeed it might be said that Coleridge read Boehme in the light of the romances and then read the Neoplatonist philosophers in the light of Boehme. What this meant in practical terms for his poetry was the growth of a language and imagery to express that confluence of genius and sensibility which Keats was to call 'the heart's imagination'. When he later writes with a particular delight of springs, or candle-flames, or running streams, or light breezes, we may trace echoes from images of nature discovered – and conjured over – long before. Charles Lamb has described how Coleridge would expound the teachings of the Neoplatonists at school, and a contemporary of his at university recorded how he came in one evening and recited passages from Maximus Tyrius and from William Lisle Bowles, a contemporary poet of sensibility.

At the same time, Coleridge could not be alive in the 1790s without an awareness of pressing contemporary issues. The French Revolution had set off a wave of political excitement in England, encouraging hopes that a new and juster society was about to emerge. The violence of subsequent events in France, on the other hand, had caused such hopes to be tempered by a cautionary note, an awareness of the dangers involved in devising any movement for reform which did not include a purification of motives and aspirations on the part of the individuals involved. The scheme of Pantisocracy, which was based on the idea that improvements in society must begin with groups of individuals who would start by trying 'the experiment of human perfectibility' within their own small circle, was an attempt by Coleridge and Southey to meet such objections. The scheme did not materialize, but Coleridge continued to reflect on the issues involved in poems such as *Religious Musings* and *Ode to the Departing Year*.

If Coleridge was drawn to write poems of political prophecy, however, he was also aware that the expression even of moderately radical opinions was, in the political climate of the time, a hazardous proceeding, laying him open to penalties which (particularly after his marriage in 1795) he could not afford to ignore. The comparatively sheltered position of England created an ambiguous environment for young men of his generation, moreover. On the one hand, portentous happenings on the other side of the Channel called for desperate remedies and new modes of thinking; on the other, English middle-class life remained little changed, so that there was considerable inducement for a young man to relax and enjoy the elegancies of contemporary civilization. The tug between the two modes sometimes resulted in the cultivation of a kind of elegant bombast, or comfortable melodrama, from which Coleridge's own poetry was not altogether immune. The disciples of Godwin, trying to pursue honesty in thought and simplicity in living, offered a middle way, but one which was not rich in possibilities for cultural development.

Factors such as these encouraged Coleridge's already existing tendency to explore and concentrate on the intellectual and moral issues underlying all political questions; in some poetry of the time, for example (as in certain passages of *The Destiny of Nations*), he explored scientific and philosophical themes directly. Considering the difficulties involved, these attempts were often surprisingly successful; the most effective of his attempts, so far as the general reader is concerned, is *The Eolian Harp*, where he managed to touch in the outlines of a philosophical theory with a lightness of imagery that allowed it to harmonize with the sensuous natural description of the opening lines.

Coleridge's growing tendency to write of society not in political but in intellectual and emotional terms led him into another form of experimentation (also foreshadowed in *The Eolian Harp*): the informal poem, usually addressed to a single person, in which some particular line of intimate thought and imagery, often involving descriptions of nature, is pursued. Such poems could express, more easily than poems addressed to the general public, his sense of possible sympathetic links between nature and the human heart. In an early example, *To a Young Friend on his proposing to domesticate with the author*, the stiffness of the title is reflected in a certain stiltedness of expression throughout, the two friends being pictured returning from a walk to receive from Mrs Coleridge (with elegant eighteenth-century symmetry) '*this* the Husband's, *that* the Brother's kiss'. The whole walk is then turned into an allegory of their friendship, culminating in the discovery of a place where

> haply, bason'd in some unsunn'd cleft,
> A beauteous spring, the rock's collected tears,
> Sleeps shelter'd there, scarce wrinkled by the gale.

This appeal to the sensibility of the heart is followed by a comparison of their relationship to that of 'neighbouring fountains' which 'image each the whole'.

Although not very successful the poem is an interesting early attempt at the *genre*. The 'heart-lore' which is handled a little awkwardly there is developed more subtly in subsequent poems: indeed, the very appearance in them of the word 'heart' (normally passed over by modern readers as a meaningless cliché) always repays close attention, as marking a moment of particular engagement. Coleridge's interest in the human heart extends to its physical workings – a fact which helps to develop the form of his poetry in a curiously apposite manner. Some years ago Albert Gérard pointed out that in many of the conversation poems an effect of 'systole' and 'diastole' could be traced. The poem, in other words, begins by focusing upon some intimate and immediate scene, which is described in careful detail; it then expands to take in some wider landscape – which occasions corresponding reflections upon larger intellectual concerns; and the poem finally returns to the local and particular scene, which is now seen to be newly illuminated by all that has been said in the poem. Such a structure may not only be traced (with variations) in direct 'conversation poems', such as *This Lime Tree Bower* . . . and *Frost at Midnight*, but extends its influence as far as *The Ancient Mariner*, where the Mariner returns to his native village endowed with new knowledge and the Guest, who hears his tale, sees the wedding-feast to which he was going in a different light. This movement of systole and diastole (which is of course the basic motion of the human heart) could take in large emotional movements, such as dilation to sublimity and contraction to pathos, for which Augustan poetry had found little room.

The writing of poetry in this mode corresponded with Coleridge's inclination to turn away from political movements and concentrate instead on the cultivation of relationships with individuals. This in turn prompted criticism and encouragement from certain friends who were themselves poets. In particular, he enjoyed a continuing intimacy with Charles Lamb, who had listened to Coleridge's early speculations and who, like him would have heard James Boyer, headmaster of Christ's Hospital, urging his pupils to prune their epithets and warning them against elaborate apostrophes and 'O thou's' as 'the grimaces of lunacy'.

As early as 1794 the two friends seem to have agreed that the most important requirement of poetry was that it should speak from the heart. In a poem addressed to Lamb that December Coleridge wrote:

> Thus far my sterile Brain hath fram'd the song
> Elaborate & swelling – but the Heart
> Not owns it.

Nearly two years later Lamb took up the same theme:

> Cultivate simplicity, Coleridge, or rather, I should say, banish elaborateness; for simplicity springs spontaneous from the heart, and carries into daylight its own modest buds and genuine, sweet, and clear flowers of expression. I allow no hot-beds in the gardens of Parnassus.

In other letters of the time (as George Whalley has shown) Lamb made many detailed suggestions about, and criticisms of, particular poems, which Coleridge heeded.

It was not until 1797, however, when William and Dorothy Wordsworth came to live near him in North Somerset, that his poetic powers really blossomed. The Wordsworths not only shared his sense of the human heart's importance but linked it with their own experience of nature. Dorothy had an openness of heart and directness of response, both to nature and to her fellow human beings, which were unusual in that decorous age; Wordsworth brought a sensibility which had (unlike Coleridge's) remained close to wild nature throughout his formative years. Together the three friends walked the countryside and studied nature, looking for points where she might be said to display a correspondence with human feeling. The poems composed by the two men, together with Dorothy Wordsworth's journals, make up a composite and complementary document of their aspirations: they were intent, evidently, on exploring the idea that exposure to nature might be one of the most beneficent moral resources available to man. At the same time this brought them necessarily face to face with the intractable problem of evil, a theme which they explored in dramas (Wordsworth's *The Borderers* and Coleridge's *Osorio*) written at the time. So far as Coleridge is concerned, the results of the discussions appear most vividly in *The Ancient Mariner* and *Kubla Khan*, poems which both carry some reference to the daemonic forces that seem to be involved in evil behaviour. Kubla Khan is, it seems, a man of commanding genius who does not understand the full destructive power of his own creative daemon; the Ancient Mariner, by his thoughtless act in shooting an albatross, unleashes equally ambiguous daemonic forces, which continue to wreak vengeance upon him until, in a sudden uprush of the heart's imagination, he glimpses the depth and significance of what he has done; after which they demand – and assist – further penance. Similar forces play a part in *Christabel*: the Geraldine whom Christabel discovers in the forest is evidently an ambiguous daemon of some kind, acting partly for Christabel's good, partly exercising a subtly malign influence.

These were essentially experimental poems, however, and their composition posed further problems. For if one accepts the implied philosophy of *The Ancient Mariner* – that men act evilly because they do not understand what they are doing – it follows that they can be redeemed from their foolish behaviour only by being taught its full implications; but if this must come about through privations such as those suffered by the Mariner, the likelihood of the mass of mankind coming to such knowledge is very small.

Coleridge's recognition of this dilemma was accompanied by a growing crisis in his domestic life. After his return from Germany, which he visited with the Wordsworths in 1798–9, he fell in love with Sara Hutchinson, Wordsworth's sister-in-law, who apparently touched his heart in a way that his own wife had never done. The result, however, was not release, but self-contradiction. According to his own philosophy, the relationship ought to have resulted in a new upsurge of creative power, yet he found himself lapsing more and more frequently into dejection. He succeeded in adding another part to *Christabel*, but the ebullience which had characterized the poetry of 1797–8 could not be regained: at its best the poetry of the time was finely drawn, but analytic rather than resonant. Its quality is well typified in the very lines from the *Letter to Sara Hutchinson* which express his condition:

> There *was* a time when tho' my path was rough,
> The Joy within me dallied with Distress;
> And all Misfortunes were but as the Stuff
> Whence Fancy made me Dreams of Happiness:
> For Hope grew round me, like the climbing Vine,
> And Leaves & Fruitage, not my own, seem'd mine!
> But now Ill Tidings bow me down to earth –
> Nor care I, that they rob me of my Mirth –

> But oh! each Visitation
> Suspends what Nature gave me at my Birth,
> My shaping Spirit of Imagination!

The man who can write lines such as these has clearly not lost all his poetic powers, but he will find it difficult to project whole new poetic structures.

Coleridge's dejection at this time was deepened by the growing success of Wordsworth, now about to enter upon a happy marriage and advancing poetically from strength to strength. While Coleridge tried vainly to complete *Christabel*, Wordsworth was producing a stream of new poetry ('Michael', 'The Brothers', and early books of *The Prelude*), rooted in his deep attachment to the Lake country and its inhabitants. In point of fact, this stream of poetry owed much to the constant stimulus of Coleridge's intelligence and psychological insight, as Wordsworth himself acknowledged, but this knowledge could be no adequate substitute for the production of poetry on his own account.

After the *Letter to Sara Hutchinson* there was a change in Coleridge's poetry, therefore. The straightforward conversational style was not to appear again – or at least not with the same ease. Having described in his poem the various contradictions which he was vainly trying to reconcile, he was now attempting to come to terms with the demands of his situation, and to maintain, side by side, his love for Sara and his domestic responsibilities.

He did not give up poetry altogether but, in a number of poems written during the whole period, he seems to have made up for the loss of his 'shaping spirit' by taking contemporary German poems and using some part of their structure as a starting point for creations of his own – an activity which might charitably be construed as 'priming the pump'. *The Picture*, for example, is based upon a rather sentimental poem by Gessner concerning a lover who retires to gloomy shades as a refuge from unhappy love only to be drawn swiftly back when he sees a girl's footprint. Coleridge's longer narrative, which deals with the relationship between nature and love more subtly, ends with the hero establishing a rôle for himself as guide to the woman he loves – a conclusion which no doubt owes something to Coleridge's own attempts at this time to sublimate his love for Sara Hutchinson. In the same way, *Hymn before Sun-rise*, the original inspiration for which, Coleridge said, came during a climb on Scafell, owes something of its form and detail to a short German poem by

Friederike Brun. From her introductory note and exclamatory stanzas, which repeat the name 'Jehovah', thundered forth from mountain streams, Coleridge takes his own introductory note and pious exclamations, but constructs a larger statement, including a reference to his belief that in the contemplation of the great forms of nature the soul is transported into an excitement and self-forgetfulness by which, through a natural sympathy, it is enabled to acknowledge the divine.

Although Coleridge could fairly claim to have transformed such originals through his development of them, he was sometimes less than ingenuous in acknowledging his German sources. The strain of trying to reconcile varying demands shows here, as in his emotional life; it may also be responsible for an uneasy mixture of poetic styles, which compares unfavourably with the flow of his best conversation poems. Some of the most interesting poems of the time are those, such as *A Sunset*, or *Hexameters*, which are ostensibly composed to experiment with an unusual metre, but which actually incorporate important observations and speculations. In his closest return to the conversational style, the poem *To William Wordsworth*, he expresses regret for lost powers – and in the act of doing so shows once again how much remains.

During these years, a more important shift in Coleridge's preferred modes of expression had already declared itself. His more direct and conversational style was now to be found mainly in his prose writings, particularly in letters and notebooks, where, in spite of their extempore composition, the mastery of rhythm and phrasing acquired over the years came effortlessly into play. In a letter of March 1801, for instance, he bemoans the loss of his powers of poetic creation: 'all sounds of similitude keep at such a distance from each other in my mind, that have I *forgotten* how to make a rhyme.' But the passage in which he goes on to make his lament, if split up into separate irregular lines, becomes a piece which might pass as reasonable modern blank verse:

> I look at the Mountains
> (That visible God Almighty that looks in
> At all my windows)
> I look at the Mountains
> Only for the Curves of their outlines;
> The Stars, as I behold them,
> Form themselves into Triangles –
> And my hands

Are scarred with scratches
From a Cat, whose back I was rubbing in the Dark
In order to see whether the sparks from it
Were refrangible by a Prism.
The Poem is dead in me –
My imagination
(Or rather the Somewhat that had been imaginative)
Lies, like a Cold Snuff
On the circular Rim of a Brass Candle-stick, without even
A stink of Tallow
To remind you that it was
Once
Cloathed and mitred with Flame.

The same facility is displayed in many other writings of the time. In a notebook entry of 1803, for example, one may see how a casual note, scribbled down in the middle of the night, can fall effortlessly into poetic lines and dramatic transitions:

> Now while I have been writing this & gazing between whiles (it is 40 M. past Two) the Break over the road is swallowed up, & the Stars gone, the Break over the House is narrowed into a rude Circle, & on the edge of its circumference one very bright Star – see! already the white mass thinning at its edge *fights* with its Brilliance – see! it has bedimmed it – & now it is gone – & the Moon is gone. The Cock-crowing too has ceased. The Greta sounds on, for ever. But I hear only the Ticking of my Watch, in the Pen-place of my Writing Desk, & the far lower note of the noise of the Fire – perpetual, yet seeming uncertain; it is the low voice of quiet change, of Destruction doing its work by little & little.

*(Notebooks*, I, 1635)

Condemned to transmit the dull pain of a ravaged sensibility, Coleridge is still contriving to turn it into music. And although he may speak of the suspension of his 'shaping spirit', that spirit is somewhere at work here, for the elements, even as they are being faithfully described, may be seen falling into a pattern: first the strange moment of unearthly brilliance in the heavens, backed by the weird voice of an untimely cock-crowing, then the three voices which provide the only subsequent sound – the voice of the Greta, the voice of his watch and the low, quiet voice from the fire-place, mirroring, respectively, the sweeping flow of life, the inexorable flow of time and the peaceful flow of that destructive process which underlies death, all continuing together. Coleridge's mind is one which naturally organizes material in this subtle manner; even the sights and sounds of a darkened room at night become emblems for the main processes that may be detected side by side in all human experience.

It is in the poetry proper that his sense of loss becomes more apparent. Coleridge has now no great unfolding theme to correspond with Wordsworth's sense of nature and man; 'If I die,' he writes in the letter quoted above,

> and the Booksellers will give you any thing for my Life, be sure to say – 'Wordsworth descended on him, like the $\Gamma\nu\tilde{\omega}\theta\iota$ $\sigma\varepsilon\alpha\upsilon\tau\acute{o}\nu$ from Heaven; by shewing to him what true Poetry was, he made him know, that he himself was no Poet.'

> (*Letters* II, 714)

The theme which had organized his work in the past had been that of the heart's imagination and its power; but cultivation of this, in his own experience, had proved self-defeating – sapping, rather than nourishing, his creative powers. Many of his later poems are in fact devoted to this strange contradiction; he writes of his gradual loss of hope, of the mutual love that has eluded him, of the 'death in life' that has been his fate; but he is unable finally to decide whether that fate is due to his own failure to find a love that could be fully requited, or to an illusory quality in the whole pursuit. To the end, therefore, the rôle of imagination remains equivocal.

## The Search for a Poetic Voice

In looking at his work as a whole, it is perhaps more accurate (as Max Schulz has maintained) to speak of 'poetic voices' than of a single 'poetic voice' in Coleridge. The age demanded a new mode of expression, yet it was hard for a single man to produce this on his own. Under the encouragement of others he developed the intimate, directly expressive mode of the conversation poems, but it was a fragile growth. In periods of isolation and insecurity it was natural to fall back on a voice more like that of the poetry he had been trying to supersede.

Other problems were involved. In the greatest and most intricate of his poems, for example, Coleridge needed to find a mode appropriate to the kind of oblique, exploratory statement that he was making. For the diction of *The Ancient Mariner* he drew upon the language of the ballads, which had been brought back into public view by works such as Thomas Percy's *Reliques of Ancient English Poetry*. He did not follow them in exact detail, however, turning rather to the contemporary long German ballads (as developed by Bürger) which were currently being translated into English. One of the ideas that he was testing, evidently, as he worked with Wordsworth on the composition of the Lyrical Ballads, was that such a language, which had in the past proved its appeal to the common people, might now exercise a wider appeal than fashionable drawing-room pieces by appealing to deeper instincts; the language which he developed there was, nevertheless, in certain important respects an artefact, for which it would be hard to find any strict historical precedent. With the archaisms there mingles a subtle appeal to the heart of the contemporary reader, mediated through a tender and cultivated sensuousness of language and images of fountains, streams and breezes. Historical authenticity was not altogether ignored; after a reviewer had criticized the phrases 'noises of a swound' and 'broad as a weft', they were changed for the 1802 edition; later, however, Coleridge restored them, recognizing, no doubt, that the true appeal of his poem had never rested upon such factors.

His later dealings with *The Ancient Mariner* are a source of interest from several points of view. Whereas many of his poems, such as *Christabel*, remained virtually untouched through the various collections of his poetry, this poem was always undergoing revision. In the earlier stages he was concerned to remove some clumsy phrasings. This is probably not the only reason, however, for his deletion of a reference to actual hypnotic power in the Mariner ('That which comes out of thine eye doth make/My body and soul to be still'); he seems to have been toning down any indication of bold metaphysical speculation. Through several editions, similarly, he changed his simile for the sun from 'like God's own head' to 'like an Angel's head'.

Further opportunities for revision came with the voyage to Malta in 1804. Seen from on board, he noticed, the behaviour of the ship's wake did not correspond to the description in his line 'The furrow followed free'; he accordingly altered it for the 1817 edition to 'The furrow streamed off free'. Once again, however, he would seem to have decided that strict accuracy of observation was dearly bought if it involved sacrificing an effective movement in the verse, for the earlier reading was later restored.

A more lasting gain for the poem came as the result of an experience on shipboard at night. Coleridge found himself indulging some 'sickly thoughts' concerning the Wordsworths and continued:

> died looking at the stars above the top mast; & when found dead, these Stars were sinking in the Horizon/ – a large Star? a road of dim Light? – Light of the Compass & rudderman's Lamp reflected with forms on the Main Sail.

(Notebooks II, 2001)

As Kathleen Coburn and others have pointed out, this experience probably provided the terms for a stanza printed first in 1817:

> We listened and looked sideways up!
> Fear at my heart, as at a cup,
> My life-blood seemed to sip!
> The stars were dim, and thick the night,
> The steersman's face by his lamp gleamed white;
> From the sails the dew did drip –

While the main drift of Coleridge's corrections was towards modernization of language and greater clarity of line, there was one respect in which his changes involved a complicated game of hide-and-seek with the poem's original significance. There can be little doubt that when he first composed it, he was using its narrative to explore the idea that in periods of extreme physical suffering the human sensibility, normally frozen into conventional attitudes by custom, became more than usually receptive to revelatory experiences – even if that experience, not fully understood, might be felt basically as terrifying. While the use of the ballad form might assist the appeal to the heart's imagination, the use of archaisms had helped to screen the full significance and implications of that appeal; and in any case, as we have seen, Coleridge had become disillusioned concerning some of his theories as time went by. With the disappearance of the archaisms, nevertheless, he evidently felt the need to offer some hints of interpretation, if still in a distancing form. Accordingly he constructed a new framing device, in the form of a series of marginal glosses (phrased as if inserted by some ancient editor) which partly elucidate and partly interpret the narrative. In this, its final structure, therefore, we find ourselves dealing with a fiction which is not only related by a fictitious hero but commented upon by a fictitious editor. The immediate effect for the general reader is to distance the narrative further, giving it still more the flavour of a remote historical romance. Nevertheless some of the glosses, such as the one that describes the daemonic nature of the albatross, leave readers with further clues to the original meaning of the poem – which they may either explore further or leave alone, as they choose.

The composition of the gloss was not simply a wilful exercise in obfuscation and tantalization. It also gave Coleridge the chance to write memorably about certain elements in the poem which, whatever his changing view of the supernatural, remained permanently valid for him. Whether or not the nightmares and visions of the poem were truly revelatory, he was intimately acquainted with nightmare as a frequent fact of his own sleep and knew the delight which sudden relief might bring, even if that relief consisted in nothing more than an awakening to the calm, on-going movements of ordinary experience. So with the Mariner's desolation:

> In his loneliness and fixedness he yearneth towards the journeying moon, and the stars that still sojourn, yet still move onward; and everywhere the blue sky belongs to them, and is their appointed rest, and their native country and their own natural homes, which they enter unannounced, as lords that are certainly expected and yet there is a silent joy at their arrival.

Still later, in the edition of 1828, he added a marvellously terse gloss for the stanza beginning 'The Sun's rim dips; the stars rush out . . . ' – simply: 'No twilight within the courts of the Sun.'

The marginal glosses are not the only striking feature of *Sibylline Leaves*; the revisions and excisions which Coleridge undertook for the collection display his critical powers at their height throughout. The same powers that he had exercised on the poetry of his predecessors and contemporaries in *Biographia Literaria* a few years before were now being used for the benefit of his own. He also added to *The Eolian Harp* a series of lines on 'the one Life', which may have been composed earlier, during the years 1797–8, when his enthusiasm for the concept was at its height, but more likely sprang from a recent resurgence of interest in the idea, after contact with similar themes in contemporary German nature-philosophy.

In his later years Coleridge would move towards a more radical view of his great poem: *The Ancient Mariner* was a 'poem of the pure imagination', he now thought, which would have been even more successful if it had been written from an amoral point of view – as in *The Arabian Nights*, where actions are often punished on the basis of some arbitrary rule which the human being who committed them could not have known or been expected to know. 'The chief fault, if I might say so, was the obtrusion of the moral sentiment so openly on the reader as a principle or cause of action in a work of such pure imagination.' When this comment to Mrs Barbauld was made is not clear; however, it should in any case be observed that in 1817 the 'moral sentiment' was still being reinforced, in the newly added marginal glosses, and that in his *Epitaph*, written shortly before his death, he was still voicing a hope that he might, in the grave, find 'life in death'. The inner debate concerning the exact moral significance of his poem was evidently never resolved; but since his audience increasingly agreed on the imaginative impact of the poem, he could safely dwell on this as its most distinctive achievement.

If we think of that achievement as expressing Coleridge's most central poetic voice, we are also forced to note that its accents were not simple. When his imagination is most powerfully at work, his voice is complex and dramatically rich, ranging from the judicious archaism of 'To Mary Queen the praise be given' to the dramatic alternation between the Two Voices. Nevertheless there are moments when simplicity breaks through memorably, as in the uprushing, directly enacted emotion of

> We drifted o'er the harbour-bar
> And I with sobs did pray –
> O let me be awake, my God!
> Or let me sleep alway.

The most characteristic note in Coleridge's voice – that of eager delight – is never far below the surface in his most imaginative poetry.

If the voice that is heard in the later poetry is a more labouring one, it is one which remains true to Coleridge's other great theme. He never lost his belief in the human heart as the key to all human experience. The rôle of imagination was harder to come to terms with: sometimes it had seemed to act as a dangerous and delusive will-o'-the-wisp, sometimes it seemed to have been no less than 'the vision and the faculty divine'. But of the heart's importance, however much its movements (and the corresponding movements of his verse) might be deadened by his gradual loss of hope, he had no doubt at all.

## The Lasting Achievement

The growing popularity of Coleridge's poetry during his lifetime was partly due to its influence upon his immediate successors, some of whom developed particular aspects or themes well beyond the point which he had reached. Keats, for example, seems to have found, in poems such as *The Eolian Harp* and *The Nightingale*, inspiration for his poetry of warm sensuousness. In the same way, Shelley was evidently encouraged by the link between natural description and metaphysical psychology (particularly in the nature-poetry) to develop a similar mode in his *Odes*. Byron, more impressed by the Oriental modes which Coleridge and Southey had begun to cultivate, actually persuaded Coleridge to publish *Kubla Khan*, and proceeded to develop the Eastern tale in a new and forceful manner.

The Victorians, also, learned much from Coleridge, particularly at those points where he tried to establish links between the heart and the imagination. The poem *Love* was much anthologized during the century. If Tennyson is to be regarded as Coleridge's major successor in this field, the influence also extends to Coventry Patmore and a host of lesser poets.

From a more recent point of view, however, Coleridge's most lasting gifts to English poetry are to be found in his insistence upon the cultivation of the informal, conversational poem to the point where it explores psychological subtleties. *The Ancient Mariner* and *Frost at Midnight* are the poems which his modern admirers would least like to lose; and these dazzling achievements are backed by a range of ideas, hints and observations which make the study of his poetry and criticism continually rewarding. His difficulty in achieving rounded and finished works was, it might be said, due precisely to his sense of the poet's predicament in a scientific age; to the modern eye, therefore, he is more profitably to be regarded as a poet of process than as a poet who should be judged exclusively by his finished products.

Coleridge's interest in subconscious and subliminal processes was at its strongest during his early years. He pursued it into the field of poetry, and displayed it particularly in his various experiments in metre. The strict metrical form favoured by previous poets seemed to him to reflect inadequately the true effects which metre, handled subtly, could have upon the feelings of the audience. 'As a medicated atmosphere, or as wine during animated conversation; they act powerfully, though themselves unnoticed,' he wrote. One area in which he indulged in metrical experiment was, of course, in the ballad form – though, as we have seen, his version of it involved a more polished usage than one would normally find in the historical examples. A more telling innovation was his introduction, in *Christabel*, of a concept of metre based not on strict patterns of syllables but on the shaping of whole lines so that the stresses reflect the flow of feeling. This development reflected a fear that the traditional system of mechanically counting syllables restricted emotional expression. Instead, he proposed a poetic form in which the metre, by following the natural run of the language as spoken in a state of excitement, should be made 'sufficiently uniform & far more malleable to the Passion & Meaning' (as he later put it) – the occasional variation in the number of syllables corresponding always to 'some transition in the nature of the imagery of passion'.

The actual achievement in *Christabel* is circumscribed by the fact that Coleridge is confining himself to a limited range of feelings – a sense of mystery and apprehension quickening towards fear, coupled with a tenderness for the young and innocent Christabel herself. Sometimes the rhythmic effect is more like that of a nursery rhyme: for example,

> A little door she opened straight,
> All in the middle of the gate . . .

(where the use of the phrase 'all in the . . .' for a place rather than a time is in any case unusual). Despite some telling moments, the total effect is more often one of charm than force. Coleridge's mastery of poetic movement is most evident, perhaps, when he is actually describing subtleties of movement in the physical world – particularly if these are also working in the mind of the observer, as in *The Ancient Mariner*, where he is specifically concerned to convey the transition from the state of a man who has lived in a fixed universe, the fixities of which have finally actualized themselves all around him, to the state of a man who feels the movements of his heart beginning to reflect those in the world outside. Broadly speaking, it is the movement from the sullen beat of

> For the sky and the sea, and the sea and the sky
> Lay like a load on my weary eye,
>     And the dead were at my feet

to the gentle onward movement of

> The moving Moon went up the sky,
>     And no where did abide:
> Softly she was going up
>     And a star or two beside –

but the whole of the fourth section of the poem needs to be read if one is to gain the full effect of the change, which then continues to the close of the poem.

Some of the best examples of Coleridge's subtlety in the handling of rhythm are to be found in the manuscript *Letter to Sara Hutchinson* – which was in fact lost to public view for more than a century. An important original feature of the poem, metrically speaking, was its use of the occasional short couplet to convey a slight tensing of the emotions. The device, as such, derives from the eighteenth-century Pindaric ode, where, following the classical model, writers would sometimes incorporate such short couplets in the sweep of their verse. In their hands, however, such usage still had the mannerist ring of the short couplets in Milton's poem *On the Morning of Christ's Nativity*. It was left to Coleridge (and to Wordsworth, in the contemporaneous *Immortality Ode*) to try the experiment of gearing this kind of movement to the motions of the human heart. The use of short lines here marks a development from the conversational mode of the earlier poems.

> My genial spirits fail –
> And what can these avail
> To lift the smoth'ring Weight from off my Breast?
> It were a vain Endeavour
> Tho' I should gaze for ever
> On that Green light, which lingers in the West!

The peroration to the letter brings this movement full circle, the short lines now simply setting off the majestic movement of the iambic lines, to convey the sense of joy as a 'Spirit' and a 'Power'.

Coleridge's fascination with subliminal processes encouraged interest in any phenomena associated with spontaneous poetic composition – as for example when a 'form' or a 'tune' might appear suddenly in the poet's mind, unbidden and unexpected. Some of his own compositions, he claimed, began in this way; the most celebrated being, of course, *Kubla Khan*. Such statements are not to be treated so literally as to suggest that particular poems flowed out in their final forms without further thought or revision, but it seems clear that certain poems were composed with extraordinary facility, while the starting-point for others was the appearance of something like a *shape* of verse, which he then elaborated. Sometimes the original idea was transformed out of all recognition, as with the *Hymn before Sun-rise*, which he claimed had begun with a hymn 'involuntarily poured forth' on Scafell: the final version, in which he transferred the whole scene to Mont Blanc and drew on Friederike Brun for images and phrases, was, as already noted, clearly the result of considerable work and thought. In the case of *Youth and Age*, many years later, he describes how the original 'air' of the poem 'whizzed right across the diameter of his brain', to become the 'Aria Spontanea' which he wrote down first:

> Flowers are lovely, Love is flower-like,
> Friendship is a shelt'ring tree –
> O the Joys, that came down shower-like,
> Of Beauty, Truth, and Liberty,
> When I was young, ere I was old (etc.)

If this is compared with the final version it will be seen that the first, basic form has been essentially retained, in the midst of a large-scale extension and reshaping.

If the waiting on inspiration becomes a permanent stance, it is of course dangerous; good art comes more often from an alternation between periods of struggle and of rest in the poet. There can be little doubt, however, that throughout his life, and particularly in his youth, Coleridge was subject to fits of inspiration of this kind, and that the rarity of their appearances in his later career made them all the more welcome.

In studying the growth of Coleridge's poetic powers, it should not be forgotten that much of his creative effort just before the writing of his greatest poems had been devoted to the production of a poetic drama. *Osorio* (which was not produced or published in full until many years later) contains various touches which show him responding to the demands of that mode (in which his chief masters were Shakespeare and Schiller), and developing skills which were then deployed in his poems of the supernatural.

Coleridge's psychological interests are again relevant. The drama evidently appealed to him at this time because it seemed to offer ways of touching an audience more directly than through the written word. The modes by which a human being's behaviour may be penetrated to the point where the springs of action are touched provides, indeed, one of the play's themes. In addition to staging direct assaults on the sensibility by a scene set in a cavern, or unusual, piercing musical sounds, Coleridge includes the unearthly strains of his *Invocation*:

> Hear, sweet spirit, hear the spell,
>   Lest a blacker charm compel!
> So shall the midnight breezes swell
> With thy deep long-lingering knell.
>
> And at evening evermore,
> In a Chapel on the shore,
> Shall the Chaunters sad and saintly,
> Yellow tapers burning faintly,
> Doleful Masses chaunt for thee,
>   Miserere Domine!
>
> Hush! the cadence dies away
>   On the quiet moonlight sea:
> The boatmen rest their oars and say,
>   Miserere Domine!

As Max Schulz has pointed out, Coleridge's handling of his verse form here seems to reflect his praise, a few months earlier, for Bowles' three-stressed 'Brōad dāy-līght' to express a captive's 'dwelling on the sight of noon — with a rapture and a kind of wonder'. It also springs from a strong interest in incantatory devices of all kinds and their possible effect upon the emotions of an audience.

Such devices reflect Coleridge's deep and abiding concern with language and its powers. Throughout a long life he never lost his sense of wonder at the extraordinary processes by which thoughts could turn into things and things into thoughts, and at the part played by language in this process. Such preoccupations led him continually to the very border of language, the point where it merges with the mystery of perceptual process itself.

For the same reason he was fascinated by all the processes of light: as he records in *Biographia Literaria*, 'the sudden charm, which accidents of light and shade, which moon-light or sun-set diffused over a known and familiar landscape' was one of the phenomena to which he and Wordsworth devoted their attention; and the fruits of such discussion may be observed in his poems of the supernatural. In *The Ancient Mariner*, the light of the sun at its most glaring emphasizes the isolatedness of everything on which it falls; moonlight, on the other hand, induces a sense of the connections between things, fostering a kind of peace and calm:

> The rock shone bright, the kirk no less
>   That stands above the rock:
> The moonlight steeped in silentness
>   The steady weathercock.

The mysterious effects that could be brought about by light also fascinated Wordsworth at this time. In *The Prelude* he displays his interest in the effect of light on mountains, which may in some lights seem insubstantial, and translucent, while other lights fix them as grossly material and intractable.

Wordsworth later came to feel that there might be something treacherous, as well as haunting, in

> The light that never was on sea or land,
>   The consecration and the poet's dream!

Coleridge, however, never lost his belief that in studying the behaviour of light man was closest to points of possible correspondence between his own powers and those of nature.

It is not surprising, then, that the imagery of light should play an important, if unobtrusive, part in so much of his thought and poetry. He was often drawn to reflect on two central, mutually suggestive, statements in the Bible: 'In the beginning was the Word', and the first recorded Word of God; 'Let there be Light'. In the same way he was fascinated by the relationship between physical light and inward 'illumination' – whether to be thought of as an actual, physiological phenomenon or as a profound metaphor. When he tried to define the nature of symbolism it was natural to him to speak of the 'translucence of the eternal through and in the temporal' as characterizing it. Joy, similarly, in the *Letter to Sara Hutchinson*, is 'This Light, this Glory, this fair luminous Mist'.

A significant moment in a poem, similarly, may be marked by some particularly attractive manifestation of light. Apart from the appearances of the sun and moon in his great poems, attention may be drawn to the stanzas describing the sun shining through the thick leaves in *The Three Graves* (ll. 505–17) and to the scene in *Alice Du Clos* when she goes riding:

> Smit by the sun the mist in glee
> Dissolves to lightsome jewelry –
> Each blossom hath its gem!

In each case Coleridge seems to be suggesting something important about the nature and rôle of his hero or heroine.

The most magical of these moments comes with Glycine's song in *Zapolya*, in which a bird, caught in a shaft of sunlight, turns into dazzling translucence:

> A sunny shaft did I behold,
>    From sky to earth it slanted:
> And poised therein a bird so bold –
>    Sweet bird, thou wert enchanted!
>
> He sank, he rose, he twinkled, he trolled
>    Within that shaft of sunny mist;
> His eyes of fire, his beak of gold,
>    All else of amethyst!

The mingled lights of fire, precious metal and jewel transmute the bird into a visionary essence of itself.

The poems, on the other hand, in which he tries to write out more explicitly the meaning of his light imagery, are less distinguished:

> Whene'er the mist, that stands 'twixt God and thee,
> Defecates to a pure transparency,
> That intercepts no light and adds no stain –
> There Reason is, and then begins her reign!

Light imagery can come to life in his poetry, it seems, only where the heart is more fully engaged. The careful, even laboured workmanship of the verse just quoted must be compared with the earlier poem *Phantom*, where a similar phenomenon is described as seen in a human being (probably Sara Hutchinson):

> There was no trace
> Of aught on that illumined face
> Uprais'd beneath the rifted stone

> But of one spirit all her own –
> She, she herself, and only she,
> Shone through her body visibly.

The mystery of personal 'radiance', whether experienced as an illumination in the mind, or as an observable physical radiance in others, was something that disturbed and attracted Coleridge all his life. At its highest it might be thought of as a key to everything: the radiating figure of the inspired poet at the end of *Kubla Khan*, fascinating mankind into a harmonic dance, was its supreme artistic embodiment. In time of disillusionment, by contrast, it was more like a delusive will-o'-the-wisp, or the visual illusion, seen by a woodman in a snow-mist, of *Constancy to an Ideal Object*:

> The enamoured rustic worships its fair hues,
> Nor knows he makes the shadow, he pursues!

It could neither be finally dismissed, nor ever fully verbalized. The imagery of light in his poetry has a corresponding ambiguous quality: it is seeking a direct access to the reader's imagination which cannot be properly mediated by the verbal structure, and its success or failure in communication will have to do with factors which are independent of the poet's skill at handling words in syntactical structures of meaning.

If we are judging Coleridge's poetry according to its success in creating sustained verbal textures (as opposed to the brilliant interplay between words and projected images in the great poems), we shall find ourselves returning to the conversation poems – and particularly to *Frost at Midnight*, his supreme achievement at this level. Nowhere else does he succeed so fully in producing his various themes and modes of thought into a single organized statement. Here his gift for rendering 'the night-side of nature' is displayed to the full; here too he shows his extraordinary power for displaying a piece of human thinking in the complexity of its shifting thrusts and shapings. Sitting awake in his cottage and looking at the sleeping infant by his side, he naturally finds himself looking before and after – both remembering his own childhood and considering Hartley's future upbringing. Images start up naturally and associate themselves with other images; while in a larger, familiar movement of systole and diastole the poet moves from the present moment, these particular things around him, to his remembered sense, in childhood, of the great appearances in nature, and to his hope that Hartley will be able to enjoy such scenes in a less restricted manner.

Finally, he can return to the icicles now forming themselves around his cottage and describe them again, this time in the context of the developed delight in nature that he envisages for Hartley.

*Frost at Midnight* is a poem which invites analysis of many features, such as the manner in which the delicate, step-by-step tracing of the argument is counterpointed by larger movements in the imagery. It is finally held together, however, by Coleridge's abiding concern for 'the sympathies of things' – ranging from the effect of beautiful landscapes upon a growing mind to the curious fact that even a small film of soot on a grate, by the simple act of moving in an otherwise silent atmosphere, can suggest 'dim sympathies with me who live'.

All this relates to one of the central mysteries that fascinated Coleridge: the mystery whereby every manifestation of life is at once unified and diverse – always existing in a separate identity, yet always linked inseparably to, and assimilating itself with, all other life-forms. The rise and fall of this particular theme (the theme of the 'one Life') is to be associated particularly with a few years of his career, and will be more appropriately traced in the separate, chronological prefaces that follow; but it should be briefly mentioned here, as the idea which proved most successful in reconciling all Coleridge's powers and interests. Among other things it brought together the work of heart and imagination: for while it could be claimed as the special office of head and mind to establish the individual in a sense of his own identity and separateness from the world of nature, the corresponding ministry of heart and imagination was to remind human beings, through an enlivened sympathy, of their links with one another. In the head each 'has a life of its own'; in the heart 'we are all one Life'.

In his later unhappiness, Coleridge found it difficult to sustain that particular, poised vision, but he did not lose his sense of the importance of the issues involved. He leaves us to wrestle with the same problem. While we look to *The Ancient Mariner, Kubla Khan* and the conversation poems as representing his most unequivocal achievements, therefore, his career also invites us to look at the whole of his work, as exhibiting the variety of processes, both creative and destructive, which, at a particular moment in English civilization, intense cultivation of heart and imagination could initiate in a man of exceptional sensitivity and intelligence.

JOHN BEER

# NOTE ON THE TEXT
## AND ACKNOWLEDGEMENTS

After all you say, I still think the chronological order the best for arranging a poet's works. All your divisions are in particular instances inadequate, and they destroy the interest which arises from watching the progress, maturity, and even the decay of genius.

So said Coleridge in the last year of his life: his advice has been followed in preparing the present selection. He himself passed through several phases in the course of his career and a general chronological arrangement helps to bring together poems of a kind. At the same time his further point has been borne in mind. Departure from strict chronological grouping sometimes helps to distinguish overlapping phases more clearly.

Further editorial decisions have been taken. After some consideration it seemed best to reprint, as a separate section, the first collection of 1796. In general a poet's later revisions should be respected, but the 1796 collection has a particular intrinsic interest. It represents Coleridge at a point in his career just before his intimacy with Wordsworth, still very much the provincial poet with an enthusiasm for effects of sublimity and pathos. His later revisions tend to destroy the fullness of this impression.

Apart from this section, the edition of 1828 has been taken as a guide in selecting poems for inclusion. A fuller edition of the poems appeared in 1834, but it seems likely that the arrangement of it was left largely to Henry Nelson Coleridge, the poet's nephew. I have not felt bound to include everything that appeared in that edition therefore. On the other hand many poems which are of considerable value appeared posthumously. The less interesting juvenilia, some ephe    occasional pieces and a number of trivial epigrams    m the 1834 collection have accordingly been omitted and the poems of 1828 supplemented by a selection indicating the range of the poet's gifts.

The poems of 1800–10 include many poems relating to Sara Hutchinson, and in arranging these I draw, with gratitude, on the work of George Whalley in *Coleridge and Sara Hutchinson and the Asra Poems*. They have not been made into a separate section, however, since they contain other themes which link them to the general poetry of the time.

Acknowledgements are due to the Oxford University Press for permission to use E. H. Coleridge's edition of the *Complete Poetical Works* (1912) as a basic text for the volume as a whole. I also wish to express thanks to Professor George Whalley and Miss Joanna Hutchinson for permission to reprint one or two poems from the text of *Sara's Poets*, a manuscript volume in Miss Hutchinson's possession; and to the Trustees of Dove Cottage for permission to reproduce the 'Letter to Sara Hutchinson' and to the Librarian of Dove Cottage for allowing me to examine the manuscript and so achieve an even greater accuracy than in previous published versions. Norman Fruman's account of Coleridge's known borrowings in his *Coleridge the Damaged Archangel* has enabled me to record ten minor debts which had previously escaped my attention. Where possible, I have also corrected poems originally published from manuscript letters or notebooks by reference to the published editions of Professor Earl Leslie Griggs and Professor Kathleen Coburn. As a result, poems such as *Limbo* and *Ne Plus Ultra* have become distinctly more intelligible. The words 'From MS' simply indicate that the poem was not published during Coleridge's lifetime, however, not necessarily that there has been an opportunity to check the text against an original manuscript.

In reorganizing the text for the 1993 resetting I have been especially indebted to Dr J. C. C. Mays, who has made available to me his datings of poems for the edition of the *Poetical Works* to appear in *The Collected Coleridge*, and so enabled me to work towards a more accurate chronological order. I am also grateful to Lorna Arnold for providing translations of the passages in classical languages.

Finally I wish to acknowledge again my debt to the University of Manchester and to the librarian and staff of the Manchester Public Libraries for providing the research facilities under which the original work on the edition took place.

# JUVENILE POEMS

Coleridge cherished from his early years the dream of becoming a great poet in the Miltonic mode. Recalling no doubt the 'nightly' visitations from the Muse that Milton had described, he was to write later of a

> divine and nightly-whispering Voice
> Which from my childhood to maturer years
> Spake to me of predestinated wreaths
> Bright with no fading colours.

In the course of his life he was to pursue many other aims, devoting his energies at different times to criticism of art and literature, political journalism, philosophy, logic and religious thought, but he always returned to poetry – even if after a certain point he recognized that the composition of a great epic poem would not be possible for him. He was writing verses from his schooldays onwards, and the poems in this section (some of which were not published until the year of his death or later) exhibit themes and interests which remained with him through life.

The *Anthem for the Children of Christ's Hospital* is a good example. Already, at the age of sixteen, he is writing of seraphs round the heavenly throne (expressing a vision of harmony at the centre of things which persists as a permanent feature of his thinking and poetry) and, still more significantly, using the sun as a symbol of love, human and divine.

Other poems express his life during these years – the life of an imaginative schoolboy in Christ's Hospital, cut off from nature except for occasional glimpses of the sky from the rooftop, deep in imaginative literature of all kinds. Return to Devonshire between school and university results in a series of satirical poems on the journey and the local church music there. He also writes humorous, domestic pieces for members of his family and for the young Mary Evans, whose family showed him great kindness during his last years at school and his first at Cambridge. The *Greek Ode on Astronomy*, however, which he submitted unsuccessfully for a prize at Cambridge in 1793 and which is here printed in Southey's translation, indicates his broader ambitions. He thought highly of it as an essay in the sublime: it reveals his inward aspirations, his desire to reach the heights attained by geniuses such as Milton or Newton. Genius he identifies with an initiation into the precincts of Heaven –

> Where round the fields of Truth
> The fiery Essences for ever feed.

By a curious irony of fate, his failure to win the prize with this poem helped to precipitate a crisis in his own affairs which resulted in flight to London, the buying of a ticket in the lottery (and the composition of a poem to express his feelings on the occasion), and his enlistment as a dragoon under the name of Silas Tomkyn Comberbache.

It was not until early in the following year that his family discovered his whereabouts and procured his discharge. His return to Cambridge proved only temporary, for during the summer of 1794 he first met Robert Southey, whose high moral idealism touched a chord in his own breast. Discovering a common disillusionment concerning the French Revolution, the two young men planned a small ideal community to be established on the banks of the Susquehanna and to be given the name of Pantisocracy. Coleridge's own interest in the scheme was closely connected with his study of human nature. But although his psychological insight enabled him to anticipate clearly some dangers of the scheme, his imagination still threw a light of enchantment over the prospect, thus veiling other difficulties. In his sonnet on the scheme, for example (on page 23 in this section), various problems of human relationship endemic in the venture are bypassed as he pictures the 'wizard passions' weaving a 'holy spell' among the inhabitants, so that the necessary harmony between them will be achieved.

As it becomes clear that the Pantisocratic scheme will not be realized, however, Coleridge turns back to English society and begins to address sonnets to figures such as Godwin and Southey whose ideals he continues to admire, at least for a time.

## Life

As late I journey'd o'er the extensive plain
   Where native Otter sports his scanty stream,
Musing in torpid woe a Sister's pain,
   The glorious prospect woke me from the dream.

At every step it widen'd to my sight –          5
   Wood, Meadow, verdant Hill, and dreary Steep,
Following in quick succession of delight, –
   Till all – at once – did my eye ravish'd sweep!

May this (I cried) my course through Life portray!
New scenes of Wisdom may each step display,      10
   And Knowledge open as my days advance!
Till what time Death shall pour the undarken'd ray,
   My eye shall dart thro' infinite expanse,
And thought suspended lie in Rapture's blissful trance.
[?1789]

## The Nose

   Ye souls unus'd to lofty verse,
      Who sweep the earth with lowly wing,
   Like sand before the blast disperse –
      A Nose! a mighty Nose I sing!
As erst Prometheus stole from heaven the fire     5
   To animate the wonder of his hand;
Thus with unhallow'd hands, O Muse, aspire,
   And from my subject snatch a burning brand!
So like the Nose I sing – my verse shall glow –
Like Phlegethon my verse in waves of fire shall flow!   10

   Light of this once all darksome spot
      Where now their glad course mortals run,
   First-born of Sirius begot
      Upon the focus of the Sun –

I'll call thee ——! for such thy earthly name –     15
    What name so high, but what too low must be?
Comets, when most they drink the solar flame
    Are but faint types and images of thee!
Burn madly, Fire! o'er earth in ravage run,
Then blush for shame more red by fiercer —— outdone!     20


    I saw when from the turtle feast
        The thick dark smoke in volumes rose!
    I saw the darkness of the mist
        Encircle thee, O Nose!
Shorn of thy rays thou shott'st a fearful gleam     25
    (The turtle quiver'd with prophetic fright)
Gloomy and sullen thro' the night of steam: –
    So Satan's Nose when Dunstan urg'd to flight,
Glowing from gripe of red-hot pincers dread
Athwart the smokes of Hell disastrous twilight shed!     30


    The Furies to madness my brain devote –
        In robes of ice my body wrap!
    On billowy flames of fire I float,
        Hear ye, my entrails how they snap?
Some power unseen forbids my lungs to breathe!     35
    What fire-clad meteors round me whizzing fly!
I vitrify thy torrid zone beneath,
    Proboscis fierce! I am calcined! I die!
Thus, like great Pliny, in Vesuvius' fire,
I perish in the blaze while I the blaze admire.     40
[1789]


## Destruction of the Bastile

    Heard'st thou yon universal cry,
        And dost thou linger still on Gallia's shore?
    Go, Tyranny! beneath some barbarous sky
        Thy terrors lost, and ruin'd power deplore!
        What tho' through many a groaning age     5

Was felt thy keen suspicious rage,
Yet Freedom rous'd by fierce Disdain
Has wildly broke thy triple chain,
And like the storm which Earth's deep entrails hide,
At length has burst its way and spread the ruins wide.          10

\*          \*          \*

IV

In sighs their sickly breath was spent; each gleam
  Of Hope had ceas'd the long long day to cheer;
Or if delusive, in some flitting dream,
  It gave them to their friends and children dear –
    Awaked by lordly Insult's sound                            15
    To all the doubled horrors round,
    Oft shrunk they from Oppression's band
    While Anguish rais'd the desperate hand
For silent death; or lost the mind's controll,
Thro' every burning vein would tides of Frenzy roll.           20

V

But cease, ye pitying bosoms, cease to bleed!
  Such scenes no more demand the tear humane;
I see, I see! glad Liberty succeed
  With every patriot virtue in her train!
    And mark yon peasant's raptur'd eyes;                       25
    Secure he views his harvests rise;
    No fetter vile the mind shall know,
    And Eloquence shall fearless glow.
Yes! Liberty the soul of Life shall reign,
Shall throb in every pulse, shall flow thro' every vein!       30

VI

Shall France alone a Despot spurn?
  Shall she alone, O Freedom, boast thy care?
Lo, round thy standard Belgia's heroes burn,
  Tho' Power's blood-stain'd streamers fire the air,

And wider yet thy influence spread,                    35
Nor e'er recline thy weary head,
Till every land from pole to pole
Shall boast one independent soul!
And still, as erst, let favour'd Britain be
First ever of the first and freest of the free!        40
[1789–91]


## To the Evening Star

O meek attendant of Sol's setting blaze,
   I hail, sweet star, thy chaste effulgent glow;
On thee full oft with fixéd eye I gaze
    Till I, methinks, all spirit seem to grow.

O first and fairest of the starry choir,                5
   O loveliest 'mid the daughters of the night,
Must not the maid I love like thee inspire
    *Pure* joy and *calm* Delight?

Must she not be, as is thy placid sphere
   Serenely brilliant? Whilst to gaze a while           10
Be all my wish 'mid Fancy's high career
    E'en till she quit this scene of earthly toil;
Then Hope perchance might fondly sigh to join
Her spirit in thy kindred orb, O Star benign!
[?1790]


## Anthem

### FOR THE CHILDREN OF CHRIST'S HOSPITAL

Seraphs! around th' Eternal's seat who throng
   With tuneful ecstasies of praise:
O! teach our feeble tongues like yours the song
   Of fervent gratitude to raise –
Like you, inspired with holy flame                      5
To dwell on that Almighty name
Who bade the child of Woe no longer sigh,
And Joy in tears o'erspread the widow's eye.

Th' all-gracious Parent hears the wretch's prayer;
   The meek tear strongly pleads on high; 10
Wan Resignation struggling with despair
   The Lord beholds with pitying eye;
Sees cheerless Want unpitied pine,
Disease on earth its head recline,
And bids Compassion seek the realms of woe 15
To heal the wounded, and to raise the low.

She comes! she comes! the meek-eyed Power I see
   With liberal hand that loves to bless;
The clouds of Sorrow at her presence flee;
   Rejoice! rejoice! ye Children of Distress! 20
The beams that play around her head
Thro' Want's dark vale their radiance spread:
The young uncultur'd mind imbibes the ray,
And Vice reluctant quits th' expected prey.

Cease, thou lorn mother! cease thy wailings drear; 25
   Ye babes! the unconscious sob forego;
Or let full Gratitude now prompt the tear
   Which erst did Sorrow force to flow.
Unkindly cold and tempest shrill
In Life's morn oft the traveller chill,
But soon his path the sun of Love shall warm; 30
And each glad scene look brighter for the storm!
[1789–91]

# From *Monody on the Death of Chatterton*

### (FIRST VERSION)
### *Lines 80–90*

       O Spirit blest!
Whether th' eternal Throne around,
Amidst the blaze of Cherubim,
Thou pourest forth the grateful hymn,
Or, soaring through the blest Domain, 5
Enraptur'st Angels with thy strain, –

Grant me, like thee, the lyre to sound,
Like thee, with fire divine to glow –
But ah! when rage the Waves of Woe,
Grant me with firmer breast t'oppose their hate,          10
And soar beyond the storms with upright eye elate!
[1790]


## With Fielding's Amelia

Virtues and Woes alike too great for man
    In the soft tale oft claim the useless sigh;
For vain the attempt to realize the plan,
    On Folly's wings must Imitation fly.
With other aim has Fielding here display'd          5
    Each social duty and each social care;
With just yet vivid colouring portray'd
    What every wife should be, what many are.
And sure the Parent of a race so sweet
    With double pleasure on the page shall dwell,          10
Each scene with sympathizing breast shall meet,
    While Reason still with smiles delights to tell
Maternal hope, that her loved progeny
In all but sorrows shall Amelias be!
[?1792]


## A Mathematical Problem

If Pegasus will let *thee* only ride him,
Spurning my clumsy efforts to o'erstride him,
Some fresh expedient the Muse will try,
And walk on stilts, although she cannot fly.

TO THE REV. GEORGE COLERIDGE

Dear Brother,
    I have often been surprised that Mathematics, the quintessence of
Truth, should have found admirers so few and so languid. Frequent
consideration and minute scrutiny have at length unravelled the cause;
viz. that though Reason is feasted, Imagination is starved: whilst Reason

is luxuriating in its proper Paradise, Imagination is wearily travelling on a dreary desert. To assist Reason by the stimulus of Imagination is the design of the following production. In the execution of it much may be objectionable. The verse (particularly in the introduction of the ode) may be accused of unwarrantable liberties, but they are liberties equally homogeneal with the exactness of Mathematical disquisition, and the boldness of Pindaric daring. I have three strong champions to defend me against the attacks of Criticism: the Novelty, the Difficulty, and the Utility of the work. I may justly plume myself that I first have drawn the nymph Mathesis from the visionary caves of abstracted idea, and caused her to unite with Harmony. The first-born of this Union I now present to you: with interested motives indeed – as I expect to receive in return the more valuable offspring of your Muse.

Thine ever,
S.T.C.

[CHRIST'S HOSPITAL] *31 March 1791*

> This is now – this was erst,
> Proposition the first – and Problem the first.

### I

> On a given finite line
> Which must no way incline;
> To describe an equi –
> – lateral Tri –
> – A, N, G, L, E.                    5
> Now let A. B.
> Be the given line
> Which must no way incline;
> The great Mathematician
> Makes this Requisition,              10
> That we describe an Equi –
> – lateral Tri –
> – angle on it:
> Aid us, Reason – aid us, Wit!

### II

> From the centre A. at the distance A. B.        15
> Describe the circle B. C. D.
> At the distance B. A. from B. the centre
> The round A. C. E. to describe boldly venture.
> (Third postulate see.)

And from the point C.                                              20
In which the circles make a pother
Cutting and slashing one another,
    Bid the straight lines a journeying go.
C. A., C. B. those lines will show.
    To the points, which by A. B. are reckon'd,          25
    And postulate the second
For Authority ye know.
            A. B. C.
        Triumphant shall be
    An Equilateral Triangle,                              30
Not Peter Pindar carp, nor Zoilus can wrangle.


                        III

Because the point A. is the centre
    Of the circular B. C. D.
And because the point B. is the centre
    Of the circular A. C. E.
A. C. to A. B. and B. C. to B. A.                         35
Harmoniously equal for ever must stay;
    Then C. A. and B. C.
Both extend the kind hand
    To the basis, A. B.                                   40
Unambitiously join'd in Equality's Band.
But to the same powers, when two powers are equal,
    My mind forbodes the sequel;
My mind does some celestial impulse teach,
    And equalises each to each.                           45
Thus C. A. with B. C. strikes the same sure alliance,
    That C. A. and B. C. had with A. B. before;
        And in mutual affiance
            None attempting to soar
            Above another,                                50
        The unanimous three
        C. A. and B. C. and A. B.
    All are equal, each to his brother,
        Preserving the balance of power so true:
Ah! the like would the proud Autocratorix[1] do!        55


[1]Empress of Russia [S.T.C.]

At taxes impending not Britain would tremble,
Nor Prussia struggle her fear to dissemble;
   Nor the Mah'met-sprung Wight
    The great Mussulman
    Would stain his Divan        60
With Urine, the soft-flowing daughter of Fright.

IV

But rein your stallion in, too daring Nine!
Should Empires bloat the scientific line?
Or with dishevell'd hair all madly do ye run
For transport that your task is done?       65
   For done it is – the cause is tried!
   And Proposition, gentle Maid,
Who soothly ask'd stern Demonstration's aid,
    Has proved her right, and A. B. C.
     Of Angles three        70
    Is shown to be of equal side.
And now our weary steed to rest in fine,
 'Tis rais'd upon A. B. the straight, the given line.
[1791]


## On Receiving an Account
## that his only Sister's Death was Inevitable

The tear which mourn'd a brother's fate scarce dry –
Pain after pain, and woe succeeding woe –
Is my heart destin'd for another blow?
O my sweet sister! and must thou too die?
Ah! how has Disappointment pour'd the tear     5
O'er infant Hope destroy'd by early frost!
How are ye gone, whom most my soul held dear!
Scarce had I lov'd you, ere I mourn'd you lost;
Say, is this hollow eye, this heartless pain,
Fated to rove thro' Life's wide cheerless plain –    10
Nor father, brother, sister meet its ken –
My woes, my joys unshared! Ah! long ere then
On me thy icy dart, stern Death, be prov'd; –
Better to die, than live and not be lov'd!
[1790–1]

## On Seeing a Youth Affectionately Welcomed
### by a Sister

I too a sister had! too cruel Death!
  How sad Remembrance bids my bosom heave!
Tranquil her soul, as sleeping Infant's breath;
  Meek were her manners as a vernal Eve.
Knowledge, that frequent lifts the bloated mind,          5
  Gave her the treasure of a lowly breast,
And Wit to venom'd Malice oft assign'd,
  Dwelt in her bosom in a Turtle's nest.
Cease, busy Memory! cease to urge the dart;
  Nor on my soul her love to me impress!                  10
For oh I mourn in anguish – and my heart
  Feels the keen pang, th' unutterable distress.
Yet wherefore grieve I that her sorrows cease,
For Life was misery, and the Grave is Peace!
[1791]


## Sonnet
#### ON QUITTING CHRIST'S HOSPITAL

Farewell parental scenes! a sad farewell!
To you my grateful heart still fondly clings,
Tho' fluttering round on Fancy's burnish'd wings
Her tales of future Joy Hope loves to tell.
Adieu, adieu! ye much-lov'd cloisters pale!                5
Ah! would those happy days return again,
When 'neath your arches, free from every stain,
I heard of guilt and wonder'd at the tale!
Dear haunts! where oft my simple lays I sang,
Listening meanwhile the echoings of my feet,              10
Lingering I quit you, with as great a pang,
As when erewhile, my weeping childhood, torn
By early sorrow from my native seat,
Mingled its tears with hers – my widow'd Parent lorn.
[1791]

## Ode to Sleep[1]

'Tis hard on Bagshot Heath to try
Unclos'd to keep the weary eye;
But ah! Oblivion's nod to get
In rattling coach is harder yet.
Slumbrous God of half-shut eye!                    5
Who lovest with limbs supine to lie;
Soother sweet of toil and care
Listen, listen to my prayer;
And to thy votary dispense
Thy soporific influence!                          10
What tho' around thy drowsy head
The seven-fold cap of night be spread,
Yet lift that drowsy head awhile
And yawn propitiously a smile;
In drizzly rains poppean dews                     15
O'er the tired inmates of the Coach diffuse;
And when thou'st charm'd our eyes to rest,
Pillowing the chin upon the breast,
Bid many a dream from thy dominions
Wave its various-painted pinions,                 20
Till ere the splendid visions close
We snore quartettes in ecstasy of nose.
While thus we urge our airy course,
O may no jolt's electric force
Our fancies from their steeds unhorse,            25
And call us from thy fairy reign
To dreary Bagshot Heath again!
[1791]

---

[1]Travelling in the Exeter Coach with three other passengers over Bagshot Heath, after some vain endeavours to compose myself I composed this Ode – August 17, 1791. [S.T.C.]

## A Devonshire Road[1]

The indignant Bard composed this furious ode,
As tired he dragg'd his way thro' Plimtree road!
  Crusted with filth and stuck in mire
  Dull sounds the Bard's bemudded lyre;
  Nathless Revenge and Ire the Poet goad        5
  To pour his imprecations on the road.
  Curst road! whose execrable way
  Was darkly shadow'd out in Milton's lay,
When the sad fiends thro' Hell's sulphureous roads
Took the first survey of their new abodes;        10
  Or when the fall'n Archangel fierce
  Dar'd through the realms of Night to pierce,
What time the Bloodhound lur'd by Human scent
Thro' all Confusion's quagmires floundering went.
Nor cheering pipe, nor Bird's shrill note        15
Around thy dreary paths shall float;
Their boding songs shall scritch-owls pour
To fright the guilty shepherds sore,
Led by the wandering fires astray
Thro' the dank horrors of thy way!        20
While they their mud-lost sandals hunt
May all the curses, which they grunt
In raging moan like goaded hog,
Alight upon thee, damnéd Bog!
[1791]


## Ode on the Ottery and Tiverton Church Music

  Hence, soul-dissolving Harmony
    That lead'st th' oblivious soul astray –
  Though thou sphere-descended be –
    Hence away! –        5

---

[1]Plimtree is about 8 miles N. of Ottery St Mary. S.T.C. must have left the mail coach at Cullompton to make his way home on foot. [E.H.C.]

Thou mightier Goddess, thou demand'st my lay,                         5
   Born when earth was seiz'd with cholic;
Or as more sapient sages say,
   What time the Legion diabolic
     Compell'd their beings to enshrine
     In bodies vile of herded swine,                         10
     Precipitate adown the steep
     With hideous rout were plunging in the deep,
And hog and devil mingling grunt and yell
   Seiz'd on the ear with horrible obtrusion; –
Then if aright old legendaries tell,                         15
   Wert thou begot by Discord on Confusion!

What though no name's sonorous power
Was given thee at thy natal hour! –
Yet oft I feel thy sacred might,
While concords wing their distant flight.                         20
   Such Power inspires thy holy son
     Sable clerk of Tiverton!
And oft where Otter sports his stream,
I hear thy banded offspring scream.
Thou Goddess! thou inspir'st each throat;                         25
'Tis thou who pour'st the scritch-owl note!
Transported hear'st thy children all
Scrape and blow and squeak and squall;
And while old Otter's steeple rings,
Clappest hoarse thy raven wings!                         30
[1791]

## An Ode in the Manner of Anacreon

    As late in wreaths gay flowers I bound,
    Beneath some roses LOVE I found,
    And by his little frolic pinion
    As quick as thought I seiz'd the minion,
    Then in my Cup the prisoner threw,                         5
    And drank him in its sparkling dew:
    And sure I feel my angry Guest
    Fluttering his Wings within my breast!
    [1792. From MS Letter]

## A Wish[1]

##### WRITTEN IN JESUS WOOD, 10 FEBRUARY 1792

Lo! thro' the dusky silence of the groves,
Thro' vales irriguous, and thro' green retreats,
With languid murmur creeps the placid stream,
   And works its secret way!

Awhile meand'ring round its native fields     5
It rolls the playful wave, and winds its flight:
Then downward flowing with awaken'd speed
   Embosoms in the Deep!

Thus thro' its silent tenor may my Life
Smooth its meek stream, by sordid Wealth unclogg'd,  10
Alike unconscious of forensic storms,
   And Glory's blood-stain'd palm!

And when dark Age shall close Life's little day,
Satiate of sport, and weary of its toils,
E'en thus may slumbrous Death my decent limbs   15
   Compose with icy hand!
[1792. From MS Letter]


## A Lover's Complaint to his Mistress

##### WHO DESERTED HIM IN QUEST OF A MORE WEALTHY
##### HUSBAND IN THE EAST INDIES

  The dubious light sad glimmers o'er the sky:
  'Tis Silence all. By lonely anguish torn
  With wandering feet to gloomy groves I fly,
  And wakeful Love still tracks my course forlorn.

[1]Translated from John Jortin's Latin 'Votum'.

Ah! will you, cruel Julia! will you go?                               5
And trust you to the Ocean's dark dismay?
Shall the wide wat'ry world between us flow?
And Winds unpitying snatch my Hopes away?

Thus could you sport with my too easy heart?
Yet tremble, lest not unavenged I grieve!                            10
The Winds may learn your own delusive art,
And faithless Ocean smile – but to deceive.
[1792. From MS Letter]


## Translation of a Greek Ode on Astronomy

WRITTEN BY S. T. COLERIDGE, FOR THE PRIZE
AT CAMBRIDGE, 1793


I

Hail, venerable NIGHT!
O first-created, hail!
Thou who art doom'd in thy dark breast to veil
The dying beam of light,
The eldest and the latest thou,                                      5
Hail, venerable NIGHT!
Around thine ebon brow,
Glittering plays with lightning rays
A wreath of flowers of fire.
The varying clouds with many a hue attire                            10
Thy many-tinted veil.
Holy are the blue graces of thy zone!
But who is he whose tongue can tell
The dewy lustres which thine eyes adorn?
Lovely to some the blushes of the morn;                              15
To some the glories of the Day,
When, blazing with meridian ray,
The gorgeous Sun ascends his highest throne;
But I with solemn and severe delight
Still watch thy constant car, immortal NIGHT!                        20

## II

For then to the celestial Palaces
Urania leads, Urania, she
The Goddess who alone
Stands by the blazing throne,
Effulgent with the light of Deity.                              25
Whom Wisdom, the Creatrix, by her side
Placed on the heights of yonder sky,
And smiling with ambrosial love, unlock'd
The depth of Nature to her piercing eye.
Angelic myriads struck their harps around,                      30
And with triumphant song
The host of Stars, a beauteous throng,
Around the ever-living Mind
In jubilee their mystic dance begun;
When at thy leaping forth, O Sun!                               35
The Morning started in affright,
Astonish'd at thy birth, her Child of Light!

## III

Hail, O Urania, hail!
Queen of the Muses! Mistress of the Song!
For thou didst deign to leave the heavenly throng.              40
As earthward thou thy steps wert bending,
A ray went forth and harbinger'd thy way:
All Ether laugh'd with thy descending.
Thou hadst wreath'd thy hair with roses,
The flower that in the immortal bower                           45
Its deathless bloom discloses.
Before thine awful mien, compelled to shrink
Fled Ignorance abash'd with all her brood
Dragons, and Hags of baleful breath,
Fierce Dreams that wont to drink                               50
The Sepulchre's black blood;
Or on the wings of storms
Riding in fury forms,
Shriek to the mariner the shriek of Death.

## IV

I boast, O Goddess to thy name                                 55
That I have raised the pile of fame;

Therefore to me be given
To roam the starry path of Heaven,
To charioteer with wings on high,
And to rein-in the Tempests of the sky.               60

### V

Chariots of happy Gods! Fountains of Light!
Ye Angel-Temples bright!
May I unblamed your flamy thresholds tread?
I leave Earth's lowly scene;
I leave the Moon serene,                              65
The lovely Queen of Night;
I leave the wide domains,
Beyond where Mars his fiercer light can fling,
And Jupiter's vast plains,
(The many-belted king;)                               70
Even to the solitude where Saturn reigns,
Like some stern tyrant to just exile driven;
Dim-seen the sullen power appears
In that cold solitude of Heaven,
And slow he drags along                               75
The mighty circle of long-lingering years.

### VI

Nor shalt thou escape my sight,
Who at the threshold of the sun-trod domes
Art trembling, . . . youngest Daughter of the Night!
And you, ye fiery-tressed strangers! you,            80
Comets who wander wide,
Will I along your pathless way pursue,
Whence bending I may view
The worlds whom elder Suns have vivified.

### VII

For Hope with loveliest visions soothes my mind,     85
That even in Man, Life's winged power,
When comes again the natal hour,
Shall on heaven-wandering feet
In undecaying youth,
Spring to the blessed seat;                           90

Where round the fields of Truth
The fiery Essences for ever feed;
And o'er the ambrosial mead,
The breezes of serenity
Silent and soothing glide for ever by.            95

### VIII

There, Priest of Nature! dost thou shine,
NEWTON! a King among the Kings divine.
Whether with harmony's mild force,
He guides along its course
The axle of some beauteous star on high            100
Or gazing, in the spring
Ebullient with creative energy,
Feels his pure breast with rapturous joy possest,
Inebriate in the holy ecstasy.

### IX

I may not call thee mortal then, my soul!            105
Immortal longings lift thee to the skies:
Love of thy native home inflames thee now,
With pious madness wise.
Know then thyself! expand thy wings divine!
Soon mingled with thy fathers thou shalt shine            110
A star amid the starry throng,
A God the Gods among.
[Translated by Robert Southey, 1802]

# To Fortune

### ON BUYING A TICKET IN THE IRISH LOTTERY

Composed during a walk to and from the Queen's Head, Gray's Inn
Lane, Holborn, and Hornsby's and Co., Cornhill.

Promptress of unnumber'd sighs,
O snatch that circling bandage from thine eyes!
O look, and smile! No common prayer
Solicits, Fortune! thy propitious care!

For, not a silken son of dress,                                          5
I clink the gilded chains of *politesse*,
Nor ask thy boon what time I scheme
Unholy Pleasure's frail and feverish dream;
Nor yet my view life's *dazzle* blinds –
Pomp! – Grandeur! Power! – I give you to the winds!      10
Let the little bosom cold
Melt only at the sunbeam ray of gold –
My pale cheeks glow – the big drops start –
The rebel *Feeling* riots at my heart!
And if, in lonely durance pent,                                          15
Thy poor mite mourn a brief imprisonment –
That mite at Sorrow's faintest sound
Leaps from its scrip with an elastic bound!
But oh! if ever song thine ear
Might soothe, O haste with fost'ring hand to rear      20
One Flower of Hope! At Love's behest,
Trembling, I plac'd it in my secret breast:
And thrice I've view'd the vernal gleam,
Since oft mine eye, with Joy's electric beam,
Illum'd it – and its sadder hue                                          25
Oft moisten'd with the Tear's ambrosial dew!
Poor wither'd floweret! on its head
Has dark Despair his sickly mildew shed!
But thou, O Fortune! canst relume
Its deaden'd tints – and thou with hardier bloom      30
May'st haply tinge its beauties pale,
And yield the unsunn'd stranger to the western gale!
[1793]


# Perspiration: A Travelling Eclogue

The Dust flies smothering, as on clatt'ring Wheels
Loath'd Aristocracy careers along;
The distant Track quick vibrates to the Eye,
And white and dazzling undulates with heat.
Where scorching to th' unwary Traveller's touch      5
The stone-fence flings its narrow Slip of Shade,

Or where the worn sides of the chalky Road
Yield their scant excavations (sultry Grots!)
Emblem of languid Patience, we behold
The fleecy Files faint-ruminating lie.                    10
[1794. From MS Letter]


## Fragment [1]

O'er the raised earth the gales of evening sigh;
And, see, a daisy peeps upon its slope!
I wipe the dimming waters from mine eye;
Even on the cold grave lights the Cherub Hope.
[1794. From MS]


# On the Prospect of Establishing a Pantisocracy in America

Whilst pale Anxiety, corrosive Care,
The Tear of Woe, the gloom of sad Despair,
    And deepen'd Anguish generous bosoms rend; –
Whilst patriot souls their country's fate lament;
Whilst mad with rage demoniac, foul intent,            5
    Embattled legions Despots vainly send
To arrest the immortal mind's expanding ray
    Of everlasting Truth; – I other climes
Where dawns, with hope serene, a brighter day
    Than e'er saw Albion in her happiest times,          10
With mental eye exulting now explore,
    And soon with kindred minds shall haste to enjoy
    (Free from the ills which here our peace destroy)
Content and Bliss on Transatlantic shore.
[1794. ?S.T.C.]

---

[1] From an 'Elegy on a Lady'.

## Pantisocracy

No more my Visionary Soul shall dwell
On Joys that were! No more endure to weigh
The Shame and Anguish of the evil Day,
Wisely forgetful! O'er the Ocean swell
Sublime of Hope I seek the cottag'd Dell,                    5
Where Virtue calm with careless step may stray,
And dancing to the moonlight Roundelay
The Wizard Passions weave an holy Spell.
Eyes that have ach'd with Sorrow! Ye shall weep
Tears of doubt-mingled Joy, like theirs who start          10
From Precipices of distemper'd Sleep,
On which the fierce-eyed Fiends their Revels keep,
And see the rising Sun, & feel it dart
New Rays of Pleasance trembling to the Heart.
[1794. From MS Letter]


## To William Godwin

### AUTHOR OF Political Justice

O form'd t' illume a sunless world forlorn,
    As o'er the chill and dusky brow of Night,
    In Finland's wintry skies the Mimic Morn[1]
Electric pours a stream of rosy light,

Pleas'd I have mark'd OPPRESSION, terror-pale,            5
    Since, thro' the windings of her dark machine,
    Thy steady eye has shot its glances keen —
And bade th' All-lovely 'scenes at distance hail'.

[1] Aurora Borealis. [S.T.C.]

Nor will I not thy holy guidance bless,
  And hymn thee, GODWIN! with an ardent lay;      10
  For that thy voice, in Passion's stormy day,
When wild I roam'd the bleak Heath of Distress,

Bade the bright Form of JUSTICE meet my way
And told me that her name was HAPPINESS!
[1794]


## To Robert Southey

OF BALLIOL COLLEGE, OXFORD, AUTHOR OF THE
'RETROSPECT', AND OTHER POEMS

Southey! thy melodies steal o'er mine ear
  Like far-off joyance, or the murmuring
  Of wild bees in the sunny showers of Spring –
Sounds of such mingled import as may cheer

The lonely breast, yet rouse a mindful tear:      5
  Wak'd by the Song doth Hope-born FANCY fling
  Rich showers of dewy fragrance from her wing,
Till sickly PASSION's drooping Myrtlēs sear

Blossom anew! But O! more thrill'd, I prize
  Thy sadder strains, that bid in MEMORY's Dream      10
The faded forms of past Delight arise;
  Then soft, on Love's pale cheek, the tearful gleam

Of Pleasure smiles – as faint yet beauteous lies
The imag'd Rainbow on a willowy stream.
[December 1794]

# THE COLLECTION OF 1796

In the following section is reprinted, with only a few minor alterations, the collection, *Poems on Various Subjects*, which Coleridge offered to the public in 1796. He afterwards made many small changes to the text of the poems, largely to meet the charge of bombastic writing which had been levelled at him, but without seriously altering the impression made by the poems as a whole. In their original state indeed, for all their defects, they possess a certain homogeneity and purity of style which are lacking in the later revisions. Together they represent a particular moment in Coleridge's development as a young poet.

At the time of publication the Pantisocratic scheme had collapsed, but he was still heavily influenced by his recent collaboration with Southey. Despite the differences which had impelled them to part company, two dominant interests remain: a yearning after the poetic sublime and a desire to influence mankind by political and religions means. The two interests are neatly represented by the first and last poems in the collection – the monody, first drafted in his schooldays, on Chatterton, whose youthful death had touched Coleridge, along with most young men of his time, and the *Religious Musings*, an attempt to find the religious significance of contemporary events. The pattern is Miltonic – first a *Lycidas*, expressing the poet's own thinly veiled aspirations, and then literary activity in the field of contemporary thought with the ultimate aim of an assault upon the epic form.

The other poems in the collection fall into very rough groups. Coleridge reprints several poems of sensibility, followed by a long series of poems which are described as 'effusions'. These include political sonnets, originally contributed to the *Morning Post*, and more poems of sensibility, including the lines 'to a young ass' which were a ready target for contemporary critics. The word 'effusion' asserts the poet's right to the expression of human emotions in his verse and also suggests a certain disregard for conventional poetic forms. Although these poems are more emotional than the preceding ones, however, sensibility is still the dominant tone. In particular, the influence of Cowper's poetry leads to the development of a conversational style. The next poems take up this style more explicitly and are entitled 'epistles'. They include two poems, *To the Author of Poems published in Bristol* and *From a Young Lady*, which enable him to repay his debt of gratitude to the benevolent, if somewhat obtuse, publisher of his early poems, Joseph Cottle.

The later poems in the collection also reflect his early married happiness. His marriage to Sarah Fricker, daughter of a Bristol schoolmistress, had taken place in October 1795. Although undertaken partly in deference to Southey's misguided insistence that he was under a moral duty to marry her, having paid attentions to her, the marriage was in its early stages happy. Coleridge's happiness, though at times expressed too self-consciously and deliberately to be entirely convincing, is evident in poems such as *Lines written at Shurton Bars* and *The Eolian Harp*.

A strong contrast to the gentle rhythms and sensitivity to nature displayed in these poems is afforded by *Religious Musings*. In this poem Coleridge deals poetically with the various calamitous events which were now shattering the peace of the late eighteenth century. In such a highly charged atmosphere it was not surprising that apocalyptic preaching was current. The atheistic activities of the French philosophers, culminating in the crowning of a whore, suggested that the signs of imminent Apocalypse promised in the Bible were now present on earth. Coleridge's references to the Book of Revelation are therefore in tune with the spirit of the time. He sees the French Revolution not as, in itself, a direct outbreak of evil but as a violent foreshadowing of the coming Apocalypse. While his verse displays the influence of Milton, moreover, the thought of his poem expresses his devotion to current scientific thought, following the discoveries of Newton, Hartley and Priestley. The final lines of the poem represent his own world-view, a variation on the mystical tradition that this world is symbolic of the supernatural order. Beyond the marvellous workings of the physical world and more particularly of the human body he sees

> . . . th' immeasurable fount
> Ebullient with creative Deity!

The whole of Nature is drawn together by the power of Love, the workings of which are expressed by the image of water thawed by the rays of the sun, and stimulated into musical flow.

The visionary conception of nature which is hinted at in these last lines is expressed more centrally in *The Eolian Harp*, the most notable piece of the collection. Coleridge himself wrote of it some years later: 'This I think the most perfect poem I ever wrote.' He was referring, presumably, to the very subtle blending of thought and imagery which characterizes it. The image of the Aeolian harp mediates perfectly between Coleridge's natural style of conversational sensitivity and his desire to present a stringent intellectual argument in his poetry – his lifelong search for a poetry that would unite heart and head.

The Aeolian harp, very fashionable in the late eighteenth century, was a stringed instrument which could be placed in the aperture of a casement window so that the touch of even a slight breeze would produce a soft dying note. That it should have been a favourite device of the time is not surprising, since it represented a happy and unusual conjunction of nature and art. Nature provided both the tone and timing of the music, with no more human intervention than was required for the initial positioning of the instrument.

More, even, than most 'men of sensibility' in his age, Coleridge delighted in the delicate tones and harmonies of nature such as bird song, the noise of wind in trees, the tenderness of human affections or the curiously harmonic power of moonlight. His own sensibility was unusually developed and refined, very largely governing his response to nature. Moreover 'sensibility' played an important part in contemporary psychological theory. Elementary conceptions of the nervous system, before the discovery of electricity facilitated knowledge of its workings, had led Hartley to formulate his theory of 'vibrations'. He held that all sensation in the human body took place by means of vibrations along the nerves, which reacted like the strings of a musical instrument. Moreover, each vibration left a small trace, called a 'vibratiuncle', which formed part of the body's apparatus for remembering. Coleridge read Hartley and was fascinated: he called his eldest son after him. And in these early poems one can see the emergence of a world-view dominated by his awareness of a universe which is filled with vibrations – and at best vibrating in harmony with the source of all its being.

This percept is at the root of all Coleridge's nature worship. It is because nature expresses directly the music of the creator that human beings ought to expose themselves to it. Their own life will be enriched, and their own response will be a harmonious music in tune with their creator. The mediation of the Aeolian harp between thought and sensibility in this poem is thus no accident. On the contrary, it is the obvious image for a communion with God and nature which is viewed in terms of vibration. The next lines (probably written many years later) provide a mature expression of this central theme:

> O! the one Life within us and abroad,
> Which meets all motion and becomes its soul,
> A light in sound, a sound-like power in light,
> Rhythm in all thought, and joyance every where –

He then advances to the vision of all nature as a vast system of wind-harps, played upon by the 'intellectual breeze' of the Creator.

The final lines of the poem recognize that such ideas are flights beyond the limits recognized by normal Christian devotion. It is this recognition that makes him diffident in expressing such speculations in public during the following years. Nevertheless, his letters and conversations show that he was constantly considering the theme of the 'one Life', intent on the notion that it might be the key to all intellectual problems. For the moment it was so satisfying as to facilitate the composition of one of his most rounded and successful poems.

## Monody on the Death of Chatterton

When faint and sad o'er Sorrow's desart wild
Slow journeys onward poor Misfortune's child;
When fades each lovely form by Fancy drest,
And inly pines the self-consuming breast;
No scourge of scorpions in thy right arm dread,                    5
No helméd terrors nodding o'er thy head,
Assume, O DEATH! the cherub wings of PEACE,
And bid the heart-sick Wanderer's anguish cease!

Thee, CHATTERTON! yon unblest stones protect
From Want, and the bleak Freezings of neglect!                    10
Escap'd the sore wounds of Affliction's rod
Meek at the Throne of Mercy, and of God,
Perchance, thou raisest high th' enraptur'd hymn
   Amid the blaze of Seraphim!

Yet oft ('tis Nature's bosom-startling call)                      15
I weep, that heaven-born Genius *so* should fall;
And oft, in Fancy's saddest hour, my soul
Averted shudders at the poison'd bowl.
Now groans my sickening heart, as still I view
   Thy corse of livid hue;                                      20
And now a flash of indignation high
Darts thro' the tear, that glistens in mine eye!

Is this the land of song-ennobled line?
Is this the land, where Genius ne'er in vain
   Pour'd forth his lofty strain?                               25
Ah me! yet SPENSER, gentlest bard divine,
   Beneath chill Disappointment's shade
His weary limbs in lonely anguish lay'd
   And o'er her darling dead
   PITY hopeless hung her head,                                 30
While 'mid the pelting of that merciless storm,'
Sunk to the cold earth OTWAY's famish'd form!

Sublime of thought, and confident of fame,
From vales where Avon[1] winds the MINSTREL came.

[1] Avon, a river near Bristol, the birth-place of Chatterton. [S.T.C.]

Light-hearted youth! aye, as he hastes along,                    35
    He meditates the future song,
How dauntless Ælla fray'd the Dacyan foes;
        And, as floating high in air,
        Glitter the sunny visions fair,
    His eyes dance rapture, and his bosom glows!                 40
Friend to the friendless, to the sick man health,
With generous joy he views th' *ideal* wealth;
He hears the widow's heaven-breath'd prayer of praise;
He marks the shelter'd orphan's tearful gaze;
Or, where the sorrow-shrivell'd captive lay,                     45
Pours the bright blaze of Freedom's noon-tide ray:
And now, indignant, 'grasps the patriot steel',
And her own iron rod he makes Oppression feel.


        Clad in Nature's rich array,
        And bright in all her tender hues,                       50
Sweet tree of Hope! thou loveliest child of Spring!
How fair didst thou disclose thine early bloom,
    Loading the west-winds with its soft perfume!
And Fancy, elfin form of gorgeous wing,
    On every blossom hung her fostering dews,                    55
        That, changeful, wanton'd to the orient day!
But soon upon thy poor unshelter'd head
Did Penury her sickly mildew shed:
And soon the scathing Lightning bade thee stand
In frowning horror o'er the blighted land!                      60


Ah! where are fled the charms of vernal Grace,
And Joy's wild gleams, that lighten'd o'er thy face?
YOUTH of tumultuous soul, and haggard eye!
Thy wasted form, thy hurried steps I view,
On thy cold forehead starts the anguish'd dew:                  65
And dreadful was that bosom-rending sigh!


    Such were the struggles of the gloomy hour,
        When CARE, of wither'd brow
    Prepar'd the poison's dea*'      power:
Already to thy lips was rais  the bowl,                          70
        When near thee stood AFFECTION meek
        (Her bosom bare, and wildly pale her cheek)

Thy sullen gaze she bade thee roll
  On scenes that well might melt thy soul;
Thy native cot she flash'd upon thy view,                    75
Thy native cot, where still, at close of day,
PEACE smiling sate, and listen'd to thy lay;
Thy Sister's shrieks she bade thee hear,
And mark thy Mother's thrilling tear;
    See, see her breast's convulsive throe,                 80
    Her silent agony of woe!
Ah! dash the poison'd chalice from thy hand!


And thou hadst dash'd it, at her soft command,
But that DESPAIR and INDIGNATION rose,
And told again the story of thy woes;                        85
Told the keen insult of th' unfeeling heart,
The dread dependence on the low-born mind;
Told every pang, with which thy soul must smart,
Neglect, and grinning Scorn, and Want combined!
Recoiling quick, thou bad'st the friend of pain             90
Roll the black tide of Death thro' every freezing vein!


Ye woods! that wave o'er Avon's rocky steep,
To Fancy's ear sweet is your murm'ring deep!
For *here* she loves the cypress wreath to weave;
Watching, with wistful eye, the sad'ning tints of eve.      95
Here, far from men, amid this pathless grove,
In solemn thought the Minstrel wont to rove,
Like star-beam on the slow sequester'd tide
Lone-glittering, thro' the high tree branching wide.
And here, in INSPIRATION's eager hour,                      100
When most the big soul feels the madning pow'r,
    These wilds, these caverns roaming o'er,
    Round which the screaming sea-gulls soar,
With wild unequal steps he pass'd along,
Oft pouring on the winds a broken song:                     105
Anon, upon some rough rock's fearful brow
Would pause abrupt – and gaze upon the waves below.


Poor CHATTERTON! *he* sorrows for thy fate
Who would have prais'd and lov'd thee, ere too late.

Poor CHATTERTON! farewell! of darkest hues          110
This chaplet cast I on thy unshap'd tomb;
But dare no longer on the sad theme muse,
Lest kindred woes persuade a kindred doom:
For oh! big gall-drops, shook from FOLLY's wing,
Have blacken'd the fair promise of my spring;          115
And the stern FATE transpierc'd with viewless dart
The last pale Hope, that shiver'd at my heart!

Hence, gloomy thoughts! no more my soul shall dwell
On joys that were! no more endure to weigh
The shame and anguish of the evil day,          120
Wisely forgetful! O'er the ocean swell
Sublime of Hope I seek the cottag'd dell
Where VIRTUE calm with careless step may stray;
And, dancing to the moon-light roundelay,
The wizard PASSIONS weave an holy spell!          125

O CHATTERTON! that thou wert yet alive!
Sure thou would'st spread the canvass to the gale,
And love, with us, the tinkling team to drive
O'er peaceful Freedom's UNDIVIDED dale;
And we, at sober eve, would round thee throng,          130
Hanging, enraptur'd, on thy stately song!
And greet with smiles the young-eyed POESY
All deftly mask'd, as hoar ANTIQUITY.

Alas vain Phantasies! the fleeting brood
Of Woe self-solac'd in her dreamy mood!          135
Yet will I love to follow the sweet dream,
Where Susquehannah pours his untam'd stream;
And on some hill, whose forest-frowning side
Waves o'er the murmurs of his calmer tide,
Will raise a solemn CENOTAPH to thee,          140
Sweet Harper of time-shrouded MINSTRELSY!
And there, sooth'd sadly by the dirgeful wind,
Muse on the sore ills I had left behind.
[1796 version]

## *To the Rev. W. J. Hort*

### WHILE TEACHING A YOUNG LADY SOME SONG-TUNES ON HIS FLUTE

#### I

Hush! ye clamorous Cares! be mute!
  Again, dear Harmonist! again
Thro' the hollow of thy flute
  Breathe that passion-warbled strain:
Till MEMORY each form shall bring      5
  The loveliest of her shadowy throng;
And HOPE, that soars on sky-lark wing,
  Carol wild her gladdest song!

#### II

O skill'd with magic spell to roll
The thrilling tones, that concentrate the soul!      10
Breathe thro' thy flute those tender notes again,
While near thee sits the chaste-eyed Maiden mild;
And bid her raise the Poet's kindred strain
In soft impassion'd voice, correctly wild.

#### III

In Freedom's UNDIVIDED dell,      15
Where *Toil* and *Health* with mellow'd *Love* shall dwell,
  Far from folly, far from men,
  In the rude romantic glen,
  Up the cliff, and thro' the glade,
  Wand'ring with the dear-lov'd maid,      20
  I shall listen to the lay,
  And ponder on thee far away!
Still, as she bids those thrilling notes aspire
('Making my fond attunéd heart her lyre')
Thy honor'd form, my Friend! shall re-appear,      25
And I will thank thee with a raptur'd tear.
[1795]

## Songs of the Pixies

The Pixies, in the superstition of Devonshire, are a race of beings invisibly small, and harmless or friendly to man. At a small distance from a village in that county, half-way up a wood-cover'd hill, is an excavation, called the Pixies' Parlour. The roots of old trees form its cieling; and on its sides are innumerable cyphers, among which the Author discovered his own cypher and those of his brothers, cut by the hand of their childhood. At the foot of the hill flows the river Otter.

To this place the Author conducted a party of young Ladies, during the Summer months of the year 1793; one of whom, of stature elegantly small, and of complexion colourless yet clear, was proclaimed the Fairy Queen: On which occasion the following Irregular Ode was written.

I

Whom the untaught Shepherds call
   PIXIES in their madrigal,
Fancy's children, here we dwell:
   Welcome, LADIES! to our cell.
Here the wren of softest note          5
   Builds it's nest and warbles well;
Here the blackbird strains his throat:
   Welcome, LADIES! to our cell.

II

When fades the moon all shadowy-pale,
And scuds the cloud before the gale,       10
Ere MORN with living gems bedight
Purples the East with streaky light,
We sip the furze-flowr's fragrant dews
Clad in robes of rainbow hues
Richer, than the deepen'd bloom,       15
That glows on Summer's lily-scented plume:
Or, sport amid the rosy gleam
Sooth'd by the distant-tinkling team,
While lusty LABOR scouting sorrow
Bids the DAME a glad good-morrow,      20
Who jogs th' accustom'd road along,
And paces cheery to her cheering song.

### III

But not our filmy pinion
We scorch amid the blaze of day,
When NOONTIDE's fiery-tresséd minion     25
    Flashes the fervid ray.
    Aye from the sultry heat
    We to the cave retreat
O'ercanopied by huge roots intertwin'd
With wildest texture, blacken'd o'er with age:     30
Round them their mantle green the ivies bind,
    Beneath whose foliage pale
    Fann'd by the unfrequent gale
We shield us from the Tyrants' mid-day rage.

### IV

Thither, while the murm'ring throng     35
Of wild-bees, hum their drowsy song,
By Indolence and Fancy brought,
A youthful BARD, 'unknown to Fame',
Wooes the Queen of solemn thought,
And heaves the gentle mis'ry of a sigh     40
    Gazing with tearful eye,
    As round our sandy grot appear
    Many a rudely sculptur'd name
    To pensive MEM'RY dear!
Weaving gay dreams of sunny-tinctur'd hue     45
    We glance before his view:
O'er his hush'd soul our soothing witch'ries shed
And twine our faery garlands round his head.

### V

When EVENING's dusky car
Crown'd with her dewy star     50
Steals o'er the fading sky in shadowy flight;
    On leaves of aspen trees
    We tremble to the breeze
Veil'd from the grosser ken of mortal sight.
    Or, haply, at the visionary hour,     55
Along our wildly-bow'rd sequestred walk,
We listen to the enamour'd rustic's talk;

Heave with the heavings of the maiden's breast,
Where young-eyed LOVES have built their turtle nest;
    Or guide of soul-subduing power      60
Th' electric flash, that from the melting eye
Darts the fond question and the soft reply.

### VI

    Or thro' the mystic ringlets of the vale
    We flash our faery feet in gamesome prank;
    Or, silent-sandal'd, pay our defter court,      65
    Circling the SPIRIT of the WESTERN GALE,
    Where, wearied with his flower-caressing sport,
    Supine he slumbers on a violet bank;
Then with quaint music hymn the parting gleam,
By lonely OTTER's sleep-persuading stream;      70
Or where his waves, with loud unquiet song
Dash'd o'er the rocky channel froths along;
Or where, his silver waters smooth'd to rest,
The tall trees' shadow sleeps upon his breast.

### VII

    Hence! thou lingerer, LIGHT!      75
    EVE saddens into NIGHT.
Mother of wildly-working dreams! we view
    The SOMBRE HOURS that round thee stand
    With down-cast eyes (a duteous band!)
Their dark robes dripping with the heavy dew.      80
    SORCRESS of the ebon throne!
    Thy power the PIXIES own,
    When round thy raven brow
    Heaven's lucent roses glow,
    And clouds, in watry colours drest,      85
Float in light drapery o'er thy sable vest:
What time the pale moon sheds a softer day
Mellowing the woods beneath its pensive beam:
For mid the quiv'ring light 'tis ours to play,
Aye-dancing to the cadence of the stream.      90

### VIII

Welcome, LADIES! to the cell,
Where the blameless PIXIES dwell.

But thou, Sweet Nymph! proclaim'd our Faery Queen,
    With what obeisance meet
      Thy presence shall we greet?                                    95
For lo! attendant on thy steps are seen
   Graceful EASE in artless stole,
   And white-robed PURITY of soul,
    With HONOR's softer mein:
   MIRTH of the loosely-flowing hair,                                 100
And meek eyed PITY eloquently fair,
   Whose tearful cheeks are lovely to the view,
     As snow-drop wet with dew.


IX

Unboastful Maid! though now the LILY pale
   Transparent grace thy beauties meek;                             105
Yet ere again along the impurpling vale,
The purpling vale and elfin-haunted grove,
Young Zephyr his fresh flowers profusely throws,
   We'll tinge with livelier hues thy cheek;
And, haply, from the nectar-breathing ROSE                              110
     Extract a BLUSH for LOVE!
[1793]


## Lines

### WRITTEN AT THE KING'S ARMS, ROSS, FORMERLY
### THE HOUSE OF THE 'MAN OF ROSS'


Richer than MISER o'er his countless hoards,
Nobler than KINGS, or king-polluted LORDS,
Here dwelt the MAN OF ROSS! O Trav'ller, hear!
Departed Merit claims a reverent tear.
Beneath this roof if thy cheer'd moments pass,                            5
Fill to the good man's name one grateful glass:
To higher zest shall MEM'RY wake thy soul,
And VIRTUE mingle in th' ennobled bowl.
But if, like me, thro' life's distressful scene
Lonely and sad thy pilgrimage hath been;                                 10

And if, thy breast with heart-sick anguish fraught,
Thou journeyest onward tempest-tost in thought;
Here cheat thy cares! in generous visions melt,
And dream of Goodness, thou hast never felt!
[1794]


## Lines

### TO A BEAUTIFUL SPRING IN A VILLAGE

Once more, sweet Stream! with slow foot wand'ring near
I bless thy milky waters cold and clear.
Escap'd the flashing of the noontide hours
With one fresh garland of Pierian flowers
(Ere from thy zephyr-haunted brink I turn)            5
My languid hand shall wreath thy mossy urn.
For not thro' pathless grove with murmur rude
Thou soothest the sad wood-nymph, SOLITUDE:
Nor thine unseen in cavern depths to well,
The HERMIT-FOUNTAIN of some dripping cell!            10
Pride of the Vale! thy useful streams supply
The scatter'd cots and peaceful hamlet nigh.
The elfin tribe around thy friendly banks
With infant uproar and soul-soothing pranks,
Releas'd from school, their little hearts at rest,            15
Launch paper navies on thy waveless breast.

The rustic here at eve with pensive look
Whistling lorn ditties leans upon his crook,
Or starting pauses with hope-mingled dread
To list the much-lov'd maid's accustom'd tread:            20
She, vainly mindful of her dame's command,
Loiters, the long-fill'd pitcher in her hand.

Unboastful Stream! thy fount with pebbled falls
The faded form of past delight recalls,
What time the morning sun of Hope arose,            25
And all was joy; save when another's woes
A transient gloom upon my soul imprest,
Like passing clouds impictur'd on thy breast.

Life's current then ran sparkling to the noon,
Or silv'ry stole beneath the pensive Moon.                    30
Ah! now it works rude brakes and thorns among,
Or o'er the rough rock bursts and foams along!
[1794]


## Epitaph on an Infant

Ere Sin could blight or Sorrow fade,
    DEATH came with friendly care;
The opening bud to Heaven convey'd
    And bade it blossom there.
[1794]


## Lines on a Friend

### WHO DIED OF A FRENZY FEVER INDUCED BY CALUMNIOUS REPORTS

Edmund! thy grave with aking eye I scan,
And inly groan for Heaven's poor outcast, Man!
'Tis tempest all or gloom: in early youth
If gifted with the Ithuriel lance of Truth
He force to start amid her feign'd caress                    5
VICE, siren-hag! in native ugliness,
A Brother's fate will haply rouse the tear,
And on he goes in heaviness and fear!
But if his fond heart call to PLEASURE's bower
Some pigmy FOLLY in a careless hour,                    10
The faithless guest shall stamp th' inchanted ground
And mingled forms of Mis'ry rise around:
Heart-fretting FEAR, with pallid look aghast,
That courts the future woe to hide the past;
REMORSE, the poison'd arrow in his side                    15
And loud lewd MIRTH, to Anguish close allied:
Till FRENZY, fierce-ey'd child of moping pain,
Darts her hot lightning flash athwart the brain.

Rest, injur'd shade! Shall SLANDER squatting near
Spit her cold venom in a DEAD MAN's ear?                         20
'Twas thine to feel the sympathetic glow
In Merit's joy, and Poverty's meek woe;
Thine all, that cheer the moment as it flies,
The *zoneless* CARES, and smiling COURTESIES.
Nurs'd in thy heart the firmer Virtues grew,                     25
And in thy heart they wither'd! Such chill dew
Wan INDOLENCE on each young blossom shed;
And VANITY her filmy net-work spread,
With eye that roll'd around in asking gaze,
And tongue that traffick'd in the trade of praise.              30
Thy follies such! the hard world mark'd them well—
Were they more wise, the PROUD who never fell?
Rest, injur'd shade! the poor man's prayer of praise
On heaven-ward wing thy wounded soul shall raise.

As oft at twilight gloom thy grave I pass,                      35
And sit me down upon its' recent grass,
With introverted eye I contemplate
Similitude of soul, perhaps of—Fate!
To me hath Heaven with bounteous hand assign'd
Energic Reason and a shaping mind,                              40
The daring ken of Truth, the Patriot's part,
And Pity's sigh, that breathes the gentle heart—
Sloth-jaundic'd all! and from my graspless hand
Drop Friendship's precious pearls, like hour-glass sand.
I weep, yet stoop not! the faint anguish flows,                 45
A dreamy pang in Morning's fev'rish doze.

Is this pil'd Earth our Being's passless mound?
Till me, cold grave! is Death with poppies crown'd?
Tired Centinel! mid fitful starts I nod,                        50
And fain would sleep, though pillow'd on a clod!
[1794]

## To a Young Lady

### WITH A POEM ON THE FRENCH REVOLUTION

Much on my early youth I love to dwell,
Ere yet I bade that friendly dome farewell,
Where first, beneath the echoing cloisters pale,
I heard of guilt and wonder'd at the tale!
Yet though the hours flew by on careless wing,                    5
Full heavily of Sorrow would I sing.
Aye as the star of evening flung its beam
In broken radiance on the wavy stream,
My soul amid the pensive twilight gloom
Mourn'd with the breeze, O LEE BOO![1] o'er thy tomb.              10
Where'er I wander'd, PITY still was near,
Breath'd from the heart and glisten'd in the tear:
No knell that toll'd, but fill'd my anxious eye,
And suff'ring Nature wept that *one* should die![2]

Thus to sad sympathies I sooth'd my breast,                        15
Calm, as the rainbow in the weeping West:
When slumb'ring FREEDOM roused by high DISDAIN
With giant fury burst her triple chain!
Fierce on her front the blasting Dog-star glow'd;
Her Banners, like a midnight Meteor, flow'd;                       20
Amid the yelling of the storm-rent skies
She came, and scatter'd battles from her eyes!
Then EXULTATION wak'd the patriot fire
And swept with wilder hand th' Alcaean lyre:
Red from the Tyrants' wound I shook the lance,                     25
And strode in joy the reeking plains of France!

In ghastly horror lie th' Oppressors low
And my heart akes, tho' MERCY struck the blow.
With wearied thought once more I seek the shade,

[1] LEE BOO, the son of ABBA THULE, Prince of the Pelew Islands came over to England with Captain Wilson, died of the small-pox, and is buried in Greenwich Church-yard. See Keate's *Account* [*of the Pelew Islands*, 1788]. [S.T.C.]
[2] 'And suffering Nature weeps that *one* should die.' – Southey's *Retrospect*. [S.T.C.]

Where peaceful Virtue weaves the MYRTLE braid.    30
And O! if EYES, whose holy glances roll,
The eloquent messengers of the pure soul;
If SMILES more winning and a gentler MIEN,
Than the love-wilder'd Maniac's brain hath seen
Shaping celestial forms in vacant air;    35
If these demand th' empassion'd Poet's care——
If MIRTH, and soften'd SENSE, and WIT refined,
The blameless features of a lovely mind;
Then haply shall my trembling hand assign
No fading wreath to BEAUTY's saintly shrine.    40
Nor, SARA! thou these early flowers refuse——
Ne'er lurk'd the snake beneath their simple hues:
No purple bloom the Child of Nature brings
From Flatt'ry's night-shade: as he feels, he sings.
[September 1794]

## Absence

### A FAREWELL ODE

Where grac'd with many a classic spoil
CAM rolls his reverend stream along,
I haste to urge the learnéd toil
That sternly chides my love-lorn song:
Ah me! too mindful of the days    5
Illum'd by PASSION's orient rays,
When Peace, and Chearfulness, and Health
Enrich'd me with the best of wealth.

Ah fair Delights! that o'er my soul
On Mem'ry's wing, like shadows, fly!    10
Ah Flowers! which Joy from Eden stole
While Innocence stood smiling by!—
But cease, fond Heart! this bootless moan.
Those Hours on rapid Pinions flown
Shall yet return, by ABSENCE crown'd,    15
And scatter livelier roses round.

The Sun, who ne'er remits his fires
On heedless eyes may pour the day:
The Moon, that oft from Heav'n retires,
Endears her renovated ray.                          20
What tho' she leave the sky unblest
To mourn awhile in murky vest?
When she relumes her lovely Light,
We bless the Wanderer of the Night.
[1791]

## Effusions

Content, as random Fancies might inspire,
If his weak harp at times or lonely lyre
He struck with desultory hand, and drew
Some soften'd tones to Nature not untrue.
                                        Bowles

I

### To the Rev. W. L. Bowles

My heart has thank'd thee, Bowles! for those soft strains
Whose sadness soothes me, like the murmuring
Of wild-bees in the sunny showers of spring!
For hence not callous to the mourner's pains
Thro' Youth's gay prime and thornless paths I went:      5
And when the *darker* day of life began,
And I did roam, a thought-bewilder'd man!
Their mild and manliest melancholy lent
A mingled charm, such as the pang consign'd
To slumber, tho' the big tear it renew'd;               10
Bidding a strange mysterious Pleasure brood
Over the wavy and tumultous mind,
As the great Spirit erst with plastic sweep
Mov'd on the darkness of the unform'd deep.
[1794–6]

## II

### *Burke*

As late I lay in slumber's shadowy vale,
With wetted cheek and in a mourner's guise
I saw the sainted form of FREEDOM rise:
She spake! not sadder moans the autumnal gale.
'Great Son of Genius! sweet to me thy name,　　　　5
Ere in an evil hour with alter'd voice
Thou badst Oppression's hireling crew rejoice
Blasting with wizard spell my laurell'd fame.
Yet never, BURKE! thou drank'st Corruption's bowl![1]
Thee stormy Pity and the cherish'd lure　　　　10
Of Pomp, and proud Precipitance of soul
Wilder'd with meteor fires. Ah Spirit pure!
That Error's mist had left thy purgéd eye:
So might I clasp thee with a Mother's joy!'
[1794]

## III

### *Pitt*

Not always should the tear's ambrosial dew
Roll its soft anguish down thy furrow'd cheek!
Not always heaven-breath'd tones of suppliance meek
Beseem thee, MERCY! Yon dark Scowler view,
Who with proud words of dear-lov'd Freedom came—　　　　5

[1]When I composed this line, I had not read the following paragraph in the *Cambridge Intelligencer* (of Saturday, 21 November 1795): –

*When Mr Burke first crossed over the House of Commons from the Opposition to the Ministry, he received a pension of £1200 a year charged on the King's Privy Purse!* When he had completed his labours, it was then a question what recompence his service deserved. Mr Burke wanting a present supply of money, it was thought that a pension of £2000 per annum *for forty years certain*, would sell for eighteen years' purchase, and bring him of course £36,000. But this pension must, by the very unfortunate act, of which Mr Burke himself was the author, have come before Parliament. Instead of this Mr Pitt suggested the idea of a pension of £2000 a year for *three lives*, to be charged on the King's Revenue of the West India 4⅛ per cents. This was tried at the market, but it was found that it would not produce the £36,000 which were wanted. In consequence of this a pension of £2500 per annum, *for three lives* on the 4½ West India Fund, the lives to be nominated by Mr Burke, that he may accommodate the purchasers, is *finally* granted to this disinterested patriot! He has thus retir'd from the trade of politics, with pensions to the amount of £3700 a year. [S.T.C.]

More blasting, than the mildew from the South!
And kiss'd his country with Iscariot mouth
(Ah! foul apostate from his Father's fame!)[1]
Then fix'd her on the cross of deep distress,
And at safe distance marks the thirsty Lance          10
Pierce her big side! But O! if some strange trance
The eye-lids of thy stern-brow'd Sister[2] press,
Seize, MERCY! thou more terrible the brand,
And hurl her thunderbolts with fiercer hand!
[1794]


IV

*Priestley*

Tho' rous'd by that dark Vizir RIOT rude
Have driven our PRIESTLEY o'er the ocean swell;
Tho' SUPERSTITION and her wolfish brood
Bay his mild radiance, impotent and fell;
Calm in his halls of Brightness he shall dwell!          5
For lo! RELIGION at his strong behest
Starts with mild anger from the Papal spell,
And flings to Earth her tinsel-glittering vest,
Her mitred state and cumbrous pomp unholy;
And JUSTICE wakes·to bid th' Oppressor wail          10
Insulting aye the wrongs of patient Folly;
And from her dark retreat by Wisdom won
Meek NATURE slowly lifts her matron veil
To smile with fondness on her gazing son!
[1794]


V

*To the Honourable Mr Erskine*

When British Freedom for an happier land
Spread her broad wings, that flutter'd with affright,
ERSKINE! thy voice she heard, and paus'd her flight
Sublime of hope! For dreadless thou didst stand
(Thy censer glowing with the hallow'd flame)          5

[1]Earl of Chatham. [S.T.C., 1797]
[2]Justice. [S.T.C., 1797]

An hireless Priest before th' insulted shrine,
And at her altar pourd'st the stream divine
Of unmatch'd eloquence. Therefore thy name
Her sons shall venerate, and cheer thy breast
With blessings heaven-ward breath'd. And when the doom    10
Of Nature bids thee die, beyond the tomb
Thy light shall shine: as sunk beneath the West
Tho' the great Summer Sun eludes our gaze,
Still burns wide Heaven with his distended blaze.
[1794]


VI

### To *Richard Brinsley Sheridan, Esq.*

It was some Spirit, SHERIDAN! that breath'd
O'er thy young mind such wildly-various power!
My soul hath mark'd thee in her shaping hour,
Thy temples with Hymettian flowrets[1] wreath'd:
And sweet thy voice, as when o'er Laura's bier    5
Sad music trembled thro' Vauclusa's glade;
Sweet, as at dawn the love-lorn Serenade
That wafts soft dreams to Slumber's list'ning ear.
Now patriot Rage and Indignation high
Swell the full tones! And now thine eye-beams dance    10
Meanings of Scorn and Wit's quaint revelry!
Writhes inly from the bosom-probing glance

---

[1] *Hymettian flowrets*. Hymettus a mountain near Athens, celebrated for its honey. This alludes to Mr Sheridan's classical attainments, and the following four lines to the exquisite sweetness and almost *Italian* delicacy of his Poetry. In Shakespeare's *Lover's Complaint* there is a fine stanza almost prophetically characteristic of Mr Sheridan:

> So on the tip of his subduing tongue
> All kind of argument and question deep,
> All replication prompt and reason strong
> For his advantage still did wake and sleep,
> To make the weeper laugh, the laugher weep:
> He had the dialect and different skill,
> Catching all passions in his craft of will:
> That he did in the general bosom reign
> Of young and old.
> [S.T.C]

Th' Apostate by the brainless rout ador'd,
As erst that elder Fiend beneath great Michael's sword.
[1795]

## VII

### Mrs Siddons[1]

As when a child on some long winter's night
Affrighted clinging to its Grandam's knees
With eager wond'ring and perturb'd delight
Listens strange tales of fearful dark decrees
Mutter'd to wretch by necromantic spell;            5
Or of those hags, who at the witching time
Of murky midnight ride the air sublime,
And mingle foul embrace with fiends of Hell:
Cold Horror drinks its blood! Anon the tear
More gentle starts, to hear the Beldame tell         10
Of pretty Babes, that lov'd each other dear,
Murder'd by cruel Uncle's mandate fell:
Even such the shiv'ring joys thy tones impart,
Even so thou, SIDDONS! meltest my sad heart!
[1794]

## VIII

### Koskiusko

O what a loud and fearful shriek[2] was there,
As tho' a thousand souls one death-groan pour'd!
Ah me! they view'd beneath an hireling's sword
Fall'n KOSKIUSKO! Thro' the burthen'd air
(As pauses the tir'd Cossac's barb'rous yell         5
Of Triumph) on the chill and midnight gale
Rises with frantic burst or sadder swell
The dirge of murder'd Hope! while Freedom pale

---

[1]This sonnet may have been altered by Coleridge, but was no doubt written by Lamb and given by him to Coleridge to make up his tale of sonnets for the *Morning Chronicle*. [E.H.C.]
[2]When *Kosciusko* was observed to fall, the Polish ranks set up a shriek. [S.T.C.]

Bends in *such* anguish o'er her destin'd bier,
As if from eldest time some Spirit meek                    10
Had gather'd in a mystic urn each tear
That ever furrow'd a sad Patriot's cheek;
And she had drain'd the sorrows of the bowl
Ev'n till she reel'd, intoxicate of soul!
[1794]


## IX

### La Fayette

As when far off the warbled strains are heard
That soar on Morning's wing the vales among,
Within his cage th' imprison'd matin bird
Swells the full chorus with a generous song:
He bathes no pinion in the dewy light,                     5
No Father's joy, no Lover's bliss he shares,
Yet still the rising radiance cheers his sight—
His Fellows' freedom soothes the Captive's cares!
Thou, FAYETTE! who didst wake with startling voice
Life's better sun from that long wintry night,            10
Thus in thy Country's triumphs shalt rejoice
And mock with raptures high the dungeon's might:
For lo! the morning struggles into day,
And Slavery's spectres shriek and vanish from the ray!
[1794]


## X

### To Earl Stanhope

Not, STANHOPE! with the Patriot's doubtful name
I mock thy worth—FRIEND OF THE HUMAN RACE!
Since scorning Faction's low and partial aim
Aloof thou wendest in thy stately pace,
Thyself redeeming from that leprous stain,                5
NOBILITY: and aye unterrify'd
Pourest thine Abdiel warnings on the train
That sit complotting with rebellious pride
'Gainst her[1] who from the Almighty's bosom leapt
With whirlwind arm, fierce Minister of Love!             10

---

[1] Gallic Liberty. [S.T.C.]

Wherefore, ere Virtue o'er thy tomb hath wept,
Angels shall lead thee to the Throne above:
And thou from forth its clouds shalt hear the voice,
Champion of FREEDOM and her God! rejoice!
[1795]

[*Effusions* XI–XIII *were contributed by Charles Lamb*]

## XIV

### *The Gentle Look*

Thou gentle LOOK, that didst my soul beguile,
Why hast thou left me? Still in some fond dream
Revisit my sad heart, auspicious SMILE!
As falls on closing flowers the lunar beam:
What time, in sickly mood, at parting day                    5
I lay me down and think of happier years;
Of Joys, that glimmer'd in Hope's twilight ray,
Then left me darkling in a vale of tears.
O pleasant days of Hope—for ever gone!
Could I recall you!—but that thought is vain.                10
Availeth not Persuasion's sweetest tone
To lure the fleet-wing'd Travellers back again:
Yet fair, tho' faint, their images shall gleam
Like the bright Rainbow on a willowy stream.
[?1793]

## XV

### *The Outcast*

Pale Roamer through the Night! thou poor Forlorn!
Remorse that man on his death-bed possess,
Who in the credulous hour of tenderness
Betrayed, then cast thee forth to Want and Scorn!
The world is pityless: the Chaste one's pride                5
Mimic of Virtue scowls on thy distress:
Thy Loves and they, that envied thee, deride:
And Vice alone will shelter Wretchedness!

O! I am sad to think, that there should be
Cold-bosom'd Lewd ones, who endure to place          10
Foul offerings on the shrine of Misery,
And force from FAMINE the caress of LOVE!
May He shed healing on thy sore disgrace,
He, the great COMFORTER that rules above!
[?1794]


### XVI

#### *Pity*

Sweet Mercy! how my very heart has bled
To see thee, poor OLD MAN! and thy gray hairs
Hoar with the snowy blast: while no one cares
To cloathe thy shrivell'd limbs and palsied head.
My father! throw away this tatter'd vest          5
That mocks thy shiv'ring! take my garment—use
A young man's arms! I'll melt these frozen dews
That hang from thy white beard and numb thy breast.
My SARA too shall tend thee, like a Child:
And thou shalt talk, in our fire side's recess,          10
Of purple Pride, that scowls on Wretchedness.—
He did not so, the GALILÆAN mild,
Who met the Lazars turn'd from rich men's doors
And call'd them Friends, and heal'd their noisome Sores!
[?1795]


### XVII

#### *Genevieve*[1]

Maid of my Love, sweet GENEVIEVE!
In Beauty's light you glide along:
Your eye is like the star of eve,
And sweet your Voice, as Seraph's song.
Yet not your heavenly Beauty gives          5
This heart with passion soft to glow:
Within your soul a VOICE there lives!

[1] This little Poem was written when the Author was a boy. [S.T.C.]

It bids you hear the tale of Woe.
When sinking low the Suff'rer wan
Beholds no hand outstretcht to save, 10
Fair, as the bosom of the Swan
That rises graceful o'er the wave,
I've seen your breast with pity heave,
And *therefore* love I you, sweet GENEVIEVE!
[1789–90]


### XVIII

### *To the Autumnal Moon*

Mild Splendor of the various-vested Night!
Mother of wildly-working visions! hail!
I watch thy gliding, while with watry light
Thy weak eye glimmers thro' a fleecy veil;
And when thou lovest thy pale orb to shroud 5
Behind the gather'd blackness lost on high;
And when thou dartest from the wind-rent cloud
Thy placid lightning o'er th' awaken'd sky.
Ah such is HOPE! as changeful and as fair!
Now dimly peering on the wistful sight; 10
Now hid behind the dragon-wing'd Despair:
But soon emerging in her radiant might
She o'er the sorrow-clouded breast of Care
Sails, like a meteor kindling in its flight.
[1788]


### XIX

### *On a Discovery Made Too Late*

Thou bleedest, my poor HEART! and thy distress
Reas'ning I ponder with a scornful smile
And probe thy sore wound sternly, tho' the while
Swoln be mine eye and dim with heaviness.
Why didst thou listen to Hope's whisper bland? 5
Or, listening, why forget the healing tale,
When Jealousy with fev'rish fancies pale
Jarr'd thy fine fibres with a maniac's hand?
Faint was that HOPE, and rayless!—Yet 'twas fair
And sooth'd with many a dream the hour of rest: 10

Thou should'st have lov'd it most, when most opprest,
And nurs'd it with an agony of Care,
Ev'n as a Mother her sweet infant heir
That wan and sickly droops upon her breast!
[1794]

## XX

### To the Author of 'The Robbers'

Schiller![1] that hour I would have wish'd to die,
If thro' the shudd'ring midnight I had sent
From the dark dungeon of the tower time-rent
That fearful voice, a famish'd Father's cry——
Lest in some after moment aught more mean                    5
Might stamp me mortal! A triumphant shout
Black HORROR scream'd, and all her *goblin* rout
Diminish'd shrunk from the more with'ring scene!
Ah Bard tremendous in sublimity!
Could I behold thee in thy loftier mood                      10
Wand'ring at eve with finely-frenzied eye
Beneath some vast old tempest-swinging wood!
Awhile with mute awe gazing I would brood:
Then weep aloud in a wild ecstacy!
[?1794]

## XXI

### Lines

COMPOSED WHILE CLIMBING THE LEFT ASCENT OF
BROCKLEY COOMB, IN THE COUNTY OF SOMERSET,
MAY, 1795

With many a pause and oft reverted eye
I climb the Coomb's ascent: sweet songsters near
Warble in shade their wild-wood melody:
Far off th' unvarying Cuckoo soothes my ear.

[1] One night in Winter, on leaving a College-friend's room, with whom I had supped, I carelessly took away with me 'The Robbers', a drama, the very name of which I had never before heard of: – A winter midnight – the wind high – and 'The Robbers' for the first time! – The readers of SCHILLER will conceive what I felt. SCHILLER introduces no supernatural beings; yet his human beings agitate and astonish more than all the *goblin* rout – even of Shakespeare. [S.T.C.]

Up scour the startling stragglers of the Flock                          5
That on green plots o'er precipices brouze:
From the forc'd fissures of the naked rock
The Yew tree bursts! Beneath its dark green boughs
(Mid which the May-thorn blends its blossoms white)
Where broad smooth stones jut out in mossy seats,                      10
I rest.—And now have gain'd the topmost site.
Ah! what a luxury of landscape meets
My gaze! Proud Towers, and Cots more dear to me,
Elm-shadow'd Fields, and prospect-bounding Sea!
Deep sighs my lonely heart: I drop the tear:                           15
Enchanting spot! O were my SARA here!


## XXII

### To a Friend
### [Charles Lamb]

#### TOGETHER WITH AN UNFINISHED POEM

Thus far my scanty brain hath built the rhyme
Elaborate and swelling: yet the heart
Not owns it. From thy spirit-breathing powers
I ask not now, my friend! the aiding verse,
Tedious to thee, and from thy anxious thought                           5
Of dissonant mood. In fancy (well I know)
From business wand'ring far and local cares,
Thou creepest round a dear-lov'd Sister's bed
With noiseless step, and watchest the faint look,
Soothing each pang with fond solicitude,                               10
And tenderest tones medicinal of love.
I too a SISTER had, an only Sister——
She lov'd me dearly, and I doted on her!
To her I pour'd forth all my puny sorrows
(As a sick Patient in his Nurse's arms)                                15
And of the heart those hidden maladies
That shrink asham'd from even Friendship's eye.
O! I have woke at midnight, and have wept,
Because SHE WAS NOT!—Cheerily, dear CHARLES!
Thou thy best friend shalt cherish many a year:                        20
Such warm presages feel I of high Hope.
For not uninterested the dear maid

I've view'd—her soul affectionate yet wise,
Her polish'd wit as mild as lambent glories
That play around a sainted infant's head.                    25
He knows (the SPIRIT that in secret sees,
Of whose omniscient and all-spreading Love
Aught to *implore*[1] were impotence of mind)
That my mute thoughts are sad before his throne,
Prepar'd, when he his healing ray vouchsafes,                30
To pour forth thanksgiving with lifted heart,
And praise Him Gracious with a BROTHER's Joy!
[1794]


XXIII

## To the Nightingale

Sister of love-lorn Poets, Philomel!
How many Bards in city garret pent,
While at their window they with downward eye
Mark the faint Lamp-beam on the kennell'd mud,
And listen to the drowsy cry of Watchmen,                    5
(Those hoarse unfeather'd Nightingales of TIME!),
How many wretched Bards address *thy* name,
And Hers, the full-orb'd Queen that shines above.
But I *do* hear thee, and the high bough mark,
Within whose mild moon-mellow'd foliage hid                  10
Thou warblest sad thy pity-pleading strains.
O! have I listen'd, till my working soul,
Wak'd by those strains to thousand phantasies,
Absorb'd hath ceas'd to listen! Therefore oft,
I hymn thy name: and with a proud delight                    15
Oft will I tell thee, MINSTREL of the MOON!
'Most musical, most melancholy' Bird!
That all thy soft diversities of tone,
Tho' sweeter far than the delicious airs
That vibrate from a white-arm'd Lady's harp,                 20

[1] I utterly recant the sentiment contained in the lines –

> Of whose omniscient and all-spreading Love
> Aught to *implore* were impotence of mind,

it being written in Scripture, 'Ask, and it shall be given you,' and my human reason being moreover convinced of the propriety of offering *petitions* as well as thanksgivings to Deity. [S.T.C., 1797]

What time the languishment of lonely love
Melts in her eye, and heaves her breast of snow,
Are not so sweet, as is the voice of her,
My SARA — best belov'd of human Kind!
When breathing the pure soul of Tenderness,                    25
She thrills me with the HUSBAND's promised name!
[1795]


XXIV

*Lines in the Manner of Spenser*

O Peace, that on a lilied bank dost love
To rest thine head beneath an Olive Tree,
I would, that from the pinions of thy Dove
One quill withouten pain ypluck'd might be!
For O! I wish my SARA's frowns to flee,                        5
And fain to her some soothing song would write,
Lest she resent my rude discourtesy,
Who vow'd to meet her ere the morning light,
But broke my plighted word—ah! false and recreant Wight!


Last night as I my weary head did pillow                       10
With thoughts of my dissever'd Fair engross'd,
Chill Fancy droop'd wreathing herself with willow,
As tho' my breast entomb'd a pining ghost.
'From some blest couch, young Rapture's bridal boast,
Rejected SLUMBER! hither wing thy way;                         15
But leave me with the matin hour, at most!
Like snowdrop opening to the solar ray,
My sad heart will expand, when I the Maid survey.'


But LOVE, who heard the silence of my thought,
Contriv'd a too successful wile, I ween:                       20
And whisper'd to himself, with malice fraught—
'Too long our Slave the Damsel's *smiles* hath seen:
Tomorrow shall he ken her alter'd mien!'
He spake, and ambush'd lay, till on my bed
The Morning shot her dewy glances keen,                        25
When as I 'gan to lift my drowsy head—
'Now, Bard! I'll work thee woe!' the laughing Elfin said.

SLEEP, softly-breathing God! his downy wing
Was flutt'ring now, as quickly to depart;
When twang'd an arrow from LOVE's mystic string,  30
With pathless wound it pierc'd him to the heart.
Was there some Magic in the Elfin's dart?
Or did he strike my couch with wizard lance?
For strait so fair a Form did upwards start
(No fairer deck'd the Bowers of old Romance)  35
That SLEEP enamour'd grew, nor mov'd from his sweet
 Trance!

My SARA came, with gentlest Look divine;
Bright shone her Eye, yet tender was its beam:
I felt the pressure of her Lip to mine!
Whispering we went, and Love was all our theme—  40
Love pure and spotless, as at first, I deem,
He sprang from Heaven! Such joys with Sleep did 'bide,
That I the living Image of my Dream
Fondly forgot. Too late I woke, and sigh'd—
'O! how shall I behold my Love at eventide!'  45
[1795]

### XXV

#### Domestic Peace

[FROM *The Fall of Robespierre*, ACT I, L. 210]

Tell me, on what holy ground
May DOMESTIC PEACE be found?
Halcyon daughter of the skies,
Far on fearful wings she flies,
From the pomp of scepter'd State,  5
From the Rebel's noisy hate.

In a cottaged vale She dwells,
Listening to the Sabbath bells!
Still around her steps are seen
Spotless HONOR's meeker mien,  10
LOVE, the sire of pleasing fears,
SORROW smiling through her tears,
And conscious of the past employ
MEMORY, bosom-spring of joy.
[1794]

XXVI[1]

*Kisses*

Cupid, if storying Legends tell aright,
Once fram'd a rich Elixir of Delight.
A Chalice o'er love-kindled flames he fix'd,
And in it Nectar and Ambrosia mix'd:
With these the magic dews, which Evening brings,                5
Brush'd from the Idalian star by faery wings:
Each tender pledge of sacred Faith he join'd,
Each gentler Pleasure of th' unspotted mind—
Day-dreams, whose tints with sportive brightness glow,
And Hope, the blameless Parasite of Woe.                       10
The eyeless Chemist heard the process rise,
The steamy Chalice bubbled up in sighs;
Sweet sounds transpir'd, as when the enamour'd Dove
Pours the soft murm'ring of responsive Love.
The finish'd work might Envy vainly blame,                     15
And 'Kisses' was the precious Compound's name.
With half the God his Cyprian Mother blest,
And breath'd on SARA's lovelier lips the rest.
[1793]

XXVII

*The Rose*

As late each flower that sweetest blows
I pluck'd, the Garden's pride!
Within the petals of a Rose
A sleeping Love I 'spied.

> [1]'Effinxit quondam blandum meditata laborem
>     Basia lascivâ Cypria Diva manu.
> Ambrosiae succos occultâ temperat arte,
>     Fragransque infuso nectare tingit opus.
> Sufficit et partem mellis, quod subdolus olim
>     Non impune favis surripuisset Amor.
> Decussos violae foliis admiscet odores
>     Et spolia aestivis plurima rapta rosis.
> Addit et illecebras et mille et mille lepores,
>     Et quot Acidalius gaudia Cestus habet.'
> Ex his composuit Dea basia; et omnia libans
>     Invenias nitidae sparsa per ora Cloës.
>                          Carm. Quad., vol. ii [S.T.C.]
> [*Carmina Quadragesimalia. Poetical Miscellanies.* Oxford, 1723–48.]

Around his brows a beamy wreath                    5
Of many a lucent hue;
All purple glow'd his cheek, beneath,
Inebriate with the dew.

I softly seiz'd th' unguarded Power,
Nor scar'd his balmy rest;                         10
And plac'd him, cag'd within the flower,
On spotless SARA's breast.

But when unweeting of the guile
Awoke the pris'ner sweet,
He struggled to escape awhile                      15
And stamp'd his faery feet.

Ah! soon the soul-entrancing sight
Subdued th' impatient boy!
He gaz'd! he thrill'd with deep delight!
Then clapp'd his wings for Joy.                    20

'And O!' he cried—'Of magic kind
What charms this Throne endear!
Some other LOVE let Venus find——
I'll fix *my* empire here.'
[1793]

### XXVIII

*The Kiss*

One kiss, dear Maid! I said and sigh'd—
Your scorn the little boon denied.
Ah why refuse the blameless bliss?
Can danger lurk within a kiss?

Yon viewless Wand'rer of the vale,                 5
The SPIRIT of the Western Gale,
At Morning's break, at Evening's close
Inhales the sweetness of the ROSE,
And hovers o'er th' uninjur'd Bloom
Sighing back the soft perfume.                     10
Vigor to the Zephyr's wing
Her nectar-breathing KISSES fling;

And He the glitter of the Dew
Scatters on the ROSE's hue.
Bashful lo! she bends her head,                    15
And darts a blush of deeper Red!

Too well those lovely lips disclose
The Triumphs of the op'ning Rose;
O fair! O graceful! bid them prove
As passive to the breath of Love.                  20
In tender accents, faint and low,
Well-pleas'd I hear the whisper'd 'No!'
The whispered 'No'——how little meant!
Sweet Falsehood, that endears Consent!
For on those lovely lips the while                 25
Dawns the soft relenting smile,
And tempts with feign'd dissuasion coy
The gentle violence of Joy.
[?1794]


XXIX

*Imitated from Ossian*[1]

The stream with languid murmur creeps,
    In LUMIN's *flowery* vale:
Beneath the dew the Lily weeps
    Slow-waving to the gale.

'Cease, restless gale! it seems to say,            5
    Nor wake me with thy sighing!
The honours of my vernal day
    On rapid wing are flying.

Tomorrow shall the Trav'ller come
    Who late beheld me blooming:                   10
His searching eye shall vainly roam
    The *dreary* vale of LUMIN.'

[1] The flower hangs its head waving at times to the gale. 'Why dost thou awake me, O Gale?' it seems to say, 'I am covered with the drops of Heaven. The time of my fading is near, the blast that shall scatter my leaves. Tomorrow shall the traveller come, he that saw me in my beauty shall come. His eyes will search the field, they will not find me. So shall they search in vain for the voice of Cona, after it has failed in the field.' – Berrathon, see Ossian's *Poems*, vol. ii. [S.T.C.]

With eager gaze and wetted cheek
   My wonted haunts along,
Thus, faithful Maiden! *thou* shalt seek          15
   The Youth of simplest song.


But I along the breeze shall roll
   The voice of feeble power;
And dwell, the Moon-beam of thy soul,
   In Slumber's nightly hour.          20
[1793]


## XXX

### *The Complaint of Ninathóma*[1]

#### [FROM THE SAME]

How long will ye round me be swelling,
   O ye blue-tumbling waves of the Sea?
Not always in Caves was my dwelling,
   Nor beneath the cold blast of the Tree.
Through the high-sounding halls of Cathlóma          5
   In the steps of my Beauty I strayed;
The warriors beheld Ninathóma,
   And they blesséd the white-bosom'd Maid!
A GHOST! by my Cavern it darted!
   In moon-beams the Spirit was drest—          10
For lovely appear the DEPARTED
   When they visit the dreams of my Rest!
But disturb'd by the Tempest's commotion
   Fleet the shadowy forms of Delight—
Ah cease, thou shrill blast of the Ocean!          15
   To howl thro' my Cavern by Night.
[1793]

[1] 'How long will ye roll around me, blue-tumbling waters of Ocean? My dwelling was not always in caves, nor beneath the whistling tree. My feast was spread in Torthoma's Hall. The youths beheld me in my loveliness. They blessed the dark-haired Nina-thóma.' – Berrathon. [S.T.C.]

XXXI

*Imitated from the Welch*

If, while my passion I impart,
    You deem my words untrue,
O place your hand upon my heart——
    Feel how it throbs for *you*!

Ah no! reject the thoughtless claim         5
    In pity to your Lover!
That thrilling touch would aid the flame
    It wishes to discover.
[?1794]


XXXII

*The Sigh*

When Youth his faery reign began
Ere Sorrow had proclaim'd me man;
While Peace the present hour beguil'd,
And all the lovely Prospect smil'd;
Then, MARY! 'mid my lightsome glee        5
I heav'd the painless SIGH for thee!

And when, along the waves of woe,
My harass'd Heart was doom'd to know
The frantic Burst of Outrage keen,
And the slow Pang that gnaws unseen;     10
Then shipwreck'd on Life's stormy sea
I heaved an anguish'd SIGH for thee!

But soon Reflection's power imprest
A stiller sadness on my breast;
And sickly Hope with waning eye         15
Was well content to droop and die:
I yielded to the stern decree,
Yet heav'd a languid SIGH for thee!

And tho' in distant climes to roam,
A Wanderer from my native home,        20

I fain would soothe the sense of Care
And lull to sleep the Joys, that were!
Thy Image may not banish'd be——
Still, MARY! still I SIGH for thee.
[June 1794]


## XXXIII

### To a Young Ass

#### ITS MOTHER BEING TETHERED NEAR IT

Poor little Foal of an oppressed Race!
I love the languid Patience of thy face:
And oft with gentle hand I give thee bread,
And clap thy ragged Coat, and pat thy head,
But what thy dulléd Spirits hath dismay'd,                    5
That never thou dost sport along the glade?
And (most unlike the nature of things young)
That earth-ward still thy moveless head is hung?
Do thy prophetic Fears anticipate,
Meek Child of Misery! thy future fate?——                    10
The starving meal, and all the thousand aches
'Which patient Merit of th' Unworthy takes?'
Or is thy sad heart thrill'd with filial pain
To see thy wretched MOTHER's shorten'd Chain?
And truly, very piteous is *her* Lot——                       15
Chain'd to a Log within a narrow spot
Where the close-eaten Grass is scarcely seen,
While sweet around her waves the tempting Green!
Poor Ass! her Master should have learnt to shew
Pity – best taught by fellowship of woe!                      20
For much I fear, that He lives, ev'n as she,
Half famish'd in a land of luxury!

How *askingly* It's footsteps t'ward me bend?
It seems to say, 'And have I then *one* Friend?'
Innocent Foal! thou poor despis'd Forlorn!                    25
I hail thee BROTHER—spite of the fool's scorn!
And fain would take thee with      in the Dell
Of Peace and mild Equality to dwell,
Where TOIL shall call the charmer HEALTH his bride,
And LAUGHTER tickle PLENTY's ribless side!                   30

How thou wouldst toss thy heels in gamesome play,
And frisk about, as Lamb or Kitten gay!
Yea! and more musically sweet to me
Thy dissonant harsh Bray of Joy would be,
Than warbled Melodies that soothe to rest          35
The tumult of some SCOUNDREL Monarch's breast!
[1794]


XXXIV

*To an Infant*

Ah cease thy Tears and Sobs, my little Life!
I did but snatch away the unclasp'd Knife:
Some safer Toy will soon arrest thine eye,
And to quick Laughter change this peevish cry!
Poor Stumbler on the rocky coast of Woe,          5
Tutor'd by Pain each source of Pain to know!
Alike the foodful fruit and scorching fire
Awake thy eager grasp and young desire:
Alike the Good, the Ill offend thy sight,
And rouse the stormy Sense of shrill Affright!     10
Untaught, yet wise! mid all thy brief alarms
Thou closely clingest to thy Mother's arms,
Nestling thy little face in that fond breast
Whose anxious Heavings lull thee to thy rest!
Man's breathing Miniature! thou mak'st me sigh—    15
A Babe art thou – and such a Thing am I!
To anger rapid and as soon appeas'd,
For trifles mourning and by trifles pleas'd,
Break Friendship's Mirror with a tetchy blow,
Yet snatch what coals of fire on Pleasure's altar glow!  20

O thou that rearest with celestial aim
The future Seraph in my mortal frame,
Thrice holy FAITH! whatever thorns I meet
As on I totter with unpractis'd feet,
Still let me stretch my arms and cling to thee,    25
Meek Nurse of Souls through their long Infancy!
[1795]

XXXV

## The Eolian Harp

COMPOSED 20 AUGUST 1795
AT CLEVEDON, SOMERSETSHIRE

My pensive SARA! thy soft cheek reclin'd
Thus on mine arm, most soothing sweet it is
To sit beside our cot, our cot o'er grown
With white-flower'd Jasmin, and the broad-leav'd Myrtle,
(Meet emblems they of Innocence and Love!)                    5
And watch the clouds, that late were rich with light,
Slow sad'ning round, and mark the star of eve
Serenely brilliant (such should Wisdom be)
Shine opposite! How exquisite the scents
Snatch'd from yon bean-field! and the world *so* hush'd!      10
The stilly murmur of the distant Sea
Tells us of Silence. And that simplest Lute,
Plac'd length-ways in the clasping casement, hark!
How by the desultory breeze caress'd,
Like some coy Maid half-yielding to her Lover,               15
It pours such sweet upbraidings, as must needs
Tempt to repeat the wrong! And now its strings
Boldlier swept, the long sequacious notes
Over delicious surges sink and rise,
Such a soft floating witchery of sound                        20
As twilight Elfins make, when they at eve
Voyage on gentle gales from Faery Land,
Where *Melodies* round honey-dropping flowers,
Footless and wild, like birds of Paradise,
Nor pause, nor perch, hovering on untam'd wing               25
[O! the one Life within us and abroad,
Which meets all motion and becomes its soul,
A light in sound, a sound-like power in light,
Rhythm in all thought, and joyance every where—
Methinks, it should have been impossible                      30
Not to love all things in a world so fill'd;
Where the breeze warbles, and the mute still air
Is Music slumbering on her instrument.][1]

---

[1] These lines, not in the 1796 edition, were first published in the errata to *Sibylline Leaves*.

And thus, my Love! as on the midway slope
Of yonder hill I stretch my limbs at noon,                          35
Whilst thro' my half-clos'd eyelids I behold
The sunbeams dance, like diamonds, on the main,
And tranquil muse upon tranquillity;
Full many a thought uncall'd and undetain'd,
And many idle flitting phantasies,                                   40
Traverse my indolent and passive brain
As wild and various, as the random gales
That swell or flutter on this subject Lute!
And what if all of animated nature
Be but organic Harps diversly fram'd,                               45
That tremble into thought, as o'er them sweeps
Plastic and vast, one intellectual Breeze,
At once the Soul of each, and God of all?
But thy more serious eye a mild reproof
Darts, O beloved Woman! nor such thoughts                           50
Dim and unhallow'd dost thou not reject,
And biddest me walk humbly with my God.


Meek Daughter in the Family of Christ,
Well hast thou said and holily disprais'd
These shapings of the unregenerate mind,
Bubbles that glitter as they rise and break                         55
On vain Philosophy's aye-babbling spring.
For never guiltless may I speak of Him,
Th' INCOMPREHENSIBLE! save when with awe
I praise him, and with Faith that inly[1] *feels*;                  60
Who with his saving mercies healéd me,
A sinful and most miserable man,
Wilder'd and dark, and gave me to possess
PEACE, and this COT, and THEE, heart-honor'd Maid!
[1795]

---

[1]'L'athée n'est point à mes yeux un faux esprit; je puis vivre avec lui aussi bien et mieux
qu'avec le dévot, car il raisonne davantage, mais il lui manque un sens, et mon âme ne se fond
point entièrement avec la sienne: il est froid au spectacle le plus ravissant, et il cherche un
syllogisme lorsque je rends une action de grâce. – 'Appel à l'impartiale postérité, par la
Citoyenne Roland', troisième partie, p. 67 [S.T.C.]. ['In my eyes the atheist is not in the least a
false person; I can live with him, as well as, and better than the devout, for he reasons further;
but he lacks a certain sense and my mind does not blend entirely with his: he is cold to the most
ravishing spectacle and he looks for a syllogism when I return a thanksgiving.']

## XXXVI

### *Written in Early Youth, the time an Autumnal Evening*

O thou wild FANCY, check thy wing! No more
Those thin white flakes, those purple clouds explore!
Nor there with happy spirits speed thy flight
Bath'd in rich amber-glowing floods of light;
Nor in yon gleam, where slow descends the day, 5
With western peasants hail the morning ray!
Ah! rather bid the perish'd pleasures move,
A shadowy train, across the soul of Love!
O'er Disappointment's wintry desart fling
Each flower, that wreath'd the dewy locks of SPRING, 10
When blushing, like a bride, from Hope's trim bower
She leapt, awaken'd by the pattering shower.

Now sheds the sinking Sun a deeper gleam,
Aid, lovely Sorceress! aid thy Poet's dream!
With faery wand O bid the MAID arise, 15
Chaste Joyance dancing in her bright blue eyes;
As erst when from the Muses' calm abode
I came, with Learning's meed not unbestowed:
When, as she twin'd a laurel round my brow,
And met my kiss, and half return'd my vow, 20
O'er all my frame shot rapid my thrill'd heart,
And every nerve confess'd the electric dart.

O dear Deceit! I see the Maiden rise,
Chaste Joyance dancing in her bright blue Eyes,
When first the lark high-soaring swells his throat, 25
Mocks the tir'd eye, and scatters the loud note,
I trace her footsteps on the accustom'd lawn,
I mark her glancing mid the gleams of dawn.
When the bent flower beneath the night-dew weeps
And on the lake the silver lustre sleeps, 30
Amid the paly radiance soft and sad
She meets my lonely path in moon-beams clad.
With her along the streamlet's brink I rove;
With her I list the warblings of the grove;
And seems in each low wind her voice to float 35
Lone-whispering Pity in each soothing note!

SPIRITS of LOVE! ye heard her name! Obey
The powerful spell, and to my haunt repair.
Whether on clust'ring pinions ye are there,
Where rich snows blossom on the Myrtle trees,          40
Or with fond languishment around my fair
Sigh in the loose luxuriance of her hair;
O heed the spell, and hither wing your way,
Like far-off music, voyaging the breeze!
SPIRITS! to you the infant Maid was given             45
Form'd by the wond'rous Alchemy of Heaven!
No fairer Maid does Love's wide empire know,
No fairer Maid e'er heav'd the bosom's snow.
A thousand Loves around her forehead fly;
A thousand Loves sit melting in her eye;              50
Love lights her smile—in Joy's red nectar dips
The flamy rose, and plants it on her lips!
Tender, serene, and all devoid of guile,
Soft is her soul, as sleeping infants' smile.
She speaks! and hark that passion-warbled song—      55
Still, Fancy! still those mazy notes prolong.
Sweet as th' angelic harps, whose rapturous falls
Awake the soften'd echoes of Heaven's Halls!


O¹ (have I sigh'd) were mine the wizard's rod,
Or mine the power of Proteus, changeful God!         60
A flower-entangled ARBOUR I would seem
To shield my Love from Noontide's sultry beam:

---

¹I entreat the Public's pardon for having carelessly suffered to be printed such intolerable stuff as this and the thirteen following lines. They have not the merit even of originality: as every thought is to be found in the Greek Epigrams. The lines in this poem from the 27th to the 36th, I have been told are a palpable imitation of the passage from the 355th to the 370th line of the Pleasures of Memory Part 3. I do not perceive so striking a similarity between the two passages; at all events I had written the Effusion several years before I had seen Mr Rogers' Poem. – It may be proper to remark that the tale of Florio in 'the Pleasures of Memory' is to be found in Lochleven, a poem of great merit by Michael Bruce. – In Mr Rogers' Poem* the names are FLORIO and JULIA; in the Lochleven Lomond and Levina – and this is all the difference. We seize the opportunity of transcribing from the Lochleven of Bruce the following exquisite passage, expressing the effects of a fine day on the human heart.

> Fat on the plain and mountain's sunny side
> Large droves of oxen and the fleecy flocks
> Feed undisturb'd, and fill the echoing air
> With Music grateful to their Master's ear.
> The Traveller stops and gazes round and round

Or bloom a MYRTLE, from whose od'rous boughs
My Love might weave gay garlands for her brows.
When Twilight stole across the fading vale,                    65
To fan my Love I'd be the EVENING GALE;
Mourn in the soft folds of her swelling vest,
And flutter my faint pinions on her breast!
Or Seraph wing I'd float a DREAM, by night,
To soothe my Love with shadows of delight: —               70
Or soar aloft to be the SPANGLED SKIES,
And gaze upon her with a thousand eyes!

As when the savage, who his drowsy frame
Had bask'd beneath the Sun's unclouded flame,
Awakes amid the troubles of the air,                          75
The skiey deluge, and white lightning's glare—
Aghast he scours before the tempest's sweep,
And sad recalls the sunny hour of sleep: —
So tossed by storms along Life's wild'ring way,
Mine eye reverted views that cloudless day,                   80
When by my native brook I wont to rove,
While Hope with kisses nurs'd the Infant Love.

Dear native brook! like PEACE, so placidly
Smoothing through fertile fields thy current meek!
Dear native brook! where first young POESY                    85
Stared wildly-eager in her noontide dream!
Where BLAMELESS PLEASURES dimple QUIET's cheek,
As water-lilies ripple a slow stream!
Dear native haunts! where Virtue still is gay:
Where Friendship's fix'd-star sheds a mellow'd ray;           90
Where LOVE a crown of thornless Roses wears:
Where soften'd SORROW smiles within her tears;

---

O'er all the plains that animate his heart
With Mirth and Music. Even the mendicant
Bow-bent with age, that on the old gray stone
Sole-sitting suns him in the public way,
Feels his heart leap, and to himself he sings.
[Poems by Michael Bruce, 1796, p. 94] [S.T.C.]

*For Coleridge's retraction of the charge of plagiarism and apology to Rogers see
'Advertisement to Supplement of 1797', pp. 244, 245. [E.H.C.]

And Mem'ry, with a VESTAL's chaste employ,
Unceasing feeds the lambent flame of Joy!
No more your sky-larks melting from the sight                    95
Shall thrill the attuned heart-string with delight: —
No more shall deck your pensive Pleasures sweet
With wreaths of sober hue my evening seat.
Yet dear to Fancy's eye your varied scene
Of wood, hill, dale, and sparkling brook between!                100
Yet sweet to Fancy's ear the warbled song,
That soars on Morning's wing your vales among.

Scenes of my Hope! the aking eye ye leave
Like yon bright hues that paint the clouds of eve!
Tearful and sad'ning with the sadden'd blaze                     105
Mine eye the gleam pursues with wistful gaze:
Sees shades on shades with deeper tint impend,
Till chill and damp the moonless night descend.
[1793]

## Poetical Epistles

Good verse *most* good, and bad verse then seems better
Receiv'd from absent friend by way of Letter.
For what so sweet can labor'd lays impart
As one rude rhyme warm from a friendly heart?

                                                                ANON

I

### Written at Shurton Bars, near Bridgewater, September 1795, in Answer to a Letter from Bristol

Nor travels my meand'ring eye
The starry wilderness on high;
    Nor now with curious sight
I mark the glow-worm, as I pass,
Move with 'green radiance'[1] through the grass,               5
    An EMERALD of Light.

O ever-present to my view!
My wafted spirit is with you,

[1] The expression 'green radiance' is borrowed from Mr WORDSWORTH, a Poet whose versification is occasionally harsh and his diction too frequently obscure; but whom I deem

And soothes your boding fears:
I see you all oppressed with gloom          10
Sit lonely in that cheerless room——
   Ah me! You are in tears!

Beloved Woman! did you fly
Chill'd Friendship's dark disliking eye,
   Or Mirth's untimely din?          15
With cruel weight these trifles press
A temper sore with Tenderness,
   When akes the Void within.

But why with sable wand unblessed
Should Fancy rouse within my breast          20
   Dim-visag'd shapes of Dread?
Untenanting its beauteous clay
My SARA's soul has wing'd its way,
   And hovers round my head!

I felt it prompt the tender Dream,          25
When slowly sunk the day's last gleam;
   You rous'd each gentler sense
As sighing o'er the Blossom's bloom
Meek Evening wakes its soft perfume
   With viewless influence.          30

And hark, my Love! The sea-breeze moans
Through yon reft house! O'er rolling stones
   In bold ambitious sweep
The onward-surging tides supply
The silence of the cloudless sky          35
   With mimic thunders deep.

Dark red'ning from the channel'd Isle[1]
(Where stands one solitary pile
   Unslated by the blast)

---

unrivalled among the writers of the present day in manly sentiment, novel imagery, and vivid colouring. [S.T.C.]

   The phrase 'green radiance' occurs in *An Evening Walk*, ll. 264–8, first published in 1793. [E.H.C.]

   [1]The Holmes, in the Bristol Channel. [S.T.C.]

The Watchfire, like a sullen star                                    40
Twinkles to many a dozing Tar
   Rude cradled on the mast.

Even there—beneath that light-house tower—
In the tumultuous evil hour
   Ere Peace with SARA came,                          45
Time was, I should have thought it sweet
To count the echoings of my feet,
   And watch the storm-vex'd flame.

And there in black soul-jaundic'd fit
A sad gloom-pamper'd Man to sit,                                     50
   And listen to the roar:
With mountain Surges bellowing deep
With an uncouth monster leap
   Plung'd foaming on the shore.

Then by the Lightning's blaze to mark                               55
Some toiling tempest-shatter'd bark:
   Her vain distress-guns hear:
And when a second sheet of light
Flash'd o'er the blackness of the night—
   To see *no* Vessel there!                          60

But Fancy now more gaily sings;
Or if awhile she droop her wings,
   As sky-larks 'mid the corn,
On summer fields she grounds her breast:
The oblivious Poppy o'er her nest                                   65
   Nods, till returning morn.

O mark those smiling tears, that swell
The open'd Rose! From heaven they fell,
   And with the sun-beam blend.
Blest visitations from above,                                       70
Such are the tender woes of Love
   Fostering the heart, they bend!

When stormy Midnight howling round
Beats on our roof with clatt'ring sound,
   To me your arms you'll stretch:                    75

Great God! you'll say—To us so kind,
O shelter from this loud bleak wind
    The houseless, friendless wretch!

The tears that tremble down your cheek,
Shall bathe my kisses chaste and meek          80
    In Pity's dew divine;
And from your heart the sighs that steal
Shall make your rising bosom feel
    The answ'ring swell of mine!

How oft, my Love! with shapings sweet          85
I paint the moment, we shall meet!
    With eager speed I dart——
I seize you in the vacant air,
And fancy, with a Husband's care
    I press you to my heart!          90

'Tis said, on Summer's evening hour
Flashes the golden-colour'd flower
    A fair electric flame.[1]
And so shall flash my love-charg'd eye
When all the heart's big ecstacy          95
    Shoots rapid thro' the frame!
[1795]

---

[1]LIGHT *from plants.* In Sweden a very curious phenomenon has been observed on certain flowers, by M. Haggern, lecturer in natural history. One evening he perceived a faint flash of light repeatedly dart from a marigold. Surprized at such an uncommon appearance, he resolved to examine it with attention; and, to be assured it was no deception of the eye, he placed a man near him, with orders to make a signal at the moment when he observed the light. They both saw it constantly at the same moment.

The light was most brilliant on marigolds of an orange or flame colour; but scarcely visible on pale ones. The flash was frequently seen on the same flower two or three times in quick succession; but more commonly at intervals of several minutes; and when several flowers in the same place emitted their light together, it could be observed at a considerable distance.

This phenomenon was remarked in the months of July and August at sun-set, and for half an hour, when the atmosphere was clear; but after a rainy day, or when the air was loaded with vapours, nothing of it was seen.

The following flowers emitted flashes, more or less vivid, in this order:

1. The marigold, *galendula officinalis.*
2. Monk's-hood, *tropaelum majus.*
3. The orange lily, *lilium bulbiferum.*
4. The Indian pink, *tagetes patula & erecta.*

From the rapidity of the flash, and other circumstances, it may be conjectured that there is something of electricity in this phenomenon. [S.T.C., from Erasmus Darwin, *The Botanical Garden.*]

II

*To a Friend, in Answer to a Melancholy Letter*

Away, those cloudy looks, that lab'ring sigh,
The peevish offspring of a sickly hour!
Nor meanly thus complain of Fortune's power,
When the blind Gamester throws a luckless die.

Yon setting Sun flashes a mournful gleam                    5
Behind those broken clouds, his stormy train:
Tomorrow shall the many-colour'd main
In brightness roll beneath his orient beam!

Wild, as th' autumnal gust, the hand of TIME
Flies o'er his mystic lyre: in shadowy dance                10
The alternate groups of Joy and Grief advance
Responsive to his varying strains sublime!

Bears on its wing each hour a load of Fate.
The swain, who, lull'd by Seine's mild murmurs, led
His weary oxen to their nightly shed,                       15
Today may rule a tempest-troubled State.

Nor shall not Fortune with a vengeful smile
Survey the sanguinary Despot's might,
And haply hurl the Pageant from his height
Unwept to wander in some savage isle.                       20

There shiv'ring sad beneath the tempest's frown
Round his tir'd limbs to wrap the purple vest;
And mix'd with nails and beads, an equal jest!
Barter for food, the jewels of his crown.
[?1795]

III

*Written After a Walk Before Supper*

Tho' much averse, dear Jack, to flicker,
To find a likeness for friend V—ker,
I've made thro' Earth, and Air, and Sea,
A Voyage of Discovery!

And let me add (to ward off strife)                    5
For V—ker and for V—ker's Wife—
SHE large and round beyond belief,
A superfluity of Beef!
Her mind and body of a piece,
And both compos'd of kitchen-grease.                  10
In short, Dame Truth might safely dub her
Vulgarity enshrin'd in blubber!
HE, meagre Bit of Littleness,
All snuff, and musk, and politesse;
So thin, that strip him of his clothing,              15
He'd totter on the edge of NOTHING!
In case of foe, he well might hide
Snug in the collops of her side.

Ah then, what simile will suit?
Spindle leg in great jack-boot?                       20
Pismire crawling in a rut?
Or a spigot in a butt?
Thus I humm'd and ha'd awhile,
When Madam Memory with a smile
Thus twitch'd my ear—'Why sure, I ween,              25
In London streets thou oft hast seen
The very image of this pair:
A little Ape with huge She-Bear
Link'd by hapless chain together:
An unlick'd mass the one – the other                 30
An antic huge[2] with nimble crupper——'
But stop, my Muse! for here comes supper.
[1792]

IV

*To the Author of Poems*[1]

PUBLISHED ANONYMOUSLY AT BRISTOL,
IN SEPTEMBER, 1795

Unboastful BARD! whose verse concise yet clear
Tunes to smooth melody unconquer'd sense,

[1]Joseph Cottle.
[2]The original MS has 'lean'.

May your fame fadeless live, as 'never-sere'
The Ivy wreathes yon Oak, whose broad defence
Embow'rs me from Noon's sultry influence!                    5
For, like that nameless Riv'let stealing by,
Your modest verse to musing Quiet dear
Is rich with tints heaven-borrow'd: the charm'd eye
Shall gaze undazzled there, and love the soften'd sky.

Circling the base of the Poetic mount                        10
A stream there is, which rolls in lazy flow
Its coal-black waters from OBLIVION's fount:
The vapor-poison'd Birds, that fly too low,
Fall with dead swoop, and to the bottom go.
Escaped that heavy stream on pinion fleet                     15
Beneath the Mountain's lofty-frowning brow,
Ere aught of perilous ascent you meet,
A mead of mildest charm delays th' unlabouring feet.
Not there the cloud-climb'd rock, sublime and vast,
That like some giant king, o'er glooms the hill;             20
Nor there the Pine-grove to the midnight blast
Makes solemn music! But th' unceasing rill
To the soft Wren or Lark's descending trill
Murmurs sweet undersong mid jasmin bowers.
In this same pleasant meadow, at your will,                  25
I ween, you wander'd—there collecting flow'rs
Of sober tint, and herbs of med'cinable powers!

There for the monarch-murder'd Soldier's tomb
You wove th' unfinish'd[1] wreath of saddest hues;
And to that holier[2] chaplet added bloom                    30
Besprinkling it with JORDAN's cleansing dews.
But lo your HENDERSON[3] awakes the Muse——
His Spirit beckon'd from the mountain's height!
You left the plain and soar'd 'mid richer views!
So Nature mourn'd when sunk the First Day's light,           35
With stars, unseen before, spangling her robe of night!
Still soar my FRIEND those richer views among,

[1]War, a Fragment. [S.T.C.]
[2]John the Baptist, a Poem. [S.T.C.]
[3]Monody on John Henderson. [S.T.C.]

Strong, rapid, fervent, flashing Fancy's beam!
Virtue and Truth shall love your gentler song;
But Poesy demands th' impassion'd theme:                          40
Waked by Heaven's silent dews at Eve's mild gleam
What balmy sweets POMONA breathes around!
But if the vext air rush a stormy stream
Or Autumn's shrill gust moan in plaintive sound,
With fruits and flowers she loads the tempest honor'd            45
    ground.
[1795]


V

[*The Silver Thimble*]

THE PRODUCTION OF A YOUNG LADY, ADDRESSED TO
THE AUTHOR OF THE POEMS ALLUDED TO IN THE
PRECEDING EPISTLE

She had lost her Silver Thimble, and her complaint being accidentally
overheard by him, her Friend, he immediately sent her four others to take
her choice of.

As oft mine eye with careless glance
Has gallop'd thro' some old romance,
Of speaking Birds and Steeds with wings,
Giants and Dwarfs, and Fiends and Kings;
Beyond the rest with more attentive care                          5
I've lov'd to read of elfin-favor'd Fair——
How if she long'd for aught beneath the sky
And suffer'd to escape one votive sigh,
Wafted along on viewless pinions aery
It lay'd itself obsequious at her Feet:                           10
Such things, I thought, one might not hope to meet
Save in the dear delicious land of Faery!
But now (by proof I know it well)
There's still some peril in free wishing——
*Politeness* is a licenc'd *spell*,                               15
And *you*, dear Sir! the Arch-magician.


You much perplex'd me by the various set:
They were indeed an elegant quartette!

My mind went to and fro, and waver'd long;
At length I've chosen (Samuel thinks me wrong)                  20
*That*, around whose azure rim
Silver figures seem to swim,
Like fleece-white clouds, that on the skiey Blue,
Waked by no breeze, the self-same shapes retain;
Or ocean Nymphs with limbs of snowy hue                        25
Slow-floating o'er the calm cerulean plain.

Just such a one, *mon cher ami*,
(The finger shield of industry)
Th' inventive Gods, I deem, to Pallas gave
What time the vain Arachne, madly brave,                       30
Challeng'd the blue-eyed Virgin of the sky
A duel in embroider'd work to try.
And hence the thimbled Finger of grave Pallas
To th' erring Needle's point was more than callous.
But ah the poor Arachne! She unarm'd                           35
Blund'ring thro' hasty eagerness, alarm'd
With all a *Rival's* hopes, a *Mortal's* fears,
Still miss'd the stitch, and stain'd the web with tears.
Unnumber'd punctures small yet sore
Full fretfully the maiden bore,                                40
Till she her lily finger found
Crimson'd with many a tiny wound;
And to her eyes, suffus'd with watery woe,
Her flower-embroider'd web danc'd dim, I wist,
Like blossom'd shrubs in a quick-moving mist:                  45
Till vanquish'd the despairing Maid sunk low.

O Bard! whom sure no common Muse inspires,
I heard your Verse that glows with vestal fires!
And I from unwatch'd needle's erring point
Had surely suffer'd on each finger joint                       50
Those wounds, which erst did poor Arachne meet;
While he, the much-lov'd Object of my Choice,
(My bosom thrilling with enthusiast heat)
Pour'd on mine ear with deep impressive voice,
How the great Prophet of the Desart stood                      55
And preach'd of Penitence by Jordan's Flood;
On WAR; or else the legendary lays

In simplest measures hymn'd to ALLA's praise;
Or what the Bard from his heart's inmost stores
O'er his *Friend's* grave in loftier numbers pours:          60
Yes, Bard Polite! you but obey'd the laws
Of Justice, when the thimble you had sent;
What wounds your thought-bewildering Muse might cause
'Tis well, your finger-shielding gifts prevent.

                                          SARA.
[1795]

## Religious Musings

### A DESULTORY POEM, WRITTEN ON CHRISTMAS' EVE,
### IN THE YEAR OF OUR LORD, 1794

                              What tho' first,
               In years unseason'd, I attun'd the Lay
               To idle Passion and unreal Woe?
               Yet serious Truth her empire o'er my song
               Hath now asserted; Falshood's evil brood,
               Vice and deceitful Pleasure, She at once
               Excluded, and my Fancy's careless toil
               Drew to the better cause!

                                          AKENSIDE

#### ARGUMENT

Introduction. Person of Christ. His Prayer on the Cross. The process
of his Doctrines on the mind of the Individual. Character of the
Elect. Superstition. Digression to the present War. Origin and Uses
of Government and Property. The present State of Society. French
Revolution. Millenium. Universal Redemption. Conclusion.

               This is the time, when most divine to hear,
               As with a Cherub's 'loud uplifted' trump
               The voice of Adoration my thrill'd heart
               Rouses! And with the rushing noise of wings
               Transports my spirit to the favor'd fields          5
               Of Bethlehem, there in shepherd's guise to sit
               Sublime of extacy, and mark entranc'd
               The glory-streaming VISION throng the night.[1]

[1] And suddenly there was with the Angel a multitude of the heavenly Host, praising God and
saying, Glory to God in the highest and on earth peace. – Luke ii. 13. [S.T.C.]

Ah not more radiant, nor loud harmonies
Hymning more unimaginably sweet                                    10
With choral songs around th' ETERNAL MIND,
The constellated company of WORLDS
Danc'd jubilant: what time the startling East
Saw from her dark womb leap her flamy Child!
Glory to God in the Highest! PEACE on Earth!                       15

Yet thou more bright than all that Angel Blaze,
Despised GALILÆAN! Man of Woes!
For chiefly in the oppressed Good Man's face
The Great Invisible (by symbols seen)
Shines with peculiar and concentred light,                         20
When all of Self regardless the scourg'd Saint
Mourns for th' oppressor. O thou meekest Man!
Meek Man and lowliest of the Sons of Men!
Who thee beheld thy imag'd Father saw.[1]
His Power and Wisdom from thy awful eye                            25
Blended their beams, and loftier Love sate there
Musing on human weal, and that dread hour
When thy insulted Anguish winged the prayer
Harp'd by Archangels, when they sing of Mercy!
Which when th' ALMIGHTY heard, from forth his Throne               30
Diviner light flash'd extacy o'er Heaven!
Heav'n's hymnings paus'd: and Hell her yawning mouth
Clos'd a brief moment.

                    Lovely was the Death
Of Him, whose Life was Love! Holy with power
He on the thought-benighted Sceptic beam'd                         35
Manifest Godhead, melting into day
What Mists dim-floating of Idolatry
Split and misshap'd the Omnipresent Sire:[2]
And first by TERROR, Mercy's startling prelude,
Uncharm'd the Spirit spell-bound with earthy lusts                 40

[1] Philip saith unto him, Lord, shew us the Father and it sufficeth us. Jesus saith unto him, Have I been so long time with you, and yet hast thou not known me, Philip? he that hath seen me hath seen the Father. – John xiv. 8, 9. [S.T.C.]

[2] Τὸ Νοητὸν διῃρήκασιν εἰς πολλῶν Θεῶν Ἰδιότητας. – DAMAS. DE MYST. AEGYPT. [S.T.C., 1797]. 'Men have split up the Intelligible One into the peculiar attributes of Gods many.' [E.H.C.] See Cudworth's *Intellectual System* (1678), p. 461.

Till of its nobler nature it 'gan feel
Dim recollections; and thence soared to HOPE,
Strong to believe whate'er of mystic good
Th' ETERNAL dooms for his IMMORTAL Sons.
From HOPE and stronger FAITH to perfect LOVE          45
Attracted and absorbed: and center'd there
GOD only to behold, and know, and feel,
Till by exclusive Consciousness of GOD
All self-annihilated it shall make[1]
GOD it's Identity: God all in all!          50
We and our Father ONE!

          And blest are they,
Who in this fleshly World, the elect of Heaven,
Their strong eye darting thro' the deeds of Men
Adore with stedfast unpresuming gaze
Him, Nature's Essence, Mind, and Energy!          55
And gazing, trembling, patiently ascend
Treading beneath their feet all visible things
As steps, that upward to their Father's Throne
Lead gradual—else nor glorified nor loved.
THEY nor Contempt imbosom nor Revenge:          60
For THEY dare know of what may seem deform
The SUPREME FAIR sole Operant: in whose sight
All things are pure, his strong controlling love
Alike from all educing perfect good.

Their's too celestial courage, inly armed——          65
Dwarfing Earth's giant brood, what time they muse
On their great Father, great beyond compare!
And marching onwards view high o'er their heads
His waving Banners of Omnipotence.

Who the Creator love, created might          70
Dread not: within their tents no Terrors walk.

---

[1]See this *demonstrated* by Hartley, vol. 1, p. 114, and vol. 2, p. 329. See it likewise proved, and freed from the charge of Mysticism, by Pistorius in his Notes and Additions to part second of Hartley on Man, Addition the 18th, the 653rd page of the third volume of Hartley, Octavo Edition. [S.T.C., 1797]

For they are Holy Things before the Lord
Aye-unprofaned, tho' Earth should league with Hell!
GOD's altar grasping with an eager hand
FEAR, the wild-visag'd, pale, eye-starting wretch,                    75
Sure-refug'd hears his hot pursuing fiends
Yell at vain distance. Soon refresh'd from Heaven
He calms the throb and tempest of his heart.
His countenance settles: a soft solemn bliss
Swims in his eye: his swimming eye uprais'd:                    80
And Faith's whole armour glitters on his limbs!
And thus transfigured with a dreadless awe,
A solemn hush of soul, meek he beholds
All things of terrible seeming. Yea, and there,
Unshudder'd, unaghasted, he shall view                    85
E'en the SEVEN SPIRITS, who in the latter day
Will shower hot pestilence on the sons of men.
For he shall know, his heart shall understand,
That kindling with intenser Deity
They from the MERCY-SEAT—like rosy flames,                    90
From God's celestial MERCY-SEAT will flash,
And at the wells of renovating LOVE
Fill their Seven Vials with salutary wrath,[1]
To sickly Nature more medicinal
Than what soft balm the weeping good man pours                    95
Into the lone despoiléd trav'ller's wounds!

Thus from the Elect, regenerate through faith,
Pass the dark Passions and what thirsty Cares[2]
Drink up the spirit, and the dim regards
Self-center. Lo they vanish! or acquire                    100
New names, new features—by supernal grace
Enrobed with Light, and naturaliz'd in Heaven.
As when a Shepherd on a vernal morn
Thro' some thick fog creeps tim'rous with slow foot,

[1] And I heard a great voice out of the Temple saying to the seven Angels, pour out the vials of
the wrath of God upon the earth. – Revelation, xvi. 1. [S.T.C.]
[2] Our evil Passions, under the influence of Religion, become innocent, and may be made to
animate our virtue – in the same manner as the thick mist melted by the Sun, increases the light
which it had before excluded. In the preceding paragraph, agreeably to this truth, we had
allegorically narrated the transfiguration of Fear into holy Awe. [S.T.C., 1797]

Darkling he fixes on th' immediate road                105
His downward eye: all else of fairest kind
Hid or deform'd. But lo, the bursting Sun!
Touched by th' enchantment of that sudden beam
Strait the black vapor melteth, and in globes
Of dewy glitter gems each plant and tree:              110
On every leaf, on every blade it hangs!
Dance glad the new-born intermingling rays,
And wide around the landscape streams with glory!


There is one Mind, one omnipresent Mind,
Omnific. His most holy name is LOVE.                   115
Truth of subliming import! with the which
Who feeds and saturates his constant soul,
He from his small particular orbit flies
With blest outstarting! From HIMSELF he flies,
Stands in the Sun, and with no partial gaze            120
Views all creation, and he loves it all,
And blesses it, and calls it very good!
This is indeed to dwell with the most High!
Cherubs and rapture-trembling Seraphim
Can press no nearer to th' Almighty's Throne.          125
But that we roam unconscious, or with hearts
Unfeeling of our universal Sire,
And that in his vast family no Cain
Injures uninjured (in her best-aim'd blow
Victorious MURDER a blind Suicide)                     130
Haply for this some younger Angel now
Looks down on Human Nature: and, behold!
A sea of blood bestrewed with wrecks, where mad
Embattling INTERESTS on each other rush
With unhelm'd Rage!


                         'Tis the sublime of man,      135
Our noontide Majesty, to know ourselves
Parts and proportions of one wond'rous whole:
This fraternises man, this constitutes
Our charities and bearings. But 'tis God
Diffused through all, that doth make all one whole;    140
This the worst superstition, him except,

Aught to desire, SUPREME REALITY![1]
The plenitude and permanence of bliss!
O Fiends of SUPERSTITION! not that oft
Your pitiless rites have floated with man's blood     145
The skull-pil'd Temple, not for this shall wrath
Thunder against you from the Holy One!
But (whether ye th' unclimbing Bigot mock
With secondary Gods, or if more pleas'd
Ye petrify th' imbrothell'd Atheist's heart,     150
The Atheist your worst slave) I o'er some plain
Peopled with Death, and to the silent Sun
Steaming with tyrant-murder'd multitudes;
Or where mid groans and shrieks loud-laughing TRADE
More hideous packs his bales of living anguish;     155
I will raise up a mourning, O ye Fiends!
And curse your spells, that film the eye of Faith,
Hiding the present God, whose presence lost,
The moral world's cohesion, we become
An Anarchy of Spirits! Toy-bewitched,     160
Made blind by lusts, disherited of soul,
No common center Man, no common sire
Knoweth! A sordid solitary thing,
Mid countless brethren with a lonely heart
Thro' courts and cities the smooth Savage roams     165
Feeling himself, his own low Self the whole,
When he by sacred sympathy might make
The whole ONE SELF! SELF, that no alien knows!
SELF, far diffus'd as Fancy's wing can travel!
SELF, spreading still! Oblivious of it's own,     170
Yet all of all possessing! This is FAITH!
This the MESSIAH's destin'd victory!

But first offences needs must come! Even now[2]
(Black Hell laughs horrible—to hear the scoff!)

---

[1]If to make aught but the Supreme Reality the object of final pursuit, be Superstition; if the attributing of sublime properties to things or persons, which those things or persons neither do or can possess, be Superstition; then Avarice and Ambition are Superstitions: and he who wishes to estimate the evils of Superstition, should transport himself, not to the temple of the Mexican Deities, but to the plains of Flanders, or the coast of Africa. – Such is the sentiment convey'd in this and the subsequent lines. [S.T.C., 1797]

[2]January 21st, 1794, in the debate on the Address to his Majesty, on the speech from the Throne, the Earl of Guildford (sic) moved an Amendment to the following effect: – 'That the

THEE to defend, meek Galilæan! THEE                    175
And thy mild laws of Love unutterable,
Mistrust and Enmity have burst the bands
Of social Peace; and list'ning Treachery lurks
With *pious* fraud to snare a brother's life;
And childless widows o'er the groaning land            180
Wail numberless; and orphans weep for bread!
THEE to defend, dear Saviour of Mankind!
THEE, Lamb of God! THEE, blameless Prince of Peace!
From all sides rush the thirsty brood of War!
AUSTRIA, and that foul WOMAN of the NORTH,             185
The lustful Murd'ress of her wedded Lord!
And he, connatural Mind![1] whom (in their songs
So bards of elder time had haply feign'd)
Some Fury fondled in her hate to man,
Bidding her serpent hair in tortuous folds             190
Lick his young face, and at his mouth imbreathe
Horrible sympathy! And leagued with these
Each petty German Princeling, nursed in gore!
Soul-harden'd barterers of human blood![2]
Death's prime Slave-merchants! Scorpion-whips of Fate! 195
Nor least in savagery of holy zeal,
Apt for the yoke, the race degenerate,
Whom Britain erst had blush'd to call her sons!
THEE to defend the Moloch Priest prefers
The prayer of hate, and bellows to the herd,           200
That Deity, ACCOMPLICE Deity
In the fierce jealousy of waken'd wrath

---

House hoped his Majesty would seize the earliest opportunity to conclude a peace with France,' &c. This motion was opposed by the Duke of Portland, who 'considered the war to be merely grounded on one principle – the preservation of the CHRISTIAN RELIGION'. May 30th, 1794, the Duke of Bedford moved a number of Resolutions, with a view to the Establishment of a Peace with France. He was opposed (among others) by Lord Abingdon in these remarkable words: 'The best road to Peace, my Lords, is WAR! and WAR carried on in the same manner in which we are taught to worship our CREATOR, namely, with all our souls, and with all our minds, and with all our hearts, and with all our strength.' [S.T.C. 1797]

[1] That Despot who received the wages of an hireling that he might act the part of a swindler, and who skulked from his impotent attacks on the liberties of France to perpetrate more successful iniquity in the plains of *Poland*. [S.T.C.]

[2] The Father of the present Prince of Hesse Cassell supported himself and his strumpets at Paris by the vast sums which he received from the British Government during the American War for the flesh of his subjects. [S.T.C.]

Will go forth with our armies and our fleets
To scatter the red ruin on their foes!
O blasphemy! to mingle fiendish deeds                    205
With blessedness! Lord of unsleeping Love,[1]
From everlasting Thou! We shall not die.
These, even these, in mercy didst thou form,
Teachers of Good thro' Evil, by brief wrong
Making Truth lovely, and her future might              210
Magnetic o'er the fix'd untrembling heart.

In the primeval age a dateless while
The vacant Shepherd wander'd with his flock,
Pitching his tent where'er the green grass wav'd.
But soon Imagination conjur'd up                        215
An host of new desires: with busy aim,
Each for himself, Earth's eager children toil'd.
So PROPERTY began, twy-streaming fount,
Whence Vice and Virtue flow, honey and gall.
Hence the soft couch, and many-colour'd robe,          220
The timbrel, and arch'd dome and costly feast,
With all th' inventive arts, that nurs'd the soul
To forms of beauty, and by sensual wants
Unsensualiz'd the mind, which in the means
Learnt to forget the grossness of the end,             225
Best-pleasur'd with it's own activity.
And hence Disease that withers manhood's arm,
The daggered Envy, spirit-quenching Want,
Warriors, and Lords, and Priests—all the sore ills[2]
That vex and desolate our mortal life.                 230
Wide-wasting ills! yet each th' immediate source

---

[1] Art thou not from everlasting, O Lord, mine Holy One? we shall not die. O Lord, thou hast ordained them for judgment; &c. – Habakkuk i. 12. [S.T.C.]

In this paragraph the Author recalls himself from his indignation against the instruments of Evil, to contemplate the *uses* of these Evils in the great process of divine Benevolence. In the first age, Men were innocent from ignorance of Vice; they fell, that by the knowledge of consequences they might attain intellectual security, i.e. Virtue, which is a wise and strong-nerv'd Innocence. [S.T.C., 1797]

[2] I deem that the teaching of the gospel for hire is wrong; because it gives the teacher an improper bias in favour of particular opinions on a subject where it is of the last importance that the mind should be perfectly unbiassed. Such is my private opinion; but I mean not to censure all hired teachers, many among whom I know, and venerate as the best and wisest of men – God forbid that I should think of these, when I use the word PRIEST, a name, after which any other term of abhorrence would appear an anti-climax. By a PRIEST I mean a man

Of mightier good. Their keen necessities
To ceaseless action goading human thought
Have made Earth's reasoning animal her Lord;
And the pale-featured Sage's trembling hand                    235
Strong as an host of arméd Deities!
From Avarice thus, from Luxury and War
Sprang heavenly Science: and from Science Freedom.
O'er waken'd realms Philosophers and Bards
Spread in concentric circles: they whose souls                 240
Conscious of their high dignities from God
Brook not Wealth's rivalry; and they who long
Enamoured with the charms of order hate
Th' unseemly disproportion; and whoe'er
Turn with mild sorrow from the victor's car                    245
And the low puppetry of thrones, to muse
On that blest triumph, when the PATRIOT SAGE[1]
Call'd the red lightnings from th' o'er-rushing cloud
And dash'd the beauteous Terrors on the earth
Smiling majestic. Such a phalanx ne'er                         250
Measur'd firm paces to the calming sound
Of Spartan flute! These on the fated day,
When stung to rage by Pity eloquent men
Have rous'd with pealing voice th' unnumbered tribes
That toil and groan and bleed, hungry and blind,               255
These hush'd awhile with patient eye serene
Shall watch the mad careering of the storm;
Then o'er the wild and wavy chaos rush
And tame th' outrageous mass, with plastic might
Moulding Confusion to such perfect forms,                      260
As erst were wont, bright visions of the day!
To float before them, when, the Summer noon,
Beneath some arch'd romantic rock reclin'd
They felt the sea-breeze lift their youthful locks,

---

who holding the scourge of power in his right hand and a bible (translated by authority) in his
left, doth necessarily cause the bible and the scourge to be associated ideas, and so produces
that temper of mind which leads to Infidelity – Infidelity which judging of Revelation by the
doctrines and practices of established Churches honors God by rejecting Christ. See 'Address
to the People', p. 57, sold by Parsons, Paternoster Row. [S.T.C.]

[1] DR FRANKLIN. [S.T.C.]

Or in the month of blossoms, at mild eve,                                  265
Wandering with desultory feet inhal'd
The wafted perfumes, and the flocks and woods
And many-tinted streams and setting Sun
With all his gorgeous company of clouds
Extatic gaz'd! then homeward as they stray'd                                270
Cast the sad eye to earth, and inly mus'd
Why there was Misery in a world so fair.


Ah far remov'd from all that glads the sense,
From all that softens or ennobles Man,
The wretched Many! Bent beneath their loads                                 275
They gape at pageant Power, nor recognize
Their cots' transmuted plunder! From the tree
Of Knowledge, ere the vernal sap had risen
Rudely disbranch'd! O *blest* Society!
Fitliest depictured by some sun-scorcht waste,                              280
Where oft majestic thro' the tainted noon
The SIMOOM sails, before whose purple pomp[1]
Who falls not prostrate dies! And where, by night,
Fast by each precious fountain on green herbs
The lion couches; or hyæna dips                                             285
Deep in the lucid stream his bloody jaws;
Or serpent rolls his vast moon-glittering bulk,
Caught in whose monstrous twine Behemoth[2] yells,
His bones loud-crashing!

                         O ye numberless,
Whom foul Oppression's ruffian gluttony                                     290
Drives from life's plenteous feast! O thou poor Wretch,
Who nurs'd in darkness and made wild by want,
Dost roam for prey, yea thy unnatural hand
Liftest to deeds of blood! O pale-eyed Form,

[1] At eleven o'clock, while we contemplated with great pleasure the rugged top of Chiggre, to which we were fast approaching, and where we were to solace ourselves with plenty of good water, IDRIS cried out with a loud voice, 'Fall upon your faces, for here is the Simoom'. I saw from the S.E. an haze come on, in colour like the purple part of the rainbow, but not so compressed or thick. – It did not occupy twenty yards in breadth, and was about twelve feet high from the ground. – We all lay flat on the ground, as if dead, till IDRIS told us it was blown over. The meteor, or purple haze, which I saw, was indeed passed; but the light air that still blew was of heat to threaten suffocation. – BRUCE's Travels, vol. 4, p. 557. [S.T.C.]

[2] Used poetically for a very large quadruped; but in general it designates the Elephant. [S.T.C.]

The victim of seduction, doom'd to know  295
Polluted nights and days of blasphemy;
Who in loath'd orgies with lewd wassailers
Must gaily laugh, while thy remember'd Home
Gnaws like a viper at thy secret heart!
O agéd Women! ye who weekly catch  300
The morsel tost by law-forc'd Charity,
And die so slowly, that none call it murder!
O loathly-visag'd Suppliants! ye that oft
Rack'd with disease, from the unopen'd gate
Of the full Lazar-house, heart-broken crawl!  305
O ye to scepter'd Glory's gore-drench'd field
Forc'd or ensnar'd, who swept by Slaughter's scythe,
(Stern nurse of Vultures!) steam in putrid heaps!
O thou poor Widow, who in dreams dost view
Thy Husband's mangled corse, and from short doze  310
Start'st with a shriek: or in thy half-thatch'd cot
Wak'd by the wintry night-storm, wet and cold,
Cow'rest o'er thy screaming baby! Rest awhile
Children of Wretchedness! More groans must rise,
More blood must steam, or ere your wrongs be full.  315
Yet is the day of Retribution nigh:
The Lamb of God hath open'd the fifth seal:[1]
And upward rush on swiftest wing of fire
Th' innumerable multitude of Wrongs
By man on man inflicted! Rest awhile,  320
Children of Wretchedness! The hour is nigh:
And lo! the Great, the Rich, the Mighty Men,
The Kings and the Chief Captains of the World,
With all that fix'd on high like stars of Heaven
Shot baleful influence, shall be cast to earth,  325
Vile and down-trodden, as the untimely fruit
Shook from the fig-tree by a sudden storm.

[1]See the sixth chapter of the Revelation of St John the Divine. – And I looked, and beheld a pale horse; and his name that sat on him was Death, and Hell followed with him. And power was given unto them over the FOURTH part of the Earth, to kill with sword, and with hunger, and with pestilence, and with the beasts of the earth. – And when he had opened the fifth seal, I saw under the altar the souls of them that were slain for the word of God, and for the testimony which they held: and white robes were given unto every one of them; and it was said unto them, that they should rest yet for a little season, until their fellow servants also, and their brethren, that should be killed as they were should be fulfilled. And I beheld when he had opened the sixth seal, the stars of Heaven fell unto the Earth, even as a fig tree casteth her untimely figs when she is shaken of a mighty wind: And the Kings of the earth, and the great men, and the rich men, and the chief captains, &c. [S.T.C.]

Ev'n now the storm begins:[1] each gentle name,
Faith and meek Piety, with fearful joy
Tremble far-off—for lo! the Giant FRENZY                        330
Uprooting empires with his whirlwind arm
Mocketh high Heaven; burst hideous from the cell
Where the old Hag, unconquerable, huge,
Creation's eyeless drudge, black RUIN, sits
Nursing th' impatient earthquake.

                                    O return!                   335
Pure FAITH! meek PIETY! The abhorred Form[2]
Whose scarlet robe was stiff with earthly pomp,
Who drank iniquity in cups of gold,
Whose names were many and all blasphemous,
Hath met the horrible judgment! Whence that cry?               340
The mighty army of foul Spirits shriek'd,
Disherited of earth! For She hath fallen
On whose black front was written MYSTERY;
She that reel'd heavily, whose wine was blood;
She that work'd whoredom with the DÆMON POWER,                 345
And from the dark embrace all evil things
Brought forth and nurtured: mitred ATHEISM;
And patient FOLLY who on bended knee
Gives back the steel that stabb'd him; and pale FEAR
Hunted by ghastlier terrors than surround                      350
Moon-blasted Madness when he yells at midnight!
Return pure FAITH! return meek PIETY!
The kingdoms of the world are your's: each heart
Self-govern'd, the vast family of Love
Rais'd from the common earth by common toil                    355
Enjoy the equal produce. Such delights
As float to earth, permitted visitants!
When on some solemn jubilee of Saints
The sapphire-blazing gates of Paradise
Are thrown wide open, and thence voyage forth                  360

[1] The French Revolution [S.T.C., 1796]. The subsequent paragraph alludes to the downfall
of Religious Establishments. I am convinced that the Babylon of the Apocalypse does not
apply to Rome exclusively; but to the union of Religion with Power and Wealth, wherever it is
found. [S.T.C., 1797]

[2] And there came one of the seven angels which had the seven vials, and talked with me,
saying unto me, come hither! I will shew unto thee the judgment of the great Whore, that
sitteth upon many waters: with whom the Kings of the earth have committed fornication, &c.
Revelation of St John the Divine, chapter the seventeenth. [S.T.C.]

Detachments wild of seraph-warbled airs
And odors snatch'd from beds of amaranth,
And they, that from the chrystal river of life
Spring up on freshen'd wing, ambrosial gales!
The favor'd good man in his lonely walk                       365
Perceives them, and his silent spirit drinks
Strange bliss which he shall recognize in heaven.
And such delights, such strange beatitude
Seize on my young anticipating heart
When that blest future rushes on my view!                     370
For in his own and in his Father's might
The SAVIOUR comes! While as to solemn strains,
The THOUSAND YEARS[1] lead up their mystic dance,
Old OCEAN claps his hands! the DESERT shouts!
And soft gales wafted from the haunts of Spring               375
Melt the primaeval North! The mighty Dead
Rise to new life, whoe'er from earliest time
With conscious zeal had urg'd Love's wond'rous plan
Coadjutors of God. To MILTON's trump
The odorous groves of earth reparadis'd                       380
Unbosom their glad echoes: inly hush'd
Adoring NEWTON his serener eye
Raises to heaven: and he of mortal kind
Wisest, he[2] first who mark'd the ideal tribes
Down the fine fibres from the sentient brain                  385
Roll subtly-surging. Pressing on his steps
Lo! Priestley there, Patriot, and Saint, and Sage,
Whom that my fleshly eye hath never seen
A childish pang of impotent regret
Hath thrill'd my heart. Him from his native land              390
Statesmen blood-stain'd and Priests idolatrous
By dark lies mad'ning the blind multitude
Drove with vain hate: calm, pitying he retir'd,
And mus'd expectant on these promis'd years.

---

[1]The Millenium: – in which I suppose, that Man will continue to enjoy the highest glory, of which his human nature is capable. – That all who in past ages have endeavoured to ameliorate the state of man will rise and enjoy the fruits and flowers, the imperceptible seeds of which they had sown in their former Life: and that the wicked will during the same period, be suffering the remedies adapted to their several bad habits. I suppose that this period will be followed by the passing away of this Earth and by our entering the state of pure intellect; when all Creation shall rest from its labours. [S.T.C., 1797]

[2]David Hartley. [S.T.C.]

O Years! the blest preeminence of Saints!                    395
Sweeping before the rapt prophetic Gaze
Bright as what glories of the jasper throne[1]
Stream from the gorgeous and face-veiling plumes
Of Spirits adoring! Ye, blest Years! must end,
And all beyond is darkness! Heights most strange!            400
Whence Fancy falls, fluttering her idle wing.
For who of woman born may paint the hour,
When seized in his mid course, the Sun shall wane
Making noon ghastly! Who of woman born
May image in his wildly-working thought,                     405
How the black-visaged, red-eyed Fiend outstretcht[2]
Beneath th' unsteady feet of Nature groans
In feverish slumbers—destin'd then to wake,
When fiery whirlwinds thunder his dread name
And Angels shout, DESTRUCTION! How his arm                   410
The mighty Spirit lifting high in air
Shall swear by Him, the ever-living ONE,
TIME IS NO MORE!

     Believe thou, O my soul,[3]
Life is a vision shadowy of Truth,
And vice, and anguish, and the wormy grave,                  415
Shapes of a dream! The veiling clouds retire,
And lo! the Throne of the redeeming God
Forth flashing unimaginable day
Wraps in one blaze earth, heaven, and deepest hell.

Contemplant Spirits! ye that hover o'er                      420
With untir'd gaze th' immeasurable fount
Ebullient with creative Deity!
And ye of plastic power, that interfus'd
Roll thro' the grosser and material mass
In organizing surge! Holies of God!                          425
(And what if Monads of the infinite mind?)
I haply journeying my immortal course

[1] Rev. iv. 2, 3.—And immediately I was in the Spirit: and behold, a Throne was set in Heaven, and one sat on the Throne. And he that sat was to look upon like a jasper and a sardine stone: &c. [S.T.C., 1797]
[2] The final Destruction impersonated. [S.T.C., 1797]
[3] This paragraph is intelligible to those, who, like the Author, believe and feel the sublime system of Berkley [sic]; and the doctrine of the final Happiness of all men. [S.T.C., 1797]

Shall sometime join your mystic choir! Till then
I discipline my young noviciate thought
In ministeries of heart-stirring song,                                    430
And aye on Meditation's heaven-ward wing
Soaring aloft I breathe th' empyreal air
Of LOVE, omnific, omnipresent LOVE,
Whose day-spring rises glorious in my soul
As the great Sun, when he his influence                                   435
Sheds on the frost-bound waters—The glad stream
Flows to the ray and warbles as it flows.
[1794–6]

# FROM CLEVEDON TO STOWEY

While the 1796 collection was going through the press Coleridge was still searching for a way of life which would enable him to combine the exercise of his poetic gifts with active intervention on the part of humanity. His first plan was to produce a periodical entitled *The Watchman*, in which he would be able to print literary productions of his own and at the same time plead the cause of freedom. Now that England was at war with France civil liberties were liable to be undermined: and it was his aim to draw attention to any undue infringements on the part of the Government and its agents. In order to be near the printer he gave up his cottage at Clevedon and moved to Bristol, commemorating the occasion by a poem entitled *Reflections on Leaving a Place of Retirement*. In this (as also in *The Watchman*) he presents the claims of conscience, arguing that the cultivation of sensibility concerning the wrongs of the world without concomitant political action is a cowardly pursuit: even good actions performed without sympathy are preferable to a sympathy that never reaches out to act.

*The Watchman* was short lived, but its numbers included several new poems, among them the *Lines on a Portrait of a Lady* (recently argued to be Coleridge's by S. F. Johnson but not hitherto printed in any collection). Coleridge's reluctance to publish it was no doubt due to the ludicrous last line, where the image in

> these I trace
> With the pencil of the Heart

recalls the one which he later ridiculed in *Biographia Literaria*:

> No more will I endure love's pleasing pain
> Or round my *heart's leg* tie his galling chain.

The earlier lines, on the other hand, foreshadow something of the rare 'entrancement' of his best work.

The failure of *The Watchman* induced disillusionment concerning practical political activity. Coleridge was beginning to realize that his talents might be better employed in the analysis of human nature and the defects in it which resulted in the sorry political scene of his day. The study of nature might in the end do more for humanity than direct political activity.

This trend had already been foreshadowed in *Reflections on Having Left a Place of Retirement*, where the best lines are not by any means those describing his entry into active life, but those in which he contemplates the view across the Bristol Channel from above Clevedon:

> It seem'd like Omnipresence! God, methought,
> Had built him there a Temple: the whole World
> Seem'd *imag'd* in its vast circumference . . .

While these considerations were moving him, his friends were urging him to raise his ambitions. 'Coleridge,' wrote Lamb in January 1797, 'I want you to write an Epic poem. Nothing short of it can satisfy the vast capacity of true poetic genius.'

The promptings fitted in with Coleridge's own dreams: but for the immediate future he had the task of providing for his household. He toyed with several schemes, including journalism and translation; the plan most attractive to him was that of becoming tutor to a number of young men, studying, as he taught them, in preparation for his great epic poem. In the meantime, his domestic responsibilities were increased by the birth of a son. The three poems composed on the occasion include a philosophical speculation concerning the immortality of the soul which looks forward to Wordsworth's *Ode*; there is also a passage of amusingly honest realism in which he describes his actual feelings at the first sight of his infant.

At the end of 1796 he settled with his wife and child in a cottage at Nether Stowey. His *Ode to the Departing Year* is another attempt at Miltonic sublimity, rising, as in his previous efforts, to passages of idiosyncratic grandeur and degenerating at worst to a sub-Miltonic bombast. At the end of the poem, however, the catalogues of wrongs and gloomy forebodings of ruin are mitigated first by an account of pastoral England, still unenslaved, 'not wholly vile', and then by an avowal that the expression of his feelings concerning his country has been acting as a purgation of his own nature so that he is now

> Cleans'd from the vaporous passions that bedim
> God's Image, sister oi tнс Seraphim.

These other themes distance the political rhetoric of the poem and show that Coleridge is beginning to be preoccupied by new ideas. In

*The Destiny of Nations* his attempts to give philosophical depth to a poetical work on Joan of Arc in which he collaborated with Southey are extracted to furnish a framework for a possible poem of his own. It is significant that in the new edition of his poems produced in 1797 the Dedication to his brother, the Reverend George Coleridge (actually one of the last poems to be written), turns out to be a poem notable for its praise of domestic pleasures.

In the same way the revision of *Religious Musings* which was undertaken for the new edition witnesses to renewed interest in the significance of natural beauty. Lines which had described the eyes of Christ, where power and wisdom and 'loftier Love' blended together, are now replaced by lines which make a similar point by way of the symbolism of nature:

> Fair the vernal mead,
> Fair the high grove, the sea, the sun, the stars;
> True impress each of their creating Sire!
> Yet nor high grove, nor many-colour'd mead,
> Nor the green ocean with his thousand isles,
> Nor the starred azure, nor the sovran sun,
> E'er with such majesty of portraiture
> Imag'd the supreme beauty uncreate,
> As thou, meek Saviour! . . .

The note of piety still holds in check more daring speculations concerning the relationship between nature and God, but a growing enthusiasm for natural beauty is unmistakable within the Miltonic mode.

# Reflections on Having Left a Place of Retirement

Sermoni propriora.[1] — HOR.

Low was our pretty Cot: our tallest Rose
Peep'd at the chamber-window. We could hear
At silent noon, and eve, and early morn,
The Sea's faint murmur. In the open air
Our Myrtles blossom'd; and across the porch          5
Thick Jasmins twined: the little landscape round
Was green and woody, and refresh'd the eye.
It was a spot which you might aptly call
The Valley of Seclusion! Once I saw
(Hallowing his Sabbath-day by quietness)             10
A wealthy son of Commerce saunter by,
Bristowa's[2] citizen: methought, it calm'd
His thirst of idle gold, and made him muse
With wiser feelings: for he paus'd, and look'd
With a pleas'd sadness, and gaz'd all around,        15
Then eyed our Cottage, and gaz'd round again,
And sigh'd, and said, it was a Blessèd Place.
And we *were* bless'd. Oft with patient ear
Long-listening to the viewless sky-lark's note
(Viewless, or haply for a moment seen               20
Gleaming on sunny wings) in whisper'd tones
I've said to my Belovèd, 'Such, sweet Girl!
The inobtrusive song of Happiness,
Unearthly minstrelsy! then only heard
When the Soul seeks to hear; when all is hush'd,     25
And the Heart listens!'

                            But the time, when first
From that low Dell, steep up the stony Mount
I climb'd with perilous toil and reach'd the top,
Oh! what a goodly scene! *Here* the bleak mount,
The bare bleak mountain speckled thin with sheep;    30
Grey clouds, that shadowing spot the sunny fields;
And river, now with bushy rocks o'er-brow'd,

---

[1]'More suitable to prose (or conversation).' Horace's original (Sat. 1. 4. 42) has 'propriora': 'nearer to prose'.

[2]'Bristol's'. These gently satirical lines recall Satan's visit to Eden in *Paradise Lost* ix, 445–66.

Now winding bright and full, with naked banks;
And seats, and lawns, the Abbey and the wood,
And cots, and hamlets, and faint city-spire;                       35
The Channel *there*, the Islands and white sails,
Dim coasts, and cloud-like hills, and shoreless Ocean –
It seem'd like Omnipresence! God, methought,
Had built him there a Temple: the whole World
Seem'd *imag'd* in its vast circumference:                          40
No *wish* profan'd my overwhelméd heart.
Blest hour! It was a luxury, – to be!

   Ah! quiet Dell! dear Cot, and Mount sublime!
I was constrain'd to quit you. Was it right,
While my unnumber'd brethren toil'd and bled,                       45
That I should dream away the entrusted hours
On rose-leaf beds, pampering the coward heart
With feelings all too delicate for use?
Sweet is the tear that from some Howard's eye
Drops on the cheek of one he lifts from earth:                      50
And he that works me good with unmov'd face,
Does it but half: he chills me while he aids,
My benefactor, not my brother man!
Yet even this, this cold beneficence
Praise, praise it, O my Soul! oft as thou scann'st                  55
The sluggard Pity's vision-weaving tribe!
Who sigh for Wretchedness, yet shun the Wretched,
Nursing in some delicious solitude
Their slothful loves and dainty sympathies!
I therefore go, and join head, heart, and hand,                     60
Active and firm, to fight the bloodless fight
Of Science, Freedom, and the Truth in Christ.

   Yet oft when after honourable toil
Rests the tir'd mind, and waking loves to dream,
My spirit shall revisit thee, dear Cot!                             65
Thy Jasmin and thy window-peeping Rose,
And Myrtles fearless of the mild sea-air.
And I shall sigh fond wishes – sweet Abode!
Ah! – had none greater! And that all had such!
It might be so – but the time is not yet.                           70
Speed it, O Father! Let thy Kingdom come!
[1795]

# Elegy

IMITATED FROM ONE OF AKENSIDE'S BLANK-VERSE
INSCRIPTIONS [NO. III]

Near the lone pile with ivy overspread,
   Fast by the rivulet's sleep-persuading sound,
Where 'sleeps the moonlight' on yon verdant bed —
   O humbly press that consecrated ground!

For there does Edmund rest, the learnéd swain!      5
   And there his spirit most delights to rove:
Young Edmund! fam'd for each harmonious strain,
   And the sore wounds of ill-requited Love.

Like some tall tree that spreads its branches wide,
   And loads the West-wind with its soft perfume,     10
His manhood blossom'd; till the faithless pride
   Of fair Matilda sank him to the tomb.

But soon did righteous Heaven her Guilt pursue!
   Where'er with wilder'd step she wander'd pale,
Still Edmund's image rose to blast her view,     15
   Still Edmund's voice accus'd her in each gale.

With keen regret, and conscious Guilt's alarms,
   Amid the pomp of Affluence she pined;
Nor all that lur'd her faith from Edmund's arms
   Could lull the wakeful horror of her mind.     20

Go, Traveller! tell the tale with sorrow fraught:
   Some tearful Maid perchance, or blooming Youth,
May hold it in remembrance; and be taught
   That Riches cannot pay for Love or Truth.
[?1794]

## *Ad Lyram*

### (CASIMIR, BOOK II. ODE 3)

The solemn-breathing air is ended –
　　Cease, O Lyre! thy kindred lay!
From the poplar-branch suspended
　　Glitter to the eye of Day!

On thy wires hov'ring, dying,　　　　　　5
　　Softly sighs the summer wind:
I will slumber, careless lying,
　　By yon waterfall reclin'd.

In the forest hollow-roaring
　　Hark! I hear a deep'ning sound –　　　10
Clouds rise thick with heavy low'ring!
　　See! th' horizon blackens round!

Parent of the soothing measure,
　　Let me seize thy wetted string!
Swiftly flies the flatterer, Pleasure,　　　15
　　Headlong, ever on the wing.
[1794]

## *Lines to Thomas Poole*[1]

. . . Joking apart, I would to God we could sit by a fireside & joke *vivâ voce,* face to face – Stella [Mrs Thelwall] and Sara [Mrs S. T. Coleridge], Jack Thelwall, & I! – as I once wrote to my dear *friend*, T. Poole, 'repeating'

　　Such Verse as Bowles, heart-honour'd Poet, sang,
　　That wakes the Tear yet steals away the Pang,
　　Then or with Berkley or with Hobbes romance it
　　Dissecting Truth with metaphysic lancet.

[1] Quoted in a letter from Coleridge to John Thelwall, dated 31 December 1796.

Or drawn from up those dark unfathom'd Wells          5
In wiser folly clink the Cap & Bells.
How many tales we told! what jokes we made!
Conundrum, Crambo, Rebus, or Charade;
Ænigmas, that had driven the Theban[1] mad,
And Puns then best when exquisitely bad;          10
And I, if aught of archer vein I hit,
With my own Laughter stifled my own Wit.
[1795–6]

## On Donne's Poetry

With Donne, whose muse on dromedary trots,
Wreathe iron pokers into true-love knots;
Rhyme's sturdy Cripple, Wit's Maze and Clue,
Thought's Forge and Furnace, Mangle-press and Screw . . .[2]
[1795 or after. Another extract from lines to Poole]

## The Hour When We Shall Meet Again
### (Composed during Illness, and in Absence)

Dim Hour! that sleep'st on pillowing clouds afar,
O rise and yoke the Turtles to thy car!
Bend o'er the traces, blame each lingering Dove,
And give me to the bosom of my Love!
My gentle Love, caressing and carest,          5
With heaving heart shall cradle me to rest!
Shed the warm tear-drop from her smiling eyes,
Lull with fond woe, and medicine me with sighs!
While finely-flushing float her kisses meek,
Like melted rubies, o'er my pallid cheek.          10
Chill'd by the night, the drooping Rose of May
Mourns the long absence of the lovely Day;

[1]Oedipus. [S.T.C.]
[2]A later version ends:
        Rhyme's sturdy cripple, fancy's maze and clue,
        Wit's forge and fire-blast, meaning's press and screw.
    See Marginalia ll, 16 and n.

Young Day returning at her promis'd hour
Weeps o'er the sorrows of her favourite Flower;
Weeps the soft dew, the balmy gale she sighs,    15
And darts a trembling lustre from her eyes.
New life and joy th' expanding flow'ret feels:
His pitying Mistress mourns, and mourning heals!
[1796]

## On Observing a Blossom
## on the First of February 1796

Sweet flower! that peeping from thy russet stem
Unfoldest timidly, (for in strange sort
This dark, frieze-coated, hoarse, teeth-chattering month
Hath borrow'd Zephyr's voice, and gazed upon thee
With blue voluptuous eye) alas, poor Flower!    5
These are but flatteries of the faithless year.
Perchance, escaped its unknown polar cave,
Even now the keen North-East is on its way.
Flower that must perish! shall I liken thee
To some sweet girl of too too rapid growth    10
Nipp'd by consumption mid untimely charms?
Or to Bristowa's bard,[1] the wondrous boy!
An amaranth, which earth scarce seem'd to own,
Till disappointment came, and pelting wrong
Beat it to earth? or with indignant grief    15
Shall I compare thee to poor Poland's hope,
Bright flower of hope killed in the opening bud?
Farewell, sweet blossom! better fate be thine
And mock my boding! Dim similitudes
Weaving in moral strains, I've stolen one hour    20
From anxious Self, Life's cruel taskmaster!
And the warm wooings of this sunny day
Tremble along my frame and harmonize
The attempered organ, that even saddest thoughts
Mix with some sweet sensations, like harsh tunes    25
Played deftly on a soft-toned instrument.
[1796]

[1]Chatterton. [S.T.C.]

## Lines on a Portrait of a Lady

Tender as the sweets of Spring
　　Wafted on the Western gale,
When the breeze with dewy wing
　　Wanders thro' the Primrose vale;

Tranquil as the hush of night                    5
　　To the Hermit's holy dream;
While the Moon with lovely light,
　　Quivers on the rippling stream;

Cheerful as the Beams of Morn,
　　Laughing on the Mountain's side;            10
Spotless as the Cygnet's form,
　　Heaving on the silver'd Tide.

Who can paint this varied grace,
　　Charms that mock the mimic art?
Yet, my Laura! these I trace                     15
　　With the pencil of the Heart.
[1796]


## On a Late Connubial Rupture in High Life[1]

### [PRINCE AND PRINCESS OF WALES]

I sigh, fair injur'd stranger! for thy fate;
　　But what shall sighs avail thee? thy poor heart,
'Mid all the 'pomp and circumstance' of state,
　　Shivers in nakedness. Unbidden, start

[1] In 1795 the Prince of Wales, who was secretly married to Mrs Fitzherbert, a Roman Catholic, agreed to marry his cousin Princess Caroline of Brunswick for the sake of his succession. They were ill-suited and a separation was arranged soon after the birth of their first child; but Caroline continued to complain at her treatment and tried unsuccessfully to gain admission to Westminster Abbey to be at his side when he was eventually crowned king in 1820.

Sad recollections of Hope's garish dream, 5
  That shaped a seraph form, and named it Love,
Its hues gay-varying, as the orient beam
  Varies the neck of Cytherea's dove.

To one soft accent of domestic joy
  Poor are the shouts that shake the high-arch'd dome; 10
Those plaudits that thy *public* path annoy,
  Alas! they tell thee – Thou'rt a wretch *at home*!

O then retire, and weep! *Their very woes*
  *Solace the guiltless*. Drop the pearly flood
On thy sweet infant, as the full-blown rose, 15
  Surcharg'd with dew, bends o'er its neighbouring bud.

And ah! that Truth some holy spell might lend
  To lure thy Wanderer from the Syren's power;
Then bid your souls inseparably blend
  Like two bright dew-drops meeting in a flower. 20
[1796]


# Verses

ADDRESSED TO J. HORNE TOOKE AND THE COMPANY WHO
MET ON 28 JUNE 1796 TO CELEBRATE HIS POLL AT THE
WESTMINSTER ELECTION

Britons! when last ye met, with distant streak
So faintly promis'd the pale Dawn to break;
So dim it stain'd the precincts of the Sky
E'en *Expectation* gaz'd with doubtful Eye.
But now such fair Varieties of Light 5
O'ertake the heavy sailing Clouds of Night;
Th' Horizon kindles with so rich a red,
That, tho' the *Sun still hides* his glorious head,
Th' impatient Matin-bird *assur'd of Day*
Leaves his low nest to meet its earliest ray; 10
Loud the sweet song of Gratulation sings,
And high in air claps his rejoicing wings!

Patriot & Sage! whose breeze-like Spirit[1] first
The lazy mists of Pedantry dispers'd,
(Mists, in which Superstition's *pigmy* band                    15
Seem'd Giant Forms, the Genii of the Land!),
Thy struggles soon shall wak'ning Britain bless,
And Truth & Freedom hail thy wish'd success.
Yes *Tooke*! tho' foul Corruption's wolfish throng
Outmalice Calumny's imposthum'd Tongue,                    20
Thy Country's noblest & *determin'd* Choice,
Soon shalt thou thrill the Senate with thy voice;
With gradual Dawn bid Error's phantoms flit,
Or wither with the lightning flash of Wit;
Or with sublimer mien & tones more deep                    25
Charm sworded Justice from mysterious Sleep,
'By violated Freedom's loud Lament,
Her Lamps extinguish'd & her Temple rent;
By the forc'd tears, her captive Martyrs shed;
By each pale Orphan's feeble cry for bread;                    30
By ravag'd Belgium's corse-impeded Flood,
And Vendée steaming still with brothers' blood!'
And if amid the strong impassion'd Tale,
Thy Tongue should falter & thy Lips turn pale;
If transient Darkness film thy aweful Eye,                    35
And thy tir'd Bosom struggle with a sigh:
Science & Freedom shall demand to hear
Who practis'd on a Life so doubly dear;
Infus'd the unwholesome anguish drop by drop
Pois'ning the sacred stream, they could not stop!                    40
Shall bid thee with recover'd strength relate
How dark & deadly is a Coward's Hate:
What seeds of Death by wan Confinement sown
When prison-echoes mock'd Disease's groan!
Shall bid th' indignant Father flash dismay,                    45
And drag th' unnatural Villain into Day
Who[2] to the sports of his flesh'd Ruffians left
Two lovely Mourners of their Sire bereft!
'Twas wrong, like this, which Rome's *first Consul* bore,

---

[1] Ἔπεα πτερόεντα. [S.T.C., quoting the title (which means 'Winged Words') of Tooke's work on etymology, the first version of which was published in 1786–1805.]

[2] 'Dundas left thief-takers in Horne Tooke's House for three days, with his two Daughters *alone*: for Horne Tooke keeps no servant.' – [S.T.C. to Estlin.]

So by th' insulted Female's name *he* swore        50
Ruin (& rais'd her reeking dagger high)
Not to the *Tyrants* but the *Tyranny*!!
[1796. From MS Letter]


# To a Friend
### [Charles Lamb]

#### WHO HAD DECLARED HIS INTENTION OF WRITING
#### NO MORE POETRY

Dear Charles! whilst yet thou wert a babe, I ween
That Genius plung'd thee in that wizard fount
Hight Castalie: and (sureties of thy faith)
That Pity and Simplicity stood by,
And promis'd for thee, that thou shouldst renounce        5
The world's low cares and lying vanities,
Steadfast and rooted in the heavenly Muse,
And wash'd and sanctified to Poesy.
Yes — thou wert plung'd, but with forgetful hand
Held, as by Thetis erst her warrior son:        10
And with those recreant unbaptizéd heels
Thou'rt flying from thy bounden minist'ries —
So sore it seems and burthensome a task
To weave unwithering flowers! But take thou heed:
For thou art vulnerable, wild-eyed boy,        15
And I have arrows[1] mystically dipped
Such as may stop thy speed. Is thy Burns dead?
And shall he die unwept, and sink to earth
'Without the meed of one melodious tear'?
Thy Burns, and Nature's own belovéd bard,        20
Who to the 'Illustrious[2] of his native Land
So properly did look for patronage.'

'Πολλά μοι ὑπ' ἀγκῶνς ὠκέα Βέλη
Ἔνδον ἐντὶ φαρέτρας
Φωνᾶντα συνετοῖσιν
['Full many a swift arrow have I beneath my arm, within my quiver, many an arrow that is vocal to the wise.'] Pind. *Olymp.* ii. 149, *K.τ.λ.* [S.T.C.]
[2]Verbatim from Burns's Dedication of his Poems to the Nobility and Gentry of the Caledonian Hunt. [S.T.C.]

Ghost of Mæcenas! hide thy blushing face!
They snatch'd him from the sickle and the plough –
To gauge ale-firkins.

            Oh! for shame return!          25
On a bleak rock, midway the Aonian mount,
There stands a lone and melancholy tree,
Whose agéd branches to the midnight blast
Make solemn music: pluck its darkest bough,
Ere yet the unwholesome night-dew be exhaled,          30
And weeping wreath it round thy Poet's tomb.
Then in the outskirts, where pollutions grow,
Pick the rank henbane and the dusky flowers
Of night-shade, or its red and tempting fruit,
These with stopped nostril and glove-guarded hand          35
Knit in nice intertexture, so to twine,
The illustrious brow of Scotch Nobility!
[1796]

## Sonnet

### ON RECEIVING A LETTER INFORMING ME
### OF THE BIRTH OF A SON

When they did greet me Father, sudden Awe
Weigh'd down my spirit! I retired and knelt
Seeking the throne of grace, but inly felt
No heavenly visitation upwards draw
My feeble mind, nor cheering ray impart.          5
Ah me! before the Eternal Sire I brought
Th' unquiet silence of confuséd Thought
And shapeless feelings: my o'erwhelmed Heart
Trembled: & vacant tears stream'd down my face.
And now once more, O Lord! to thee I bend,          10
Lover of souls! and groan for future grace,
That, ere my Babe youth's perilous maze have trod,
Thy overshadowing Spirit may descend
And he be born again, a child of God!
[20 September 1796. From MS Letter]

## Sonnet

COMPOSED ON A JOURNEY HOMEWARD; THE AUTHOR
HAVING RECEIVED INTELLIGENCE OF THE BIRTH OF A
SON, 20 SEPTEMBER 1796

Oft o'er my brain does that strange fancy roll
   Which makes the present (while the flash doth last)
   Seem a mere semblance of some unknown past,
Mixed with such feelings, as perplex the soul
Self-questioned in her sleep; and some have said[1]     5
   We liv'd, ere yet this robe of flesh we wore.[2]
   O my sweet baby! when I reach my door,
If heavy looks should tell me thou art dead,
(As sometimes, through excess of hope, I fear)
I think that I should struggle to believe     10
   Thou wert a spirit, to this nether sphere
Sentenc'd for some more venial crime to grieve;
Did'st scream, then spring to meet Heaven's quick reprieve,
   While we wept idly o'er thy little bier!
[1796]

## Sonnet

TO A FRIEND WHO ASKED HOW I FELT WHEN THE NURSE
FIRST PRESENTED MY INFANT TO ME

Charles! my slow heart was only sad, when first
   I scann'd that face of feeble infancy:
For dimly on my thoughtful spirit burst
   All I had been, and all my child might be!
But when I saw it on its mother's arm,     5

[1] Ἦν που ἡμῶν ἡ ψυχὴ πρὶν ἐν τῷδε τῷ ἀνθρωπίνῳ εἴδει γενέσθαι. ['Our soul existed somewhere before it was born in this human form'.] – Plat. *Phaedon.* Cap. xviii. 72 e. [S.T.C.]
[2] Almost all the followers of Fénelon believe that men are degraded Intelligences who had all once existed together in a paradisiacal or perhaps heavenly state. The first four lines express a feeling which I have often had – the present has appeared like a vivid dream or exact similitude of some past circumstances. [S.T.C.]

And hanging at her bosom (she the while
　　Bent o'er its features with a tearful smile)
Then I was thrill'd and melted, and most warm
Impress'd a father's kiss: and all beguil'd
　　Of dark remembrance and presageful fear,          10
　　I seem'd to see an angel-form appear –
'Twas even thine, belovéd woman mild!
　　So for the mother's sake the child was dear,
And dearer was the mother for the child.
[1796]


## Sonnet

### [TO CHARLES LLOYD]

The piteous sobs that choke the Virgin's breath
　　For him, the fair betrothéd Youth, who lies
　　Cold in the narrow dwelling, or the cries
With which a Mother wails her darling's death,
These from our nature's common impulse spring,          5
　　Unblam'd, unprais'd; but o'er the piléd earth
　　Which hides the sheeted corse of grey-hair'd Worth,
If droops the soaring Youth with slacken'd wing;
If he recall in saddest minstrelsy
　　Each tenderness bestow'd, each truth imprest,          10
Such grief is Reason, Virtue, Piety!
And from the Almighty Father shall descend
　　Comforts on his late evening, whose young breast
Mourns with no transient love the Agéd Friend.
[1796]


## To a Young Friend

### ON HIS PROPOSING TO DOMESTICATE WITH THE AUTHOR

### Composed in 1796

A mount, not wearisome and bare and steep,
　　But a green mountain variously up-piled,

Where o'er the jutting rocks soft mosses creep,
Or colour'd lichens with slow oozing weep;
   Where cypress and the darker yew start wild;     5
And, 'mid the summer torrent's gentle dash
Dance brighten'd the red clusters of the ash;
   Beneath whose boughs, by those still sounds beguil'd,
Calm Pensiveness might muse herself to sleep;
   Till haply startled by some fleecy dam,     10
That rustling on the bushy cliff above
With melancholy bleat of anxious love,
   Made meek enquiry for her wandering lamb:
   Such a green mountain 'twere most sweet to climb,
E'en while the bosom ach'd with loneliness –     15
How more than sweet, if some dear friend should bless
   The adventurous toil, and up the path sublime
Now lead, now follow: the glad landscape round,
Wide and more wide, increasing without bound!

   O then 'twere loveliest sympathy, to mark     20
The berries of the half-uprooted ash
Dripping and bright; and list the torrent's dash, –
   Beneath the cypress, or the yew more dark,
Seated at ease, on some smooth mossy rock;
In social silence now, and now to unlock     25
The treasur'd heart; arm linked in friendly arm,
Save if the one, his muse's witching charm
Muttering brow-bent, at unwatch'd distance lag;
   Till high o'er head his beckoning friend appears,
And from the forehead of the topmost crag     30
   Shouts eagerly: for haply *there* uprears
That shadowing Pine its old romantic limbs,
   Which latest shall detain the enamour'd sight
Seen from below, when eve the valley dims,
   Tinged yellow with the rich departing light;     35
   And haply, bason'd in some unsunn'd cleft,
A beauteous spring, the rock's collected tears,
Sleeps shelter'd there, scarce wrinkled by the gale!
   Together thus, the world's vain turmoil left,
Stretch'd on the crag, and shadow'd by the pine,    40
   And bending o'er the clear delicious fount,
Ah! dearest youth! it were a lot divine

To cheat our noons in moralizing mood,
While west-winds fann'd our temples toil-bedew'd:
   Then downwards slope, oft pausing, from the mount,    45
To some lone mansion, in some woody dale,
Where smiling with blue eye, Domestic Bliss
Gives *this* the Husband's, *that* the Brother's kiss!


   Thus rudely vers'd in allegoric lore,
The Hill of Knowledge I essayed to trace;    50
That verdurous hill with many a resting-place,
And many a stream, whose warbling waters pour
   To glad, and fertilize the subject plains;
That hill with secret springs, and nooks untrod,
And many a fancy-blest and holy sod    55
   Where Inspiration, his diviner strains
Low-murmuring, lay; and starting from the rock's
Stiff evergreens, (whose spreading foliage mocks
Want's barren soil, and the bleak frosts of age,
And Bigotry's mad fire-invoking rage!)    60
O meek retiring spirit! we will climb,
Cheering and cheered, this lovely hill sublime;
   And from the stirring world up-lifted high
(Whose noises, faintly wafted on the wind,
To quiet musings shall attune the mind,    65
   And oft the melancholy *theme* supply),
   There, while the prospect through the gazing eye
   Pours all its healthful greenness on the soul,
We'll smile at wealth, and learn to smile at fame,
Our hopes, our knowledge, and our joys the same,    70
   As neighbouring fountains image each the whole:
Then when the mind hath drunk its fill of truth
   We'll discipline the heart to pure delight,
Rekindling sober joy's domestic flame.
They whom I love shall love thee, honour'd youth!    75
   Now may Heaven realize this vision bright!

[1796]

## Addressed to a Young Man of Fortune

### [Charles Lloyd]

#### WHO ABANDONED HIMSELF TO AN INDOLENT AND CAUSELESS MELANCHOLY

Hence that fantastic wantonness of woe,
  O Youth to partial Fortune vainly dear!
To plunder'd Want's half-shelter'd hovel go,
  Go, and some hunger-bitten infant hear
  Moan haply in a dying mother's ear:          5
Or when the cold and dismal fog-damps brood
O'er the rank church-yard with sear elm-leaves strew'd,
Pace round some widow's grave, whose dearer part
  Was slaughter'd, where o'er his uncoffin'd limbs
The flocking flesh-birds scream'd! Then, while thy heart    10
  Groans, and thine eye a fiercer sorrow dims,
Know (and the truth shall kindle thy young mind)
What Nature makes thee mourn, she bids thee heal!
  O abject! if, to sickly dreams resign'd,
All effortless thou leave Life's common-weal        15
  A prey to Tyrants, Murderers of Mankind.
[1796]

## The Destiny of Nations

### A VISION

Auspicious Reverence! Hush all meaner song,
Ere we the deep preluding strain have poured
To the Great Father, only Rightful King,
Eternal Father! King Omnipotent!
To the Will Absolute, the One, the Good!        5
The I AM, the Word, the Life, the Living God!

  Such symphony requires best instrument.
Seize, then, my soul! from Freedom's trophied dome

The Harp which hangeth high between the Shields
Of Brutus and Leonidas! With that                                    10
Strong music, that soliciting spell, force back
Man's free and stirring spirit that lies entranced.

    For what is Freedom, but the unfettered use
Of all the powers which God for use had given?
But chiefly this, him First, him Last to view                        15
Through meaner powers and secondary things
Effulgent, as through clouds that veil his blaze.
For all that meets the bodily sense I deem
Symbolical, one almighty alphabet
For infant minds; and we in this low world                           20
Placed with our backs to bright Reality,
That we may learn with young unwounded ken
The substance from its shadow. Infinite Love,
Whose latence is the plenitude of All,
Thou with retracted beams, and self-eclipse                          25
Veiling, revealest thine eternal Sun.

    But some there are who deem themselves most free
When they within this gross and visible sphere
Chain down the wingéd thought, scoffing ascent,
Proud in their meanness: and themselves they cheat                   30
With noisy emptiness of learnéd phrase,
Their subtle fluids, impacts, essences,
Self-working tools, uncaused effects, and all
Those blind Omniscients, those Almighty Slaves,
Untenanting creation of its God.                                     35

    But Properties are God: the naked mass
(If mass there be, fantastic guess or ghost)
Acts only by its inactivity.
Here we pause humbly. Others boldlier think
That as one body seems the aggregate                                 40
Of atoms numberless, each organized;
So by a strange and dim similitude
Infinite myriads of self-conscious minds
Are one all-conscious Spirit, which informs
With absolute ubiquity of thought                                    45
(His one eternal self-affirming act!)

All his involvéd Monads, that yet seem
With various province and apt agency
Each to pursue its own self-centering end.
Some nurse the infant diamond in the mine;                    50
Some roll the genial juices through the oak;
Some drive the mutinous clouds to clash in air,
And rushing on the storm with whirlwind speed,
Yoke the red lightnings to their volleying car.
Thus these pursue their never-varying course,                    55
No eddy in their stream. Others, more wild,
With complex interests weaving human fates,
Duteous or proud, alike obedient all,
Evolve the process of eternal good.

   And what if some rebellious, o'er dark realms                    60
Arrogate power? yet these train up to God,
And on the rude eye, unconfirmed for day,
Flash meteor-lights better than total gloom.
As ere from Lieule-Oaive's vapoury head
The Laplander beholds the far-off Sun                    65
Dart his slant beam on unobeying snows,
While yet the stern and solitary Night
Brooks no alternate sway, the Boreal Morn
With mimic lustre substitutes its gleam,
Guiding his course or by Niemi lake                    70
Or Balda Zhiok,[1] or the mossy stone
Of Solfar-kapper,[2] while the snowy blast
Drifts arrowy by, or eddies round his sledge,
Making the poor babe at its mother's back[3]

[1]Balda-Zhiok, i.e. mons altitudinis, the highest mountain in Lapland. [S.T.C.]

[2]Solfar-kapper: capitium Solfar, hic locus omnium, quotquot veterum Lapponum super-
stitio sacrificiisque religiosoque cultui dedicavit, celebratissimus erat, in parte sinus australis
situs, semimilliaris spatio a mari distans. Ipse locus, quem curiositatis gratia aliquando me
invisisse memini, duabus praealtis lapidibus, sibi invicem oppositis, quorum alter musco
circumdatus erat, constabat. ['Cape Solfar, this place was the most frequented of all that
superstition dedicated to the Lapps' sacrifices and religious worship, situated on the southern
side of the bay, about half a mile from the sea. The place itself, which I remember I once visited
out of curiosity, consisted of two very high stones, facing each other, one of them covered with
moss.'] – LEEMIUS, De Lapponibus. [S.T.C.]

[3]The Lapland women carry their infants at their backs in a piece of excavated wood which
serve them for a cradle: opposite to the infant's mouth there is a hole for it to breathe through.

Mirandum prorsus est et vix credibile nisi cui vidisse contigit. Lappones hyeme iter facientes
per vastos montes, perque horrida et invia tesqua, eo praesertim tempore quo omnia perpetuis
nivibus obtecta sunt et nives ventis agitantur et in gyros aguntur, viam ad destinata loca

Scream in its scanty cradle: he the while                           75
Wins gentle solace as with upward eye
He marks the streamy banners of the North,
Thinking himself those happy spirits shall join
Who there in floating robes of rosy light
Dance sportively. For Fancy is the power                            80
That first unsensualizes the dark mind,
Giving it new delights; and bids it swell
With wild activity; and peopling air,
By obscure fears of Beings invisible,
Emancipates it from the grosser thrall                              85
Of the present impulse, teaching Self-control,
Till Superstition with unconscious hand
Seat Reason on her throne. Wherefore not vain,
Nor yet without permitted power impressed,
I deem those legends terrible, with which                           90
The polar ancient thrills his uncouth throng:
Whether of pitying Spirits that make their moan
O'er slaughter'd infants, or that Giant Bird
Vuokho, of whose rushing wings the noise
Is Tempest, when the unutterable Shape                              95
Speeds from the mother of Death, and utters once[1]
That shriek, which never murderer heard, and lived.

    Or if the Greenland Wizard in strange trance
Pierces the untravelled realms of Ocean's bed
Over the abysm, even to that uttermost cave                         100
By mis-shaped prodigies beleaguered, such
As Earth ne'er bred, nor Air, nor the upper Sea:
Where dwells the Fury Form, whose unheard name
With eager eye, pale cheek, suspended breath,

---

absque errore invenire posse, lactantem autem infantem, si quem habeat, ipsa mater in dorso
baiulat, in excavato ligno (Gieed'k ipsi vocant) quod pro cunis utuntur, in hoc infans pannis et
pellibus convolutus colligatus iacet. ['It is very remarkable and hardly credible unless one has
seen it. When the Lapps journey in winter through rough and pathless wastes, even at the time
when everything is covered by perpetual snows, and the snow is stirred up by the winds and
driven around in circles, they are able to find their way, unerringly, to their destinations, and
the mother of any breast-fed infant carries it on her back, in a hollowed-out log which they call
Gieed'k and use instead of a cradle; in this the infant lies bound in cloths and furs.'] –
LEEMIUS, De Lapponibus. [S.T.C.]
    [1] Jaibme Aibno. [S.T.C.]

And lips half-opening with the dread of sound,                    105
Unsleeping Silence guards, worn out with fear
Lest haply 'scaping on some treacherous blast
The fateful word let slip the Elements
And frenzy Nature. Yet the wizard her,
Arm'd with Torngarsuck's power, the Spirit of Good,[1]    110
Forces to unchain the foodful progeny
Of the Ocean stream; — thence thro' the realm of Souls,
Where live the Innocent, as far from cares
As from the storms and overwhelming waves
That tumble on the surface of the Deep,                          115
Returns with far-heard pant, hotly pursued
By the fierce Warders of the Sea, once more,
Ere by the frost foreclosed, to repossess
His fleshly mansion, that had staid the while
In the dark tent within a cow'ring group                        120
Untenanted. — Wild phantasies! yet wise,
On the victorious goodness of high God
Teaching reliance, and medicinal hope,
Till from Bethabra northward, heavenly Truth
With gradual steps, winning her difficult way,                  125
Transfer their rude Faith perfected and pure.


If there be Beings of higher class than Man,
I deem no nobler province they possess,
Than by disposal of apt circumstance
To rear up kingdoms: and the deeds they prompt,                 130
Distinguishing from mortal agency,
They choose their human ministers from such states
As still the Epic song half fears to name,
Repelled from all the minstrelsies that strike
The palace-roof and soothe the monarch's pride.                 135


    And such, perhaps, the Spirit, who (if words
Witnessed by answering deeds may claim our faith)

[1] They call the Good Spirit, Torngarsuck. The other great but malignant spirit is a nameless female; she dwells under the sea in a great house where she can detain in captivity all the animals of the ocean by her magic power. When a dearth befalls the Greenlanders, an Angekok or magician must undertake a journey thither: he passes through the kingdom of souls, over an horrible abyss into the Palace of this phantom, and by his enchantments causes the captive creatures to ascend directly to the surface of the ocean. — See CRANTZ, *History of Greenland*, vol. 1, p. 206. [S.T.C.]

Held commune with that warrior-maid of France
Who scourged the Invader. From her infant days,
With Wisdom, mother of retired thoughts,                    140
Her soul had dwelt; and she was quick to mark
The good and evil thing, in human lore
Undisciplined. For lowly was her birth,
And Heaven had doomed her early years to toil
That pure from Tyranny's least deed, herself               145
Unfeared by Fellow-natures, she might wait
On the poor labouring man with kindly looks,
And minister refreshment to the tired
Way-wanderer, when along the rough-hewn bench
The sweltry man had stretched him, and aloft               150
Vacantly watched the rudely-pictured board
Which on the Mulberry-bough with welcome creak
Swung to the pleasant breeze. Here, too, the Maid
Learnt more than Schools could teach: Man's shifting mind,
His vices and his sorrows! And full oft                    155
At tales of cruel wrong and strange distress
Had wept and shivered. To the tottering Eld
Still as a daughter would she run: she placed
His cold limbs at the sunny door, and loved
To hear him story, in his garrulous sort,                  160
Of his eventful years, all come and gone.

    So twenty seasons past. The Virgin's form,
Active and tall, nor Sloth nor Luxury
Had shrunk or paled. Her front sublime and broad,
Her flexile eye-brows wildly haired and low,              165
And her full eye, now bright, now unillumed,
Spake more than Woman's thought; and all her face
Was moulded to such features as declared
That Pity there had oft and strongly worked,
And sometimes Indignation. Bold her mien,                 170
And like an haughty huntress of the woods
She moved: yet sure she was a gentle maid!
And in each motion her most innocent soul
Beamed forth so brightly, that who saw would say
Guilt was a thing impossible in her!                      175
Nor idly would have said – for she had lived

In this bad World, as in a place of Tombs,
And touched not the pollutions of the Dead.

'Twas the cold season when the Rustic's eye
From the drear desolate whiteness of his fields          180
Rolls for relief to watch the skiey tints
And clouds slow-varying their huge imagery;
When now, as she was wont, the healthful Maid
Had left her pallet ere one beam of day
Slanted the fog-smoke. She went forth alone          185
Urged by the indwelling angel-guide, that oft,
With dim inexplicable sympathies
Disquieting the heart, shapes out Man's course
To the predoomed adventure. Now the ascent
She climbs of that steep upland, on whose top          190
The Pilgrim-man, who long since eve had watched
The alien shine of unconcerning stars,
Shouts to himself, there first the Abbey-lights
Seen in Neufchâtel's vale; now slopes adown
The winding sheep-track vale-ward: when, behold          195
In the first entrance of the level road
An unattended team! The foremost horse
Lay with stretched limbs; the others, yet alive
But stiff and cold, stood motionless, their manes
Hoar with the frozen night-dews. Dismally          200
The dark-red dawn now glimmered; but its gleams
Disclosed no face of man. The maiden paused,
Then hailed who might be near. No voice replied.
From the thwart wain at length there reached her ear
A sound so feeble that it almost seemed          205
Distant: and feebly, with slow effort pushed,
A miserable man crept forth: his limbs
The silent frost had eat, scathing like fire.
Faint on the shafts he rested. She, meantime,
Saw crowded close beneath the coverture          210
A mother and her children – lifeless all,
Yet lovely! not a lineament was marred –
Death had put on so slumber-like a form!
It was a piteous sight; and one, a babe,
The crisp milk frozen on its innocent lips,          215
Lay on the woman's arm, its little hand
Stretched on her bosom.

                          Mutely questioning,
The Maid gazed wildly at the living wretch.
He, his head feebly turning, on the group
Looked with a vacant stare, and his eye spoke          220
The drowsy calm that steals on worn-out anguish.
She shuddered; but, each vainer pang subdued,
Quick disentangling from the foremost horse
The rustic bands, with difficulty and toil
The stiff cramped team forced homeward. There arrived,   225
Anxiously tends him she with healing herbs,
And weeps and prays – but the numb power of Death
Spreads o'er his limbs; and ere the noon-tide hour,
The hovering spirits of his Wife and Babes
Hail him immortal! Yet amid his pangs,                 230
With interruptions long from ghastly throes,
His voice had faltered out this simple tale.

   The Village, where he dwelt an husbandman,
By sudden inroad had been seized and fired
Late on the yester-evening. With his wife              235
And little ones he hurried his escape.
They saw the neighbouring hamlets flame, they heard
Uproar and shrieks! and terror-struck drove on
Through unfrequented roads, a weary way!
But saw nor house nor cottage. All had quenched        240
Their evening hearth-fire: for the alarm had spread.
The air clipt keen, the night was fanged with frost,
And they provisionless! The weeping wife
Ill hushed her children's moans; and still they moaned,
Till Fright and Cold and Hunger drank their life.      245
They closed their eyes in sleep, nor knew 'twas Death.
He only, lashing his o'er-wearied team,
Gained a sad respite, till beside the base
Of the high hill his foremost horse dropped dead.
Then hopeless, strengthless, sick for lack of food,    250
He crept beneath the coverture, entranced,
Till wakened by the maiden. – Such his tale.

   Ah! suffering to the height of what was suffered
Stung with too keen a sympathy, the Maid
Brooded with moving lips, mute, startful, dark!        255

And now her flushed tumultous features shot
Such strange vivacity, as fires the eye
Of Misery fancy-crazed! and now once more
Naked, and void, and fixed, and all within
The unquiet silence of confused thought                    260
And shapeless feelings. For a mighty hand
Was strong upon her, till in the heat of soul
To the high hill-top tracing back her steps,
Aside the beacon, up whose smouldered stones
The tender ivy-trails crept thinly, there,                 265
Unconscious of the driving element,
Yea, swallowed up in the ominous dream, she sate
Ghastly as broad-eyed Slumber! a dim anguish
Breathed from her look! and still with pant and sob,
Inly she toiled to flee, and still subdued,               270
Felt an inevitable Presence near.

Thus as she toiled in troublous ecstasy,
A horror of great darkness wrapt her round,
And a voice uttered forth unearthly tones,
Calming her soul, – 'O Thou of the Most High              275
Chosen, whom all the perfected in Heaven
Behold expectant —— '

[The following fragments were intended to form part of the
poem when finished.]

                    'Maid beloved of Heaven!
(To her the tutelary Power exclaimed)
Of Chaos the adventurous progeny                           280
Thou seest; foul missionaries of foul sire,
Fierce to regain the losses of that hour
When Love rose glittering, and his gorgeous wings
Over the abyss fluttered with such glad noise,
As what time after long and pestful calms,                285
With slimy shapes and miscreated life
Poisoning the vast Pacific, the fresh breeze
Wakens the merchant-sail uprising. Night
An heavy unimaginable moan
Sent forth, when she the Protoplast beheld                290
Stand beauteous on Confusion's charméd wave.

Moaning she fled, and entered the Profound
That leads with downward windings to the Cave
Of Darkness palpable, Desert of Death
Sunk deep beneath Gehenna's massy roots.                         295
There many a dateless age the Beldame lurked
And trembled; till engendered by fierce Hate,
Fierce Hate and gloomy Hope, a Dream arose,
Shaped like a black cloud marked with streaks of fire.
It roused the Hell-Hag: she the dew-damp wiped            300
From off her brow, and through the uncouth maze
Retraced her steps; but ere she reached the mouth
Of that drear labyrinth, shuddering she paused,
Nor dared re-enter the diminished Gulph.
As through the dark vaults of some mouldered Tower         305
(Which, fearful to approach, the evening hind
Circles at distance in his homeward way)
The winds breathe hollow, deemed the plaining groan
Of prisoned spirits: with such fearful voice
Night murmured, and the sound through Chaos went.       310
Leaped at her call her hideous-fronted brood!
A dark behest they heard, and rushed on earth;
Since that sad hour, in Camps and Courts adored,
Rebels from God, and Tyrants o'er Mankind!'

———————————

From his obscure haunt                              315
Shrieked Fear, of Cruelty the ghastly Dam,
Feverous yet freezing, eager-paced yet slow,
As she that creeps from forth her swampy reeds,
Ague, the biform Hag! when early Spring
Beams on the marsh-bred vapours.                        320

———————————

'Even so (the exulting Maiden said)
The sainted Heralds of Good Tidings fell,
And thus they witnessed God! But now the clouds
Treading, and storms beneath their feet, they soar
Higher, and higher soar, and soaring sing              325
Loud songs of triumph! O ye Spirits of God,
Hover around my mortal agonies!'

She spake, and instantly faint melody
Melts on her ear, soothing and sad, and slow,
Such measures, as at calmest midnight heard          330
By agéd Hermit in his holy dream,
Foretell and solace death; and now they rise
Louder, as when with harp and mingled voice
The white-robed multitude[1] of slaughtered saints
At Heaven's wide-open'd portals gratulant            335
Receive some martyred patriot. The harmony
Entranced the Maid, till each suspended sense
Brief slumber seized, and confused ecstasy.

    At length awakening slow, she gazed around:
And through a mist, the relict of that trance        340
Still thinning as she gazed, an Isle appeared,
Its high, o'er-hanging, white, broad-breasted cliffs,
Glassed on the subject ocean. A vast plain
Stretched opposite, where ever and anon
The ploughman following sad his meagre team          345
Turned up fresh sculls unstartled, and the bones
Of fierce hate-breathing combatants, who there
All mingled lay beneath the common earth,
Death's gloomy reconcilement! O'er the fields
Stept a fair Form, repairing all she might,          350
Her temples olive-wreathed; and where she trod,
Fresh flowerets rose, and many a foodful herb.
But wan her cheek, her footsteps insecure,
And anxious pleasure beamed in her faint eye,
As she had newly left a couch of pain,               355
Pale Convalescent! (Yet some time to rule
With power exclusive o'er the willing world,
That blessed prophetic mandate then fulfilled –
Peace be on Earth!) An happy while, but brief,
She seemed to wander with assiduous feet,            360
And healed the recent harm of chill and blight,
And nursed each plant that fair and virtuous grew.

---

[1]Rev. vi. 9, 11. – And when he had opened the fifth seal, I saw under the altar the souls of them that were slain for the word of God and for the testimony which they held. And white robes were given unto every one of them; and it was said unto them, that they should rest yet for a little season, until their fellow-servants also and their brethren, that should be killed as they were, should be fulfilled. [S.T.C.]

But soon a deep precursive sound moaned hollow:
Black rose the clouds, and now, (as in a dream)
Their reddening shapes, transformed to Warrior-hosts,        365
Coursed o'er the sky, and battled in mid-air.
Nor did not the large blood-drops fall from Heaven
Portentous! while aloft were seen to float,
Like hideous features looming on the mist,
Wan stains of ominous light! Resigned, yet sad,        370
The fair Form bowed her olive-crownéd brow,
Then o'er the plain with oft-reverted eye
Fled till a place of Tombs she reached, and there
Within a ruined Sepulchre obscure
Found hiding-place.

           The delegated Maid        375
Gazed through her tears, then in sad tones exclaimed; —
'Thou mild-eyed Form! wherefore, ah! wherefore fled?
The Power of Justice, like a name all light,
Shone from thy brow; but all they, who unblamed
Dwelt in thy dwellings, call thee Happiness.        380
Ah! why, uninjured and unprofited,
Should multitudes against their brethren rush?
Why sow they guilt, still reaping misery?
Lenient of care, thy songs, O Peace! are sweet,
As after showers the perfumed gale of eve,        385
That flings the cool drops on a feverous cheek;
And gay thy grassy altar piled with fruits.
But boasts the shrine of Dæmon War one charm,
Save that with many an orgie strange and foul,
Dancing around with interwoven arms,        390
The Maniac Suicide and Giant Murder
Exult in their fierce union! I am sad,
And know not why the simple peasants crowd
Beneath the Chieftains' standard!' Thus the Maid.

  To her the tutelary Spirit said:        395
'When Luxury and Lust's exhausted stores
No more can rouse the appetites of kings;
When the low flattery of their reptile lords
Falls flat and heavy on the accustomed ear;
When eunuchs sing, and fools buffoonery make,        400

And dancers writhe their harlot-limbs in vain;
Then War and all its dread vicissitudes
Pleasingly agitate their stagnant hearts;
Its hopes, its fears, its victories, its defeats,
Insipid Royalty's keen condiment!                              405
*Therefore* uninjured and unprofited
(Victims at once and executioners),
The congregated Husbandmen lay waste
The vineyard and the harvest. As along
The Bothnic coast, or southward of the Line,                   410
Though hushed the winds and cloudless the high noon,
Yet if Leviathan, weary of ease,
In sports unwieldy toss his island-bulk,
Ocean behind him billows, and before
A storm of waves breaks foamy on the strand.                   415
And hence, for times and seasons bloody and dark,
Short Peace shall skin the wounds of causeless War,
And War, his strainéd sinews knit anew,
Still violate the unfinished works of Peace.
But yonder look! for more demands thy view!'                   420
He said: and straightway from the opposite Isle
A vapour sailed, as when a cloud, exhaled
From Egypt's fields that steam hot pestilence,
Travels the sky for many a trackless league,
Till o'er some death-doomed land, distant in vain,             425
It broods incumbent. Forthwith from the plain,
Facing the Isle, a brighter cloud arose,
And steered its course which way the vapour went.

    The Maiden paused, musing what this might mean.
But long time passed not, ere that brighter cloud              430
Returned more bright; along the plain it swept;
And soon from forth its bursting sides emerged
A dazzling form, broad-bosomed, bold of eye,
And wild her hair, save where with laurels bound.
Not more majestic stood the healing God,[1]                    435
When from his bow the arrow sped that slew
Huge Python. Shriek'd Ambition's giant throng,
And with them hissed the locust-fiends that crawled

[1] The Apollo Belvedere.

And glittered in Corruption's slimy track.

Great was their wrath, for short they knew their reign;        440
And such commotion made they, and uproar,
As when the mad Tornado bellows through
The guilty islands of the western main,
What time departing from their native shores,[1]
Eboe, or Koromantyn's plain of palms,        445
The infuriate spirits of the murdered make
Fierce merriment, and vengeance ask of Heaven.
Warmed with new influence, the unwholesome plain
Sent up its foulest fogs to meet the morn:
The Sun that rose on Freedom, rose in Blood!        450

'Maiden beloved, and Delegate of Heaven!
(To her the tutelary Spirit said)
Soon shall the Morning struggle into Day,
The stormy Morning into cloudless Noon.
Much hast thou seen, nor all canst understand—        455
But this be thy best omen – Save thy Country!'

[1]The Slaves in the West-India Islands consider Death as a passport to their native country.
The Sentiment is thus expressed in the Introduction to a Greek Prize Ode on the Slave-Trade,
of which the Ideas are better than the Language or Metre, in which they are conveyed:

> Ὦ σκότου πύλας, θάνατε, προλείπων
> Ἐς γένος σπεύδοις ὑποζευχθὲν Ἄτᾳ*·
> Οὐ ξενισθήσῃ γενύων σπαραγμοῖς
>           Οὐδ᾽ ὀλολυγμῷ,
> Ἀλλὰ καὶ κύκλοισι χοροιτύποισι
> Κἀσμάτων χαρᾷ· φοβερὸς μὲν ἐσσί,
> Ἀλλ᾽ ὅμως Ἐλευθερίᾳ συνοικεῖς,
>           Στυγνὲ Τύραννε!
> Δασκίοις ἐπὶ πτερύγεσσι σῇοι
> Ἆ! Θαλάσσιον καθορῶντες οἶδμα
> Αἰθεροπλάγκτοις ὑπὸ πόσσ᾽ ἀνεῖσι
>           Πατρίδ᾽ ἐπ᾽ αἶαν,
> Ἔνθα μὰν Ἐρασταὶ Ἐρωμένῃσιν
> Ἀμφὶ πηγῆσιν κιτρίνων ὑπ᾽ ἀλσῶν,
> Ὅσσ᾽ ὑπὸ Βροτοῖς ἔπαθον Βροτοί, τὰ
>           Δεινὰ λέγοντι.

*ο before ζ ought to have been made long; ὁοῖς ὑπὸζ is an Amphimacer not (as the metre here
requires) a Dactyl. [S.T.C.]

### LITERAL TRANSLATION

Leaving the gates of Darkness, O Death! hasten thou to a Race yoked to Misery! Thou wilt not
be received with lacerations of Cheeks, nor with funereal ululation, but with circling Dances
and the joy of Songs. Thou art terrible indeed, yet thou dwellest with LIBERTY, stern GENIUS!
Borne on thy dark pinions over the swelling of Ocean they return to their native country. There
by the side of fountains beneath Citron groves, the Lovers tell to their Beloved, what horrors,
being Men, they had endured from Men. [S.T.C.]

Thus saying, from the answering Maid he passed,
And with him disappeared the heavenly Vision.

   'Glory to Thee, Father of Earth and Heaven!
All-conscious Presence of the Universe!                    460
Nature's vast ever-acting Energy!
In will, in deed, Impulse of All to All!
Whether thy Love with unrefracted ray
Beam on the Prophet's purgéd eye, or if
Diseasing realms the Enthusiast, wild of thought,          465
Scatter new frenzies on the infected throng,
Thou both inspiring and predooming both,
Fit instruments and best, of perfect end:
Glory to Thee, Father of Earth and Heaven!'

---

           And first a landscape rose      470
More wild and waste and desolate than where
The white bear, drifting on a field of ice,
Howls to her sundered cubs with piteous rage
And savage agony.
[1796–7. Revised 1816–34]

## *Sonnet*

### TO THE RIVER OTTER

Dear native Brook! wild Streamlet of the West!
  How many various-fated years have past,
   What happy and what mournful hours, since last
I skimm'd the smooth thin stone along thy breast,
Numbering its light leaps! yet so deep imprest                5
Sink the sweet scenes of childhood, that mine eyes
  I never shut amid the sunny ray,
But straight with all their tints thy waters rise,
  Thy crossing plank, thy marge with willows grey,
And bedded sand that vein'd with various dyes                10
Gleam'd through thy bright transparence! On my way,
  Visions of Childhood! oft have ye beguil'd
Lone manhood's cares, yet waking fondest sighs:
  Ah! that once more I were a careless Child!
[?1793–?1796]

## *Ode on the Departing Year*[1]

Ἰού, ἰού, ὢ ὢ κακά.
Ὑπ᾽ αὖ με δεινὸς ὀρθομαντείας πόνος
Στροβεῖ, ταράσσων φροιμίοις δυσφροιμίοις.

. . . . .

Τὸ μέλλον ἥξει. Καὶ σύ μ᾽ ἐν τάχει παρὼν
Ἄγαν ἀληθόμαντιν οἰκτείρας ἐρεῖς.
ÆSCHY. AGAMEM. 1225.[2]

### ARGUMENT

The Ode commences with an address to the Divine Providence that regulates into one vast harmony all the events of time, however calamitous some of them may appear to mortals. The second Strophe calls on men to suspend their private joys and sorrows, and devote them for a while to the cause of human nature in general. The first Epode speaks of the Empress of Russia, who died of an apoplexy on the 17th of November 1796; having just concluded a subsidary treaty with the Kings combined against France. The first and second Antistrophe describe the Image of the Departing Year, etc., as in a vision. The second Epode prophesies, in anguish of spirit, the downfall of this country.

I

Spirit who sweepest the wild Harp of Time!
  It is most hard, with an untroubled ear
  Thy dark inwoven harmonies to hear!
Yet, mine eye fix'd on Heaven's unchanging clime,
Long had I listen'd, free from mortal fear,
  With inward stillness, and a bowéd mind;          5
  When lo! its folds far waving on the wind,
I saw the train of the Departing Year!

---

[1] This Ode was written on the 24th, 25th and ⟶ days of December, 1796; and published separately on the last day of the year. [S.T.C.]

[2] "Ha, ha! Oh, oh, the agony. Once more the dreadful throes of true prophecy whirl and distract me with their boding onset . . . Soon thou, present here thyself, shalt [of thy pity] pronounce me all too true a prophet.'

Starting from my silent sadness
   Then with no unholy madness,                                    10
Ere yet the enter'd cloud foreclos'd my sight,
I rais'd the impetuous song, and solemniz'd his flight.


II

   Hither, from the recent tomb,
   From the prison's direr gloom,
   From Distemper's midnight anguish;                                15
And thence, where Poverty doth waste and languish;
   Or where, his two bright torches blending,
     Love illumines Manhood's maze;
   Or where o'er cradled infants bending,
     Hope has fix'd her wishful gaze;                            20
    Hither, in perplexéd dance,
  Ye Woes! ye young-eyed Joys! advance!
  By Time's wild harp, and by the hand
    Whose indefatigable sweep
    Raises its fateful strings from sleep,                        25
I bid you haste, a mix'd tumultuous band!
    From every private bower,
     And each domestic hearth,
    Haste for one solemn hour;
   And with a loud and yet a louder voice,                        30
O'er Nature struggling in portentous birth,
    Weep and rejoice!
Still echoes the dread Name that o'er the earth[1]
Let slip the storm, and woke the brood of Hell:
   And now advance in saintly Jubilee                             35
Justice and Truth! They too have heard thy spell,
  They too obey thy name, divinest Liberty!


III

   I mark'd Ambition in his war-array!
    I heard the mailéd Monarch's troublous cry —
  'Ah! wherefore does the Northern Conqueress stay!               40

---

[1] The Name of Liberty, which at the commencement of the French Revolution was both the occasion and the pretext of unnumbered crimes and horrors. [S.T.C., 1803]

Groans not her chariot on its onward way?'
      Fly, mailéd Monarch, fly!
      Stunn'd by Death's twice mortal mace,
      No more on Murder's lurid face
The insatiate Hag shall gloat with drunken eye!                45
      Manes of the unnumber'd slain!
      Ye that gasp'd on Warsaw's plain!
      Ye that erst at Ismail's tower,
When human ruin choked the streams,
      Fell in Conquest's glutted hour,                          50
Mid women's shrieks and infants' screams!
      Spirits of the uncoffin'd slain,
            Sudden blasts of triumph swelling,
      Oft, at night, in misty train,
            Rush around her narrow dwelling!                     55
The exterminating Fiend is fled —
(Foul her life, and dark her doom)
Mighty armies of the dead
      Dance, like death-fires, round her tomb!
Then with prophetic song relate,                                60
Each some Tyrant-Murderer's fate!


                            IV

Departing Year! 'twas on no earthly shore
      My soul beheld thy Vision! Where alone,
      Voiceless and stern, before the cloudy throne,
Aye Memory sits: thy robe inscrib'd with gore,                  65
With many an unimaginable groan
      Thou storied'st thy sad hours! Silence ensued,
      Deep silence o'er the ethereal multitude,
Whose locks with wreaths, whose wreaths with glories shone.
      Then, his eye wild ardours glancing,                      70
      From the choiréd gods advancing,
The Spirit of the Earth made reverence meet,
And stood up, beautiful, before the cloudy seat.


                            V

      Throughout the blissful throng,
      Hush'd were harp and song:                                75
Till wheeling round the throne the Lampads seven,

(The mystic Words of Heaven)
   Permissive signal make:
The fervent Spirit bow'd, then spread his wings and spake!
    'Thou in stormy blackness throning                    80
    Love and uncreated Light,
  By the Earth's unsolaced groaning,
    Seize thy terrors, Arm of might!
  By Peace with proffer'd insult scared,
    Masked Hate and envying Scorn!                    85
    By years of Havoc yet unborn!
And Hunger's bosom to the frost-winds bared!
    But chief by Afric's wrongs,
      Strange, horrible, and foul!
    By what deep guilt belongs                    90
To the deaf Synod, "Full of gifts and lies!"
By Wealth's insensate laugh! by Torture's howl!
      Avenger, rise!
   For ever shall the thankless Island scowl,
  Her quiver full, and with unbroken bow?                    95
Speak! from thy storm-black Heaven O speak aloud!
     And on the darkling foe
Open thine eye of fire from some uncertain cloud!
  O dart the flash! O rise and deal the blow!
The Past to thee, to thee the Future cries!                    100
  Hark! how wide Nature joins her groans below!
   Rise, God of Nature! rise.'


## VI

The voice had ceas'd, the Vision fled;
Yet still I gasp'd and reel'd with dread.
And ever, when the dream of night                    105
Renews the phantom to my sight,
Cold sweat-drops gather on my limbs;
  My ears throb hot; my eye-balls start;
My brain with horrid tumult swims;
  Wild is the tempest of my heart;                    110
And my thick and struggling breath
Imitates the toil of death!
No stranger agony confounds
  The Soldier on the war-field spread,

When all foredone with toil and wounds,       115
  Death-like he dozes among heaps of dead!
(The strife is o'er, the day-light fled,
  And the night-wind clamours hoarse!
See! the starting wretch's head
  Lies pillow'd on a brother's corse!)       120

### VII

Not yet enslaved, not wholly vile,
O Albion! O my mother Isle!
Thy valleys, fair as Eden's bowers,
Glitter green with sunny showers;
Thy grassy uplands' gentle swells       125
  Echo to the bleat of flocks;
(Those grassy hills, those glittering dells
  Proudly ramparted with rocks)
And Ocean mid his uproar wild
Speaks safety to his Island-child!       130
  Hence for many a fearless age
  Has social Quiet lov'd thy shore;
Nor ever proud Invader's rage
Or sack'd thy towers, or stain'd thy fields with gore.

### VIII

Abandon'd of Heaven! mad Avarice thy guide,       135
At cowardly distance, yet kindling with pride –
Mid thy herds and thy corn-fields secure thou hast stood,
And join'd the wild yelling of Famine and Blood!
The nations curse thee! They with eager wondering
  Shall hear Destruction, like a vulture, scream!       140
  Strange-eyed Destruction! who with many a dream
Of central fires through nether seas up-thundering
  Soothes her fierce solitude; yet as she lies
By livid fount, or red volcanic stream,
  If ever to her lidless dragon-eyes,       145
  O Albion! thy predestin'd ruins rise,
The fiend-hag on her perilous couch doth leap,
Muttering distemper'd triumph in her charmèd sleep.

### IX

Away, my soul, away!
In vain, in vain the Birds of warning sing –          150
And hark! I hear the famish'd brood of prey
Flap their lank pennons on the groaning wind!
Away, my soul, away!
I unpartaking of the evil thing,
With daily prayer and daily toil          155
Soliciting for food my scanty soil,
Have wail'd my country with a loud Lament.
Now I recentre my immortal mind
In the deep Sabbath of meek self-content;
Cleans'd from the vaporous passions that bedim          160
God's Image, sister of the Seraphim.
[1796]

## The Raven

#### A CHRISTMAS TALE, TOLD BY A SCHOOL-BOY TO HIS LITTLE BROTHERS AND SISTERS

Underneath an old oak tree
There was of swine a huge company,
That grunted as they crunched the mast:
For that was ripe, and fell full fast.
Then they trotted away, for the wind grew high:          5
One acorn they left, and no more might you spy.
Next came a Raven, that liked not such folly:
He belonged, they did say, to the witch Melancholy!
Blacker was he than blackest jet,
Flew low in the rain, and his feathers not wet.          10
He picked up the acorn and buried it straight
By the side of a river both deep and great.
Where then did the Raven go?
He went high and low,
Over hill, over dale, did the black Raven go.          15
Many Autumns, many Springs
Travelled[1] he with wandering wings:

[1]Seventeen or eighteen years ago an artist of some celebrity was so pleased with this doggerel that he amused himself with the thought of making a Child's Picture Book of it; but he could not hit on a picture for these four lines. I suggested a *Round-about* with four seats, and the four seasons, as Children, with Time for the shew-man. [S.T.C., 1817]

Many Summers, many Winters —
I can't tell half his adventures.
At length he came back, and with him a She,     20
And the acorn was grown to a tall oak tree.
They built them a nest in the topmost bough,
And young ones they had, and were happy enow.
But soon came a Woodman in leathern guise,
His brow, like a pent-house, hung over his eyes.     25
He'd an axe in his hand, not a word he spoke,
But with many a hem! and a sturdy stroke,
At length he brought down the poor Raven's own oak.
His young ones were killed; for they could not depart,
And their mother did die of a broken heart.     30

The boughs from the trunk the Woodman did sever;
And they floated it down on the course of the river.
They sawed it in planks, and its bark they did strip,
And with this tree and others they made a good ship.
The ship, it was launched; but in sight of the land     35
Such a storm there did rise as no ship could withstand.
It bulged on a rock, and the waves rush'd in fast:
Round and round flew the raven, and cawed to the blast.
He heard the last shriek of the perishing souls —
See! see! o'er the topmast the mad water rolls!     40
Right glad was the Raven, and off he went fleet,
And Death riding home on a cloud he did meet,
And he thank'd him again and again for this treat:
They had taken his all, and REVENGE IT WAS SWEET![1]
[1797]

---

[1] In *Sibylline Leaves* (1817) Coleridge added two lines at this point:

> We must not think so; but forget and forgive,
> And what Heaven gives life to, we'll still let it live.

In a manuscript note, however, he reacted angrily against that decision:

Added thro' cowardly fear of the Goody! What a Hollow, where the Heart of Faith ought to be, does it not betray? this alarm concerning Christian morality, that will not permit even a Raven to be a Raven, nor a Fox a Fox, but demands conventicular justice to be inflicted on their unchristian conduct, or at least an antidote to be annexed.

## On the Christening of a Friend's Child

This day among the faithful plac'd
   And fed with fontal manna,
O with maternal title grac'd,
   Dear Anna's dearest Anna!

While others wish thee wise and fair,       5
   A maid of spotless fame,
I'll breathe this more compendious prayer
   May'st thou deserve thy name!

Thy mother's name, a potent spell,
   That bids the Virtues hie       10
From mystic grove and living cell,
   Confess'd to Fancy's eye;

Meek Quietness without offence;
   Content in homespun kirtle;
True Love; and True Love's Innocence,       15
   White Blossom of the Myrtle!

Associates of thy name, sweet Child!
   These Virtues may'st thou win;
With face as eloquently mild
   To say, they lodge within.       20

So, when her tale of days all flown,
   Thy mother shall be miss'd here;
When Heaven at length shall claim its own
   And Angels snatch their Sister;

Some hoary-headed friend, perchance,       25
   May gaze with stifled breath;
And oft, in momentary trance,
   Forget the waste of death.

Even thus a lovely rose I've view'd
   In summer-swelling pride;                 30
Nor mark'd the bud, that green and rude
   Peep'd at the rose's side.


It chanc'd I pass'd again that way
   In Autumn's latest hour,
And wond'ring saw the selfsame spray         35
   Rich with the selfsame flower.


Ah fond deceit! the rude green bud
   Alike in shape, place, name,
Had bloom'd where bloom'd its parent stud,
   Another and the same!              40
[1797]


## To an Unfortunate Woman at the Theatre

Maiden, that with sullen brow
   Sitt'st behind those virgins gay,
Like a scorch'd and mildew'd bough,
   Leafless 'mid the blooms of May!


Him who lur'd thee and forsook,          5
   Oft I watch'd with angry gaze,
Fearful saw his pleading look,
   Anxious heard his fervid phrase.


Soft the glances of the Youth,
   Soft his speech, and soft his sigh;      10
But no sound like simple Truth,
   But no *true* love in his eye.


Loathing thy polluted lot,
   Hie thee, Maiden, hie thee hence!
Seek thy weeping Mother's cot,         15
   With a wiser innocence.

Thou hast known deceit and folly,
   Thou hast *felt* that Vice is woe:
With a musing melancholy
   Inly arm'd, go, Maiden! go.                    20

Mother sage of Self-dominion,
   Firm thy steps, O Melancholy!
The strongest plume in Wisdom's pinion
   Is the memory of past folly.

Mute the sky-lark and forlorn,                    25
   While she moults the firstling plumes,
That had skimm'd the tender corn,
   Or the beanfield's odorous blooms.

Soon with renovated wing
   Shall she dare a loftier flight,                    30
Upward to the Day-Star spring,
   And embathe in heavenly light.
[1797]


## To an Unfortunate Woman

### WHOM THE AUTHOR HAD KNOWN IN THE DAYS
### OF HER INNOCENCE

Myrtle-leaf that, ill besped,
   Pinest in the gladsome ray,
Soil'd beneath the common tread
   Far from thy protecting spray!

When the Partridge o'er the sheaf                    5
   Whirr'd along the yellow vale,
Sad I saw thee, heedless leaf!
   Love the dalliance of the gale.

Lightly didst thou, foolish thing!
   Heave and flutter to his sighs,                    10
While the flatterer, on his wing,
   Woo'd and whisper'd thee to rise.

Gaily from thy mother-stalk
    Wert thou danc'd and wafted high –
Soon on this unshelter'd walk
    Flung to fade, to rot and die.        15
[1797]

# To the Rev. George Coleridge

## OF OTTERY ST MARY, DEVON

### With some Poems

Notus in fratres animi paterni.[1]
        HOR. *Carm.* lib. II. 2.

A blessed lot hath he, who having passed
His youth and early manhood in the stir
And turmoil of the world, retreats at length,
With cares that move, not agitate the heart,
To the same dwelling where his father dwelt;       5
And haply views his tottering little ones
Embrace those agéd knees and climb that lap,
On which first kneeling his own infancy
Lisp'd its brief prayer. Such, O my earliest Friend!
Thy lot, and such thy brothers too enjoy.       10
At distance did ye climb Life's upland road,
Yet cheer'd and cheering: now fraternal love
Hath drawn you to one centre. Be your days
Holy, and blest and blessing may ye live!

  To me the Eternal Wisdom hath dispens'd       15
A different fortune and more different mind –
Me from the spot where first I sprang to light
Too soon transplanted, ere my soul had fix'd
Its first domestic loves; and hence through life
Chasing chance-started friendships. A brief while       20
Some have preserv'd me from life's pelting ills;
But, like a tree with leaves of feeble stem,

[1] 'Notable to his brothers for his fatherly disposition.'

If the clouds lasted, and a sudden breeze
Ruffled the boughs, they on my head at once
Dropped the collected shower; and some most false,          25
False and fair-foliag'd as the Manchineel,
Have tempted me to slumber in their shade
E'en mid the storm; then breathing subtlest damps,
Mix'd their own venom with the rain from Heaven,
That I woke poison'd! But, all praise to Him          30
Who gives us all things, more have yielded me
Permanent shelter; and beside one Friend,
Beneath the impervious covert of one oak,
I've rais'd a lowly shed, and know the names
Of Husband and of Father; not unhearing          35
Of that divine and nightly-whispering Voice,
Which from my childhood to maturer years
Spake to me of predestinated wreaths,
Bright with no fading colours!

                                        Yet at times
My soul is sad, that I have roam'd through life          40
Still most a stranger, most with naked heart
At mine own home and birth-place: chiefly then,
When I remember thee, my earliest Friend!
Thee, who didst watch my boyhood and my youth;
Didst trace my wanderings with a father's eye;          45
And boding evil yet still hoping good,
Rebuk'd each fault, and over all my woes
Sorrow'd in silence! He who counts alone
The beatings of the solitary heart,
That Being knows, how I have lov'd thee ever,          50
Lov'd as a brother, as a son rever'd thee!
Oh! 'tis to me an ever new delight,
To talk of thee and thine: or when the blast
Of the shrill winter, rattling our rude sash,
Endears the cleanly hearth and social bowl;          55
Or when, as now, on some delicious eve,
We in our sweet sequester'd orchard-plot
Sit on the tree crook'd earth-ward; whose old boughs,
That hang above us in an arborous roof,
Stirr'd by the faint gale of departing May,          60
Send their loose blossoms slanting o'er our heads!

   Nor dost not thou sometimes recall those hours,
When with the joy of hope thou gavest thine ear
To my wild firstling-lays. Since then my song
Hath sounded deeper notes, such as beseem                    65
Or that sad wisdom folly leaves behind,
Or such as, tuned to these tumultuous times,
Cope with the tempest's swell!

                         These various strains,
Which I have fram'd in many a various mood,
Accept, my Brother! and (for some perchance                  70
Will strike discordant on thy milder mind)
If aught of error or intemperate truth
Should meet thine ear, think thou that riper age
Will calm it down, and let thy love forgive it!

          NETHER-STOWEY, SOMERSET, 26TH MAY 1797

# FRIENDSHIP WITH WORDSWORTH

In the lines to his brother which concluded the last section, Coleridge lingered over his descriptions of nature in a way which indicated the direction of his thought. Those lines were dated 26 May 1797; by July he was writing to J. P. Estlin: 'I am wearied with politics even to soreness – I never knew a passion for politics exist for a long time without swallowing up, or absolutely excluding, a passion for Religion –' In March of the following year he could write to his brother that he had withdrawn himself almost totally from the consideration of 'immediate causes' (i.e. current political arguments) and proclaim his ambitions as follows: 'in poetry, to elevate the imagination & set the affections in right tune by the beauty of the inanimate impregnated, as with a living soul, by the presence of Life – in prose, to the seeking with patience & a slow, very slow mind . . . What our faculties are & what they are capable of becoming.'

This last statement is an important indication of the direction given to his thought by a new force. During the spring of 1797 he had become intimate with William and Dorothy Wordsworth, whom he had known for some time, and who were now living at Racedown, only a few miles from Nether Stowey. For the first time, Coleridge found himself in the company of a poet whose powers matched his own and who shared his interest in the beauties of external nature, the mystery of man's internal nature, and the relation of both to the place of human beings in the universe. Several important results ensued. The various subjects discussed in the *The Eolian Harp* came into prominence once more. In that poem, indeed, Wordsworth may well have found not only a stimulus for his thinking about nature but a model for the conversational style he was to adopt in *Tintern Abbey*. For Coleridge, the intercourse meant that the philosophical questions which had preoccupied him during the writing of the earlier poems were now endowed with new significance by inter-action with a powerful mind that had reflected upon them from the standpoint of a different experience.

Coleridge began to look more closely at nature itself. In this respect he owed much to the delicate observation of Dorothy Wordsworth, whom he characterized as follows: 'Her information various – her eye watchful in minutest observation of nature – and her taste a perfect electrometer – it bends, protrudes, and draws in, at subtlest beauties & most recondite faults.' In his poem *This Lime-Tree Bower my Prison*, written while the Wordsworths and Lamb were enjoying a walk, leaving him confined to the garden, he devotes himself to minute description of the scene around him and the scenes which will be visible to them. He imagines the sunset:

> Shine in the slant beams of the sinking orb,
> Ye purple heath-flowers! Richlier burn, ye clouds!

In the spring of the next year William Hazlitt, visiting Stowey, was to see a similar sunset:

> . . . Wordsworth, looking out of the low, latticed window, said, 'How beautifully the sun sets on that yellow bank!' I thought within myself, 'With what eyes these poets see nature!'

The closing lines of the same poem are addressed to the Wordsworths and Lamb, 'to whom/ No sound is dissonant, which tells of Life.' They bring out a further interest. His interest in the interrelationship between all forms of life – the 'one Life within us and abroad' as he was to call it in a later version of *The Eolian Harp* – is now becoming the dominant theme of his poetic writing. The idea that 'we are all *one Life*' lies behind even the theory of the *Lyrical Ballads* – for the ballad form, coming as it does out of the people, is well fitted to convey the themes of universal humanity. Coleridge's enthusiasm for writing in the common idiom reinforced Wordsworth's concern for the life of ordinary men. The two poets even went so far as to join in the writing of a long ballad-poem entitled *The Three Graves*, of which some parts are extant, and were planning a more ambitious work, *The Wanderings of Cain*, of which a single piece of verse and several prose drafts were later preserved by Coleridge.

Concern with 'life' led naturally to an interest in children. It is notable that one of Coleridge's rare contributions to Wordsworth's poetry consisted in completing the first stanza of 'We are Seven':

> A simple child, dear brother Jim,
> That lightly draws its breath,
> And feels its life in every limb,
> What should it know of death?

This immediate sense of the liveliness of young children was helped by observation of his own son, named after the philosopher David Hartley, who was beginning to show the first signs of an awakening intelligence. Stimulated also by the revolutionary educational theories of the time, Coleridge became fascinated by the conception of the 'child of nature'. His drama *Osorio* contained two passages which he liked well enough to print, under the titles of *The Foster-Mother's Tale* and *The Dungeon* respectively, in *Lyrical Ballads*. The first tells of a youth who, after having been brought up within the influences of nature, is taken away to be educated in convent and castle, resists the restraints involved and is flung into a dungeon for indulging in heretical speculations. A final glimpse shows him setting off alone in the moonlight up a tropical river, never again to be heard of apart from a rumour that he lives and dies among primitive men.

In the following act of *Osorio*, the doctrine of Nature's healing power is stated with great force in the second passage to be extracted, which argues against contemporary theories of punishment and asserts that the only effective treatment of the criminal is to place him under the influences of nature until he 'can no more endure/ To be a jarring and a dissonant thing,/ Amid this general dance and minstrelsy'. By now the theory is being carried to extraordinary lengths, but the extract shows the poets' current concern to reconcile the fact of evil and crime with their theories of nature.

The doctrine of submission to nature appears more convincingly in *Frost at Midnight* and *The Nightingale*. In the first of these, Coleridge sits in his cottage, sensitive to the almost undetectable manifestations of life in the countryside beyond:

> Sea, and hill, and wood,
> With all the numberless goings-on of life
> Inaudible as dreams!

Inside the cottage, the only sign of life comes from the fluttering film on the grate, which reminds him of his schooldays and then leads him to reflect on the lack of natural beauty in the buildings and city where he was educated and to determine that his own child will be exposed as much as possible to that beauty, which is the language of God himself. The natural descriptions of this poem show his gifts at their best. *The Nightingale* again argues the case for exposing human beings to the influences of nature. Milton's description of the nightingale as 'most musical, most melancholy' is opposed by the assertion that these birds express most potently the joy in Nature.

The poem ends with the portrayal of another 'child of nature', this time a 'gentle Maid', who ('Even like a Lady vowed and dedicate/ To something more than Nature in the grove') goes out at night to listen to the nightingales, responding to the joy and the sudden spontaneous bursts of 'choral minstrelsy,/ As if some sudden gale had swept at once/ A hundred airy harps'.

During the period of collaboration with Wordsworth, Coleridge's critical faculties had sharpened in certain respects. Thus, the *Sonnets Attempted in the Manner of Contemporary Writers* display a refreshingly satirical attitude towards some of the mannerisms of his earlier style. On the other hand, a somewhat uncritical belief in the ultimate benevolence of nature actively helped towards the elaboration of his ideas. The figure of the gentle Maid already foreshadows the hermit who worships at an oak in *The Ancient Mariner* and the Christabel who goes out into a wood in order to pray for her absent lover. Coleridge, at this and many other points, shows himself fully possessed by his avowed poetic aim of setting the affections in right tune 'by the beauty of the inanimate impregnated, as with a living soul, by the presence of Life . . .' Basic themes of the great poems are already in motion. For a time, natural religion and the 'one Life' will hold undisputed sway.

# The Foster-Mother's Tale[1]

### A DRAMATIC FRAGMENT

*Foster-Mother.* I never saw the man whom you describe.
  *Maria.* 'Tis strange! he spake of you familiarly
As mine and Albert's common Foster-mother.
  *Foster-Mother.* Now blessings on the man, whoe'er he be,
That joined your names with mine! O my sweet lady,      5
As often as I think of those dear times
When you two little ones would stand at eve
On each side of my chair, and make me learn
All you had learnt in the day; and how to talk
In gentle phrase, then bid me sing to you –           10
'Tis more like heaven to come than what *has* been.
  *Maria.* O my dear Mother! this strange man has left me
Troubled with wilder fancies, than the moon
Breeds in the love-sick maid who gazes at it,
Till lost in inward vision, with wet eye               15
She gazes idly! – But that entrance, Mother!
  *Foster-Mother.* Can no one hear? It is a perilous tale!
  *Maria.* No one.
  *Foster-Mother.* My husband's father told it me,
Poor old Leoni! – Angels rest his soul!
He was a woodman, and could fell and saw              20
With lusty arm. You know that huge round beam
Which props the hanging wall of the old Chapel?
Beneath that tree, while yet it was a tree,
He found a baby wrapt in mosses, lined
With thistle-beards, and such small locks of wool      25
As hang on brambles. Well, he brought him home,
And rear'd him at the then Lord Velez' cost.
And so the babe grew up a pretty boy,
A pretty boy, but most unteachable –
And never learnt a prayer, nor told a bead,           30
But knew the names of birds, and mock'd their notes,
And whistled, as he were a bird himself:
And all the autumn 'twas his only play

---

[1]From *Osorio*, Act IV. The title and text are here printed from *Lyrical Ballads*, 1798. [E.H.C.]

To get the seeds of wild flowers, and to plant them
With earth and water, on the stumps of trees.                    35
A Friar, who gather'd simples in the wood,
A grey-haired man – he lov'd this little boy,
The boy lov'd him – and, when the Friar taught him,
He soon could write with the pen: and from that time,
Lived chiefly at the Convent or the Castle.                      40
So he became a very learnéd youth.
But Oh! poor wretch! – he read, and read, and read,
Till his brain turn'd – and ere his twentieth year,
He had unlawful thoughts of many things:
And though he prayed, he never lov'd to pray                     45
With holy men, nor in a holy place –
But yet his speech, it was so soft and sweet,
The late Lord Velez ne'er was wearied with him.
And once, as by the north side of the Chapel
They stood together, chain'd in deep discourse,                  50
The earth heav'd under them with such a groan,
That the wall totter'd, and had well-nigh fallen
Right on their heads. My Lord was sorely frighten'd;
A fever seiz'd him, and he made confession
Of all the heretical and lawless talk                           55
Which brought this judgment: so the youth was seiz'd
And cast into that hole. My husband's father
Sobb'd like a child – it almost broke his heart:
And once as he was working in the cellar,
He heard a voice distinctly; 'twas the youth's,                 60
Who sung a doleful song about green fields,
How sweet it were on lake or wild savannah,
To hunt for food, and be a naked man,
And wander up and down at liberty.
He always doted on the youth, and now                           65
His love grew desperate; and defying death,
He made that cunning entrance I describ'd:
And the young man escap'd.
    *Maria*.                              'Tis a sweet tale:
Such as would lull a listening child to sleep,
His rosy face besoil'd with unwiped tears. –                    70
And what became of him?
    *Foster-Mother*.              He went on shipboard
With those bold voyagers, who made discovery

Of golden lands. Leoni's younger brother
Went likewise, and when he return'd to Spain,
He told Leoni, that the poor mad youth,                        75
Soon after they arriv'd in that new world,
In spite of his dissuasion, seiz'd a boat,
And all alone, set sail by silent moonlight
Up a great river, great as any sea,
And ne'er was heard of more: but 'tis suppos'd,               80
He liv'd and died among the savage men.
[1797]


## The Dungeon[1]

And this place our forefathers made for man!
This is the process of our love and wisdom,
To each poor brother who offends against us –
Most innocent, perhaps – and what if guilty?
Is this the only cure? Merciful God!                           5
Each pore and natural outlet shrivell'd up
By Ignorance and parching poverty,
His energies roll back upon his heart,
And stagnate and corrupt; till chang'd to poison,
They break out on him, like a loathsome plague-spot;         10
Then we call in our pamper'd mountebanks –
And this is their best cure! uncomforted
And friendless solitude, groaning and tears,
And savage faces, at the clanking hour
Seen through the steams and vapour of his dungeon,           15
By the lamp's dismal twilight! So he lies
Circled with evil, till his very soul
Unmoulds its essence, hopelessly deform'd
By sights of ever more deformity!


With other ministrations thou, O nature!                      20
Healest thy wandering and distemper'd child:
Thou pourest on him thy soft influences,

[1]From *Osorio*, Act V; and *Remorse*, Act V, Scene i. The title and text are here printed from *Lyrical Ballads*, 1798. [E.H.C.]

Thy sunny hues, fair forms, and breathing sweets,
Thy melodies of woods, and winds, and waters,
Till he relent, and can no more endure                          25
To be a jarring and a dissonant thing,
Amid this general dance and minstrelsy;
But, bursting into tears, wins back his way,
His angry spirit heal'd and harmoniz'd
By the benignant touch of love and beauty.                      30
[1797]


## Melancholy

### A FRAGMENT

Stretch'd on a moulder'd Abbey's broadest wall,
    Where ruining ivies propp'd the ruins steep –
Her folded arms wrapping her tatter'd pall,
    Had Melancholy mus'd herself to sleep.
    The fern was press'd beneath her hair,                       5
    The dark green Adder's Tongue[1] was there;
And still as pass'd the flagging sea-gale weak,
The long lank leaf bow'd fluttering o'er her cheek.

    That pallid cheek was flush'd: her eager look
Beam'd eloquent in slumber! Inly wrought,                        10
    Imperfect sounds her moving lips forsook,
And her bent forehead work'd with troubled thought.
    Strange was the dream –
[?1797]


## Some Fragments

### MAINLY FROM MANUSCRIPTS OF 1797–8

                terrible and loud
As the strong Voice that from the Thunder-cloud
Speaks to the startled Midnight.

---

[1] A botanical mistake. The plant which the poet here describes is called the Hart's Tongue.
[S.T.C.]

The swallows interweaving there mid the paired
Sea-mews, at distance wildly-wailing –

------------------------

           On the broad mountain-top
The neighing wild-colt races with the wind
O'er fern & heath-flowers –

------------------------

                A long deep Lane
So overshadow'd, it might seem one bower –
The damp Clay banks were furr'd with mouldy moss.

------------------------

Broad-breasted Pollards with broad-branching head.

------------------------

'Twas sweet to know it only possible –
Some *wishes* cross'd my mind & dimly cheer'd it –
And one or two poor melancholy Pleasures[;]
In these, the pale unwarming light of Hope
Silv'ring their flimsy wing flew silent by,         5
Moths in the Moonlight –

------------------------

            Behind the thin
Grey cloud that cover'd but not hid the sky
The round full moon look'd small. –[1]

------------------------

The Sun-shine lies on the cottage-wall,
Ashining thro' the snow –

------------------------

The reed-roof'd Village, still bepatch'd with snow
Smok'd in the sun-thaw.[2]

------------------------

[1]Compare *Christabel*, lines 16–19.
[2]Compare *Frost at Midnight*, lines 69–70.

'Twas not a mist, nor was it quite a cloud,
But it pass'd smoothly on towards the Sea
Smoothly & lightly betwixt Earth & Heaven.
                    So thin a cloud –
It scarce bedimm'd the Star that shone behind it.                    5
                    And Hesper now
Paus'd on the welkin's blue and cloudless brink,
A golden circlet! while the Star of Jove,
That other lovely star, high o'er my head
Shone whitely in the centre of his Haze                    10
                    . . . one black-blue Cloud
Stretch'd, like the heavens o'er all the cope of Heaven.
[1797–8. From MS]


## This Lime-Tree Bower my Prison[1]

### [ADDRESSED TO CHARLES LAMB, OF THE INDIA HOUSE, LONDON]

In the June of 1797 some long-expected friends paid a visit to the author's cottage; and on the morning of their arrival, he met with an accident, which disabled him from walking during the whole time of their stay. One evening, when they had left him for a few hours, he composed the following lines in the garden-bower.

Well, they are gone, and here must I remain,
This lime-tree bower my prison! I have lost
Beauties and feelings, such as would have been
Most sweet to my remembrance even when age
Had dimm'd mine eyes to blindness! They, meanwhile,                    5
Friends, whom I never more may meet again,
On springy heath, along the hill-top edge,
Wander in gladness, and wind down, perchance,
To that still roaring dell, of which I told;
The roaring dell, o'erwooded, narrow, deep,                    10
And only speckled by the mid-day sun;
Where its slim trunk the ash from rock to rock
Flings arching like a bridge; - that branchless ash,
Unsunn'd and damp, whose few poor yellow leaves
Ne'er tremble in the gale, yet tremble still,                    15

[1]This poem, which is first known from letters of July 1797, when it was addressed as a whole to the 'friends', underwent many small revisions.

Fann'd by the water-fall! and there my friends
Behold the dark green file of long lank weeds,[1]
That all at once (a most fantastic sight!)
Still nod and drip beneath the dripping edge
Of the blue clay-stone.

             Now, my friends emerge          20
Beneath the wide wide Heaven – and view again
The many-steepled tract magnificent
Of hilly fields and meadows, and the sea,
With some fair bark, perhaps, whose sails light up
The slip of smooth clear blue betwixt two Isles          25
Of purple shadow! Yes! they wander on
In gladness all; but thou, methinks, most glad,
My gentle-hearted Charles! for thou hast pined
And hunger'd after Nature, many a year,
In the great City pent, winning thy way          30
With sad yet patient soul, through evil and pain
And strange calamity! Ah! slowly sink
Behind the western ridge, thou glorious Sun!
Shine in the slant beams of the sinking orb,
Ye purple heath-flowers! richlier burn, ye clouds!          35
Live in the yellow light, ye distant groves!
And kindle, thou blue Ocean! So my friend
Struck with deep joy may stand, as I have stood,
Silent with swimming sense; yea, gazing round
On the wide landscape, gaze till all doth seem          40
Less gross than bodily; and of such hues
As veil the Almighty Spirit, when yet he makes
Spirits perceive his presence.

              A delight
Comes sudden on my heart, and I am glad
As I myself were there! Nor in this bower,          45
This little lime-tree bower, have I not mark'd
Much that has sooth'd me. Pale beneath the blaze
Hung the transparent foliage; and I watch'd
Some broad and sunny leaf, and lov'd to see

[1]The *Asplenium Scolopendrium*, called in some countries the Adder's Tongue, in others the Hart's Tongue: but Withering gives the Adder's Tongue as the trivial name of the *Ophioglossum* only. [S.T.C.]

The shadow of the leaf and stem above                    50
Dappling its sunshine! And that walnut-tree
Was richly ting'd, and a deep radiance lay
Full on the ancient ivy, which usurps
Those fronting elms, and now, with blackest mass
Makes their dark branches gleam a lighter hue            55
Through the late twilight: and though now the bat
Wheels silent by, and not a swallow twitters,
Yet still the solitary humble-bee
Sings in the bean-flower! Henceforth I shall know
That Nature ne'er deserts the wise and pure;             60
No plot so narrow, be but Nature there,
No waste so vacant, but may well employ
Each faculty of sense, and keep the heart
Awake to Love and Beauty! and sometimes
'Tis well to be bereft of promis'd good,                 65
That we may lift the soul, and contemplate
With lively joy the joys we cannot share.
My gentle-hearted Charles! when the last rook
Beat its straight path along the dusky air
Homewards, I blest it! deeming its black wing            70
(Now a dim speck, now vanishing in light)
Had cross'd the mighty Orb's dilated glory,
While thou stood'st gazing; or, when all was still,
Flew creeking o'er thy head, and had a charm[1]
For thee, my gentle-hearted Charles, to whom             75
No sound is dissonant which tells of Life.
[1797–1829]


## Sonnet to William Linley

### WHILE HE SANG A SONG TO PURCELL'S MUSIC

While my young cheek retains its healthful hues,
And I have many friends who hold me dear,

---

[1] Some months after I had written this line, it gave me pleasure to find that Bartram had observed the same circumstance of the Savanna Crane. 'When these Birds move their wings in flight, their strokes are slow, moderate and regular; and even when at a considerable distance or high above us, we plainly hear the quill-feathers: their shafts and webs upon one another creek as the joints or working of a vessel in a tempestuous sea.' [S.T.C.]

Linley! methinks, I would not often hear
Such melodies as thine, lest I should lose
All memory of the wrongs and sore distress                          5
    For which my miserable brethren weep!
    But should uncomforted misfortunes steep
My daily bread in tears and bitterness;
And if at Death's dread moment I should lie
    With no belovéd face at my bed-side,                            10
To fix the last glance of my closing eye,
    Methinks such strains, breathed by my angel-guide,
Would make me pass the cup of anguish by,
    Mix with the blest, nor know that I had died!
[1797]


## Sonnets Attempted in the Manner of Contemporary Writers[1]

### [SIGNED: 'NEHEMIAH HIGGINBOTTOM']

#### I

Pensive at eve on the *hard* world I mus'd,
And *my poor* heart was sad: so at the Moon
I gaz'd – and sigh'd, and sigh'd! – for, ah! how soon
Eve darkens into night. Mine eye perus'd
With tearful vacancy the *dampy* grass                              5
Which wept and glitter'd in the *paly* ray;
And *I did pause me* on my lonely way,
And *mused me* on those *wretched ones* who pass
*O'er the black heath* of Sorrow. But, alas!
Most of *Myself* I thought: when it befell                          10

[1] 'I sent [to the *Monthly Magazine*] three mock sonnets in ridicule of my own, & Charles Lloyd's, & Lamb's, &c., &c. – in ridicule of that affectation of unaffectedness, of jumping & misplaced accent on commonplace epithets, flat lines forced into poetry by italics (signifying how well & *mouthishly* the Author would read them), puny pathos, &c., &c. – the instances are almost all taken from mine & Lloyd's poems – I signed them Nehemiah Higginbottom. I think they may do good to our young Bards.' [S.T.C., Letter, 1797] 'I contributed three sonnets, the first of which had for its object to excite a good-natured laugh at the spirit of doleful egotism and at the recurrence of favourite phrases, with the double defect of being at once trite and licentious. The second, on low, creeping language and thoughts, under the pretence of *simplicity*. And the third, the phrases of which were borrowed entirely from my own poems, on the indiscriminate use of elaborate and swelling language and imagery.' [S.T.C., *Biographia Literaria*, ch. i]

That the *sooth* Spirit of the breezy wood
Breath'd in mine ear – 'All this is very well;
But much of *one* thing is for *no* thing good.'
Ah! my *poor heart's* INEXPLICABLE SWELL!

## II

### TO SIMPLICITY

O! I do love thee, meek *Simplicity*!
For of thy lays the lulling simpleness
Goes to my heart and soothes each small distress,
Distress though small, yet haply great to me!
'Tis true on Lady Fortune's gentlest pad          5
I amble on; yet, though I know not why,
*So* sad I am! – but should a friend and I
Grow cool and *miff*, O! I am *very* sad!
And then with sonnets and with sympathy
My dreamy bosom's mystic woes I pall;          10
Now of my false friend plaining plaintively,
Now raving at mankind in general;
But, whether sad or fierce, 'tis simple all,
All very simple, meek Simplicity!

## III

### ON A RUINED HOUSE IN A ROMANTIC COUNTRY

And this reft house is that the which he built,
Lamented Jack! And here his malt he pil'd,
Cautious in vain! These rats that squeak so wild,
Squeak, not unconscious of their father's guilt.
Did ye not see her gleaming thro' the glade?          5
Belike, 'twas she, the maiden all forlorn.
What though she milk no cow with crumpled horn,
Yet *aye* she haunts the dale where *erst* she stray'd;
And *aye* beside her stalks her amorous knight!
Still on his thighs their wonted brogues are worn,          10
And thro' those brogues, still tatter'd and betorn,
His hindward charms gleam an unearthly white;
As when thro' broken clouds at night's high noon
Peeps in fair fragments forth the full-orb'd harvest-moon!
[1797]

# The Three Graves

A FRAGMENT OF A SEXTON'S TALE

The Author has published the following humble fragment, encouraged by the decisive recommendation of more than one of our most celebrated living Poets. The language was intended to be dramatic; that is, suited to the narrator; and the metre corresponds to the homeliness of the diction. It is therefore presented as the fragment, not of a Poem, but of a common Ballad-tale. Whether this is sufficient to justify the adoption of such a style, in any metrical composition not professedly ludicrous, the Author is himself in some doubt. At all events, it is not presented as poetry, and it is in no way connected with the Author's judgment concerning poetic diction. Its merits, if any, are exclusively psychological. The story which must be supposed to have been narrated in the first and second parts [given below from MS – Ed.] is as follows: –

Edward, a young farmer, meets at the house of Ellen her bosom-friend Mary, and commences an acquaintance, which ends in a mutual attachment. With her consent, and by the advice of their common friend Ellen, he announces his hopes and intentions to Mary's mother, a widow-woman bordering on her fortieth year, and from constant health, the possession of a competent property, and from having had no other children but Mary and another daughter (the father died in their infancy), retaining for the greater part her personal attractions and comeliness of appearance; but a woman of low education and violent temper. The answer which she at once returned to Edward's application was remarkable – 'Well, Edward! you are a handsome young fellow, and you shall have my daughter.' From this time all their wooing passed under the mother's eye; and, in fine, she became herself enamoured of her future son-in-law, and practised every art, both of endearment and of calumny, to transfer his affections from her daughter to herself. (The outlines of the Tale are positive facts, and of no very distant date, though the author has purposely altered the names and the scene of action, as well as invented the characters of the parties and the detail of the incidents.) Edward, however, though perplexed by her strange detractions from her daughter's good qualities, yet in the innocence of his own heart still mistook her increasing fondness for motherly affection; she at length, overcome by her miserable passion, after much abuse of Mary's temper and moral tendencies, exclaimed with violent emotion – 'O Edward, indeed, indeed, she is not fit for you – she has not a heart to love you as you deserve. It is I that love you! Marry me, Edward! and I will this very day settle all my property on you.' The Lover's eyes were now opened: and thus taken by surprise, whether from the effect of the horror which he felt, acting as it were hysterically on his nervous system, or that at the first moment he lost the sense of the guilt of the proposal in the feeling of its strangeness and absurdity, he flung her from him and burst into a fit of laughter. Irritated by this almost to frenzy, the woman fell on her knees, and in a loud voice that approached to a scream, she prayed for a curse both on him and on her own child. Mary happened to be in the room directly above them, heard Edward's laugh, and her mother's blasphemous prayer, and fainted away. He, hearing the fall, ran upstairs, and taking her in his arms, carried her off to Ellen's home; and after some fruitless attempts on her part toward a reconciliation with her mother, she was married to him. – And here the third part of the Tale begins.

I was not led to choose this story from any partiality to tragic, much less to monstrous events (though at the time that I composed the verses, somewhat more than twelve years ago, I was less averse to such subjects than at present), but from finding in it a striking proof of the possible effect on the imagination, from an idea violently and suddenly impressed on it. I had been reading Bryan Edwards's account of the effects of the *Oby* witchcraft on the Negroes in the West Indies, and Hearne's deeply interesting anecdotes of similar workings on the imagination of the Copper Indians (those of my readers who have it in their power will be well repaid for the trouble of referring to those works for the passages alluded to); and I conceived the design of shewing that instances of this kind are not peculiar to savage or barbarous tribes, and of illustrating the mode in which the mind is affected in these cases, and the progress and symptoms of the morbid action on the fancy from the beginning.

The Tale is supposed to be narrated by an old Sexton, in a country church-yard, to a Traveller whose curiosity had been awakened by the appearance of three graves, close by each other, to two only of which there were grave-stones. On the first of these was the name, and dates, as usual: on the second, no name, but only a date, and the words, 'The Mercy of God is infinite.'

## [*Part I. From MS*][1]

Beneath this thorn when I was young,
    This thorn that blooms so sweet,
We loved to stretch our lazy limbs
    In summer's noon-tide heat.


And hither too the old man came,        5
    The maiden and her feer,
'Then tell me, Sexton, tell me why
    The toad has harbour here.


'The Thorn is neither dry nor dead,
    But still it blossoms sweet;        10
Then tell me why all round its roots .
    The dock and nettle meet.


'Why here the hemlock, &c. [*sic in* MS]


'Why these three graves all side by side,
    Beneath the flow'ry thorn,        15
Stretch out so green and dark a length,
    By any foot unworn.'


There, there a ruthless mother lies
    Beneath the flowery thorn;
And there a barren wife is laid,        20
    And there a maid forlorn.


The barren wife and maid forlorn
    Did love each other dear;
The ruthless mother wrought the woe,
    And cost them many a tear.        25

[1] Wordsworth claimed that he gave Coleridge the subject of this poem, and an earlier version of lines 78 to 199 appears in one of his notebooks. Besides making a present of these lines to Coleridge, he may well have contributed elsewhere to the poem, therefore. See Wordsworth, *Poems* (ed. E. de Selincourt), 1940, i, 308–12 and note, p. 374. [Ed.]

Fair Ellen was of serious mind,
   Her temper mild and even,
And Mary, graceful as the fir
   That points the spire to heaven.

Young Edward he to Mary said,          30
   'I would you were my bride,'
And she was scarlet as he spoke,
   And turned her face to hide.

'You know my mother she is rich,
   And you have little gear;          35
And go and if she say not Nay,
   Then I will be your feer.'

Young Edward to the mother went,
   To him the mother said;
'In truth you are a comely man;       40
   You shall my daughter wed.'

[In Mary's joy fair Eleanor
   Did bear a sister's part;
For why, though not akin in blood,
   They sisters were in heart.]        45

Small need to tell to any man
   That ever shed a tear
What passed within the lover's heart
   The happy day so near.

The mother, more than mothers use,    50
   Rejoiced when they were by;
And all the 'course of wooing' passed
   Beneath the mother's eye.

And here within the flowering thorn
   How deep they drank of joy:     55
The mother fed upon the sight,
   Nor . . .        [*sic in* MS]

[*Part II. From MS*]

And now the wedding day was fix'd,
  The wedding-ring was bought;
The wedding-cake with her own hand          60
  The ruthless mother brought.

'And when tomorrow's sun shines forth
  The maid shall be a bride';
Thus Edward to the mother spake
  While she sate by his side.          65

Alone they sate within the bower:
  The mother's colour fled,
For Mary's foot was heard above –
  She decked the bridal bed.

And when her foot was on the stairs          70
  To meet her at the door,
With steady step the mother rose,
  And silent left the bower.

She stood, her back against the door,
  And when her child drew near –          75
'Away! away!' the mother cried,
  'Ye shall not enter here.

'Would ye come here, ye maiden vile,
  And rob me of my mate?'
And on her child the mother scowled          80
  A deadly leer of hate.

Fast rooted to the spot, you guess,
  The wretched maiden stood,
As pale as any ghost of night
  That wanteth flesh and blood.          85

She did not groan, she did not fall,
  She did not shed a tear,
Nor did she cry, 'Oh! mother, why
  May I not enter here?'

But wildly up the stairs she ran,                    90
   As if her sense was fled,
And then her trembling limbs she threw
   Upon the bridal bed.


The mother she to Edward went
   Where he sate in the bower,
And said, 'That woman is not fit                     95
   To be your paramour.


'She is my child – it makes my heart
   With grief and trouble swell;
I rue the hour that gave her birth,                  100
   For never worse befel.


'For she is fierce and she is proud,
   And of an envious mind;
A wily hypocrite she is,
   And giddy as the wind.                       105


'And if you go to church with her,
   You'll rue the bitter smart;
For she will wrong your marriage-bed,
   And she will break your heart.


'Oh God, to think that I have shared                 110
   Her deadly sin so long;
She is my child, and therefore I
   As mother held my tongue.


'She is my child, I've risked for her
   My living soul's estate:                     115
I cannot say my daily prayers,
   The burthen is so great.


'And she would scatter gold about
   Until her back was bare;
And should you swing for lust of hers               120
   In truth she'd little care.'

Then in a softer tone she said,
　　And took him by the hand:
'Sweet Edward, for one kiss of yours
　　I'd give my house and land.                    125

'And if you'll go to church with me,
　　And take me for your bride,
I'll make you heir of all I have –
　　Nothing shall be denied.'

Then Edward started from his seat,                    130
　　And he laughed loud and long –
'In truth, good mother, you are mad,
　　Or drunk with liquor strong.'

To him no word the mother said,
　　But on her knees she fell,                    135
And fetched her breath while thrice your hand
　　Might toll the passing-bell.

'Thou daughter now above my head,
　　Whom in my womb I bore,
May every drop of thy heart's blood                    140
　　Be curst for ever more.

'And curséd be the hour when first
　　I heard thee wawl and cry;
And in the Church-yard curséd be
　　The grave where thou shalt lie!'                    145

And Mary on the bridal-bed
　　Her mother's curse had heard;
And while the cruel mother spake
　　The bed beneath her stirred.

In wrath young Edward left the hall,                    150
　　And turning round he sees
The mother looking up to God
　　And still upon her knees.

Young Edward he to Mary went
　　When on the bed she lay:                               155
'Sweet love, this is a wicked house –
　　Sweet love, we must away.'


He raised her from the bridal-bed,
　　All pale and wan with fear;
'No Dog,' quoth he, 'if he were mine,                       160
　　No Dog would kennel here.'


He led her from the bridal-bed,
　　He led her from the stairs.
[Had sense been hers she had not dar'd
　　To venture on her prayers. MS *erased*]


The mother still was in the bower,
　　And with a greedy heart                                 165
She *drank perdition* on her knees,
　　Which never may depart.


But when their steps were heard below
　　On God she did not call;
She did forget the God of Heaven,                           170
　　For they were in the hall.


She started up – the servant maid
　　Did see her when she rose;
And she has oft declared to me
　　The blood within her froze.                             175


As Edward led his bride away
　　And hurried to the door,
The ruthless mother springeth forth
　　Stopped midway on the floor.


What did she mean? What did she mean?                       180
　　For with a smile she cried:
'Unblest ye shall not pass my door,
　　The bride-groom and his bride.

'Be blithe as lambs in April are,
　As flies when fruits are red;　　　　　185
May God forbid that thought of me
　Should haunt your marriage-bed.

'And let the night be given to bliss,
　The day be given to glee:
I am a woman weak and old,　　　　　190
　Why turn a thought on me?

'What can an agéd mother do,
　And what have ye to dread?
A curse is wind, it hath no shape
　To haunt your marriage-bed.'　　　　195

When they were gone and out of sight
　She rent her hoary hair,
And foamed like any Dog of June
　When sultry sun-beams glare.

　　　*　　　*　　　*

Now ask you why the barren wife,　　　200
　And why the maid forlorn
And why the ruthless mother lies
　Beneath the flowery thorn?

Three times, three times this spade of mine,
　In spite of bolt or bar,　　　　　　　205
Did from beneath the belfry come,
　When spirits wandering are.

And when the mother's soul to Hell
　By howling fiends was borne,
This spade was seen to mark her grave　210
　Beneath the flowery thorn.

And when the death-knock at the door
　Called home the maid forlorn,
This spade was seen to mark her grave
　Beneath the flowery thorn.　　　　　215

And 'tis a fearful, fearful tree;
    The ghosts that round it meet,
'Tis they that cut the rind at night,
    Yet still it blossoms sweet.

\*          \*          \*

[*End of* MS]

## Part III

The grapes upon the Vicar's wall                        220
    Were ripe as ripe could be;
And yellow leaves in sun and wind
    Were falling from the tree.


On the hedge-elms in the narrow lane
    Still swung the spikes of corn:                      225
Dear Lord! it seems but yesterday —
    Young Edward's marriage-morn.


Up through that wood behind the church,
    There leads from Edward's door
A mossy track, all over boughed,                         230
    For half a mile or more.


And from their house-door by that track
    The bride and bridegroom went;
Sweet Mary, though she was not gay,
    Seemed cheerful and content.                         235


But when they to the church-yard came,
    I've heard poor Mary say,
As soon as she stepped into the sun,
    Her heart it died away.


And when the Vicar join'd their hands,                   240
    Her limbs did creep and freeze:
But when they prayed, she thought she saw
    Her mother on her knees.

And o'er the church-path they returned –
    I saw poor Mary's back,             245
Just as she stepped beneath the boughs
    Into the mossy track.

Her feet upon the mossy track
    The married maiden set:
That moment – I have heard her say –        250
    She wished she could forget.

The shade o'er-flushed her limbs with heat –
    Then came a chill like death:
And when the merry bells rang out,
    They seemed to stop her breath.       255

Beneath the foulest mother's curse
    No child could ever thrive:
A mother is a mother still,
    The holiest thing alive.

So five months passed: the mother still     260
    Would never heal the strife;
But Edward was a loving man
    And Mary a fond wife.

'My sister may not visit us,
    My mother says her nay:       265
O Edward! you are all to me,
I wish for your sake I could be
    More lifesome and more gay.

'I'm dull and sad! indeed, indeed
    I know I have no reason!       270
Perhaps I am not well in health,
    And 'tis a gloomy season.'

'Twas a drizzly time – no ice, no snow!
    And on the few fine days
She stirred not out, lest she might meet     275
    Her mother in the ways.

But Ellen, spite of miry ways
    And weather dark and dreary,
Trudged every day to Edward's house,
    And made them all more cheery.                    280

Oh! Ellen was a faithful friend,
    More dear than any sister!
As cheerful too as singing lark;
And she ne'er left them till 'twas dark,
    And then they always missed her.                  285

And now Ash Wednesday came – that day
    But few to church repair:
For on that day you know we read
    The Commination prayer.

Our late old Vicar, a kind man,                        290
    Once, Sir, he said to me,
He wished that service was clean out
    Of our good Liturgy.

The mother walked into the church –
    To Ellen's seat she went:                          295
Though Ellen always kept her church
    All church-days during Lent.

And gentle Ellen welcomed her
    With courteous looks and mild:
Thought she, 'What if her heart should melt,           300
    And all be reconciled!'

The day was scarcely like a day –
    The clouds were black outright:
And many a night, with half a moon,
    I've seen the church more light.                   305

The wind was wild; against the glass
    The rain did beat and bicker;
The church-tower swinging over head,
    You scarce could hear the Vicar!

And then and there the mother knelt,                310
   And audibly she cried –
'Oh! may a clinging curse consume
   This woman by my side!

'O hear me, hear me, Lord in Heaven,
   Although you take my life –                315
O curse this woman, at whose house
   Young Edward woo'd his wife.

'By night and day, in bed and bower,
   O let her curséd be!!!'
So having prayed, steady and slow,                320
   She rose up from her knee!
And left the church, nor e'er again
   The church-door entered she.

I saw poor Ellen kneeling still,
   So pale! I guessed not why:
When she stood up, there plainly was                325
   A trouble in her eye.

And when the prayers were done, we all
   Came round and asked her why:
Giddy she seemed, and sure, there was                330
   A trouble in her eye.

But ere she from the church-door stepped
   She smiled and told us why:
'It was a wicked woman's curse,'
   Quoth she, 'and what care I?'                335

She smiled, and smiled, and passed it off
   Ere from the door she stept –
But all agree it would have been
   Much better had she wept.

And if her heart was not at ease,                340
   This was her constant cry –
'It was a wicked woman's curse –
   God's good, and what care I?'

There was a hurry in her looks,
　　Her struggles she redoubled:                              345
'It was a wicked woman's curse,
　　And why should I be troubled?'


These tears will come – I dandled her
　　When 'twas the merest fairy –
Good creature! and she hid it all:                              350
　　She told it not to Mary.


But Mary heard the tale: her arms
　　Round Ellen's neck she threw;
'O Ellen, Ellen, she cursed me,
　　And now she hath cursed you!'                              355


I saw young Edward by himself
　　Stalk fast adown the lee,
He snatched a stick from every fence,
　　A twig from every tree.


He snapped them still with hand or knee,                       360
　　And then away they flew!
As if with his uneasy limbs
　　He knew not what to do!


You see, good sir! that single hill?
　　His farm lies underneath:                                  365
He heard it there, he heard it all,
　　And only gnashed his teeth.


Now Ellen was a darling love
　　In all his joys and cares:
And Ellen's name and Mary's name                              370
Fast-linked they both together came,
　　Whene'er he said his prayers.


And in the moment of his prayers
　　He loved them both alike:
Yea, both sweet names with one sweet joy                       375
　　Upon his heart did strike!

He reach'd his home, and by his looks
    They saw his inward strife:
And they clung round him with their arms,
    Both Ellen and his wife.                                    380

And Mary could not check her tears,
    So on his breast she bowed;
Then frenzy melted into grief,
    And Edward wept aloud.

Dear Ellen did not weep at all,                                 385
    But closelier did she cling,
And turned her face and looked as if
    She saw some frightful thing.

*Part IV*

To see a man tread over graves
    I hold it no good mark;                                     390
'Tis wicked in the sun and moon,
    And bad luck in the dark!

You see that grave? The Lord he gives,
    The Lord, he takes away:
O Sir! the child of my old age                                 395
    Lies there as cold as clay.

Except that grave, you scarce see one
    That was not dug by me;
I'd rather dance upon 'em all
    Than tread upon these three!                               400

'Aye, Sexton! 'tis a touching tale.'
    You, Sir! are but a lad;
This month I'm in my seventieth year,
    And still it makes me sad.

And Mary's sister told it me,                                   405
    For three good hours and more;
Though I had heard it, in the main,
    From Edward's self, before.

Well! it passed off! the gentle Ellen
   Did well nigh dote on Mary;         410
And she went oftener than before,
And Mary loved her more and more:
   She managed all the dairy.

To market she on market-days,
   To church on Sundays came;         415
All seemed the same: all seemed so, Sir!
   But all was not the same!

Had Ellen lost her mirth? Oh! no!
   But she was seldom cheerful;
And Edward looked as if he thought         420
   That Ellen's mirth was fearful.

When by herself, she to herself
   Must sing some merry rhyme;
She could not now be glad for hours,
   Yet silent all the time.         425

And when she soothed her friend, through all
   Her soothing words 'twas plain
She had a sore grief of her own,
   A haunting in her brain.

And oft she said, I'm not grown thin!         430
   And then her wrist she spanned;
And once when Mary was down-cast,
   She took her by the hand,
And gazed upon her, and at first
   She gently pressed her hand;         435

Then harder, till her grasp at length
   Did gripe like a convulsion!
'Alas!' said she, 'we ne'er can be
   Made happy by compulsion!'

And once her both arms suddenly         440
   Round Mary's neck she flung,
And her heart panted, and she felt
   The words upon her tongue.

She felt them coming, but no power
 Had she the words to smother;                445
And with a kind of shriek she cried,
 'Oh Christ! you're like your mother!'

So gentle Ellen now no more
 Could make this sad house cheery;
And Mary's melancholy ways                450
 Drove Edward wild and weary.

Lingering he raised his latch at eve,
 Though tired in heart and limb;
He loved no other place, and yet
 Home was no home to him.                455

One evening he took up a book,
 And nothing in it read;
Then flung it down, and groaning cried,
 'O! Heaven! that I were dead.'

Mary looked up into his face,                460
 And nothing to him said;
She tried to smile, and on his arm
 Mournfully leaned her head.

And he burst into tears, and fell
 Upon his knees in prayer:                465
'Her heart is broke! O God! my grief,
 It is too great to bear!'

'Twas such a foggy time as makes
 Old sextons, Sir! like me,
Rest on their spades to cough; the spring                470
 Was late uncommonly.

And then the hot days, all at once,
 They came, we know not how:
You looked about for shade, when scarce
 A leaf was on a bough.                475

It happened then ('twas in the bower,
 A furlong up the wood:
Perhaps you know the place, and yet
 I scarce know how you should,)

No path leads thither, 'tis not nigh                 480
   To any pasture-plot;
But clustered near the chattering brook,
   Lone hollies marked the spot.

Those hollies of themselves a shape
   As of an arbour took,                            485
A close, round arbour; and it stands
   Not three strides from a brook.

Within this arbour, which was still
   With scarlet berries hung,
Were these three friends, one Sunday morn,     490
   Just as the first bell rung.

'Tis sweet to hear a brook, 'tis sweet
   To hear the Sabbath-bell,
'Tis sweet to hear them both at once,
   Deep in a woody dell.                             495

His limbs along the moss, his head
   Upon a mossy heap,
With shut-up senses, Edward lay:
That brook e'en on a working day
   Might chatter one to sleep.                       500

And he had passed a restless night,
   And was not well in health;
The women sat down by his side,
   And talked as 'twere by stealth.

'The Sun peeps through the close thick leaves,    505
   See, dearest Ellen! see!
'Tis in the leaves, a little sun
   No bigger than your ee;

'A tiny sun, and it has got
   A perfect glory too;                              510
Ten thousand threads and hairs of light,
Make up a glory gay and bright
   Round that small orb, so blue.'

And then they argued of those rays,
    What colour they might be;         515
Says this, 'They're mostly green'; says that,
    'They're amber-like to me.'


So they sat chatting, while bad thoughts
    Were troubling Edward's rest;
But soon they heard his hard quick pants,     520
    And the thumping in his breast.


'A mother too!' these self-same words
 --Did Edward mutter plain;
His face was drawn back on itself,
    With horror and huge pain.         525


Both groaned at once, for both knew well
    What thoughts were in his mind;
When he waked up, and stared like one
    That hath been just struck blind.


He sat upright; and ere the dream     530
    Had had time to depart,
'O God, forgive me!' (he exclaimed)
    'I have torn out her heart.'


Then Ellen shrieked, and forthwith burst,
    Into ungentle laughter;     535
And Mary shivered, where she sat,
    And never she smiled after.

*Carmen reliquum in futurum tempus relegatum.*[1] Tomorrow!
and Tomorrow! and Tomorrow! [Note by S.T.C., 1815]
[1797–8]

---

[1] 'The rest of the poem was postponed to a future time.'

# The Wanderings of Cain

A prose composition, one not in metre at least, seems *primâ facie* to require explanation or apology. It was written in the year 1798, near Nether Stowey, in Somersetshire, at which place (*sanctum et amabile nomen!* ['sacred and lovable name!'] rich by so many associations and recollections) the author had taken up his residence in order to enjoy the society and close neighbourhood of a dear and honoured friend, T. Poole, Esq. The work was to have been written in concert with another [Wordsworth], whose name is too venerable within the precincts of genius to be unnecessarily brought into connection with such a trifle, and who was then residing at a small distance from Nether Stowey. The title and subject were suggested by myself, who likewise drew out the scheme and the contents for each of the three books or cantos, of which the work was to consist, and which, the reader is to be informed, was to have been finished in one night! My partner undertook the first canto: I the second: and which ever had *done first*, was to set about the third. Almost thirty years have passed by; yet at this moment I cannot without something more than a smile moot the question which of the two things was the more impracticable, for a mind so eminently original to compose another man's thoughts and fancies, or for a taste so austerely pure and simple to imitate the Death of Abel? Methinks I see his grand and noble countenance as at the moment when having despatched my own portion of the task at full finger-speed, I hastened to him with my manuscript — that look of humourous despondency fixed on his almost blank sheet of paper, and then its silent mock-piteous admission of failure struggling with the sense of the exceeding ridiculousness of the whole scheme — which broke up in a laugh: and the Ancient Mariner was written instead.

Years afterward, however, the draft of the plan and proposed incidents, and the portion executed, obtained favour in the eyes of more than one person, whose judgment on a poetic work could not but have weighed with me, even though no parental partiality had been thrown into the same scale, as a make-weight: and I determined on commencing anew, and composing the whole in stanzas, and made some progress in realizing this intention, when adverse gales drove my bark off the 'Fortunate Isles' of the Muses: and then other and more momentous interests prompted a different voyage, to firmer anchorage and a securer port. I have in vain tried to recover the lines from the palimpsest tablet of my memory: and I can only offer the introductory stanza, which had been committed to writing for the purpose of procuring a friend's judgment on the metre, as a specimen:

Encinctured with a twine of leaves,
That leafy twine his only dress!
A lovely Boy was plucking fruits,
By moonlight, in a wilderness.
The moon was bright, the air was free,
And fruits and flowers together grew
On many a shrub and many a tree:
And all put on a gentle hue,
Hanging in the shadowy air
Like a picture rich and rare.
It was a climate where, they say,
The night is more belov'd than day.
But who that beauteous Boy beguil'd,
That beauteous Boy to linger here?
Alone, by night, a little child,
In place so silent and so wild –
Has he no friend, no loving mother near?

I have here given the birth, parentage, and premature decease of the 'Wanderings of Cain, a poem', – intreating, however, my Readers not to think so meanly of my judgment as to suppose that I either regard or offer it as any excuse for the publication of the following fragment (and I may add, of one or two others in its neighbourhood) in its primitive crudity. But I should find still greater difficulty in forgiving myself were I to record pro *taedio* publico ['for the public *tedium*'] a set of petty mishaps and annoyances which I myself wish to forget. I must be content therefore with assuring the friendly Reader, that the less he attributes its appearance to the Author's will, choice, or judgment, the nearer to the truth he will be.

S. T. COLERIDGE (1828)

# The Wanderings of Cain

'A little further, O my father, yet a little further, and we shall come into the open moonlight.' Their road was through a forest of fir-trees; at its entrance the trees stood at distances from each other, and the path was broad, and the moonlight and the moonlight shadows reposed upon it, and appeared quietly to inhabit that solitude. But soon the path winded and became narrow; the sun at high noon sometimes speckled, but never illumined it, and now it was dark as a cavern.

'It is dark, O my father!' said Enos, 'but the path under our feet is smooth and soft, and we shall soon come out into the open moonlight.'

'Lead on, my child!' said Cain: 'guide me, little child!' And the innocent little child clasped a finger of the hand which had murdered the righteous Abel; and he guided his father. 'The fir branches drip upon thee, my son.' 'Yea, pleasantly, father, for I ran fast and eagerly to bring thee the pitcher and the cake, and my body is not yet cool. How happy the squirrels are that feed on these fir-trees! they leap from bough to bough, and the old squirrels play round their young ones in the nest. I clomb a tree yesterday at noon, O my father, that I might play with them, but they leaped away from the branches, even to the slender twigs did they leap, and in a moment I beheld them on another tree. Why, O my father, would they not play with me? I would be good to them as thou art good to me: and I groaned to them even as thou groanest when thou givest me to eat, and when thou coverest me at evening, and as often as I stand at thy knee and thine eyes look at me?' Then Cain stopped, and stifling his groans he sank to the earth, and the child Enos stood in the darkness beside him.

And Cain lifted up his voice and cried bitterly, and said, 'The Mighty One that persecuteth me is on this side and on that; he pursueth my soul like the wind, like the sandblast he passeth through me; he is around me even as the air! O that I might be utterly no more! I desire to die – yea, the things that never had life, neither move they upon the earth – behold! they seem precious to mine eyes. O that a man might live without the breath of his nostrils. So I might abide in darkness, and blackness, and an empty space! Yea, I would lie down, I would not rise, neither would I stir my limbs till I became as a rock in the den of the lion, on which the young lion resteth his head whilst he sleepeth. For the torrent that roareth far off hath a voice: and the clouds in heaven look terribly on me; the Mighty One who is against me speaketh in the wind of the cedar grove; and in silence am I dried up.' Then Enos spake to his father, 'Arise, my father, arise, we are but a little way from the place where I found the cake and the pitcher.' And Cain said, 'How knowest thou!' and the child answered – 'Behold the bare rocks are a few of thy strides distant from the forest; and while even now thou wert lifting up thy voice, I heard the echo.' Then the child took hold of his father, as if he would raise him: and Cain being faint and feeble rose slowly on his knees and pressed himself against the trunk of a fir, and stood upright and followed the child.

The path was dark till within three strides' length of its termination, when it turned suddenly; the thick black trees formed a low arch, and the moonlight appeared for a moment like a dazzling portal. Enos ran before and stood in the open air; and when Cain, his father, emerged from the darkness, the child was affrighted. For the mighty limbs of Cain were wasted as by fire; his hair was as the matted curls on the bison's forehead, and so glared his fierce and sullen eye beneath: and the black abundant locks on either side, a rank and tangled mass, were stained and scorched, as though the grasp of a burning iron hand had striven to rend them; and his countenance told in a strange and terrible language of agonies that had been, and were, and were still to continue to be.

The scene around was desolate; as far as the eye could reach it was desolate: the bare rocks faced each other, and left a long and wide interval of thin white sand. You might wander on and look round and round, and peep into the crevices of the rocks and discover nothing that acknowledged the influence of the seasons. There was no spring, no summer, no autumn: and the winter's snow, that would have been lovely, fell not on these hot rocks and scorching sands. Never morning lark had poised himself over this desert; but the huge serpent often hissed there beneath the talons of the vulture, and the vulture screamed, his

wings imprisoned within the coils of the serpent. The pointed
and shattered summits of the ridges of the rocks made a rude
mimicry of human concerns, and seemed to prophesy mutely of
80    things that then were not; steeples, and battlements, and ships
with naked masts. As far from the wood as a boy might sling a
pebble of the brook, there was one rock by itself at a small
distance from the main ridge. It had been precipitated there
perhaps by the groan which the Earth uttered when our first
85    father fell. Before you approached, it appeared to lie flat on the
ground, but its base slanted from its point, and between its
point and the sands a tall man might stand upright. It was here
that Enos had found the pitcher and cake, and to this place he
led his father. But ere they had reached the rock they beheld a
90    human shape: his back was towards them, and they were
advancing unperceived, when they heard him smite his breast
and cry aloud, 'Woe is me! woe is me! I must never die again,
and yet I am perishing with thirst and hunger.'

Pallid, as the reflection of the sheeted lightning on the heavy-
95    sailing night-cloud, became the face of Cain; but the child Enos
took hold of the shaggy skin, his father's robe, and raised his
eyes to his father, and listening whispered, 'Ere yet I could
speak, I am sure, O my father, that I heard that voice. Have not
I often said that I remembered a sweet voice? O my father! this
100    is it'; and Cain trembled exceedingly. The voice was sweet
indeed, but it was thin and querulous, like that of a feeble slave
in misery, who despairs altogether, yet can not refrain himself
from weeping and lamentation. And, behold! Enos glided
forward, and creeping softly round the base of the rock, stood
105    before the stranger, and looked up into his face. And the Shape
shrieked, and turned round, and Cain beheld him, that his
limbs and his face were those of his brother Abel whom he had
killed! And Cain stood like one who struggles in his sleep
because of the exceeding terribleness of a dream.

110    Thus as he stood in silence and darkness of soul, the Shape
fell at his feet, and embraced his knees, and cried out with a
bitter outcry, 'Thou eldest born of Adam, whom Eve, my
mother, brought forth, cease to torment me! I was feeding my
flocks in green pastures by the side of quiet rivers, and thou
115    killedst me; and now I am in misery.' Then Cain closed his eyes,
and hid them with his hands; and again he opened his eyes, and
looked around him, and said to Enos, 'What beholdest thou?

Didst thou hear a voice, my son?' 'Yes, my father, I beheld a
man in unclean garments, and he uttered a sweet voice, full
of lamentation.' Then Cain raised up the Shape that was like    120
Abel, and said: – 'The Creator of our father, who had respect
unto thee, and unto thy offering, wherefore hath he forsaken
thee?' Then the Shape shrieked a second time, and rent his
garment, and his naked skin was like the white sands beneath
their feet; and he shrieked yet a third time, and threw himself    125
on his face upon the sand that was black with the shadow of the
rock, and Cain and Enos sate beside him; the child by his right
hand, and Cain by his left. They were all three under the rock,
and within the shadow. The Shape that was like Abel raised
himself up, and spake to the child: 'I know where the cold    130
waters are, but I may not drink, wherefore didst thou then take
away my pitcher?' But Cain said, 'Didst thou not find favour in
the sight of the Lord thy God?' The Shape answered, 'The Lord
is God of the living only, the dead have another God.' Then the
child Enos lifted up his eyes and prayed; but Cain rejoiced    135
secretly in his heart. 'Wretched shall they be all the days of their
mortal life,' exclaimed the Shape, 'who sacrifice worthy and
acceptable sacrifices to the God of the dead; but after death
their toil ceaseth. Woe is me, for I was well beloved by the God
of the living, and cruel wert thou, O my brother, who didst    140
snatch me away from his power and his dominion.' Having
uttered these words, he rose suddenly, and fled over the sands:
and Cain said in his heart, 'The curse of the Lord is on me; but
who is the God of the dead?' and he ran after the Shape, and the
Shape fled shrieking over the sands, and the sands rose like    145
white mists behind the steps of Cain, but the feet of him that
was like Abel disturbed not the sands. He greatly outrun Cain,
and turning short, he wheeled round, and came again to the
rock where they had been sitting, and where Enos still stood;
and the child caught hold of his garment as he passed by, and he    150
fell upon the ground. And Cain stopped, and beholding him
not, said, 'He has passed into the dark woods,' and he walked
slowly back to the rocks; and when he reached it the child told
him that he had caught hold of his garment as he passed by, and
that the man had fallen upon the ground: and Cain once more    155
sate beside him, and said, 'Abel, my brother, I would lament for
thee, but that the spirit within me is withered, and burnt up
with extreme agony. Now, I pray thee, by thy flocks, and by

thy pastures, and by the quiet rivers which thou lovedst, that
160  thou tell me all that thou knowest. Who is the God of the dead?
where doth he make his dwelling? what sacrifices are accept-
able unto him? for I have offered, but have not been received;
I have prayed, and have not been heard; and how can I be
afflicted more than I already am?' The Shape arose and
165  answered, 'O that thou hadst had pity on me as I will have pity
on thee. Follow me, Son of Adam! and bring thy child with
thee!'

And they three passed over the white sands between the
rocks, silent as the shadows.
170                                                      [1797–8]


## Parliamentary Oscillators

Almost awake? Why, what is this, and whence,
    O ye right loyal men, all undefiléd?
Sure, 'tis not possible that Common-Sense
    Has hitch'd her pullies to each heavy eye-lid?

Yet wherefore else that start, which discomposes          5
    The drowsy waters lingering in your eye?
    And are you *really* able to descry
That precipice three yards beyond your noses?

Yet flatter you I cannot, that your wit
    Is much improved by this long loyal dozing;           10
And I admire, no more than Mr Pitt,
    Your jumps and starts of patriotic prosing –

Now cluttering to the Treasury Cluck, like chicken,
    Now with small beaks the ravenous *Bill* opposing;[1]
With serpent-tongue now stinging, and now licking,        15
    Now semi-sibilant, now smoothly glozing –

---

[1] Pitt's 'treble assessment at seven millions' which formed part of the budget for 1798. The grant was carried in the House of Commons, 4 January 1798. [E.H.C.]

Now having faith implicit that he can't err,
   Hoping his hopes, alarm'd with his alarms;
And now believing him a sly inchanter,
   Yet still afraid to break his brittle charms,       20

Lest some mad Devil suddenly unhamp'ring,
   Slap-dash! the imp should fly off with the steeple,
On revolutionary broom-stick scampering. –
   O ye soft-headed and soft-hearted people,

If you can stay so long from slumber free,       25
   My muse shall make an effort to salute 'c:
For lo! a very dainty simile
   Flash'd sudden through my brain, and 'twill just suit 'e!

You know that water-fowl that cries, Quack! Quack!?
   Full often have I seen a waggish crew       30
Fasten the Bird of Wisdom on its back,
   The ivy-haunting bird, that cries, To-whoo!

Both plung'd together in the deep mill-stream,
   (Mill-stream, or farm-yard pond, or mountain-lake,)
Shrill, as a *Church and Constitution* scream,       35
   Tu-whoo! quoth Broad-face, and down dives the Drake!

The green-neck'd Drake once more pops up to view,
   Stares round, cries Quack! and makes an angry pother;
Then shriller screams the Bird with eye-lids blue,
   The broad-faced Bird! and deeper dives the other.      40
Ye *quacking* Statesmen! 'tis even so with you –
   One Peasecod is not liker to another.

Even so on Loyalty's Decoy-pond, each
   Pops up his head, as fir'd with British blood,
Hears once again the Ministerial screech,       45
   And once more seeks the bottom's blackest mud!
[1797]
                         (*Signed:* LABERIUS)

## Fire, Famine, and Slaughter

### A WAR ECLOGUE

The Scene a desolated Tract in La Vendée. FAMINE is discovered lying on the ground; to her enter FIRE and SLAUGHTER.

*Fam*.  Sisters! sisters! who sent you here?
*Slau*.  [*to Fire*]. I will whisper it in her ear.
*Fire*.  No! no! no!
Spirits hear what spirits tell:
'Twill make a holiday in Hell.                                   5
   No! no! no!
Myself, I named him once below,
And all the souls, that damnéd be,
Leaped up at once in anarchy,
Clapped their hands and danced for glee.                        10
They no longer heeded me;
But laughed to hear Hell's burning rafters
Unwillingly re-echo laughters!
   No! no! no!
Spirits hear what spirits tell:                                 15
'Twill make a holiday in Hell!
 *Fam*.  Whisper it, sister! so and so!
In a dark hint, soft and slow.
 *Slau*.  Letters four do form his name —
And who sent you?
 *Both*.   The same! the same!                 20
 *Slau*.  He came by stealth, and unlocked my den,
And I have drunk the blood since then
Of thrice three hundred thousand men.
 *Both*.  Who bade you do't?
 *Slau*.    The same! the same!
Letters four do form his name.                                  25
He let me loose, and cried Halloo!
To him alone the praise is due.
 *Fam*.  Thanks, sister, thanks! the men have bled,
Their wives and their children faint for bread.
I stood in a swampy field of battle;                           30

With bones and skulls I made a rattle,
To frighten the wolf and carrion-crow
And the homeless dog – but they would not go.
So off I flew: for how could I bear
To see them gorge their dainty fare?                    35
I heard a groan and a peevish squall,
And through the chink of a cottage-wall –
Can you guess what I saw there?
    *Both.* Whisper it, sister! in our ear.
    *Fam.* A baby beat its dying mother:                    40
I had starved the one and was starving the other!
    *Both.* Who bade you do't?
    *Fam.*             The same! the same!
Letters four do form his name.
He let me loose, and cried, Halloo!
To him alone the praise is due.                    45
    *Fire.* Sisters! I from Ireland came!
Hedge and corn-fields all on flame,
I triumph'd o'er the setting sun!
And all the while the work was done,
On as I strode with my huge strides,                    50
I flung back my head and I held my sides,
It was so rare a piece of fun
To see the sweltered cattle run
With uncouth gallop through the night,
Scared by the red and noisy light!                    55
By the light of his own glazing cot
Was many a naked Rebel shot:
The house-stream met the flame and hissed,
While crash! fell in the roof, I wist,
On some of those old bed-rid nurses,                    60
That deal in discontent and curses.
    *Both.* Who bade you do't?
    *Fire.*             The same! the same!
Letters four do form his name.
He let me loose, and cried Halloo!
To him alone the praise is due.                    65
    *All.* He let us loose, and cried Halloo!
How shall we yield him honour due?
    *Fam.* Wisdom comes with lack of food.
I'll gnaw, I'll gnaw the multitude,

Till the cup of rage o'erbrim:                              70
They shall seize him and his brood –
  *Slau.*  They shall tear him limb from limb!
  *Fire.*  O thankless beldames and untrue!
And is this all that you can do
For him, who did so much for you?                           75
Ninety months he, by my troth!
Hath richly catered for you both;
And in an hour would you repay
An eight years' work? – Away! away!
I alone am faithful! I                                      80
Cling to him everlastingly.
[1797]


# The Old Man of the Alps

Stranger! whose eyes a look of pity shew,
Say, will you listen to a tale of woe?
A tale in no unwonted horrors drest;
But sweet is pity to an agéd breast.
This voice did falter with old age before;                  5
Sad recollections make it falter more.
Beside the torrent and beneath a wood,
High in these Alps my summer cottage stood;
One daughter still remain'd to cheer my way,
The evening-star of life's declining day:                  10
Duly she hied to fill her milking-pail,
Ere shout of herdsmen rang from cliff or vale;
When she return'd, before the summer shiel,
On the fresh grass she spread the dairy meal;
Just as the snowy peaks began to lose                      15
In glittering silver lights their rosy hues.
Singing in woods or bounding o'er the lawn,
No blither creature hail'd the early dawn;
And if I spoke of hearts by pain oppress'd,
When every friend is gone to them that rest;               20
Or of old men that leave, when they expire,
Daughters, that should have perish'd with their sire –
Leave them to toil all day through paths unknown,

And house at night behind some sheltering stone;
Impatient of the thought, with lively cheer                    25
She broke half-closed the tasteless tale severe.
*She* play'd with fancies of a gayer hue,
Enamour'd of the scenes her *wishes* drew;
And oft she prattled with an eager tongue
Of promised joys that would not loiter long,                   30
Till with her tearless eyes so bright and fair,
She seem'd to see them realiz'd in air!
In fancy oft, within some sunny dell,
Where never wolf should howl or tempest yell,
She built a little home of joy and rest,                       35
And fill'd it with the friends whom she lov'd best:
She named the inmates of her fancied cot,
And gave to each his own peculiar lot;
Which with our little herd abroad should roam,
And which should tend the dairy's toil at home,               40
And now the hour approach'd which should restore
Her lover from the wars, to part no more.
Her whole frame fluttered with uneasy joy;
I long'd myself to clasp the valiant boy;
And though I strove to calm *her* eager mood,                 45
It was my own sole thought in solitude.
I told it to the Saints amid my hymns –
For O! you know not, on an old man's limbs
How thrillingly the pleasant sun-beams play,
That shine upon his daughter's wedding-day.                   50
I hoped, that those fierce tempests, soon to rave
Unheard, unfelt, around *my* mountain grave,
Not undelightfully would break *her* rest,
While she lay pillow'd on her lover's breast;
Or join'd his pious prayer for pilgrims driven               55
Out to the mercy of the winds of heaven.
Yes! now the hour approach'd that should restore
Her lover from the wars to part no more.
Her thoughts were wild, her soul was in her eye,
She wept and laugh'd as if she knew not why;                  60
And she had made a song about the wars,
And sang it to the sun and to the stars!
But while she look'd and listen'd, stood and ran,
And saw him plain in every distant man,

By treachery stabbed, on NANSY's murderous day,[1]    65
A senseless corse th' expected husband lay.
A wounded man, who met us in the wood,
Heavily ask'd her where *my* cottage stood,
And told us all: she cast her eyes around
As if his words had been but empty sound.    70
Then look'd to Heav'n, like one that would deny
That such a thing *could be* beneath the sky.
*Again* he ask'd her if she knew my name,
And instantly an anguish wrench'd her frame,
And left her mind imperfect. No delight    75
Thenceforth she found in any cheerful sight,
Not ev'n in those time-haunted wells and groves,
Scenes of past joy, and birth-place of her loves.
If to her spirit any sound was dear,
'Twas the deep moan that spoke the tempest near;    80
Or sighs which chasms of icy vales outbreathe,
Sent from the dark, imprison'd floods beneath.
She wander'd up the crag and down the slope,
But not, as in her happy days of hope,
To seek the churning-plant of sovereign power,    85
That grew in clefts and bore a scarlet flower!
She roam'd, without a purpose, all alone,
Thro' high grey vales unknowing and unknown.

Kind-hearted stranger! patiently you hear
A tedious tale: I thank you for that tear.    90
May never other tears o'ercloud your eye,
Than those which gentle Pity can supply!
Did you not mark a towering convent hang,
Where the huge rocks with sounds of torrents rang?
Ev'n yet, methinks, its spiry turrets swim    95
Amid yon purple gloom ascending dim!
For thither oft would my poor child repair,
To ease her soul by penitence and prayer.
I knew that peace at good men's prayers returns
Home to the contrite heart of him that mourns,    100
And check'd her not; and often there she found
A timely pallet when the evening frown'd.

[1]The mutiny at Nancy in August 1790, quelled with much loss of life.

And there I trusted that my child would light
On shelter and on food, one dreadful night,
When there was uproar in the element,                    105
And she was absent. To my rest I went:
I thought her safe, yet often did I wake
And felt my very heart within me ache.
No daughter near me, at this very door,
Next morn I listen'd to the dying roar.                  110
Above, below, the prowling vulture wail'd,
And down the cliffs the heavy vapour sail'd.
Up by the wide-spread waves in fury torn,
Homestalls and pines along the vale were borne.
The Dalesmen in thick crowds appear'd below             115
Clearing the road, o'erwhelm'd with hills of snow.
At times to the proud gust's ascending swell,
A pack of blood-hounds flung their doleful yell:
For after nights of storm, that dismal train
The pious convent sends, with hope humane,              120
To find some out-stretch'd man – perchance to save,
Or give, at least, that last good gift, a grave!
But now a gathering crowd did I survey,
That slowly up the pasture bent their way;
Nor could I doubt but that their care had found         125
Some pilgrim in th' unchannel'd torrent drown'd.
And down the lawn I hasten'd to implore
That they would bring the body to my door;
But soon exclaim'd a boy, who ran before,
'Thrown by the last night's waters from their bed,      130
Your daughter has been found, and she is dead!'

The old man paused – May he who, sternly just,
Lays at his will his creatures in the dust;
Some ere the earliest buds of hope be blown,
And some, when every bloom of joy is flown;             135
May he the parent to his child restore
In that unchanging realm, where Love reigns evermore!
[1797–8]

                                    NICIAS ERYTHRAEUS

## The Snow-Drop[1]

### I

Fear no more, thou timid Flower!
Fear thou no more the winter's might,
The whelming thaw, the ponderous shower,
The silence of the freezing night!
Since Laura murmur'd o'er thy leaves          5
The potent sorceries of song,
To thee, meek Flowret! gentler gales
    And cloudless skies belong.

### II

Her eye with tearful meanings fraught,
She gaz'd till all the body mov'd          10
Interpreting the Spirit's thought —
The Spirit's eager sympathy
Now trembled with thy trembling stem,
And while thou droopedst o'er thy bed,
With sweet unconscious sympathy          15
    Inclin'd the drooping head.

### III

She droop'd her head, she stretch'd her arm,
She whisper'd low her witching rhymes,
Fame unreluctant heard the charm,
And bore thee to Pierian climes!          20
Fear thou no more the Matin Frost
That sparkled on thy bed of snow:
For there, mid laurels ever green,
    Immortal thou shalt blow.

[1]The MS bears the following heading: LINES WRITTEN IMMEDIATELY AFTER THE PERUSAL OF MRS ROBINSON'S SNOW DROP. [E.H.C.] Cf. Mary Robinson, *Poetical Works*, 1806, i. 123.

### IV

Thy petals boast a white more soft,                    25
The spell hath so perfuméd thee,
That careless Love shall deem thee oft
A blossom from his Myrtle tree.
Then, laughing at the fair deceit,
Shall race with some Etesian wind                    30
To seek the woven arboret
    Where Laura lies reclin'd.

### V

All them whom Love and Fancy grace,
When grosser eyes are clos'd in sleep,
The gentle spirits of the place                    35
Waft up the insuperable steep,
On whose vast summit broad and smooth
Her nest the Phœnix Bird conceals,
And where by cypresses o'erhung
    The heavenly Lethe steals.                    40

### VI

A sea-like sound the branches breathe,
Stirr'd by the Breeze that loiters there;
And all that stretch their limbs beneath,
Forget the coil of mortal care.
Strange mists along the margins rise,                    45
To heal the guests who thither come,
And fit the soul to re-endure
    Its earthly martyrdom.

### VII

The margin dear to moonlight elves
Where Zephyr-trembling Lilies grow,                    50
And bend to kiss their softer selves
That tremble in the stream below: –
There nightly borne does Laura lie
A magic Slumber heaves her breast:
Her arm, white wanderer of the Harp,                    55
    Beneath her cheek is prest.

## VIII

The Harp uphung by golden chains
Of that low wind which whispers round,
With coy reproachfulness complains,
In snatches of reluctant sound:                                    60
The music hovers half-perceiv'd,
And only moulds the slumberer's dreams;
Remember'd LOVES relume her cheek
        With Youth's returning gleams.
[December 1797]

## Frost at Midnight

The Frost performs its secret ministry,
Unhelped by any wind. The owlet's cry
Came loud – and hark, again! loud as before.
The inmates of my cottage, all at rest,
Have left me to that solitude, which suits                         5
Abstruser musings: save that at my side
My cradled infant slumbers peacefully.
'Tis calm indeed! so calm, that it disturbs
And vexes meditation with its strange
And extreme silentness. Sea, hill, and wood,                       10
This populous village! Sea, and hill, and wood,
With all the numberless goings-on of life,
Inaudible as dreams! the thin blue flame
Lies on my low-burnt fire, and quivers not;
Only that film,[1] which fluttered on the grate,                   15
Still flutters there, the sole unquiet thing.
Methinks, its motion in this hush of nature
Gives it dim sympathies with me who live,
Making it a companionable form,
Whose puny flaps and freaks the idling Spirit                      20
By its own moods interprets, every where
Echo or mirror seeking of itself,
And makes a toy of Thought.

[1]In all parts of the kingdom these films are called *strangers* and supposed to portend the
arrival of some absent friend. [S.T.C.] The passage echoes a similar one in Cowper's *The Task*
iv, 286–98.

                        But O! how oft,
How oft, at school, with most believing mind,
Presageful, have I gazed upon the bars,          25
To watch that fluttering *stranger*! and as oft
With unclosed lids, already had I dreamt
Of my sweet birth-place, and the old church-tower,
Whose bells, the poor man's only music, rang
From morn to evening, all the hot Fair-day,      30
So sweetly, that they stirred and haunted me
With a wild pleasure, falling on mine ear
Most like articulate sounds of things to come!
So gazed I, till the soothing things, I dreamt,
Lulled me to sleep, and sleep prolonged my dreams!    35
And so I brooded all the following morn,
Awed by the stern preceptor's face, mine eye
Fixed with mock study on my swimming book:
Save if the door half opened, and I snatched
A hasty glance, and still my heart leaped up,     40
For still I hoped to see the *stranger's* face,
Townsman, or aunt, or sister more beloved,
My play-mate when we both were clothed alike!

   Dear Babe, that sleepest cradled by my side,
Whose gentle breathings, heard in this deep calm,    45
Fill up the intersperséd vacancies
And momentary pauses of the thought!
My babe so beautiful! it thrills my heart
With tender gladness, thus to look at thee,
And think that thou shalt learn far other lore,    50
And in far other scenes! For I was reared
In the great city, pent 'mid cloisters dim,
And saw nought lovely but the sky and stars.
But *thou*, my babe! shalt wander like a breeze
By lakes and sandy shores, beneath the crags    55
Of ancient mountain, and beneath the clouds,
Which image in their bulk both lakes and shores
And mountain crags: so shalt thou see and hear
The lovely shapes and sounds intelligible
Of that eternal language, which thy God    60
Utters who from eternity doth teach
Himself in all, and all things in himself.

Great universal Teacher! he shall mould
Thy spirit, and by giving make it ask.

Therefore all seasons shall be sweet to thee,          65
Whether the summer clothe the general earth
With greenness, or the redbreast sit and sing
Betwixt the tufts of snow on the bare branch
Or mossy apple-tree, while the nigh thatch
Smokes in the sun-thaw; whether the eave-drops fall     70
Heard only in the trances of the blast,
Or if the secret ministry of frost
Shall hang them up in silent icicles,
Quietly shining to the quiet Moon.[1]
[February 1798]

## *Lewti*[2]

### OR THE CIRCASSIAN LOVE-CHAUNT

At midnight by the stream I roved,
To forget the form I loved,
Image of Lewti! from my mind
Depart; for Lewti is not kind.

The Moon was high, the moonlight gleam          5
    And the shadow of a star
Heaved upon Tamaha's stream;
    But the rock shone brighter far,
The rock half sheltered from my view
By pendent boughs of tressy yew. –             10

---

[1]When the poem was first published it ended:

> Quietly shining to the quiet moon,
> Like those, my babe! which ere tomorrow's warmth
> Have capp'd their sharp keen points with pendulous drops,
> Will catch thine eye, and with their novelty
> Suspend thy little soul; then make thee shout,
> And stretch and flutter from thy mother's arms
> As thou wouldst fly for very eagerness.

In 1808–9 Coleridge removed the last six lines, contending in a marginal annotation that they destroyed the 'rondo, and return upon itself of the Poem'.

[2]Some lines are taken or adapted from Wordsworth's early 'Beauty and Moonlight'.

So shines my Lewti's forehead fair,
Gleaming through her sable hair.
Image of Lewti! from my mind
Depart; for Lewti is not kind.

I saw a cloud of palest hue,                                    15
   Onward to the moon it passed;
Still brighter and more bright it grew,
With floating colours not a few,
   Till it reached the moon at last:
Then the cloud was wholly bright,                              20
With a rich and amber light!
And so with many a hope I seek,
   And with such joy I find my Lewti;
And even so my pale wan cheek
   Drinks in as deep a flush of beauty!                      25
Nay, treacherous image! leave my mind,
If Lewti never will be kind.

The little cloud – it floats away,
   Away it goes; away so soon?
Alas! it has no power to stay:                                 30
Its hues are dim, its hues are grey –
   Away it passes from the moon!
How mournfully it seems to fly,
   Ever fading more and more,
To joyless regions of the sky –                               35
   And now 'tis whiter than before!
As white as my poor cheek will be,
   When, Lewti! on my couch I lie,
A dying man for love of thee.
Nay, treacherous image! leave my mind –                       40
And yet, thou didst not look unkind.

   I saw a vapour in the sky,
   Thin, and white, and very high;
I ne'er beheld so thin a cloud:
   Perhaps the breezes that can fly                          45
   Now below and now above,
Have snatched aloft the lawny shroud

Of Lady fair – that died for love.
For maids, as well as youths, have perished
From fruitless love too fondly cherished.          50
Nay, treacherous image! leave my mind –
For Lewti never will be kind.

Hush! my heedless feet from under
  Slip the crumbling banks for ever:
Like echoes to a distant thunder,          55
  They plunge into the gentle river.
The river-swans have heard my tread,
And startle from their reedy bed.
O beauteous birds! methinks ye measure
  Your movements to some heavenly tune!          60
O beauteous birds' 'tis such a pleasure
  To see you move beneath the moon,
I would it were your true delight
To sleep by day and wake all night.

I know the place where Lewti lies,          65
When silent night has closed her eyes:
  It is a breezy jasmine-bower,
The nightingale sings o'er her head:
  Voice of the Night! had I the power
That leafy labyrinth to thread,          70
And creep, like thee, with soundless tread,
I then might view her bosom white
Heaving lovely to my sight,
As these two swans together heave
On the gently swelling wave.          75

Oh! that she saw me in a dream,
  And dreamt that I had died for care;
All pale and wasted I would seem,
  Yet fair withal, as spirits are!
I'd die indeed, if I might see          80
Her bosom heave, and heave for me!
Soothe, gentle image! soothe my mind!
To-morrow Lewti may be kind.
[1798]

## *To a Young Lady*

[*Miss Lavinia Poole*]

### ON HER RECOVERY FROM A FEVER

Why need I say, Louisa dear!
How glad I am to see you here,
   A lovely convalescent;
Risen from the bed of pain and fear,
   And feverish heat incessant.       5

The sunny showers, the dappled sky,
The little birds that warble high,
   Their vernal loves commencing,
Will better welcome you than I
   With their sweet influencing.       10

Believe me, while in bed you lay,
Your danger taught us all to pray:
   You made us grow devouter!
Each eye looked up and seemed to say,
   How can we do without her?       15

Besides, what vexed us worse, we knew,
They have no need of such as you
   In the place where you were going:
This World has angels all too few,
   And Heaven is overflowing!       20
[31 March 1798]

## *The Nightingale*

### A CONVERSATION POEM, APRIL 1798

No cloud, no relique of the sunken day
Distinguishes the West, no long thin slip
Of sullen light, no obscure trembling hues.

Come, we will rest on this old mossy bridge!
You see the glimmer of the stream beneath, 5
But hear no murmuring: it flows silently,
O'er its soft bed of verdure. All is still,
A balmy night! and though the stars be dim,
Yet let us think upon the vernal showers
That gladden the green earth, and we shall find 10
A pleasure in the dimness of the stars.
And hark! the Nightingale begins its song,
'Most musical, most melancholy' bird![1]
A melancholy bird? Oh! idle thought!
In Nature there is nothing melancholy. 15
But some night-wandering man whose heart was pierced
With the remembrance of a grievous wrong,
Or slow distemper, or neglected love,
(And so, poor wretch! filled all things with himself,
And made all gentle sounds tell back the tale 20
Of his own sorrow) he, and such as he,
First named these notes a melancholy strain.
And many a poet echoes the conceit;
Poet who hath been building up the rhyme
When he had better far have stretched his limbs 25
Beside a brook in mossy forest-dell,
By sun or moon-light, to the influxes
Of shapes and sounds and shifting elements
Surrendering his whole spirit, of his song
And of his fame forgetful! so his fame 30
Should share in Nature's immortality,
A venerable thing! and so his song
Should make all Nature lovelier, and itself
Be loved like Nature! But 'twill not be so;
And youths and maidens most poetical, 35
Who lose the deepening twilights of the spring
In ball-rooms and hot theatres, they still
Full of meek sympathy must heave their sighs
O'er Philomela's pity-pleading strains.

---

[1] '*Most musical, most melancholy.*' This passage in Milton possesses an excellence far superior to that of mere description; it is spoken in the character of the melancholy Man, and has therefore a *dramatic* propriety. The Author makes this remark, to rescue himself from the charge of having alluded with levity to a line in Milton; a charge than which none could be more painful to him, except perhaps that of having ridiculed his Bible. [S.T.C.]

My Friend, and thou, our Sister! we have learnt          40
A different lore: we may not thus profane
Nature's sweet voices, always full of love
And joyance! 'Tis the merry Nightingale
That crowds, and hurries, and precipitates
With fast thick warble his delicious notes,               45
As he were fearful that an April night
Would be too short for him to utter forth
His love-chant, and disburthen his full soul
Of all its music!

            And I know a grove
Of large extent, hard by a castle huge,                   50
Which the great lord inhabits not; and so
This grove is wild with tangling underwood,
And the trim walks are broken up, and grass,
Thin grass and king-cups grow within the paths.
But never elsewhere in one place I knew                   55
So many nightingales; and far and near,
In wood and thicket, over the wide grove,
They answer and provoke each other's song,
With skirmish and capricious passagings,
And murmurs musical and swift jug jug,                    60
And one low piping sound more sweet than all –
Stirring the air with such a harmony,
That should you close your eyes, you might almost
Forget it was not day! On moonlight bushes,
Whose dewy leaflets are but half-disclosed,               65
You may perchance behold them on the twigs,
Their bright, bright eyes, their eyes both bright and full,
Glistening, while many a glow-worm in the shade
Lights up her love-torch.

              A most gentle Maid,
Who dwelleth in her hospitable home                       70
Hard by the castle, and at latest eve
(Even like a Lady vowed and dedicate
To something more than Nature in the grove)
Glides through the pathways; she knows all their notes,
That gentle Maid! and oft, a moment's space,              75
What time the moon was lost behind a cloud,

Hath heard a pause of silence; till the moon
Emerging, hath awakened earth and sky
With one sensation, and those wakeful birds
Have all burst forth in choral minstrelsy,                    80
As if some sudden gale had swept at once
A hundred airy harps! And she hath watched
Many a nightingale perch giddily
On blossomy twig still swinging from the breeze,
And to that motion tune his wanton song                      85
Like tipsy Joy that reels with tossing head.

    Farewell, O Warbler! till tomorrow eve,
And you, my friends! farewell, a short farewell!
We have been loitering long and pleasantly,
And now for our dear homes. – That strain again!             90
Full fain it would delay me! My dear babe,
Who, capable of no articulate sound,
Mars all things with his imitative lisp,
How he would place his hand beside his ear,
His little hand, the small forefinger up,                    95
And bid us listen! And I deem it wise
To make him Nature's play-mate. He knows well
The evening-star; and once, when he awoke
In most distressful mood (some inward pain
Had made up that strange thing, an infant's dream –)        100
I hurried with him to our orchard-plot,
And he beheld the moon, and, hushed at once,
Suspends his sobs, and laughs most silently,
While his fair eyes, that swam with undropped tears,
Did glitter in the yellow moon-beam! Well! –                105
It is a father's tale: But if that Heaven
Should give me life, his childhood shall grow up
Familiar with these songs, that with the night
He may associate joy. – Once more, farewell,
Sweet Nightingale! once more, my friends! farewell.         110
[1798]

## The Ballad of the Dark Ladié

### A FRAGMENT

Beneath yon birch with silver bark,
And boughs so pendulous and fair,
The brook falls scatter'd down the rock:
    And all is mossy there!

And there upon the moss she sits,         5
The Dark Ladié in silent pain;
The heavy tear is in her eye,
    And drops and swells again.

Three times she sends her little page
Up the castled mountain's breast,        10
If he might find the Knight that wears
    The Griffin for his crest.

The sun was sloping down the sky,
And she had linger'd there all day,
Counting moments, dreaming fears –      15
    Oh wherefore can he stay?

She hears a rustling o'er the brook,
She sees far off a swinging bough!
'Tis He! 'Tis my betrothéd Knight!
    Lord Falkland, it is Thou!'       20

She springs, she clasps him round the neck,
She sobs a thousand hopes and fears,
Her kisses glowing on his cheeks
    She quenches with her tears.

     *     *     *

'My friends with rude ungentle words     25
They scoff and bid me fly to thee!
O give me shelter in thy breast!
    O shield and shelter me!

'My Henry, I have given thee much,
I gave what I can ne'er recall,                    30
I gave my heart, I gave my peace,
    O Heaven! I gave thee all.'

The Knight made answer to the Maid,
While to his heart he held her hand,
'Nine castles hath my noble sire,                 35
    None statelier in the land.

'The fairest one shall be my love's,
The fairest castle of the nine!
Wait only till the stars peep out,
    The fairest shall be thine:                  40

'Wait only till the hand of eve
Hath wholly closed yon western bars,
And through the dark we two will steal
    Beneath the twinkling stars!' –

'The dark? the dark? No! not the dark?           45
The twinkling stars? How, Henry? How?'
O God! 'twas in the eye of noon
    He pledged his sacred vow!

And in the eye of noon my love
Shall lead me from my mother's door,              50
Sweet boys and girls all clothed in white
    Strewing flowers before:

But first the nodding minstrels go
With music meet for lordly bowers,
The children next in snow-white vests,            55
    Strewing buds and flowers!

And then my love and I shall pace,
My jet black hair in pearly braids,
Between our comely bachelors
    And blushing bridal maids.                    60

\*    \*    \*

[1798–?1800]

# KUBLA KHAN

When Coleridge published this poem in 1816 he attached a note declaring that the publication was undertaken at Lord Byron's request and, so far as his own opinions were concerned, 'rather as a psychological curiosity, than on the ground of any supposed *poetic* merits'. He also attached an account of the composition of the poem which, like the account tacked on to the early manuscript poem also reproduced here, ascribed the composition of the poem to the effects of a dose of opium taken for medicinal reasons. The existence of that earlier evidence supports Coleridge's assertion that the poem (or perhaps some part of it) was written in a half-waking condition. But this does not, of course, mean that the poem is devoid of meaning. On the contrary, the language of the poem seems overdetermined by the pressures of meaning behind some of the words, and to contain the fruits of Coleridge's thinking and reading on certain topics which had long fascinated him.[1]

Some of these he shared with his age. The late eighteenth century had shown deep interest in all the phenomena of 'genius', seeing in such powers an element which might pass beyond ordinary human faculties and guard against the ultimate sterility of an 'age of reason'. The genius need not be an artist. He might be a scientist, penetrating the inward meaning of the universe, or a priest, bringing heaven before men's eyes, or a ruler, controlling his people not by physical coercion but by a wisdom which was also imaginative enough to make an appeal to their total nature and so educe a willing co-operation from them. In each case, the result was the same. Men are most fully compelled, not by physical coercion, but by the imaginative power of the genius, which makes an irresistible and completely satisfying appeal to the whole man.

Coleridge enlarged upon the nature of genius by drawing a

[1]The interpretations of Coleridge's major poems which are sketched in this and the following prefaces are more fully worked out in my books, *Coleridge the Visionary* (1959) and *Coleridge's Poetic Intelligence* (1977). [Ed.]

comparison between the man of 'absolute genius' and the man of 'commanding genius'.

The man of commanding genius is under a curse. Like the Satan of *Paradise Lost*, he can command intense devotion and create mighty works

> with the sound
> Of Dulcet Symphonies and voices sweet.

Yet because he is cut off from the central harmony of Heaven his efforts are doomed. His power will eventually be stunted into meanness; his love, corrupted from its true pride, will crawl as lust.

The man of absolute genius, on the other hand, is restored to the mountain paradise of Milton's poem. He brings his vision into physical being and fascinates his followers into harmony by reason of the primal truth which possesses him:

> For he on honey-dew hath fed,
> And drunk the milk of paradise.

*Kubla Khan*, to sum up, is a poem with two major themes: genius and the lost paradise. In the first stanza the man of commanding genius, the fallen but demonic man, strives to rebuild the lost paradise in a world which is, like himself, fallen. In the second stanza, the other side of the demonic re-asserts itself – the mighty fountain in the savage place, the wailing woman beneath the waning moon, the demon-lover. The third stanza is a moment of miraculous unity between the contending forces – the sunny dome and the caves of ice, the fountain and the caves, the dome and the waves all being counterpoised in one harmony. Finally, in the last stanza, there is a vision of paradise regained – of man revisited by that absolute genius which corresponds to his original, unfallen state, of the honey-dew fountain of immortality re-established in the garden, of complete harmony between Apollo with his lyre and the damsel with the dulcimer, of the established dome, and of the multitude, reconciled by the terrible fascination of the genius into complete harmony.

The compression of meaning within the poem is intense, and this tends to confirm Coleridge's account that it was composed in a state of mind which was not fully conscious. A large resource of already achieved speculation was tapped as soon as Coleridge set eyes upon the words 'In *Xamdu* did *Cublai Can* build a stately Palace'. And in particular reminiscence of one particular line in *Paradise Lost,* 'Of *Cambalu,* seat of *Cathaian Can*', helped to set in motion memories of speculation about the symbolic meaning of Milton's poem. Around this nucleus of speculation, other images gathered, some common, some recondite, coalescing into a single pattern.

The paradox of the poem, however, is that its immediate shape and verbal structure were dictated more by Coleridge's own poetic experience, as developed in the writing of his previous poetry. Thus the texture of the poem has a life of its own. The bare anatomy of meaning is covered by a clothing of exotic language, glimmering and glittering by turns. The various appeals to the senses in ice and moonlight, mighty fountain and mazy river, paradise milk and paradise honey are skilfully deployed. Crystalline and drowsy by turns, the poem, as a verbal structure, exists in a total mood of dreamy enchantment.

As a result, the poem may be read as a pattern of compressed imaginative speculation or as a texture of enchantment, according to whether attention is directed upon the meaning or the wording. And this curious combination of intense speculation and sensuous appeal makes *Kubla Khan*, more than any other of his poems, symbolic of the man who created it. When he remembered Coleridge talking, Carlyle found himself moved to sensuous imagery:

> Glorious islets, too, I have seen rise out of the haze; but they were few, and soon swallowed in the general element again. Balmy sunny islets, islets of the blest and the intelligible . . .

Yet the listener who cared to listen and investigate more closely would have been impressed less by the sweet eloquence of the speaker than by the breadth of his thinking. Few men have read so much, thought so much, or tried more consistently to work the sum of human experience into a total pattern. Often his thinking and his musical sense refused to interlock completely, just as they do in the first stanzas of this poem. It is only in the last stanza, when the poet turns from his problem to himself to express his complete aims, that a perfect fusion is reached. But this fusion creates fresh problems – indeed, the remainder of his career may be viewed as the quest for an ideal community, an ideal woman, an ideal poem, each eluding him by turns.

The two versions of *Kubla Khan* presented here consist of a manuscript version apparently written down soon after the time of composition and a polished version (beginning on the opposite page) published nearly twenty years later on the encouragement of Lord Byron. The descriptions of the circumstances of composition, one at the beginning, the other at the end, agree in stating that the poem was composed in 1797 (in the summer or autumn) and that Coleridge was at the time of composition experiencing the effects of opium prescribed for an indisposition; the more elaborate 1816 version may have been written up slightly in an attempt to disguise the nature of his own aspirations as suggested in the last stanza of the poem.

The manuscript came to light in 1934 and was acquired in 1962 by the British Library. It is unlikely that it was the original on which Coleridge first wrote down his poem if the note at the end was written at the same time, since that has a retrospective quality: Coleridge would surely have given the exact date had he been writing on the spot. There are some corrections on the manuscript: 'From forth' (line 17) was corrected from 'And from', 'far' (line 29) from 'fear' and 'Amara' from 'Amora'. The 1816 version (pp. 203–7 below) was probably prepared from an earlier one which still retained 'And from' and 'Amora': a comparison between the 1816 text and the manuscript will show further alterations, mostly of style. In the Crewe manuscript the space after 'Caves of Ice!' (line 36) is indicated decisively but it is not at all clear that stanza divisions were meant to occur earlier. Since there is some indication of a break in the writing at those points, however, and since the divisions were made in every edition during Coleridge's lifetime, I have retained them, but with a half-line break in each case.

The only clue to the history of the manuscript is a pencilled note 'Sent by Mrs Southey, as an Autograph of Coleridge'. The manuscript is untitled.

# Kubla Khan

## Or, A Vision in a Dream

### A FRAGMENT

The following fragment is here published at the request of a poet of great and deserved celebrity [Lord Byron], and, as far as the Author's own opinions are concerned, rather as a psychological curiosity, than on the ground of any supposed *poetic* merits.

In the summer of the year 1797, the Author, then in ill health, had retired to a lonely farm-house between Porlock and Linton, on the Exmoor confines of Somerset and Devonshire. In consequence of a slight indisposition, an anodyne had been prescribed, from the effects of which he fell asleep in his chair at the moment that he was reading the following sentence, or words of the same substance, in 'Purchas's Pilgrimage': 'Here the Khan Kubla commanded a palace to be built, and a stately garden thereunto. And thus ten miles of fertile ground were inclosed with a wall.'[1] The Author continued for about three hours in a profound sleep, at least of the external senses, during which time he has the most vivid confidence, that he could not have composed less than from two to three hundred lines; if that indeed can be called composition in which all the images rose up before him as *things*, with a parallel production of the correspondent expressions, without any sensation or consciousness of effort. On awaking he appeared to himself to have a distinct recollection of the whole, and taking his pen, ink, and paper, instantly and eagerly wrote down the lines that are here preserved. At this moment he was unfortunately called out by a person on business from Porlock, and detained by him above an hour, and on his return to his room found, to his no small surprise and mortification, that though he still retained some vague and dim recollection of the general purport of the vision, yet, with the exception of some eight or ten scattered lines and images, all the rest had passed away like the images on the surface of a stream into which a stone has been cast, but, alas! without the after restoration of the latter!

[1]'In Xamdu did Cublai Can build a stately Palace, encompassing sixteene miles of plaine ground with a wall, wherein are fertile Meddowes, pleasant Springs, delightfull Streames, and all sorts of beasts of chase and game, and in the middest thereof a sumptuous house of pleasure.' – *Purchas his Pilgrimage*: Lond. fol. 1626, Bk. IV, chap. xiii, p. 418.

## *The Crewe Manuscript of* Kubla Khan

In Xannadù did Cubla Khan
A stately Pleasure-Dome decree;
Where Alph, the sacred River, ran
Thro' Caverns measureless to Man
Down to a sunless Sea.       5
So twice six miles of fertile ground
With Walls and Towers were compass'd round:
And here were Gardens bright with sinuous Rills
Where blossom'd many an incense-bearing Tree,
And here were Forests ancient as the Hills       10
Enfolding sunny Spots of Greenery.

But o! that deep romantic Chasm, that slanted
Down a green Hill athwart a cedarn Cover,
A savage Place, as holy and inchanted
As e'er beneath a waning Moon was haunted       15
By Woman wailing for her Dæmon Lover:
From forth this Chasm with hideous Turmoil seething,
As if this Earth in fast thick Pants were breathing,

> Then all the charm
> Is broken – all that phantom-world so fair
> Vanishes, and a thousand circlets spread,
> And each mis-shape[s] the other. Stay awhile,
> Poor youth! who scarcely dar'st lift up thine eyes –
> The stream will soon renew its smoothness, soon
> The visions will return! And lo, he stays,
> And soon the fragments dim of lovely forms
> Come trembling back, unite, and now once more
> The pool becomes a mirror.[1]

Yet from the still surviving recollections in his mind, the Author has frequently purposed to finish for himself what had been originally, as it were, given to him. Σαμερον αδιον ασω[2]: but the to-morrow is yet to come.

As a contrast to this vision, I have annexed a fragment of a very different character, describing with equal fidelity the dream of pain and disease.[3]


In Xanadu did Kubla Khan
A stately pleasure-dome decree:
Where Alph, the sacred river, ran
Through caverns measureless to man
  Down to a sunless sea.                                    5
So twice five miles of fertile ground
With walls and towers were girdled round:
And here were gardens bright with sinuous rills,
Where blossomed many an incense-bearing tree;
And here were forests ancient as the hills,                       10
Enfolding sunny spots of greenery.

But oh! that deep romantic chasm which slanted
Down the green hill athwart a cedarn cover!
A savage place! as holy and enchanted
As e'er beneath a waning moon was haunted                         15
By woman wailing for her demon-lover!
And from this chasm, with ceaseless turmoil seething,
As if this earth in fast thick pants were breathing,

---

[1]From *The Picture; or, the Lover's Resolution*, ll. 91–100, below.
[2]'Tomorrow I shall sing more sweetly'. After Theocritus i. 145. [E.H.C.]
[3]See *The Pains of Sleep*, below.

A mighty Fountain momently was forc'd,
Amid whose swift half-intermitted Burst                    20
Huge Fragments vaulted like rebounding Hail,
Or chaffy Grain beneath the Thresher's Flail:
And mid these dancing Rocks at once & ever
It flung up momently the sacred River.
Five miles meandering with a mazy Motion                  25
Thro' Wood and Dale the sacred River ran,
Then reach'd the Caverns measureless to Man
And sank in Tumult to a lifeless Ocean;
And mid this Tumult Cubla heard from far
Ancestral Voices prophesying War.                         30

 The Shadow of the Dome of Pleasure
 Floated midway on the Wave
 Where was heard the mingled Measure
 From the Fountain and the Cave.
It was a miracle of rare Device,                          35
A sunny Pleasure-Dome with Caves of Ice!

 A Damsel with a Dulcimer
 In a Vision once I saw:
It was an Abyssinian Maid,
And on her Dulcimer she play'd                            40
Singing of Mount Amara.
Could I revive within me
Her Symphony & Song,
To such a deep Delight 'twould win me,
That with Music loud and long                             45
I would build that Dome in Air,
That sunny Dome! those Caves of Ice!
And all, who heard, should see them there,
And all should cry, Beware! Beware!
His flashing Eyes! his floating Hair!                     50
Weave a circle round him thrice,
And close your Eyes in holy Dread:
For He on Honey-dew hath fed
And drank the Milk of Paradise.

This fragment with a good deal more, not recoverable, composed, in
a sort of Reverie brought on by two grains of Opium, taken to check a
dysentery, at a Farm House between Porlock & Linton, a quarter of a
mile from Culbone Church, in the fall of the year, 1797.

            S. T. Coleridge

A mighty fountain momently was forced:
Amid whose swift half-intermitted burst                    20
Huge fragments vaulted like rebounding hail,
Or chaffy grain beneath the thresher's flail:
And 'mid these dancing rocks at once and ever
It flung up momently the sacred river.
Five miles meandering with a mazy motion                   25
Through wood and dale the sacred river ran,
Then reached the caverns measureless to man,
And sank in tumult to a lifeless ocean:
And 'mid this tumult Kubla heard from far
Ancestral voices prophesying war!                          30

   The shadow of the dome of pleasure
    Floated midway on the waves;
   Where was heard the mingled measure
    From the fountain and the caves.
It was a miracle of rare device,                           35
A sunny pleasure-dome with caves of ice!

   A damsel with a dulcimer
   In a vision once I saw:
   It was an Abyssinian maid,
   And on her dulcimer she played,                     40
   Singing of Mount Abora.
   Could I revive within me
   Her symphony and song,
   To such a deep delight 'twould win me,
That with music loud and long,                             45
I would build that dome in air,
That sunny dome! those caves of ice!
And all who heard should see them there,
And all should cry, Beware! Beware!
His flashing eyes, his floating hair!                      50
Weave a circle round him thrice,
And close your eyes with holy dread,
For he on honey-dew hath fed,
And drunk the milk of Paradise.
[1816]

# THE ANCIENT MARINER

On 13 November 1797 Coleridge set out with William and Dorothy Wordsworth, late in the afternoon, to walk over the Quantocks to Watchet. They were planning an expedition together: and in order to defray the expenses they had decided to write a series of poems, to be submitted to the *New Monthly Magazine*. During the evening Coleridge's contribution, which was to be a ballad, began to take shape. Wordsworth, intending to collaborate, found that their two styles would not assimilate and so contributed only a few lines. But already one or two suggestions of his had set Coleridge's imagination to work.

We know something of the projects with which he had been toying during previous months. A long poem on the Origin of Evil; a poem on the wanderings of Cain; or 'a poem on delirium, confounding its own dream scenery with external things, and connected with the imagery of high latitudes'.

Each of these ideas worked hard in the new poem: but the actual starting point of the plot was a dream related to Coleridge by a neighbour of his, Mr Cruikshank, in which he had seen a skeleton ship, with figures in it. Wordsworth, who had been reading Shelvocke's *Voyages* a day or two before, remembered accounts of large albatrosses in the South Seas, and suggested that the shooting of an albatross, as recorded in Shelvocke, might be the cause of the ship's troubles. He also suggested that the ship might be navigated by the dead men. From this point Coleridge's imagination took over and began to shape the entire poem as we know it.

The theme of the shooting gave him an opportunity to explore the idea of the 'one Life' which had been haunting his thinking in previous months. For here was a perfect example of a crime against the one Life – thoughtless and motiveless, possible only to a man who had not seen the unity of all life in the world. Such a man must do penance until he has learnt a proper reverence for living things, after which he will be sent abroad to tell chosen individuals of what he has learnt.

For Coleridge, however, reverence for life consisted of something more than kindness to living creatures. Life was not simply a biological phenomenon, existing on a small planet in the mighty universe. It was in itself a reflection of the God who had created all things. The workings of this life Coleridge found reflected in the ancient Egyptian hieroglyphic of the sun, the serpent and the wings. This he apparently saw as a telling emblem of the relationship between God and the creation. The light of the divine, imaged in the sun, goes forth into the universe and works also as energy, symbolized by the serpent. Energy, however, cannot exist autonomously; it must constantly be connected back to its source if it is to retain its meaning and not degenerate into evil. This connection is made by love, symbolized in the soaring wings of the Egyptian hieroglyph.

Coleridge throughout his career constantly used the traditional image of the sun for God. He also used the image of winged Love. A passage in *The Destiny of Nations* bears further on the imagery of *The Ancient Mariner* by picturing Love as a winged presence on the ocean:

> . . . Love rose glittering, and his gorgeous wings
> Over the abyss fluttered with such glad noise,
> As what time after long and pestful calms,
> With slimy shapes and miscreated life
> Poisoning the vast Pacific, the fresh breeze
> Wakens the merchant-sail uprising.

Thus the events and landscape of the poem lend symbolic depth to its meaning. It was a favourite idea of Coleridge's (an idea which he took over from previous mystic philosophers) that human beings cannot endure unmodified exposure to the divine. Time and space are a creation of the divine mercy to shield human beings from the power of God which, without protection, would appear purely as wrath.

The Wedding-Guest, having heard the tale, heeds the moral – that men should turn to the source of life and love and that their best form of prayer to that source is to love all living creatures until they are completely at home within the harmony of the 'one Life'. The shooting of the albatross is only one blatant example of all the offences against life by which human beings cut themselves off from the central harmony of the creation.

The Mariner himself is evidently an allegorical figure – he has even been compared with the *poète maudit* of Rimbaud's *Bâteau Ivre*. The comparison is fair, but with one important difference. Rimbaud's poet is under compulsion to sail farther and farther, just as he himself departed from civilization until he found himself in the wilds of Abyssinia. Coleridge's Mariner, on the other hand, returns by an equally powerful necessity to his own country. For Coleridge, the main result of experiencing the sublime is that the domestic is illuminated: and so the Mariner's piercing eye, that 'glittering eye' which had frightened the Wedding-Guest, now turns out to be in addition the 'bright eye' of childlike innocence and recaptured vision.

At the time when Coleridge was writing, the two most fashionable poetic modes were those of pathos and sublimity. This poem is uniquely successful in achieving both qualities, passing from the world of the senses first to a landscape of the sublime and then to a world where sensibility has been illuminated and transfigured by that terror and glory. Charles Lamb readily perceived the achievement: in reply to Southey's satiric description of the poem as 'a Dutch attempt at German sublimity', he asserted indignantly that it was 'a right English attempt, and a successful one, to dethrone German sub-limity'. And a line or two later, he stressed the other achievement of the poem: 'I never so deeply felt the pathetic as in that part, "A spring of love gush'd from my heart, And I bless'd them unaware . . ."'

For modern readers, on the other hand, the main achievement of the poem lies in a quality which Coleridge himself recognized when, in late life, he described *The Ancient Mariner* as 'a poem of the pure imagination'. The occasional awkwardnesses and circumlocutions of his early poems now finally drop away, giving place to a liquid flow of imagery which makes an instant appeal. Sometimes the appeal is vividly to the eye – there is a certain isolation of the vividnesses, so that each stanza stands away from the next, requiring something like a moment of darkness before the reader has assimilated it and is ready to pass on. At other times response is evoked from other senses, ranging from the refined –

> Her beams bemocked the sultry main,
> Like April hoar-frost spread

to the grossly physical –

> We could not speak, no more than if
> We had been choked with soot.

But Coleridge's mastery in this poem is due above all to the fact that he has created a landscape which obeys other laws beyond those of nature. When ice-drifts loom, or the sun fixes the ship to the ocean, we become aware of a structuring that appeals directly to our imagination. The same imaginative genius is displayed in the use of language. The word 'silly', which we tend to use in situations where we have complete control, breaks into the Mariner's enslavement and so evokes, suddenly, a whole world of relief:

> The silly buckets on the deck,
> That had so long remained,
> I dreamt that they were filled with dew;
> And when I awoke, it rained.

Crystalline, pure, impulsive in clarity of colour, the language of the poem evokes the full quality of Coleridge's sensibility, responsive equally to vivid brightness and to softer sensations such as the noises of hidden streams, the feeling of a breeze on the cheek, refreshing sleep or summer birdsong. The poet himself appears, fully and apparently, in this, his finest work: it has also a timeless anonymous quality which transcends the individual personality of the man who wrote it.

It was difficult for him to know exactly what he had done in writing the poem. Read in terms of the imagery discussed above it has a symbolic structure which shows a man glimpsing briefly the meaning of a universe which he lacks the full equipment to understand. The one thing that he takes from the experience is a sense of the crucial importance of love in the scheme of things. But while those who penetrate the symbolism of the poem may be led to apprehend the harmonic quality in the universe that is suggested particularly in the dawn vision of the spirits, travelling back and forth between the earth and the sun, the poem can, for others who read it simply as a straightforward narrative, display rather the riddling nature of a universe where self-contradictions abound: where at one moment spirits seem to be settling one's fate by playing dice and at another a series of disasters occur which might seem to be a disproportionate punishment for a thoughtless act by a single member of society. It was for this reason, no doubt, that to his later versions of the poem Coleridge attached the prose glosses, written in the persona of a later scribe, which explain the events of the poem in terms of a more orthodox Christian set of doctrines.

Coleridge's own position, caught between the attractions of a set of doctrines that gave an imaginative interpretation of human experience and a more sceptical self which could sympathize with those who read the poem simply as a dramatization of the self-contradictory nature of the universe, was in some respects similar to, though not identical with, that of his own hero. John Sterling, writing thirty years later, was to see the figure of the Mariner as a key to an essential quality in the poet's own character – and even in his manner:

> It is painful to observe in Coleridge, that, with all the kindness and glorious far-seeing intelligence of his eye, there is a glare in it, a light half unearthly, half morbid. It is the glittering eye of the Ancient Mariner.

More recently, T. S. Eliot has put the same point in a different way:

> . . . for a few years Coleridge had been visited by the Muse (I know of no poet to whom this hackneyed metaphor is better applicable) and thenceforth was a haunted man.

# The Rime of the Ancyent Marinere,[1]

## in Seven Parts

### Argument

How a Ship having passed the Line was driven by Storms to the cold
Country towards the South Pole; and how from thence she made her
course to the tropical Latitude of the Great Pacific Ocean; and of the
strange things that befell; and in what manner the Ancyent Marinere
came back to his own Country.

I

It is an ancient Marinere,
   And he stoppeth one of three:
'By thy long grey beard and thy glittering eye
   'Now wherefore stoppest me?

'The Bridegroom's doors are open'd wide       5
   'And I am next of kin;
'The Guests are met, the Feast is set, –
   'May'st hear the merry din.

But still he holds the wedding-guest –
   There was a Ship, quoth he –       10
'Nay, if thou'st got a laughsome tale,
   'Marinere! come with me.'

He holds him with his skinny hand,
   Quoth he, there was a Ship –
'Now get thee hence, thou grey-beard Loon!       15
   'Or my Staff shall make thee skip.

[1]The text on the left-hand pages here follows the first version, published in 1798, that on the
right-hand the version in *Sibylline Leaves* (1817), as reprinted, with minor alterations, in the
*Poetical Works* of 1828. This was a poem that Coleridge constantly revised: Jack Stillinger has
counted thirteen separate states. ('How many Mariners did Coleridge write?' *Studies in
Romanticism* XXXI (1992) 127–46). The differences between the versions here display the
two major areas of revision: the modernizing of the language and the introduction of the
interpreting glosses. See the Appendix (p. 491) for further notes, including one on his use of
older words.

# The Rime of the Ancient Mariner

## in Seven Parts

Facile credo, plures esse Naturas invisibiles quam visibiles in rerum universitate. Sed horum omnium familiam quis nobis enarrabit? et gradus et cognationes et discrimina et singulorum munera? Quid agunt? quae loca habitant? Harum rerum notitiam semper ambivit ingenium humanum, nunquam attigit. Juvat, interea, non diffiteor, quandoque in animo, tanquam in Tabulâ, majoris et melioris mundi imaginem contemplari: ne mens assuefacta hodiernae vitae minutiis se contrahat nimis, & tota subsidat in pusillas cogitationes. Sed veritati interea invigilandum est, modusque servandus, ut certa ab incertis, diem a nocte, distinguamus. – T. BURNET, *Archaeol. Phil.* p. 68.[1]

### PART THE FIRST

An ancient Mariner meeteth three Gallants bidden to a wedding-feast, and detaineth one.

It is an ancient Mariner,
And he stoppeth one of three.
'By thy long grey beard and glittering eye,
Now wherefore stopp'st thou me?

The Bridegroom's doors are opened wide,    5
And I am next of kin;
The guests are met, the feast is set:
May'st hear the merry din.'

He holds him with his skinny hand,
'There was a ship,' quoth he.    10
'Hold off! unhand me, greybeard loon!'
Eftsoons his hand dropt he.

---

[1]Tr.: I can easily believe, that there are more invisible than visible beings in the universe . . . But who will explain to us this great family – their ranks, their relationships, their differences and their respective functions? [What do they do, and where do they live? – *S.T.C.'s addition*] Human cleverness has always sought knowledge of these things, never attained it. At the same time I do not deny the pleasure of sometimes contemplating, as in a picture, the image of a greater and better world; lest the mind, inured to the details of everyday life, should contract and sink down into paltry thoughts. But meanwhile we must be vigilant for truth and observe proportion, so that we can distinguish the certain from the uncertain, day from night.

He holds him with his glittering eye —
  The wedding guest stood still
And listens like a three year's child;
  The Marinere hath his will.                    20

The wedding-guest sate on a stone,
  He cannot chuse but hear:
And thus spake on that ancyent man,
  The bright-eyed Marinere.

The Ship was cheer'd, the Harbour clear'd —     25
  Merrily did we drop
Below the Kirk, below the Hill,
  Below the Light-house top.

The Sun came up upon the left,
  Out of the Sea came he:                        30
And he shone bright, and on the right
  Went down into the Sea.

Higher and higher every day,
  Till over the mast at noon —
The wedding-guest here beat his breast,          35
  For he heard the loud bassoon.

The Bride hath pac'd into the Hall,
  Red as a rose is she;
Nodding their heads before her goes
  The merry Minstralsy.                          40

The wedding-guest he beat his breast,
  Yet he cannot chuse but hear:
And thus spake on that ancyent Man,
  The bright-eyed Marinere.

Listen, Stranger! Storm and Wind,               45
  A Wind and Tempest strong!
For days and weeks it play'd us freaks —
  Like Chaff we drove along.

The Wedding-Guest is spellbound by the eye of the old sea-faring man, and constrained to hear his tale.

He holds him with his glittering eye —
The Wedding-Guest stood still,
And listens like a three years child:                    15
The Mariner hath his will.

The Wedding-Guest sat on a stone:
He cannot chuse but hear;
And thus spake on that ancient man,
The bright-eyed Mariner.                                  20

The ship was cheered, the harbour cleared,
Merrily did we drop
Below the kirk, below the hill,
Below the light house top.

The Mariner tells how the ship sailed southward with a good wind and fair weather, till it reached the Line.

The Sun came up upon the left,                            25
Out of the sea came he!
And he shone bright, and on the right
Went down into the sea.

Higher and higher every day,
Till over the mast at noon —                              30
The Wedding-Guest here beat his breast,
For he heard the loud bassoon.

The Wedding-Guest heareth the bridal music; but the Mariner continueth his tale.

The bride hath paced into the hall,
Red as a rose is she;
Nodding their heads before her goes                       35
The merry minstrelsy.

The Wedding-Guest he beat his breast,
Yet he cannot chuse but hear;
And thus spake on that ancient man,
The bright-eyed Mariner.                                   40

The ship drawn by a storm toward the south pole

And now the STORM-BLAST came, and he
Was tyrannous and strong:
He struck with his o'ertaking wings,
And chased us south along.

Listen, Stranger! Mist and Snow,
    And it grew wond'rous cauld:                    50
And Ice mast-high came floating by
    As green as Emerauld.

And thro' the drifts the snowy clifts,
    Did send a dismal sheen;
Ne shapes of men ne beasts we ken –              55
    The Ice was all between.

The Ice was here, the Ice was there,
    The ice was all around:
It crack'd and growl'd, and roar'd and
        howl'd –
    Like noises of a swound.                       60

At length did cross an Albatross,
    Thorough the Fog it came;
And an it were a Christian Soul,
    We hail'd it in God's name.

The Marineres gave it biscuit-worms,             65
    And round and round it flew:
The Ice did split with a Thunder-fit;
    The Helmsman steer'd us thro'.

And a good south wind sprung up behind,
    The Albatross did follow;                      70
And every day for food or play
    Came to the Marinere's hollo!

In mist or cloud on mast or shroud
    It perch'd for vespers nine,
Whiles all the night thro' fog smoke-white        75
    Glimmer'd the white moon-shine.

With sloping masts and dipping prow,          45
As who pursued with yell and blow
Still treads the shadow of his foe,
And forward bends his head,
The ship drove fast, loud roared the blast,
And southward aye we fled                     50

And now there came both mist and snow,
And it grew wondrous cold:
And ice, mast-high, came floating by,
As green as emerald.

The land of ice, and
of fearful sounds
where no living thing
was to be seen.
And through the drifts the snowy clifts        55
Did send a dismal sheen:
Nor shapes of men nor beasts we ken –
The ice was all between.

The ice was here, the ice was there,
The ice was all around:                        60
It cracked and growled, and roared and
          howled,
Like noises in a swound!

Till a great sea-bird,
called the Albatross,
came through the
snow-fog, and was
received with great
joy and hospitality.
At length did cross an Albatross,
Thorough the fog it came;
As if it had been a Christian soul,            65
We hailed it in God's name.

It ate the food it ne'er had eat,
And round and round it flew.
The ice did split with a thunder-fit;
The helmsman steered us through!               70

And lo! the Albatross
proveth a bird of
good omen, and
followeth the ship as
it returned north-
ward through fog
and floating ice.
And a good south wind sprung up behind;
The Albatross did follow,
And every day, for food or play,
Came to the mariners' hollo!

In mist or cloud, on mast or shroud,           75
It perched for vespers nine;
Whiles all the night, through fog-smoke white,
Glimmered the white Moon-shine.

'God save thee, ancient Marinere!
  'From the fiends that plague thee thus –
'Why look'st thou so?' – with my cross bow
  I shot the Albatross.                                    80


II

The Sun came up upon the right,
  Out of the Sea came he;
And broad as a weft upon the left
  Went down into the Sea.


And the good south wind still blew behind,         85
  But no sweet Bird did follow
Ne any day for food or play
  Came to the Marinere's hollo!


And I had done a hellish thing
  And it would work 'em woe;                             90
For all averr'd, I had kill'd the Bird,
  That made the Breeze to blow.


Ne dim ne red, like God's own head,
  The glorious Sun uprist:
Then all averr'd, I had kill'd the Bird               95
  That brought the fog and mist.
'Twas right, said they, such birds to slay
  That bring the fog and mist.


The breezes blew, the white foam flew
  The furrow follow'd free:                            100
We were the first that ever burst
  Into that silent Sea.


Down dropt the breeze, the Sails dropt down,
  'Twas sad as sad could be
And we did speak only to break                       105
  The silence of the Sea.

The ancient Mariner inhospitably killeth the pious bird of good omen.

'God save thee, ancient Mariner!
From the fiends, that plague thee thus! –                    80
Why look'st thou so?' – With my cross-bow
I shot the ALBATROSS.


### PART THE SECOND

The Sun now rose upon the right:
Out of the sea came he,
Still hid in mist, and on the left                          85
Went down into the sea.

And the good south wind still blew behind,
But no sweet bird did follow,
Nor any day for food or play
Came to the mariners' hollo!                                90

His shipmates cry out against the ancient Mariner, for killing the bird of good luck.

And I had done a hellish thing,
And it would work 'em woe:
For all averred, I had killed the bird
That made the breeze to blow.
Ah wretch! said they, the bird to slay                      95
That made the breeze to blow!

But when the fog cleared off, they justify the same, and thus make themselves accomplices in the crime.

Nor dim nor red, like God's own head,
The glorious Sun uprist:
Then all averred, I had killed the bird
That brought the fog and mist.                              100
'Twas right, said they, such birds to slay,
That bring the fog and mist.

The fair breeze continues; the ship enters the Pacific Ocean, and sails northward, even till it reaches the Line.

The fair breeze blew, the white foam flew,
The furrow followed free;
We were the first that ever burst                           105
Into that silent sea.

The ship hath been suddenly becalmed.

Down dropt the breeze, the sails dropt down,
'Twas sad as sad could be;
And we did speak only to break
The silence of the sea!                                     110

All in a hot and copper sky
　　The bloody sun at noon,
Right up above the mast did stand,
　　No bigger than the moon.                                        110

Day after day, day after day,
　　We stuck, ne breath ne motion,
As idle as a painted Ship
　　Upon a painted Ocean.

Water, water, every where                                          115
　　And all the boards did shrink;
Water, water every where,
　　Ne any drop to drink.

The very deeps did rot: O Christ!
　　That ever this should be!                                      120
Yea, slimy things did crawl with legs
　　Upon the slimy Sea.

About, about, in reel and rout
　　The Death-fires danc'd at night;
The water, like a witch's oils,                                    125
　　Burnt green and blue and white.

And some in dreams assured were
　　Of the Spirit that plagued us so:
Nine fathom deep he had follow'd us
　　From the Land of Mist and Snow.                                130

And every tongue thro' utter drouth
　　Was wither'd at the root;
We could not speak no more than if
　　We had been choked with soot.

Ah wel-a-day! what evil looks                                      135
　　Had I from old and young;
Instead of the Cross the Albat̲ ̲s
　　About my neck was hung.

All in a hot and copper sky,
The bloody Sun, at noon,
Right up above the mast did stand,
No bigger than the Moon.

Day after day, day after day,                    115
We stuck, nor breath nor motion;
As idle as a painted ship
Upon a painted ocean.

And the Albatross
begins to be avenged.

Water, water, every where,
And all the boards did shrink;                    120
Water, water, every where,
Nor any drop to drink.

The very deep did rot: O Christ!
That ever this should be!
Yea, slimy things did crawl with legs            125
Upon the slimy sea.

About, about, in reel and rout
The death-fires danced at night;
The water, like a witch's oils,
Burnt green, and blue and white.                  130

A Spirit had followed
them; one of the
invisible inhabitants
of this planet, neither
departed souls nor
angels; concerning

And some in dreams assuréd were
Of the spirit that plagued us so;
Nine fathom deep he had followed us
From the land of mist and snow.

whom the learned Jew, Josephus, and the Platonic Constantinopolitan, Michael Psellus, may
be consulted. They are very numerous, and there is no climate or element without one or more.

And every tongue, through utter drought,         135
Was withered at the root;
We could not speak, no more than if
We had been choked with soot.

The shipmates, in
their sore distress,
would fain throw the
whole guilt on the
ancient Mariner: in
sign whereof they

Ah! well a-day! what evil looks
Had I from old and young!                         140
Instead of the cross, the Albatross
About my neck was hung.

hang the dead sea-bird round his neck.

### III

I saw a something in the Sky
   No bigger than my fist;                   140
At first it seem'd a little speck
   And then it seem'd a mist:
It mov'd and mov'd, and took at last
   A certain shape, I wist.

A speck, a mist, a shape, I wist!            145
   And still it ner'd and ner'd;
And, an it dodg'd a water-sprite,
   It plung'd and tack'd and veer'd.

With throat unslack'd, with black lips bak'd
   Ne could we laugh, ne wail:          150
Then while thro' drouth all dumb they stood
I bit my arm and suck'd the blood
   And cry'd, A sail! a sail!

With throat unslack'd, with black lips bak'd
   Agape they hear'd me call:         155
Gramercy! they for joy did grin
And all at once their breath drew in
   As they were drinking all.

She doth not tack from side to side –
   Hither to work us weal           160
Withouten wind, withouten tide
   She steddies with upright keel.

The western wave was all a flame,
   The day was well nigh done!
Almost upon the western wave
   Rested the broad bright Sun;      165
When that strange shape drove suddenly
   Betwixt us and the Sun.

PART THE THIRD

There passed a weary time. Each throat
Was parched, and glazed each eye.
A weary time! a weary time!                          145
How glazed each weary eye,
When looking westward, I beheld
A something in the sky.

At first it seemed a little speck,
And then it seemed a mist;                           150
It moved and moved, and took at last
A certain shape, I wist.

A speck, a mist, a shape, I wist!
And still it neared and neared:
As if it dodged a water-sprite,                      155
It plunged and tacked and veered.

With throats unslaked, with black lips baked,
We could nor laugh nor wail;
Through utter drought all dumb we stood!
I bit my arm, I sucked the blood,                    160
And cried, A sail! a sail!

With throats unslaked, with black lips baked,
Agape they heard me call:
Gramercy! they for joy did grin,
And all at once their breath drew in,                165
As they were drinking all.

See! see! (I cried) she tacks no more!
Hither to work us weal;
Without a breeze, without a tide,
She steadies with upright keel!                      170

The western wave was all a-flame.
The day was well nigh done!
Almost upon the western wave
Rested the broad bright Sun;
When that strange shape drove suddenly               175
Betwixt us and the Sun.

The ancient Mariner beholdeth a sign in the element afar off.

At its nearer approach, it seemeth to him to be a ship; and at a dear ransom he freeth his speech from the bonds of thirst.

A flash of joy;

And horror follows. For can it be a ship that comes onward without wind or tide?

And strait the Sun was fleck'd with bars
   (Heaven's mother send us grace)                    170
As if thro' a dungeon grate he peer'd
   With broad and burning face.

Alas! (thought I, and my heart beat loud)
   How fast she neres and neres!
Are those *her* Sails that glance in the Sun           175
   Like restless gossameres?

Are those *her* naked ribs, which fleck'd
   The sun that did behind them peer?
And are these two all, all the crew,
   That woman and her fleshless Pheere?                180

*His* bones were black with many a crack,
   All black and bare, I ween;
Jet-black and bare, save where with rust
Of mouldy damps and charnel crust
   They're patch'd with purple and green.              185

*Her* lips are red, *her* looks are free,
   *Her* locks are yellow as gold:
Her skin is as white as leprosy,
And she is far liker Death than he;
   Her flesh makes the still air cold.                 190

The naked Hulk alongside came
   And the Twain were playing dice;
'The Game is done! I've won, I've won!'
   Quoth she, and whistled thrice.

A gust of wind sterte up behind,                       195
   And whistled thro' his bones;
Thro' the holes of his eyes and the hole of his mouth
   Half-whistles and half-groans.

With never a whisper in the Sea
   Oft darts the Spectre-ship;                        200
While clombe above the Eastern bar
The horned Moon, with one bright Star
   Almost atween the tips.

And straight the Sun was flecked with bars,
(Heaven's Mother send us grace!)
As if through a dungeon-grate he peered
With broad and burning face.                    180

*It seemeth him but the skeleton of a ship.*

Alas! (thought I, and my heart beat loud)
How fast she nears and nears!
Are those *her* sails that glance in the Sun,
Like restless gossameres?

Are those *her* ribs through which the Sun    185
Did peer, as through a grate?
And is that Woman all her crew?
Is that a DEATH? and are there two?
Is DEATH that woman's mate?

*And its ribs are seen as bars on the face of the setting Sun.*

*The spectre-woman and her death-mate, and no other on board the skeleton ship.*

*Like vessel, like crew!*

*Her* lips were red, *her* looks were free,         190
Her locks were yellow as gold:
Her skin was as white as leprosy,
The Night-mare LIFE-IN-DEATH was she,
Who thicks man's blood with cold.

*DEATH and LIFE-IN-DEATH have diced for the ship's crew, and she (the latter) winneth the ancient Mariner.*

The naked hulk alongside came,                  195
And the twain were casting dice;
'The game is done! I've won! I've won!'
Quoth she, and whistles thrice.

*No twilight within the courts of the sun.*

The Sun's rim dips; the stars rush out:
At one stride comes the dark;                    200
With far-heard whisper, o'er the sea,
Off shot the spectre-bark.

*At the rising of the Moon,*

We listened and looked sideways up!
Fear at my heart, as at a cup,
My life-blood seemed to sip!                      205
The stars were dim, and thick the night,
The steersman's face by his lamp gleamed
          white;
From the sails the dew did drip —
Till clomb above the eastern bar
The hornéd Moon, with one bright star          210
Within the nether tip.

One after one by the horned Moon
   (Listen, O Stranger! to me)             205
Each turn'd his face with a ghastly pang
   And curs'd me with his ee.

Four times fifty living men,
   With never a sigh or groan,
With heavy thump, a lifeless lump         210
   They dropp'd down one by one.

Their souls did from their bodies fly, –
   They fled to bliss or woe;
And every soul it pass'd me by,
   Like the whiz of my Cross-bow.       215

IV

'I fear thee, ancyent Marinere!
   'I fear thy skinny hand;
'And thou art long and lank and brown
   'As is the ribb'd Sea-sand.

'I fear thee and thy glittering eye       220
   'And thy skinny hand so brown –
Fear not, fear not, thou wedding guest!
   This body dropt not down.

Alone, alone, all all alone
   Alone on the wide wide Sea;       225
And Christ would take no pity on
   My soul in agony.

The many men so beautiful,
   And they all dead did lie!
And a million million slimy things      230
   Liv'd on – and so did I.

One after another,

> One after one, by the star-dogged Moon,
> Too quick for groan or sigh,
> Each turned his face with a ghastly pang,
> And cursed me with his eye.                    215

His shipmates drop down dead.

> Four times fifty living men,
> (And I heard nor sigh nor groan)
> With heavy thump, a lifeless lump,
> They dropped down one by one.

But LIFE-IN-DEATH begins her work on the ancient Mariner.

> The souls did from their bodies fly, —          220
> They fled to bliss or woe!
> And every soul, it passed me by,
> Like the whizz of my cross-bow!

## PART THE FOURTH

The wedding-guest feareth that a spirit is talking to him;

> 'I fear thee, ancient Mariner!
> I fear thy skinny hand!                          225
> And thou art long, and lank, and brown,
> As is the ribbed sea-sand.[1]

> I fear thee and thy glittering eye,
> And thy skinny hand, so brown.' —

But the ancient Mariner assureth him of his bodily life, and proceedeth to relate his horrible penance.

> Fear not, fear not, thou Wedding-Guest!          230
> This body dropt not down.

> Alone, alone, all, all alone,
> Alone on a wide wide sea!
> And never a saint took pity on
> My soul in agony.                                235

He despiseth the creatures of the calm,

> The many men, so beautiful!
> And they all dead did lie:
> And a thousand thousand slimy things
> Lived on; and so did I.

---

[1] For the last two lines of this stanza, I am indebted to Mr WORDSWORTH. It was on a delightful walk from Nether Stowey to Dulverton, with him and his sister, in the Autumn of 1797, that this Poem was planned, and in part composed. [S.T.C.]

I look'd upon the rotting Sea,
   And drew my eyes away;
I look'd upon the eldritch deck,
   And there the dead men lay.                        235

I look'd to Heaven, and try'd to pray;
   But or ever a prayer had gusht,
A wicked whisper came and made
   My heart as dry as dust.

I clos'd my lids and kept them close,              240
   Till the balls like pulses beat;
For the sky and the sea, and the sea and the
      sky
Lay like a load on my weary eye,
   And the dead were at my feet.

The cold sweat melted from their limbs,           245
   Ne rot, ne reek did they;
The look with which they look'd on me,
   Had never pass'd away.

An orphan's curse would drag to Hell
   A spirit from on high:                           250
But O! more horrible than that
   Is the curse in a dead man's eye!
Seven days, seven nights I saw that curse,
   And yet I could not die.

The moving Moon went up the sky                    255
   And no where did abide:
Softly she was going up
   And a star or two beside —

Her beams bemock'd the sultry main
   Like morning frosts yspread;                     260
But where the ship's huge shadow lay,
The charmed water burnt alway
   A still and awful red.

And envieth that
they should live, and
so many lie dead.

I looked upon the rotting sea,                    240
And drew my eyes away;
I looked upon the rotting deck,
And there the dead men lay.

I looked to Heaven, and tried to pray;
But or ever a prayer had gusht,                   245
A wicked whisper came, and made
My heart as dry as dust.

I closed my lids, and kept them close,
And the balls like pulses beat;
For the sky and the sea, and the sea and the
        sky                                       250
Lay like a load on my weary eye,
And the dead were at my feet.

But the curse liveth
for him in the eye of
the dead men.

The cold sweat melted from their limbs,
Nor rot nor reek did they:
The look with which they looked on me             255
Had never passed away.

An orphan's curse would drag to Hell
A spirit from on high;
But oh! more horrible than that
Is the curse in a dead man's eye!                 260
Seven days, seven nights, I saw that curse,
And yet I could not die.

In his loneliness and
fixedness he yearneth
towards the journey-
ing Moon, and the
stars that still
sojourn, yet still
move onward; and

The moving Moon went up the sky,
And no where did abide:
Softly she was going up,                          265
And a star or two beside –

every where the blue sky belongs to them, and is their appointed rest, and their native country
and their own natural homes, which they enter unannounced, as lords that are certainly
expected and yet there is a silent joy at their arrival.

Her beams bemocked the sultry main,
Like April hoar-frost spread;
But where the ship's huge shadow lay,
The charméd water burnt alway                     270
A still and awful red.

Beyond the shadow of the ship
  I watch'd the water-snakes:            265
They mov'd in tracks of shining white;
And when they rear'd, the elfish light
  Fell off in hoary flakes.

Within the shadow of the ship
  I watch'd their rich attire:            270
Blue, glossy green, and velvet black
They coil'd and swam; and every track
  Was a flash of golden fire.

O happy living things! no tongue
  Their beauty might declare:            275
A spring of love gusht from my heart,
  And I bless'd them unaware!
Sure my kind saint took pity on me,
  And I bless'd them unaware.

The self-same moment I could pray;         280
  And from my neck so free
The Albatross fell off, and sank
  Like lead into the sea.

### V

O sleep, it is a gentle thing
  Belov'd from pole to pole!           285
To Mary-queen the praise be yeven
She sent the gentle sleep from heaven
  That slid into my soul.

The silly buckets on the deck
  That had so long remain'd,          290
I dreamt that they were fill'd with dew
  And when I awoke it rain'd.

My lips were wet, my throat was cold,
  My garments all were dank;
Sure I had drunken in my dreams         295
  And still my body drank.

By the light of the
Moon he beholdeth
God's creatures of
the great calm.

Beyond the shadow of the ship,
I watched the water-snakes:
They moved in tracks of shining white,
And when they reared, the elfish light          275
Fell off in hoary flakes.

Within the shadow of the ship
I watched their rich attire:
Blue, glossy green, and velvet black,
They coiled and swam; and every track          280
Was a flash of golden fire.

Their beauty and
their happiness.

O happy living things! no tongue
Their beauty might declare:
A spring of love gushed from my heart,

He blesseth them in
his heart.

And I blessed them unaware:                     285
Sure my kind saint took pity on me,
And I blessed them unaware.

The spells begins to
break.

The self same moment I could pray;
And from my neck so free
The Albatross fell off, and sank                290
Like lead into the sea.

## PART THE FIFTH

O sleep! it is a gentle thing,
Beloved from pole to pole!
To Mary Queen the praise be given!
She sent the gentle sleep from Heaven,          295
That slid into my soul.

By grace of the holy
Mother, the ancient
Mariner is refreshed
with rain.

The silly buckets on the deck,
That had so long remained,
I dreamt that they were filled with dew;
And when I awoke, it rained.                     300

My lips were wet, my throat was cold,
My garments all were dank;
Sure I had drunken in my dreams,
And still my body drank.

I mov'd and could not feel my limbs,
  I was so light, almost
I thought that I had died in sleep,
  And was a blessed Ghost.                                    300

The roaring wind! it roar'd far off,
  It did not come anear;
But with its sound it shook the sails
  That were so thin and sere.

The upper air bursts into life,                               305
  And a hundred fire-flags sheen
To and fro they are hurried about;
And to and fro, and in and out
  The stars dance on between.

The coming wind doth roar more loud;                          310
  The sails do sigh, like sedge:
The rain pours down from one black cloud
  And the Moon is at its edge.

Hark! hark! the thick black cloud is cleft,
  And the Moon is at its side:                                315
Like waters shot from some high crag,
The lightning falls with never a jag
  A river steep and wide.

The strong wind reach'd the ship: it roar'd
  And dropp'd down, like a stone!                             320
Beneath the lightning and the moon
  The dead men gave a groan.

They groan'd, they stirr'd, they all uprose,
  Ne spake, ne mov'd their eyes:
It had been strange, even in a dream                          325
  To have seen those dead men rise.

The helmsman steerd, the ship mov'd on;
  Yet never a breeze up-blew;
The Marineres all 'gan work the ropes,
  Where they were wont to do:                                 330
They rais'd their limbs like lifeless tools —
  We were a ghastly crew.

I moved, and could not feel my limbs:           305
I was so light – almost
I thought that I had died in sleep,
And was a blesséd ghost.

He heareth sounds
and seeth strange
sights and commo-
tions in the sky and
the element.

And soon I heard a roaring wind:
It did not come anear;                          310
But with its sound it shook the sails,
That were so thin and sere.

The upper air burst into life!
And a hundred fire-flags sheen,
To and fro they were hurried about!             315
And to and fro, and in and out,
The wan stars danced between.

And the coming wind did roar more loud,
And the sails did sigh like sedge;
And the rain poured down from one black
        cloud;
The Moon was at its edge.                       320

The thick black cloud was cleft, and still
The Moon was at its side:
Like waters shot from some high crag,
The lightning fell with never a jag,            325
A river steep and wide.

The bodies of the
ship's crew are
inspirited, and the
ship moves on;

The loud wind never reached the ship,
Yet now the ship moved on!
Beneath the lightning and the Moon
The dead men gave a groan.                      330

They groaned, they stirred, they all uprose,
Nor spake, nor moved their eyes;
It had been strange, even in a dream,
To have seen those dead men rise.

The helmsman steered, the ship moved on;        335
Yet never a breeze up blew;
The mariners all 'gan work the ropes,
Where they were wont to do;
They raised their limbs like lifeless tools –
We were a ghastly crew.                         340

The body of my brother's son
  Stood by me knee to knee:
The body and I pull'd at one rope,                    335
  But he said nought to me —
And I quak'd to think of my own voice
  How frightful it would be!


The day-light dawn'd — they drop'd their
    arms,
  And cluster'd round the mast:                   340
Sweet sounds rose slowly thro' their mouths
  And from their bodies pass'd.


Around, around, flew each sweet sound,
  Then darted to the sun:
Slowly the sounds came back again                     345
  Now mix'd, now one by one.


Sometimes a dropping from the sky
  I heard the Lavrock sing;
Sometimes all little birds that are
How they seem'd to fill the sea and air               350
  With their sweet jargoning,


And now 'twas like all instruments,
  Now like a lonely flute;
And now it is an angel's song
  That makes the heavens be mute.                  355


It ceas'd: yet still the sails made on
  A pleasant noise till noon,
A noise like of a hidden brook
  In the leafy month of June,
That to the sleeping woods all night                  360
  Singeth a quiet tune.

The body of my brother's son
Stood by me, knee to knee:
The body and I pulled at one rope,
But he said nought to me.

'I fear thee, ancient Mariner!'                    345
Be calm, thou Wedding-Guest!
'Twas not those souls that fled in pain,
Which to their corses came again,
But a troop of spirits blest:

For when it dawned – they dropped their
        arms,
And clustered round the mast;                      350
Sweet sounds rose slowly through their
        mouths,
And from their bodies passed.

Around, around, flew each sweet sound,
Then darted to the Sun;
Slowly the sounds came back again,                 355
Now mixed, now one by one.

Sometimes a-dropping from the sky
I heard the sky-lark sing;
Sometimes all little birds that are,               360
How they seemed to fill the sea and air
With their sweet jargoning!

And now 'twas like all instruments,
Now like a lonely flute;
And now it is an angel's song,                     365
That makes the Heavens be mute.

It ceased; yet still the sails made on
A pleasant noise till noon,
A noise like of a hidden brook
In the leafy month of June,                        370
That to the sleeping woods all night
Singeth a quiet tune.

*But not by the souls of the men, nor by dæmons of earth or middle air, but by a blessed troop of angelic spirits, sent down by the invocation of the guardian saint.*

Listen, O listen, thou Wedding-guest!
  'Marinere! thou hast thy will:
'For that, which comes out of thine eye, doth make
  'My body and soul to be still.'          365

Never sadder tale was told
  To a man of woman born:
Sadder and wiser thou wedding-guest!
  Thou'lt rise to morrow morn.

Never sadder tale was heard          370
  By a man of woman born:
The Marineres all return'd to work
  As silent as beforne.

The Marineres all 'gan pull the ropes,
  But look at me they n'old:          375
Thought I, I am as thin as air —
  They cannot me behold.

Till noon we silently sail'd on
  Yet never a breeze did breathe:
Slowly and smoothly went the ship          380
  Mov'd onward from beneath.

Under the keel nine fathom deep
  From the land of mist and snow
The spirit slid: and it was He
  That made the Ship to go.          385
The sails at noon left off their tune
  And the Ship stood still also.

The sun right up above the mast
  Had fix'd her to the ocean:
But in a minute she 'gan stir          390
  With a short uneasy motion —
Backwards and forwards half her length
  With a short uneasy motion.

Then, like a pawing horse let go,
  She made a sudden bound:          395
It flung the blood into my head,
  And I fell into a swound.

Till noon we quietly sailed on,
Yet never a breeze did breathe:
Slowly and smoothly went the ship,                 375
Moved onward from beneath.

The lonesome spirit
from the south pole
carries on the ship
as far as the line,
in obedience to
the angelic troop,
but still requireth
vengeance.

Under the keel nine fathom deep,
From the land of mist and snow,
The spirit slid: and it was he
That made the ship to go.                          380
The sails at noon left off their tune,
And the ship stood still also.

The Sun, right up above the mast,
Had fixed her to the ocean:
But in a minute she 'gan stir,                     385
With a short uneasy motion –
Backwards and forwards half her length
With a short uneasy motion.

Then like a pawing horse let go,
She made a sudden bound:                            390
It flung the blood into my head,
And I fell down in a swound.

How long in that same fit I lay,
    I have not to declare;
But ere my living life return'd,
I heard and in my soul discern'd                    400
    Two voices in the air,

'Is it he? quoth one, 'Is this the man?
    'By him who died on cross,
'With his cruel bow he lay'd full low             405
    'The harmless Albatross.

'The spirit who bideth by himself
    'In the land of mist and snow,
'He lov'd the bird that lov'd the man
    'Who shot him with his bow.                    410

The other was a softer voice,
    As soft as honey-dew:
Quoth he the man hath penance done,
    And penance more will do.

## VI

### FIRST VOICE

'But tell me, tell me! speak again,               415
    'Thy soft response renewing —
'What makes that ship drive on so fast?
    'What is the Ocean doing?

### SECOND VOICE

'Still as a Slave before his Lord,
    'The Ocean hath no blast:                      420
'His great bright eye most silently
    'Up to the moon is cast —

'If he may know which way to go,
    'For she guides him smooth or grim.
'See, brother, see! how graciously               425
    'She looketh down on him.

The Polar Spirit's
fellow dæmons, the
invisible inhabitants
of the element, take
part in his wrong;
and two of them re-
late, one to the other,
that penance long
and heavy for the
ancient Mariner hath
been accorded to the
Polar Spirit, who re-
turneth southward.

How long in that same fit I lay,
I have not to declare;
But ere my living life returned,                    395
I heard and in my soul discerned
TWO VOICES in the air.

'Is it he?' quoth one. 'Is this the man?
By him who died on cross,
Wth his cruel bow he laid full low               400
The harmless Albatross.

The spirit who bideth by himself
In the land of mist and snow,
He loved the bird that loved the man
Who shot him with his bow.'                       405

The other was a softer voice,
As soft as honey-dew:
Quoth he, 'The man hath penance done,
And penance more will do.'

## PART THE SIXTH

### FIRST VOICE

But tell me, tell me! speak again,                 410
Thy soft response renewing –
What makes that ship drive on so fast?
What is the OCEAN doing?

### SECOND VOICE

Still as a slave before his lord,
The OCEAN hath no blast;                           415
His great bright eye most silently
Up to the Moon is cast –

If he may know which way to go;
For she guides him smooth or grim.
See, brother, see! how graciously                  420
She looketh down on him.

### FIRST VOICE

'But why drives on that ship so fast
　'Withouten wave or wind?

### SECOND VOICE

'The air is cut away before,
　'And closes from behind.                                    430

'Fly, brother, fly! more high, more high,
　'Or we shall be belated:
'For slow and slow that ship will go,
　'When the Marinere's trance is abated.'

I woke, and we were sailing on                               435
　As in a gentle weather:
'Twas night, calm night, the moon was high;
　The dead men stood together.

All stood together on the deck,
　For a charnel-dungeon fitter:                              440
All fix'd on me their stony eyes
　That in the moon did glitter.

The pang, the curse, with which they died,
　Had never pass'd away:
I could not draw my een from theirs                          445
　Ne turn them up to pray.

And in its time the spell was snapt,
　And I could move my een:
I look'd far-forth, but little saw
　Of what might else be seen.                                450

Like one, that on a lonely road
　Doth walk in fear and dread,
And having once turn'd round, walks on
　And turns no more his head:
Because he knows, a frightful fiend                          455
　Doth close behind him tread.

FIRST VOICE

*The Mariner hath been cast into a trance; for the angelic power causeth the vessel to drive northward faster than human life could endure.*

But why drives on that ship so fast,
Without or wave or wind?

SECOND VOICE

The air is cut away before,
And closes from behind.                    425

Fly, brother, fly! more high, more high!
Or we shall be belated:
For slow and slow that ship will go,
When the Mariner's trance is abated.

*The supernatural motion is retarded; the Mariner awakes, and his penance begins anew.*

I woke, and we were sailing on           430
As in a gentle weather:
'Twas night, calm night, the Moon was high;
The dead men stood together.

All stood together on the deck,
For a charnel-dungeon fitter:            435
All fixed on me their stony eyes,
That in the Moon did glitter.

The pang, the curse, with which they died,
Had never passed away:
I could not draw my eyes from theirs,    440
Nor turn them up to pray.

*The curse is finally expiated.*

And now this spell was snapt: once more
I viewed the ocean green,
And looked far forth, yet little saw
Of what had else been seen –            445

Like one, that on a lonesome road
Doth walk in fear and dread,
And having once turned round walks on,
And turns no more his head;
Because he knows, a frightful fiend      450
Doth close behind him tread.

But soon there breath'd a wind on me,
   Ne sound ne motion made:
Its path was not upon the sea
   In ripple or in shade.                                    460

It rais'd my hair, it fann'd my cheek,
   Like a meadow-gale of spring —
It mingled strangely with my fears,
   Yet it felt like a welcoming.

Swiftly, swiftly flew the ship,                                 465
   Yet she sail'd softly too:
Sweetly, sweetly blew the breeze —
   On me alone it blew.

O dream of joy! is this indeed
   The light-house top I see?                              470
Is this the Hill? Is this the Kirk?
   Is this mine own countrée?

We drifted o'er the Harbour-bar,
   And I with sobs did pray —
'O let me be awake, my God!                                     475
   'Or let me sleep alway!'

The harbour-bay was clear as glass,
   So smoothly it was strewn!
And on the bay the moon light lay,
   And the shadow of the moon.                             480

The moonlight bay was white all o'er,
   Till rising from the same,
Full many shapes, that shadows were,
   Like as of torches came.

A little distance from the prow                                 485
   Those dark-red shadows were;
But soon I saw that my own flesh
   Was red as in a glare.

But soon there breathed a wind on me,
Nor sound nor motion made:
Its path was not upon the sea,
In ripple or in shade.                                    455

It raised my hair, it fanned my cheek
Like a meadow-gale of spring –
It mingled strangely with my fears,
Yet it felt like a welcoming.

Swiftly, swiftly flew the ship,                           460
Yet she sailed softly too:
Sweetly, sweetly blew the breeze –
On me alone it blew.

And the ancient Mariner beholdeth his native country.

Oh! dream of joy! is this indeed
The light-house top I see?                                465
Is this the hill? is this the kirk?
Is this mine own countree?

We drifted o'er the harbour-bar,
And I with sobs did pray –
O let me be awake, my God!                                470
Or let me sleep alway.

The harbour-bay was clear as glass,
So smoothly it was strewn!
And on the bay the moonlight lay,
And the shadow of the Moon.                               475

I turn'd my head in fear and dread,
   And by the holy rood,               490
The bodies had advanc'd, and now
   Before the mast they stood.

They lifted up their stiff right arms,
   They held them strait and tight;
And each right-arm burnt like a torch,     495
   A torch that's borne upright.
Their stony eye-balls glitter'd on
   In the red and smoky light.

I pray'd and turn'd my head away
   Forth looking as before.            500
There was no breeze upon the bay,
   No wave against the shore.

The rock shone bright, the kirk no less
   That stands above the rock:
The moonlight steep'd in silentness     505
   The steady weathercock.

And the bay was white with silent light,
   Till rising from the same
Full many shapes, that shadows were,
   In crimson colours came.         510

A little distance from the prow
   Those crimson shadows were:
I turn'd my eyes upon the deck —
   O Christ! what saw I there?

Each corse lay flat, lifeless and flat;     515
   And by the Holy rood
A man all light, a seraph-man,
   On every corse there stood.

This seraph-band, each wav'd his hand:
   It was a heavenly sight:
They stood as signals to the land,     520
   Each one a lovely light:

The rock shone bright, the kirk no less,
That stands above the rock:
The moonlight steeped in silentness
The steady weathercock.

And the bay was white with silent light,          480
Till rising from the same,
Full many shapes, that shadows were,
In crimson colours came.

A little distance from the prow
Those crimson shadows were:                        485
I turned my eyes upon the deck –
Oh, Christ! what saw I there!

Each corse lay flat, lifeless and flat,
And, by the holy rood!
A man all light, a seraph-man,                     490
On every corse there stood.

This seraph-band, each waved his hand:
It was a heavenly sight!
They stood as signals to the land,
Each one a lovely light:                           495

The angelic spirits leave the dead bodies,

And appear in their own forms of light.

This seraph-band, each wav'd his hand,
    No voice did they impart —
No voice; but O! the silence sank,                              525
    Like music on my heart.

Eftsones I heard the dash of oars,
    I heard the pilot's cheer:
My head was turn'd perforce away
    And I saw a boat appear.                                    530

Then vanish'd all the lovely lights;
    The bodies rose anew:
With silent pace, each to his place,
    Came back the ghastly crew.
The wind, that shade nor motion made,                          535
    On me alone it blew.

The pilot, and the pilot's boy
    I heard them coming fast:
Dear Lord in Heaven! it was a joy,
    The dead men could not blast.                              540

I saw a third — I heard his voice:
    It is the Hermit good!
He singeth loud his godly hymns
    That he makes in the wood.
He'll shrieve my soul, he'll wash away                         545
    The Albatross's blood.

## VII

This Hermit good lives in that wood
    Which slopes down to the Sea.
How loudly his sweet voice he rears!
He loves to talk with Marineres                                550
    That come from a far Contrée.

He kneels at morn and noon and eve —
    He hath a cushion plump:
It is the moss, that wholly hides
    The rotted old Oak-stump.                                  555

This seraph-band, each waved his hand,
No voice did they impart –
No voice; but oh! the silence sank
Like music on my heart.

But soon I heard the dash of oars,                    500
I heard the Pilot's cheer;
My head was turned perforce away,
And I saw a boat appear.

The Pilot, and the Pilot's boy,
I heard them coming fast:                              505
Dear Lord in Heaven! it was a joy
The dead men could not blast.

I saw a third – I heard his voice:
It is the Hermit good!
He singeth loud his godly hymns                        510
That he makes in the wood.
He'll shrieve my soul, he'll wash away
The Albatross's blood.

### PART THE SEVENTH

The Hermit of the
Wood,

This Hermit good lives in that wood
Which slopes down to the sea.                          515
How loudly his sweet voice he rears!
He loves to talk with marineres
That come from a far countree.

He kneels at morn, and noon and eve –
He hath a cushion plump:                               520
It is the moss that wholly hides
The rotted old oak-stump.

The Skiff-boat ne'rd: I heard them talk,
   'Why, this is strange, I trow!
'Where are those lights so many and fair
   'That signal made but now?

'Strange, by my faith! the Hermit said —        560
   'And they answer'd not our cheer.
'The planks look warp'd, and see those sails
   'How thin they are and sere!
'I never saw aught like to them
   'Unless perchance it were        565

'The skeletons of leaves that lag
   'My forest brook along:
'When the Ivy-tod is heavy with snow,
'And the Owlet whoops to the wolf below
   'That eats the she-wolf's young.        570

'Dear Lord! it has a fiendish look —
   (The Pilot made reply)
'I am a-fear'd. — 'Push on, push on![']
   Said the Hermit cheerily.

The Boat came closer to the Ship,        575
   But I ne spake ne stirr'd!
The Boat came close beneath the Ship,
   And strait a sound was heard!

Under the water it rumbled on,
   Still louder and more dread:        580
It reach'd the Ship, it split the bay;
   The Ship went down like lead.

Stunn'd by that loud and dreadful sound,
   Which sky and ocean smote:
Like one that hath been seven days drown'd        585
   My body lay afloat:
But, swift as dreams, myself I found
   Within the Pilot's boat.

The skiff-boat neared: I heard them talk,
'Why, this is strange, I trow!
Where are those lights so many and fair,    525
That signal made but now?'

Approacheth the
ship with wonder.

'Strange, by my faith!' the Hermit said —
'And they answered not our cheer!
The planks looked warped! and see those
    sails,
How thin they are and sere!    530
I never saw aught like to them,
Unless perchance it were

Brown skeletons of leaves that lag
My forest-brook along;
When the ivy-tod is heavy with snow,    535
And the owlet whoops to the wolf below,
That eats the she-wolf's young.'

'Dear Lord! it hath a fiendish look —
(The Pilot made reply)
I am a-feared' — 'Push on, push on!'    540
Said the Hermit cheerily.

The boat came closer to the ship,
But I nor spake nor stirred;
The boat came close beneath the ship,
And straight a sound was heard.    545

The ship suddenly
sinketh.

Under the water it rumbled on,
Still louder and more dread:
It reached the ship, it split the bay;
The ship went down like lead.

The ancient Mariner
is saved in the
Pilot's boat.

Stunned by that loud and dreadful sound,    550
Which sky and ocean smote,
Like one that hath been seven days drowned
My body lay afloat;
But swift as dreams, myself I found
Within the Pilot's boat.    555

Upon the whirl, where sank the Ship,
    The boat spun round and round:                                 590
And all was still, save that the hill
    Was telling of the sound.

I mov'd my lips: the Pilot shriek'd
    And fell down in a fit.
The Holy Hermit rais'd his eyes                                   595
    And pray'd where he did sit.

I took the oars: the Pilot's boy,
    Who now doth crazy go,
Laugh'd loud and long, and all the while
    His eyes went to and fro,                                     600
'Ha! ha!' quoth he – 'full plain I see,
    'The devil knows how to row.'

And now all in mine own Countrée
    I stood on the firm land!
The Hermit stepp'd forth from the boat,                           605
    And scarcely he could stand.

'O shrieve me, shrieve me, holy Man!
    The Hermit cross'd his brow –
'Say quick,' quoth he, 'I bid thee say
    'What manner man art thou?                                    610

Forthwith this frame of mine was wrench'd
    With a woeful agony,
Which forc'd me to begin my tale
    And then it left me free.

Since then at an uncertain hour,                                  615
    Now oftimes and now fewer,
That anguish comes and makes me tell
    My ghastly aventure.

I pass, like night, from land to land;
    I have strange power of speech;                               620
The moment that his face I see
I know the man that must hear me;
    To him my tale I teach.

Upon the whirl, where sank the ship,
The boat spun round and round;
And all was still, save that the hill
Was telling of the sound.

I moved my lips – the Pilot shrieked                    560
And fell down in a fit;
The holy Hermit raised his eyes,
And prayed where he did sit.

I took the oars: the Pilot's boy,
Who now doth crazy go,                                  565
Laughed loud and long, and all the while
His eyes went to and fro.
'Ha! ha!' quoth he, 'full plain I see,
The Devil knows how to row.'

And now, all in my own countree,                        570
I stood on the firm land!
The Hermit stepped forth from the boat,
And scarcely he could stand.

*The ancient Mariner earnestly entreateth the Hermit to shrieve him; and the penance of life falls on him.*

'O shrieve me, shrieve me, holy man!'
The Hermit crossed his brow.                            575
'Say quick,' quoth he, 'I bid thee say –
What manner of man art thou?'

Forthwith this frame of mine was wrenched
With a woeful agony,
Which forced me to begin my tale;                       580
And then it left me free.

*And ever and anon throughout his future life an agony constraineth him to travel from land to land,*

Since then, at an uncertain hour,
The agony returns:
And till my ghastly tale is told,
This heart within me burns.                             585

I pass, like night, from land to land;
I have strange power of speech;
That moment that his face I see,
I know the man that must hear me:
To him my tale I teach.                                 590

What loud uproar bursts from that door!
   The Wedding-guests are there;         625
But in the Garden-bower the Bride
   And Bride-maids singing are:
And hark the little Vesper-bell
   Which biddeth me to prayer.

O Wedding-guest! this soul hath been        630
   Alone on a wide wide sea:
So lonely 'twas, that God himself
   Scarce seemed there to be.

O sweeter than the Marriage-feast,
   'Tis sweeter far to me         635
To walk together to the Kirk
   With a goodly company.

To walk together to the Kirk
   And all together pray,
While each to his great father bends,      640
Old men, and babes, and loving friends,
   And Youths, and Maidens gay.

Farewell, farewell! but this I tell
   To thee, thou wedding-guest!
He prayeth well who loveth well,       645
   Both man and bird and beast.

He prayeth best who loveth best,
   All things both great and small:
For the dear God, who loveth us,
   He made and loveth all.        650

The Marinere, whose eye is bright,
   Whose beard with age is hoar,
Is gone; and now the wedding-guest
   Turn'd from the bridegroom's door.

He went, like one that hath been stunn'd   655
   And is of sense forlorn:
A sadder and a wiser man
   He rose the morrow morn.
[1797–8]

What loud uproar bursts from that door!
The wedding-guests are there:
But in the garden-bower the bride
And bride-maids singing are:
And hark the little vesper bell,                                        595
Which biddeth me to prayer!

O Wedding-Guest! this soul hath been
Alone on a wide wide sea:
So lonely 'twas, that God himself
Scarce seeméd there to be.                                             600

O sweeter than the marriage-feast,
'Tis sweeter far to me,
To walk together to the kirk
With a goodly company! –

To walk together to the kirk,                                          605
All all together pray,
While each to his great Father bends,
Old men, and babes, and loving friends
And youths and maidens gay!

*And to teach, by his own example, love and reverence to all things that God made and loveth.*

Farewell, farewell! but this I tell                                    610
To thee, thou Wedding-Guest!
He prayeth well, who loveth well
Both man and bird and beast.

He prayeth best, who loveth best
All things both great and small;                                       615
For the dear God who loveth us,
He made and loveth all.'

The Mariner, whose eye is bright,
Whose beard with age is hoar,
Is gone: and now the Wedding-Guest                                     620
Turned from the bridegroom's door.

He went like one that hath been stunned,
And is of sense forlorn:
A sadder and a wiser man,
He rose the morrow morn.                                               625
[1817–34]

# CHRISTABEL

In *Biographia Literaria* Coleridge records the poetic task to which he was addressing himself at the time of his association with Wordsworth:

> ... it was agreed that my endeavours should be directed to persons and characters supernatural, or at least romantic; yet so as to transfer from our inward nature a human interest and a semblance of truth sufficient to procure for these shadows of imagination that willing suspension of disbelief for the moment, which constitutes poetic faith.

With this view, he goes on, he had written *The Ancient Mariner*, and was hoping, in *Christabel*, to realize his ideal more nearly than he had done in his first attempt.

Even a cursory glance at this poem will show that it is very different from the one which preceded it. If *The Ancient Mariner* is a poem which has gradually crystallized around a given structure of ideas, it owes much of its force to the evocation of remembered images. *Christabel*, on the other hand, was evidently planned more completely from the beginning and relies more on present imagination for its shaping and colouring.

The point of departure for the poem was the 'child of nature' motif which had been used for a series of figures, including the foundling in *The Foster-Mother's Tale*, the child, Enos, in *The Wanderings of Cain* and the 'gentle Maid' in *The Nightingale*. Christabel is discovered at the beginning of the poem in the wood near her home, where she has gone to pray 'for the weal of her lover who's far away'. But why should she have forsaken the security of the castle to make her devotions? She needs to escape from a castle which, as we learn later, is more like a deathly prison. But also, evidently, like the 'gentle Maid' of the earlier poem, she goes out into nature

> Even like a Lady vowed and dedicate
> To something more than Nature in the grove.

The atmospheres of the two poems are in strong contrast, however.

Whereas the nightingales were made into symbols of joy, and their song broke out

> As if some sudden gale had swept at once
> A hundred airy harps!

the atmosphere of *Christabel* is sombre and brooding, with owls hooting beneath a veiled moon.

The reason for the changed atmosphere is that Coleridge now wished to carry into his nature poetry the questions of guilt and evil which he had been discussing with Wordsworth and which had resulted in such experiments as *Osorio*, *The Wanderings of Cain* and *The Ancient Mariner*. The basic problem can be simply stated. If the state of grace corresponds to an innocent vision of nature and the fall of man is a fall away from that vision, is it ever possible for the innocent to redeem the experienced?

This was the problem that pervaded *The Wanderings of Cain*, where Enos, the innocent child of nature, leads his father through the wilderness; he faces it again in this poem. There is also a personal reference. Coleridge had determined that Hartley should be brought up as a child of nature and during this period he must constantly have been looking for any signs that his child's innocence was being clouded by evil. The epilogue to Part Two is very clearly about Hartley: and one can perceive that a good deal of the reference to 'eyes' in the poem may result from observation of his own child.

In *The Ancient Mariner* the Mariner whose 'long grey beard and glittering eye' were so terrifying to the Wedding-Guest was also the 'bright-eyed Mariner'. Like the genius in *Kubla Khan*, his eyes were frightening because he was one who had plumbed the mysteries of existence and knew how terrible they could be. Yet he was frightening only at first sight, for the vision of which he had to tell was, rightly understood, one of restored innocence, or a regained paradise in which the passions of experience were restrained by the harmonizing power of vision.

In *Christabel*, Coleridge uses this imagery in a different way. In this poem, innocence is symbolized by the dove, experience by the serpent. The serpent imagery is used as in *Paradise Lost*: if the daemonic energies begin to exist separately and autonomously, they necessarily become energies of evil. Yet innocence cannot reach maturity without mastering and subsuming them. For Christabel, young and relatively untried, her mother embodies the maturity of innocent vision, while Geraldine stands for the autonomous energies of sex and power. Geraldine herself is ambiguous. She detests and fears Christabel's mother ('Off, wandering mother! Peak and pine!') – yet when she drinks the wild-flower wine made by her, she is restored to her full heavenly stature and beauty. Characteristically, it is her eyes that reflect the change:

> Her fair large eyes 'gan glitter bright,
> And from the floor whereon she sank,
> The lofty lady stood upright:
> She was most beautiful to see,
> Like a lady of a far countrée.

Conversely, when Christabel comes temporarily under Geraldine's spell, the change is equally reflected in her eyes, which 'passively did imitate' the look which she had seen in Geraldine's:

> A snake's small eye blinks dull and shy,
> And the lady's eyes they shrunk in her head,
> Each shrunk up to a serpent's eye,
> And with somewhat of malice and more of dread,
> At Christabel she looked askance!

The observation is fine; and its importance in the symbolic structure of the poem is underlined by the fact that two of the adjectives used for the snake's eye, 'small' and 'dull', are also used for the moon at the beginning of the poem:

> The moon is behind, and at the full;
> And yet she looks both small and dull.

Throughout this poem, evil is represented primarily as the veiling and hiding of good. The minimal light of the clouded moon and the half-hidden eye of the snake both speak of a vision that has been obscured until it no longer controls human energies, which are left to the caprice of the passion of the moment.

It is impossible to know how Coleridge would have concluded the poem, but it seems clear that Christabel would finally have overcome the peril of the forces represented by Geraldine and that her victory, reconciling the dove and the eagle, would have acted 'for the weal of her lover'. Eventually, one can see, the atmosphere of death would have disappeared from the castle to be replaced by life – the 'one Life'.

The language of the poem, with its direct appeal to the sensibility of the drawing-room, has sometimes been criticized. The use of nursery rhyme metres, which fitted *The Ancient Mariner*, is not quite so happy in this setting. Moreover, a good deal of lesser poetry which has since been written under its shadow has debased the currency. Yet despite such uneasinesses, Coleridge succeeds remarkably well in his attempt to achieve the 'sudden charm, which accidents of light and shade, which moon-light or sun-set diffuse over a known and familiar landscape'. The success is more marked in the first section, where landscape and atmosphere both contribute to the sense of an obscure evil, always just out of sight. In the second stanza, Coleridge has set himself the more difficult task of representing 'witchery by daylight.' Yet here also he contrives to create a landscape corresponding to the type of evil being described. If clouded moonlight helps to suggest the insidious enchantment of Geraldine, the hard light of common day is an appropriate medium for the level-headed lack of imagination and perception displayed by Sir Leoline, which prove natural allies for the forces represented by Geraldine and enable them to carry out their work.

In a preface to the published version, Coleridge drew attention to the early date of composition, in order that he might not be charged with plagiarism, particularly in respect of the metre employed. Scott and Byron, who had heard the poem recited, had already produced verse in a similar vein – it was, indeed, this fact which had prompted publication of the poem in its unfinished state. In his preface, Coleridge also described the 'new principle' involved in the metre of the poem, 'namely, that of counting in each line the accents, not the syllables'. 'Nevertheless,' he went on, 'this occasional variation in number of syllables is not introduced wantonly, or for the mere ends of convenience, but in correspondence with some transition in the nature of the imagery or passion.'

# Christabel

## PART I

'Tis the middle of night by the castle clock,
And the owls have awakened the crowing cock;
Tu–whit! — tu–whoo!
And hark, again! the crowing cock,
How drowsily it crew.                                            5

Sir Leoline, the Baron rich,
Hath a toothless mastiff bitch;
From her kennel beneath the rock
She maketh answer to the clock,
Four for the quarters, and twelve for the hour;            10
Ever and aye, by shine and shower,
Sixteen short howls, not over loud;
Some say, she sees my lady's shroud.

Is the night chilly and dark?
The night is chilly, but not dark.                            15
The thin gray cloud is spread on high,
It covers but not hides the sky.
The moon is behind, and at the full;
And yet she looks both small and dull.
The night is chill, the cloud is gray:                       20
'Tis a month before the month of May,
And the Spring comes slowly up this way.

The lovely lady, Christabel,
Whom her father loves so well,
What makes her in the wood so late,                          25
A furlong from the castle gate?
She had dreams all yesternight
Of her own betrothéd knight;
And she in the midnight wood will pray
For the weal of her lover that's far away.                   30

She stole along, she nothing spoke,
The sighs she heaved were soft and low,
And naught was green upon the oak
But moss and rarest mistletoe:

She kneels beneath the huge oak tree,                      35
And in silence prayeth she.

The lady sprang up suddenly,
The lovely lady, Christabel!
It moaned as near, as near can be,
But what it is she cannot tell. –                          40
On the other side it seems to be,
Of the huge, broad-breasted, old oak tree.

The night is chill; the forest bare;
Is it the wind that moaneth bleak?
There is not wind enough in the air                        45
To move away the ringlet curl
From the lovely lady's cheek –
There is not wind enough to twirl
The one red leaf, the last of its clan,
That dances as often as dance it can,                      50
Hanging so light, and hanging so high,
On the topmost twig that looks up at the sky.

Hush, beating heart of Christabel!
Jesu, Maria, shield her well!
She folded her arms beneath her cloak,                     55
And stole to the other side of the oak.
        What sees she there?

There she sees a damsel bright,
Drest in a silken robe of white,
That shadowy in the moonlight shone:                       60
The neck that made that white robe wan,
Her stately neck, and arms were bare;
Her blue-veined feet unsandal'd were,
And wildly glittered here and there
The gems entangled in her hair.                            65
I guess, 'twas frightful there to see
A lady so richly clad as she –
Beautiful exceedingly!

Mary mother, save me now!
(Said Christabel,) And who art thou?                       70

The lady strange made answer meet,
And her voice was faint and sweet: —
Have pity on my sore distress,
I scarce can speak for weariness:
Stretch forth thy hand, and have no fear!      75
Said Christabel, How camest thou here?
And the lady, whose voice was faint and sweet,
Did thus pursue her answer meet: —

My sire is of a noble line,
And my name is Geraldine:      80
Five warriors seized me yestermorn,
Me, even me, a maid forlorn:
They choked my cries with force and fright,
And tied me on a palfrey white.
The palfrey was as fleet as wind,      85
And they rode furiously behind.
They spurred amain, their steeds were white:
And once we crossed the shade of night.
As sure as Heaven shall rescue me,
I have no thought what men they be;      90
Nor do I know how long it is
(For I have lain entranced I wis)
Since one, the tallest of the five,
Took me from the palfrey's back,
A weary woman, scarce alive.      95
Some muttered words his comrades spoke:
He placed me underneath this oak;
He swore they would return with haste;
Whither they went I cannot tell —
I thought I heard, some minutes past,      100
Sounds as of a castle bell.
Stretch forth thy hand (thus ended she),
And help a wretched maid to flee.

Then Christabel stretched forth her hand,
And comforted fair Geraldine:      105
O well, bright dame! may you command
The service of Sir Leoline;
And gladly our stout chivalry
Will he send forth and friends withal

To guide and guard you safe and free          110
Home to your noble father's hall.

She rose: and forth with steps they passed
That strove to be, and were not, fast.
Her gracious stars the lady blest,
And thus spake on sweet Christabel:          115
All our household are at rest,
The hall as silent as the cell;
Sir Leoline is weak in health,
And may not well awakened be,
But we will move as if in stealth,          120
And I beseech your courtesy,
This night, to share your couch with me.

They crossed the moat, and Christabel
Took the key that fitted well;
A little door she opened straight,          125
All in the middle of the gate;
The gate that was ironed within and without,
Where an army in battle array had marched out.
The lady sank, belike through pain,
And Christabel with might and main          130
Lifted her up, a weary weight,
Over the threshold of the gate:
Then the lady rose again,
And moved, as she were not in pain.

So free from danger, free from fear,          135
They crossed the court: right glad they were.
And Christabel devoutly cried
To the lady by her side,
Praise we the Virgin all divine
Who hath rescued thee from thy distress!          140
Alas, alas! said Geraldine,
I cannot speak for weariness.
So free from danger, free from fear,
They crossed the court: right glad they were.

Outside her kennel, the mastiff old          145
Lay fast asleep, in moonshine cold.

The mastiff old did not awake,
Yet she an angry moan did make!
And what can ail the mastiff bitch?
Never till now she uttered yell                                    150
Beneath the eye of Christabel.
Perhaps it is the owlet's scritch:
For what can ail the mastiff bitch?


They passed the hall, that echoes still,
Pass as lightly as you will!                                       155
The brands were flat, the brands were dying,
Amid their own white ashes lying;
But when the lady passed, there came
A tongue of light, a fit of flame;
And Christabel saw the lady's eye,                                 160
And nothing else saw she thereby,
Save the boss of the shield of Sir Leoline tall,
Which hung in a murky old niche in the wall.
O softly tread, said Christabel,
My father seldom sleepeth well.                                    165


Sweet Christabel her feet doth bare,
And jealous of the listening air
They steal their way from stair to stair,
Now in glimmer, and now in gloom,
And now they pass the Baron's room,                                170
As still as death, with stifled breath!
And now have reached her chamber door;
And now doth Geraldine press down
The rushes of the chamber floor.


The moon shines dim in the open air,                               175
And not a moonbeam enters here.
But they without its light can see
The chamber carved so curiously,
Carved with figures strange and sweet,
All made out of the carver's brain,                                180
For a lady's chamber meet:
The lamp with twofold silver chain
Is fastened to an angel's feet.

The silver lamp burns dead and dim;
But Christabel the lamp will trim.                    185
She trimmed the lamp, and made it bright,
And left it swinging to and fro,
While Geraldine, in wretched plight,
Sank down upon the floor below.

O weary lady, Geraldine,                              190
I pray you, drink this cordial wine!
It is a wine of virtuous powers;
My mother made it of wild flowers.

And will your mother pity me,
Who am a maiden most forlorn?                         195
Christabel answered — Woe is me!
She died the hour that I was born.
I have heard the grey-haired friar tell
How on her death-bed she did say,
That she should hear the castle-bell                  200
Strike twelve upon my wedding-day.
O mother dear! that thou wert here!
I would, said Geraldine, she were!

But soon with altered voice, said she —
'Off, wandering mother! Peak and pine!                205
I have power to bid thee flee.'
Alas! what ails poor Geraldine?
Why stares she with unsettled eye?
Can she the bodiless dead espy?
And why with hollow voice cries she,                  210
'Off, woman, off! this hour is mine —
Though thou her guardian spirit be,
Off, woman, off! 'tis given to me.'

Then Christabel knelt by the lady's side,
And raised to heaven her eyes so blue —              215
Alas! said she, this ghastly ride —
Dear lady! it hath wildered you!
The lady wiped her moist cold brow,
And faintly said, ''Tis over now!'

Again the wild-flower wine she drank:                 220
Her fair large eyes 'gan glitter bright,

And from the floor whereon she sank,
The lofty lady stood upright:
She was most beautiful to see,
Like a lady of a far countrée.                                    225

And thus the lofty lady spake —
'All they who live in the upper sky,
Do love you, holy Christabel!
And you love them, and for their sake
And for the good which me befel,                                   230
Even I in my degree will try,
Fair maiden, to requite you well.
But now unrobe yourself; for I
Must pray, ere yet in bed I lie.'

Quoth Christabel, so let it be!                                    235
And as the lady bade, did she.
Her gentle limbs did she undress,
And lay down in her loveliness.

But through her brain of weal and woe
So many thoughts moved to and fro,                                 240
That vain it were her lids to close;
So half-way from the bed she rose,
And on her elbow did recline
To look at the lady Geraldine.

Beneath the lamp the lady bowed,                                   245
And slowly rolled her eyes around;
Then drawing in her breath aloud,
Like one that shuddered, she unbound
The cincture from beneath her breast:
Her silken robe, and inner vest,                                   250
Dropt to her feet, and full in view,
Behold! her bosom and half her side — [1]
A sight to dream of, not to tell!
O shield her! shield sweet Christabel!

Yet Geraldine nor speaks nor stirs;                                255
Ah! what a stricken look was hers!

[1] In at least one copy this line is followed by another, pencilled in by Coleridge: 'It was dark
& rough as the Sea-Wolf's hide.'

Deep from within she seems half-way
To lift some weight with sick assay,
And eyes the maid and seeks delay;
Then suddenly, as one defied,                              260
Collects herself in scorn and pride,
And lay down by the Maiden's side! –
And in her arms the maid she took,
       Ah wel-a-day!
And with low voice and doleful look                        265
These words did say:
'In the touch of this bosom there worketh a spell,
Which is lord of thy utterance, Christabel!
Thou knowest to-night, and wilt know to-morrow
This mark of my shame, this seal of my sorrow;            270
      But vainly thou warrest,
        For this is alone in
      Thy power to declare,
        That in the dim forest
        Thou heard'st a low moaning,       275
And found'st a bright lady, surpassingly fair;
And didst bring her home with thee in love and in
    charity,
To shield her and shelter her from the damp air.'


## The Conclusion to Part I

It was a lovely sight to see
The lady Christabel, when she                               280
Was praying at the old oak tree.
    Amid the jaggéd shadows
    Of mossy leafless boughs,
    Kneeling in the moonlight,
    To make her gentle vows;                          285
Her slender palms together prest,
Heaving sometimes on her breast;
Her face resigned to bliss or bale –
Her face, oh call it fair not pale,
And both blue eyes more bright than clear,                 290
Each about to have a tear.

With open eyes (ah woe is me!)
Asleep, and dreaming fearfully,
Fearfully dreaming, yet, I wis,
Dreaming that alone, which is –                 295
O sorrow and shame! Can this be she,
The lady, who knelt at the old oak tree?
And lo! the worker of these harms,
That holds the maiden in her arms,
Seems to slumber still and mild,                 300
As a mother with her child.

A star hath set, a star hath risen,
O Geraldine! since arms of thine
Have been the lovely lady's prison.
O Geraldine! one hour was thine –             305
Thou'st had thy will! By tairn[1] and rill,
The night-birds all that hour were still.
But now they are jubilant anew,
From cliff and tower, tu–whoo! tu–whoo!
Tu–whoo! tu–whoo! from wood and fell!        310

And see! the lady Christabel
Gathers herself from out her trance;
Her limbs relax, her countenance
Grows sad and soft; the smooth thin lids
Close o'er her eyes; and tears she sheds –       315
Large tears that leave the lashes bright!
And oft the while she seems to smile
As infants at a sudden light!

Yea, she doth smile, and she doth weep,
Like a youthful hermitess,                    320
Beauteous in a wilderness,
Who, praying always, prays in sleep.
And, if she move unquietly,

[1] Tairn or Tarn (derived by Lye from the Icelandic *Tiorn*, stagnum, palus) is rendered in our dictionaries as synonymous with Mere or Lake; but it is properly a large Pool or Reservoir in the Mountains, commonly the Feeder of some Mere in the valleys. Tarn Watling and Blellum Tarn, though on lower ground than other Tarns, are yet not exceptions, for both are on elevations, and Blellum Tarn feeds the Wynander Mere. [S.T.C.]

Perchance, 'tis but the blood so free
Comes back and tingles in her feet.                          325
No doubt, she hath a vision sweet.
What if her guardian spirit 'twere,
What if she knew her mother near?
But this she knows, in joys and woes,
That saints will aid if men will call:                       330
For the blue sky bends over all!
[1797]


## Part II

Each matin bell, the Baron saith,
Knells us back to a world of death.
These words Sir Leoline first said,
When he rose and found his lady dead:                        335
These words Sir Leoline will say
Many a morn to his dying day!

And hence the custom and law began
That still at dawn the sacristan,
Who duly pulls the heavy bell,                               340
Five and forty beads must tell
Between each stroke – a warning knell,
Which not a soul can choose but hear
From Bratha Head to Wyndermere.

Saith Bracy the bard, So let it knell!                       345
And let the drowsy sacristan
Still count as slowly as he can!
There is no lack of such, I ween,
As well fill up the space between.
In Langdale Pike and Witch's Lair,                           350
And Dungeon-ghyll so foully rent,
With ropes of rock and bells of air
Three sinful sextons' ghosts are pent,
Who all give back, one after t'other,
The death-note to their living brother;                      355
And oft too, by the knell offended,
Just as their one! two! three! is ended,
The devil mocks the doleful tale
With a merry peal from Borodale.

The air is still! through mist and cloud      360
That merry peal comes ringing loud;
And Geraldine shakes off her dread,
And rises lightly from the bed;
Puts on her silken vestments white,
And tricks her hair in lovely plight,      365
And nothing doubting of her spell
Awakens the lady Christabel.
'Sleep you, sweet lady Christabel?
I trust that you have rested well.'

And Christabel awoke and spied      370
The same who lay down by her side –
O rather say, the same whom she
Raised up beneath the old oak tree!
Nay, fairer yet! and yet more fair!
For she belike hath drunken deep      375
Of all the blessedness of sleep!
And while she spake, her looks, her air
Such gentle thankfulness declare,
That (so it seemed) her girded vests
Grew tight beneath her heaving breasts.      380
'Sure I have sinn'd!' said Christabel.
'Now heaven be praised if all be well!'
And in low faltering tones, yet sweet,
Did she the lofty lady greet
With such perplexity of mind      385
As dreams too lively leave behind.

So quickly she rose, and quickly arrayed
Her maiden limbs, and having prayed
That He, who on the cross did groan,
Might wash away her sins unknown,      390
She forthwith led fair Geraldine
To meet her sire, Sir Leoline.

The lovely maid and the lady tall
Are pacing both into the hall,
And pacing on through page and groom,      395
Enter the Baron's presence-room.

The Baron rose, and while he prest
His gentle daughter to his breast,
With cheerful wonder in his eyes
The lady Geraldine espies,                                    400
And gave such welcome to the same,
As might beseem so bright a dame!

But when he heard the lady's tale,
And when she told her father's name,
Why waxed Sir Leoline so pale,                               405
Murmuring o'er the name again,
Lord Roland de Vaux of Tryermaine?

Alas! they had been friends in youth;
But whispering tongues can poison truth;
And constancy lives in realms above;                        410
And life is thorny; and youth is vain;
And to be wroth with one we love
Doth work like madness in the brain.
And thus it chanced, as I divine,
With Roland and Sir Leoline.                                 415
Each spake words of high disdain
And insult to his heart's best brother:
They parted — ne'er to meet again!
But never either found another
To free the hollow heart from paining —                     420
They stood aloof, the scars remaining,
Like cliffs which had been rent asunder;
A dreary sea now flows between; —
But neither heat, nor frost, nor thunder,
Shall wholly do away, I ween,                               425
The marks of that which once hath been.

Sir Leoline, a moment's space,
Stood gazing on the damsel's face:
And the youthful Lord of Tryermaine
Came back upon his heart again.                             430

O then the Baron forgot his age,
His noble heart swelled high with rage;
He swore by the wounds in Jesu's side,

He would proclaim it far and wide
With trump and solemn heraldry,        435
That they, who thus had wronged the dame,
Were base as spotted infamy!
'And if they dare deny the same,
My herald shall appoint a week,
And let the recreant traitors seek        440
My tourney court – that there and then
I may dislodge their reptile souls
From the bodies and forms of men!'
He spake: his eye in lightning rolls!
For the lady was ruthlessly seized; and he kenned        445
In the beautiful lady the child of his friend!

And now the tears were on his face,
And fondly in his arms he took
Fair Geraldine, who met the embrace,
Prolonging it with joyous look.        450
Which when she viewed, a vision fell
Upon the soul of Christabel,
The vision of fear, the touch and pain!
She shrunk and shuddered, and saw again –
(Ah, woe is me! Was it for thee,        455
Thou gentle maid! such sights to see?)

Again she saw that bosom old,
Again she felt that bosom cold,
And drew in her breath with a hissing sound:
Whereat the Knight turned wildly round,        460
And nothing saw, but his own sweet maid
With eyes upraised, as one that prayed.

The touch, the sight, had passed away,
And in its stead that vision blest,
Which comforted her after-rest,        465
While in the lady's arms she lay,
Had put a rapture in her breast,
And on her lips and o'er her eyes
Spread smiles like light!
                    With new surprise,
'What ails then my belovéd child?'        470

The Baron said – His daughter mild
Made answer, 'All will yet be well!'
I ween, she had no power to tell
Aught else: so mighty was the spell.

Yet he, who saw this Geraldine, 475
Had deemed her sure a thing divine,
Such sorrow with such grace she blended,
As if she feared, she had offended
Sweet Christabel, that gentle maid!
And with such lowly tones she prayed, 480
She might be sent without delay
Home to her father's mansion.
                                        'Nay!
Nay, by my soul!' said Leoline.
'Ho! Bracy the bard, the charge be thine!
Go thou, with music sweet and loud, 485
And take two steeds with trappings proud,
And take the youth whom thou lov'st best
To bear thy harp, and learn thy song,
And clothe you both in solemn vest,
And over the mountains haste along, 490
Lest wandering folk, that are abroad,
Detain you on the valley road.

'And when he has crossed the Irthing flood,
My merry bard! he hastes, he hastes
Up Knorren Moor, through Halegarth Wood, 495
And reaches soon that castle good
Which stands and threatens Scotland's wastes.

'Bard Bracy! bard Bracy! your horses are fleet,
Ye must ride up the hall, your music so sweet,
More loud than your horses' echoing feet! 500
And loud and loud to Lord Roland call,
Thy daughter is safe in Langdale hall!
Thy beautiful daughter is safe and free –
Sir Leoline greets thee thus through me.
He bids thee come without delay 505
With all thy numerous array
And take thy lovely daughter home:

And he will meet thee on the way
With all his numerous array
White with their panting palfreys' foam:                          510
And, by mine honour! I will say,
That I repent me of the day
When I spake words of fierce disdain
To Roland de Vaux of Tryermaine! –
– For since that evil hour hath flown,                            515
Many a summer's sun hath shone;
Yet ne'er found I a friend again
Like Roland de Vaux of Tryermaine.'


The lady fell, and clasped his knees,
Her face upraised, her eyes o'erflowing;                          520
And Bracy replied, with faltering voice,
His gracious Hail on all bestowing! –
'Thy words, thou sire of Christabel,
Are sweeter than my harp can tell;
Yet might I gain a boon of thee,                                  525
This day my journey should not be,
So strange a dream hath come to me,
That I had vowed with music loud
To clear yon wood from thing unblest,
Warned by a vision in my rest!                                    530
For in my sleep I saw that dove,
That gentle bird, whom thou dost love,
And call'st by thy own daughter's name –
Sir Leoline! I saw the same
Fluttering, and uttering fearful moan,                           535
Among the green herbs in the forest alone.
Which when I saw and when I heard,
I wonder'd what might ail the bird;
For nothing near it could I see,
Save the grass and green herbs underneath the old
    tree.                                                         540


'And in my dream methought I went
To search out what might there be found;
And what the sweet bird's trouble meant,
That thus lay fluttering on the ground.

I went and peered, and could descry 545
No cause for her distressful cry;
But yet for her dear lady's sake
I stooped, methought, the dove to take,
When lo! I saw a bright green snake
Coiled around its wings and neck. 550
Green as the herbs on which it couched,
Close by the dove's its head it crouched;
And with the dove it heaves and stirs,
Swelling its neck as she swelled hers!
I woke; it was the midnight hour, 555
The clock was echoing in the tower;
But though my slumber was gone by,
This dream it would not pass away –
It seems to live upon my eye!
And thence I vowed this self-same day, 560
With music strong and saintly song
To wander through the forest bare,
Lest aught unholy loiter there.'

Thus Bracy said: the Baron, the while,
Half-listening heard him with a smile;
Then turned to Lady Geraldine, 565
His eyes made up of wonder and love;
And said in courtly accents fine,
'Sweet maid, Lord Roland's beauteous dove,
With arms more strong than harp or song,
Thy sire and I will crush the snake!' 570
He kissed her forehead as he spake,
And Geraldine in maiden wise,
Casting down her large bright eyes,
With blushing cheek and courtesy fine 575
She turned her from Sir Leoline;
Softly gathering up her train,
That o'er her right arm fell again;
And folded her arms across her chest,
And couched her head upon her breast, 580
And looked askance at Christabel —
Jesu, Maria, shield her well!

A snake's small eye blinks dull and shy,
And the lady's eyes they shrunk in her head,

Each shrunk up to a serpent's eye,                                    585
And with somewhat of malice, and more of dread,
At Christabel she looked askance! –
One moment – and the sight was fled!
But Christabel in dizzy trance
Stumbling on the unsteady ground                                      590
Shuddered aloud, with a hissing sound;
And Geraldine again turned round,
And like a thing, that sought relief,
Full of wonder and full of grief,
She rolled her large bright eyes divine                               595
Wildly on Sir Leoline.

The maid, alas! her thoughts are gone,
She nothing sees – no sight but one!
The maid, devoid of guile and sin,
I know not how, in fearful wise,                                      600
So deeply had she drunken in
That look, those shrunken serpent eyes,
That all her features were resigned
To this sole image in her mind:
And passively did imitate                                            605
That look of dull and treacherous hate!
And thus she stood, in dizzy trance,
Still picturing that look askance
With forced unconscious sympathy
Full before her father's view —                                      610
As far as such a look could be,
In eyes so innocent and blue!

And when the trance was o'er, the maid
Paused awhile, and inly prayed:
Then falling at the Baron's feet,                                     615
'By my mother's soul do I entreat
That thou this woman send away!'
She said: and more she could not say:
For what she knew she could not tell,
O'er-mastered by the mighty spell.                                   620

Why is thy cheek so wan and wild,
Sir Leoline? Thy only child

Lies at thy feet, thy joy, thy pride,
So fair, so innocent, so mild;
The same, for whom thy lady died!                              625
O by the pangs of her dear mother
Think thou no evil of thy child!
For her, and thee, and for no other,
She prayed the moment ere she died:
Prayed that the babe for whom she died,                        630
Might prove her dear lord's joy and pride!
   That prayer her deadly pangs beguiled,
       Sir Leoline!
   And wouldst thou wrong thy only child,
       Her child and thine?                                 635

Within the Baron's heart and brain
If thoughts, like these, had any share,
They only swelled his rage and pain,
And did but work confusion there.
His heart was cleft with pain and rage,                        640
His cheeks they quivered, his eyes were wild,
Dishonoured thus in his old age;
Dishonoured by his only child,
And all his hospitality
To the wronged daughter of his friend                          645
By more than woman's jealousy
Brought thus to a disgraceful end –
He rolled his eye with stern regard
Upon the gentle minstrel bard,
And said in tones abrupt, austere –                            650
'Why, Bracy! dost thou loiter here?
I bade thee hence!' The bard obeyed;
And turning from his own sweet maid,
The agéd knight, Sir Leoline,
Led forth the lady Geraldine!                                  655
[1800]

## The Conclusion to Part II

A little child, a limber elf,
Singing, dancing to itself,
A fairy thing with red round cheeks,

That always finds, and never seeks,
Makes such a vision to the sight 660
As fills a father's eyes with light;
And pleasures flow in so thick and fast
Upon his heart, that he at last
Must needs express his love's excess
With words of unmeant bitterness. 665
Perhaps 'tis pretty to force together
Thoughts so all unlike each other;
To mutter and mock a broken charm,
To dally with wrong that does no harm.
Perhaps 'tis tender too and pretty 670
At each wild word to feel within
A sweet recoil of love and pity.
And what, if in a world of sin
(O sorrow and shame should this be true!)
Such giddiness of heart and brain 675
Comes seldom save from rage and pain,
So talks as it's most used to do.
[1801]

# FROM STOWEY TO KESWICK

In the early part of 1798, while still writing his great poems, Coleridge again found himself preoccupied with political issues. The Swiss cantons had been suppressed by the French Government. The event was of considerable importance ideologically, for it was the first occasion on which the Government could be said to have acted deliberately in a way which ran counter to the principles of the Revolution. From now on, any indulgence with which Coleridge might have regarded the shortcomings of French rulers finally disappeared. His new attitude was expressed in a poem composed on the occasion which was originally entitled *Recantation* and later *France: an Ode*.

Criticism of the French Government in no way involved uncritical acceptance of his own country's policy, however. By April he was writing *Fears in Solitude*, in which feeling for the safety of his countrymen was accompanied by the reflection that they were not worthy of liberty. Liberty remained the ideal: his new attitude consisted simply in facing the factual situation which had now been revealed in France. The point is expressed in a satirical poem, also entitled *Recantation*. He concludes the other poems with the reflection that liberty may sometimes exist in human affairs but is truly to be found only in nature.

Early in 1798 the generous grant of a pension by the Wedgwood brothers gave him unexpected freedom from financial worry. Together with William and Dorothy Wordsworth, he formed the plan of wintering in Germany, from which country interesting intellectual events of various sorts were reported. Some time after their arrival, however, they separated. William and Dorothy preferred the cheapness of Goslar, while Coleridge, feeling the necessity of intellectual stimulus in a university town, stayed at Göttingen. The main poetic fruit of the trip was a series of translations and imitations from German which Coleridge undertook both then and afterwards, but his encounter with the new critical philosophy also affected his poetry obliquely, by way of its effect on his modes of thinking.

The German experience had an unexpected result, in addition. Coleridge realized for the first time how essential intimate affection was for his personal happiness. Some of his poems reflect directly a mood of homesickness or longing for the company of William and Dorothy; while the *Lines Written in an Album* range more widely, commenting on the importance of 'the Life within' for a true enjoyment of Nature. This theme, which was to receive fuller treatment in *Dejection: an Ode*, looks forward to the stress placed on domestic affection in subsequent years.

On his return to England, Coleridge spent a good deal of time working in London. Metre still fascinated him: his notebooks of the time are dotted with metrical experiments – which are not necessarily of low poetic quality. At the end of 1799 he received a proposal from Longman that he should translate two plays by Schiller, *The Piccolomini* and *The Death of Wallenstein*, which were about to be published. He set to work and finally finished the translations in April of the new year. His later attitudes to this work varied. He blamed the disgust engendered by it for his poetic decline, yet he also spoke of it as 'a specimen of my happiest attempt, during the prime manhood of my intellect, before I had been buffeted by adversity or crossed by fatality'. Lamb, who visited him sometimes, was to recall how he would sit in a dressing gown, and look like a conjuror; the translation in fact contains one or two touches of Coleridge the 'magical' poet. The passages reprinted in this section are two which he himself spoke of as original, owing little or nothing to Schiller. The second is particularly interesting as showing the sophistication of Coleridge's attitude towards mythology. He sees that the ancient myths often made a direct appeal to the imagination and so to the whole man: with the total rejection of mythology on the grounds that it is not *factually* true, men have cut themselves off from these resources. It was both his own experience as a poet and his contact with German thinking, probably, which helped him to see so clearly the issues involved, while his contemporaries were not even aware that a problem existed. In their defence of the inspired man, and their picture of a world which has been spiritually diminished by its loss of mythology, the two passages could, in fact, be regarded as comments on the first and most brilliant period of his poetic career.

## *France: An Ode*

### I

Ye Clouds! that far above me float and pause,
   Whose pathless march no mortal may controul!
   Ye Ocean-Waves! that, wheresoe'er ye roll,
Yield homage only to eternal laws!
Ye Woods! that listen to the night-birds singing,         5
   Midway the smooth and perilous slope reclined,
Save when your own imperious branches swinging,
   Have made a solemn music of the wind!
Where, like a man beloved of God,
Through glooms, which never woodman trod,         10
    How oft, pursuing fancies holy,
My moonlight way o'er flowering weeds I wound,
    Inspired, beyond the guess of folly,
By each rude shape and wild unconquerable sound!
O ye loud Waves! and O ye Forests high!         15
   And O ye Clouds that far above me soared!
Thou rising Sun! thou blue rejoicing Sky!
   Yea, every thing that is and will be free!
   Bear witness for me, wheresoe'er ye be,
   With what deep worship I have still adored         20
   The spirit of divinest Liberty.

### II

When France in wrath her giant-limbs upreared,
   And with that oath, which smote air, earth, and sea,
   Stamped her strong foot and said she would be free,
Bear witness for me, how I hoped and feared!         25
With what a joy my lofty gratulation
   Unawed I sang, amid a slavish band:
And when to whelm the disenchanted nation,
   Like fiends embattled by a wizard's wand,
    The Monarchs marched in evil day,         30
    And Britain joined the dire array;
   Though dear her shores and circling ocean,

Though many friendships, many youthful loves
    Had swoln the patriot emotion
And flung a magic light o'er all her hills and groves;        35
Yet still my voice, unaltered, sang defeat
    To all that braved the tyrant-quelling lance,
And shame too long delayed and vain retreat!
For ne'er, O Liberty! with partial aim
I dimmed thy light or damped thy holy flame;        40
    But blessed the paeans of delivered France,
And hung my head and wept at Britain's name.

### III

'And what,' I said, 'though Blasphemy's loud scream
    With that sweet music of deliverance strove!
    Though all the fierce and drunken passions wove        45
A dance more wild than e'er was maniac's dream!
    Ye storms, that round the dawning East assembled,
The Sun was rising, though ye hid his light!'
    And when, to soothe my soul, that hoped and trembled,
The dissonance ceased, and all seemed calm and bright;        50
    When France her front deep-scarr'd and gory
    Concealed with clustering wreaths of glory;
        When, insupportably advancing,
    Her arm made mockery of the warrior's ramp;
        While timid looks of fury glancing,        55
    Domestic treason, crushed beneath her fatal stamp,
Writhed like a wounded dragon in his gore;
    Then I reproached my fears that would not flee;
'And soon,' I said, 'shall Wisdom teach her lore
In the low huts of them that toil and groan!        60
And, conquering by her happiness alone,
    Shall France compel the nations to be free,
Till Love and Joy look round, and call the Earth their own.'

### IV

Forgive me, Freedom! O forgive those dreams!
    I hear thy voice, I hear thy loud lament,        65
    From bleak Helvetia's icy caverns sent –
I hear thy groans upon her blood-stained streams!
    Heroes, that for your peaceful country perished,

And ye that, fleeing, spot your mountain-snows
   With bleeding wounds; forgive me, that I cherished     70
One thought that ever blessed your cruel foes!
    To scatter rage, and traitorous guilt,
    Where Peace her jealous home had built;
      A patriot-race to disinherit
Of all that made their stormy wilds so dear;     75
     And with inexpiable spirit
To taint the bloodless freedom of the mountaineer –
O France, that mockest Heaven, adulterous, blind,
   And patriot only in pernicious toils!
Are these thy boasts, Champion of human kind?     80
   To mix with Kings in the low lust of sway,
Yell in the hunt, and share the murderous prey;
To insult the shrine of Liberty with spoils
   From freemen torn; to tempt and to betray?

V

   The Sensual and the Dark rebel in vain,     85
   Slaves by their own compulsion! In mad game
   They burst their manacles and wear the name
    Of Freedom, graven on a heavier chain!
   O Liberty! with profitless endeavour
Have I pursued thee, many a weary hour;     90
   But thou nor swell'st the victor's strain, nor ever
Didst breathe thy soul in forms of human power.
    Alike from all, howe'er they praise thee,
    (Nor prayer, nor boastful name delays thee)
     Alike from Priestcraft's harpy minions,     95
    And factious Blasphemy's obscener slaves,
     Thou speedest on thy subtle pinions,
The guide of homeless winds, and playmate of the waves!
And there I felt thee! – on that sea-cliff's verge,
   Whose pines, scarce travelled by the breeze above,     100
Had made one murmur with the distant surge!
Yes, while I stood and gazed, my temples bare,
And shot my being through earth, sea, and air,
   Possessing all things with intensest love,
   O Liberty! my spirit felt thee there.     105
[March–April 1798]

## *Fears in Solitude*

WRITTEN IN APRIL 1798, DURING THE ALARM
OF AN INVASION

A green and silent spot, amid the hills,
A small and silent dell! O'er stiller place
No singing sky-lark ever poised himself.
The hills are heathy, save that swelling slope,
Which hath a gay and gorgeous covering on,                    5
All golden with the never-bloomless furze,
Which now blooms most profusely: but the dell,
Bathed by the mist, is fresh and delicate
As vernal corn-field, or the unripe flax,
When, through its half-transparent stalks, at eve,           10
The level sunshine glimmers with green light.
Oh! 'tis a quiet spirit-healing nook!
Which all, methinks, would love; but chiefly he,
The humble man, who, in his youthful years,
Knew just so much of folly, as had made                      15
His early manhood more securely wise!
Here he might lie on fern or withered heath,
While from the singing-lark (that sings unseen
The minstrelsy that solitude loves best),
And from the sun, and from the breezy air,                   20
Sweet influences trembled o'er his frame;
And he, with many feelings, many thoughts,
Made up a meditative joy, and found
Religious meanings in the forms of Nature!
And so, his senses gradually wrapt                           25
In a half sleep, he dreams of better worlds,
And dreaming hears thee still, O singing-lark,
That singest like an angel in the clouds!


    My God! it is a melancholy thing
For such a man, who would full fain preserve                 30
His soul in calmness, yet perforce must feel
For all his human brethren – O my God!
It weighs upon the heart, that he must think
What uproar and what strife may now be stirring
This way or that way o'er these silent hills –               35

Invasion, and the thunder and the shout,
And all the crash of onset; fear and rage,
And undetermined conflict – even now,
Even now, perchance, and in his native isle:
Carnage and groans beneath this blessed sun!          40
We have offended, Oh! my countrymen!
We have offended very grievously,
And been most tyrannous. From east to west
A groan of accusation pierces Heaven!
The wretched plead against us; multitudes             45
Countless and vehement, the sons of God,
Our brethren! Like a cloud that travels on,
Steamed up from Cairo's swamps of pestilence,
Even so, my countrymen! have we gone forth
And borne to distant tribes slavery and pangs,        50
And, deadlier far, our vices, whose deep taint
With slow perdition murders the whole man,
His body and his soul! Meanwhile, at home,
All individual dignity and power
Engulfed in Courts, Committees, Institutions,         55
Associations and Societies,
A vain, speech-mouthing, speech-reporting Guild,
One Benefit-Club for mutual flattery,
We have drunk up, demure as at a grace,
Pollutions from the brimming cup of wealth;           60
Contemptuous of all honourable rule,
Yet bartering freedom and the poor man's life
For gold, as at a market! The sweet words
Of Christian promise, words that even yet
Might stem destruction, were they wisely preached,    65
Are muttered o'er by men, whose tones proclaim
How flat and wearisome they feel their trade:
Rank scoffers some, but most too indolent
To deem them falsehoods or to know their truth.
Oh! blasphemous! the Book of Life is made             70
A superstitious instrument, on which
We gabble o'er the oaths we mean to break;
For all must swear – all and in every place,
College and wharf, council and justice-court;
All, all must swear, the briber and the bribed,       75
Merchant and lawyer, senator and priest,

The rich, the poor, the old man and the young;
All, all make up one scheme of perjury,
That faith doth reel; the very name of God
Sounds like a juggler's charm; and, bold with joy,          80
Forth from his dark and lonely hiding-place,
(Portentous sight!) the owlet Atheism,
Sailing on obscene wings athwart the noon,
Drops his blue-fringèd lids, and holds them close,
And hooting at the glorious sun in Heaven,          85
Cries out, 'Where is it?'
                 Thankless too for peace,
(Peace long preserved by fleets and perilous seas)
Secure from actual warfare, we have loved
To swell the war-whoop, passionate for war!
Alas! for ages ignorant of all          90
Its ghastlier workings, (famine or blue plague,
Battle, or siege, or flight through wintry snows),
We, this whole people, have been clamorous
For war and bloodshed; animating sports,
The which we pay for as a thing to talk of,          95
Spectators and not combatants! No guess
Anticipative of a wrong unfelt,
No speculation on contingency,
However dim and vague, too vague and dim
To yield a justifying cause; and forth,          100
(Stuffed out with big preamble, holy names,
And adjurations of the God in Heaven,)
We send our mandates for the certain death
Of thousands and ten thousands! Boys and girls,
And women, that would groan to see a child          105
Pull off an insect's leg, all read of war,
The best amusement for our morning-meal!
The poor wretch, who has learnt his only prayers
From curses, who knows scarcely words enough
To ask a blessing from his Heavenly Father,          110
Becomes a fluent phraseman, absolute
And technical in victories and defeats,
And all our dainty terms for fratricide;
Terms which we trundle smoothly o'er our tongues
Like mere abstractions, empty sounds to which          115
We join no feeling and attach no form!

As if the soldier died without a wound;
As if the fibres of this godlike frame
Were gored without a pang; as if the wretch,
Who fell in battle, doing bloody deeds,                    120
Passed off to Heaven, translated and not killed;
As though he had no wife to pine for him,
No God to judge him! Therefore, evil days
Are coming on us, O my countrymen!
And what if all-avenging Providence,                       125
Strong and retributive, should make us know
The meaning of our words, force us to feel
The desolation and the agony
Of our fierce doings?
                          Spare us yet awhile,
Father and God! O! spare us yet awhile!                    130
Oh! let not English women drag their flight
Fainting beneath the burthen of their babes,
Of the sweet infants, that but yesterday
Laughed at the breast! Sons, brothers, husbands, all
Who ever gazed with fondness on the forms                  135
Which grew up with you round the same fire-side,
And all who ever heard the sabbath-bells
Without the infidel's scorn, make yourselves pure!
Stand forth! be men! repel an impious foe,
Impious and false, a light yet cruel race,                 140
Who laugh away all virtue, mingling mirth
With deeds of murder; and still promising
Freedom, themselves too sensual to be free,
Poison life's amities, and cheat the heart
Of faith and quiet hope, and all that soothes              145
And all that lifts the spirit! Stand we forth;
Render them back upon the insulted ocean,
And let them toss as idly on its waves
As the vile sea-weed, which some mountain-blast
Swept from our shores! And oh! may we return              150
Not with a drunken triumph, but with fear,
Repenting of the wrongs with which we stung
So fierce a foe to frenzy!
                          I have told,
O Britons! O my brethren! I have told
Most bitter truth, but without bitterness.                 155

Nor deem my zeal or factious or mis-timed;
For never can true courage dwell with them,
Who, playing tricks with conscience, dare not look
At their own vices. We have been too long
Dupes of a deep delusion! Some, belike,                      160
Groaning with restless enmity, expect
All change from change of constituted power;
As if a Government had been a robe
On which our vice and wretchedness were tagged
Like fancy-points and fringes, with the robe               165
Pulled off at pleasure. Fondly these attach
A radical causation to a few
Poor drudges of chastising Providence,
Who borrow all their hues and qualities
From our own folly and rank wickedness,                    170
Which gave them birth and nursed them. Others,
    meanwhile,
Dote with a mad idolatry; and all
Who will not fall before their images,
And yield them worship, they are enemies
Even of their country!
                        Such have I been deemed –          175
But, O dear Britain! O my Mother Isle!
Needs must thou prove a name most dear and holy
To me, a son, a brother, and a friend,
A husband, and a father! who revere
All bonds of natural love, and find them all               180
Within the limits of thy rocky shores.
O native Britain! O my Mother Isle!
How shouldst thou prove aught else but dear and holy
To me, who from thy lakes and mountain-hills,
Thy clouds, thy quiet dales, thy rocks and seas,           185
Have drunk in all my intellectual life,
All sweet sensations, all ennobling thoughts,
All adoration of the God in nature,
All lovely and all honourable things,
Whatever makes this mortal spirit feel                     190
The joy and greatness of its future being!
There lives nor form nor feeling in my soul
Unborrowed from my country! O divine
And beauteous island! thou hast been my sole

And most magnificent temple, in the which                    195
I walk with awe, and sing my stately songs,
Loving the God that made me! –
                                    May my fears,
My filial fears, be vain! and may the vaunts
And menace of the vengeful enemy
Pass like the gust, that roared and died away                200
In the distant tree: which heard, and only heard
In this low dell, bowed not the delicate grass.


   But now the gentle dew-fall sends abroad
The fruit-like perfume of the golden furze:
The light has left the summit of the hill,                   205
Though still a sunny gleam lies beautiful,
Aslant the ivied beacon. Now farewell,
Farewell, awhile, O soft and silent spot!
On the green sheep-track, up the heathy hill,
Homeward I wind my way; and lo! recalled                     210
From bodings that have well nigh wearied me,
I find myself upon the brow, and pause
Startled! And after lonely sojourning
In such a quiet and surrounded nook,
This burst of prospect, here the shadowy main,               215
Dim tinted, there the mighty majesty
Of that huge amphitheatre of rich
And elmy fields, seems like society –
Conversing with the mind, and giving it
A livelier impulse and a dance of thought!                   220
And now, belovéd Stowey! I behold
Thy church-tower, and, methinks, the four huge elms
Clustering, which mark the mansion of my friend;
And close behind them, hidden from my view,
Is my own lowly cottage, where my babe                       225
And my babe's mother dwell in peace! With light
And quickened footsteps thitherward I tend,
Remembering thee, O green and silent dell!
And grateful, that by nature's quietness
And solitary musings, all my heart                           230
Is softened, and made worthy to indulge
Love, and the thoughts that yearn for human kind.

NETHER STOWEY, 28TH APRIL 1798

## *Recantation*[1]

### ILLUSTRATED IN THE STORY OF THE MAD OX

#### I

An Ox, long fed with musty hay,
   And work'd with yoke and chain,
Was turn'd out on an April day,
When fields are in their best array,
And growing grasses sparkle gay           5
   At once with Sun and rain.

#### II

The grass was fine, the Sun was bright –
   With truth I may aver it;
The ox was glad, as well he might,
Thought a green meadow no bad sight,       10
And frisk'd, to shew his huge delight,
   Much like a beast of spirit.

#### III

'*Stop, neighbours, stop, why these alarms?*
   *The ox is only glad!*'
But still they pour from cots and farms –    15
'Halloo!' the parish is up in arms,
(A *hoaxing*-hunt has always charms)
   'Halloo! the ox is mad.'

#### IV

The frighted beast scamper'd about –
   Plunge! through the hedge he drove:    20
The mob pursue with hideous rout,
A bull-dog fastens on his snout;
'He gores the dog! his tongue hangs out!
   He's mad, he's mad, by Jove!'

[1]'Written when fears were entertained of an invasion, and Mr Sheridan and Mr Tierney were absurdly represented as having *recanted* because to [The French Revolution (?)] in its origin they, [having been favourable, changed their opinion when the Revolutionists became unfaithful to their principles (?)].' [S.T.C., 1800]

### V

'STOP, NEIGHBOURS, STOP!' aloud did call 25
  A sage of sober hue.
But all at once, on him they fall,
And women squeak and children squall,
'What? would you have him toss us all?
  And dam'me, who are you?' 30

### VI

Oh! hapless sage! his ears they stun,
  And curse him o'er and o'er!
'You bloody-minded dog! (cries one),
To slit your windpipe were good fun,
'Od blast you for an *impious* son 35
  Of a Presbyterian wh—re!'

### VII

'You'd have him gore the Parish-priest,
  And run against the altar!
You fiend!' the sage his warnings ceas'd,
And north and south, and west and east, 40
Halloo! they follow the poor beast,
  Mat, Dick, Tom, Bob and Walter.

### VIII

Old Lewis ('twas his evil day),
  Stood trembling in his shoes;
The ox was his — what cou'd he say? 45
His legs were stiffen'd with dismay,
The ox ran o'er him mid the fray,
  And gave him his death's bruise.

### IX

The frighted beast ran on — but here,
  (No tale, tho' in print, more true is) 50
My Muse stops short in mid career —
Nay, gentle Reader, do not sneer!
I cannot chuse but drop a tear,
  A tear for good old Lewis!

X

The frighted beast ran through the town,                    55
    All follow'd, boy and dad,
Bull-dog, parson, shopman, clown:
The publicans rush'd from the Crown,
'Halloo! hamstring him! cut him down!'
    THEY DROVE THE POOR OX MAD.                              60

XI

Should you a Rat to madness tease
    Why ev'n a Rat may plague you:
There's no Philosopher but sees
That Rage and Fear are one disease —
Though that may burn, and this may freeze,                   65
    They're both alike the Ague.

XII

And so this Ox, in frantic mood,
    Fac'd round like any Bull!
The mob turn'd tail, and he pursued,
Till they with heat and fright were stew'd,                  70
And not a chick of all this brood
    But had his belly full!

XIII

Old Nick's astride the beast, 'tis clear!
    Old Nicholas, to a tittle!
But all agree he'd disappear,                                75
Would but the Parson venture near,
And through his teeth,[1] right o'er the steer,
    Squirt out some fasting-spittle.

XIV

Achilles was a warrior fleet,
    The Trojans he could worry:                              80
Our Parson too was swift of feet,

[1]According to the superstition of the West-Countries, if you meet the Devil, you may either cut him in half with a straw, or force him to disappear by spitting over his horns. [S.T.C.]

But shew'd it chiefly in retreat:
The victor Ox scour'd down the street,
  The mob fled hurry-scurry.

### XV

Through gardens, lanes and fields new plough'd,    85
  Through *his* hedge, and through *her* hedge,
He plung'd and toss'd and bellow'd loud –
Till in his madness he grew proud
To see this helter-skelter crowd
  That had more wrath than courage!    90

### XVI

Alas! to mend the breaches wide
  He made for these poor ninnies,
They all must work, whate'er betide,
Both days and months, and pay beside
(Sad news for Av'rice and for Pride),    95
  A *sight* of golden guineas!

### XVII

But here once more to view did pop
  The man that kept his senses;
And now he cried, – 'Stop, neighbours, stop!
The Ox is mad! I would not swop,    100
No! not a school-boy's farthing top
  For all the parish-fences.'

### XVIII

'The Ox is mad! Ho! Dick, Bob, Mat!'
  What means this coward fuss?
'Ho! stretch this rope across the plat –    105
'Twill trip him up – or if not that,
Why, dam'me! we must lay him flat –
  See! here's my blunderbuss.'

### XIX

'*A lying dog! just now he said
  The Ox was only glad –*    110

*Let's break his Presbyterian head!'*
'Hush!' quoth the sage, 'you've been misled;
No quarrels now! let's all make head,
    YOU DROVE THE POOR OX MAD.'


### XX

As thus I sat, in careless chat,                    115
    With the morning's wet newspaper,
In eager haste, without his hat,
As blind and blund'ring as a bat,
In came that fierce Aristocrat,
    Our pursy Woollen-draper.                        120


### XXI

And so my Muse perforce drew bit;
    And in he rush'd and panted!
'Well, have you heard?' No, not a whit.
'What, *ha'nt* you heard?' Come, out with it!
'That Tierney votes for Mister PITT,                 125
    And Sheridan's *recanted*!'
[1798]

## A Silent City

The silence of a City – How awful at midnight –
Mute as the battlements & crags & towers
That fancy makes in the clouds – yea as mute
As the moonlight that sleeps on the steady Vanes –
The cell of a departed Anchoret,                          5
His skeleton & flitting ghost are there,
Sole tenants –
And all the City, silent as the moon
That steeps in quiet light the steady Vanes
Of her huge temples –                                     10
[?September 1798. From MS]

## Hexameters[1]

William, my teacher, my friend! dear William and dear
    Dorothea!
Smooth out the folds of my letter, and place it on desk or on
    table;
Place it on table or desk; and your right hands loosely half-
    closing,[2]
Gently sustain them in air, and extending the digit didactic,
Rest it a moment on each of the forks of the five-forkéd left
    hand,                                                5
Twice on the breadth of the thumb, and once on the tip of each
    finger;
Read with a nod of the head in a humouring recitativo;
And, as I live, you will see my hexameters hopping before you.
This is a galloping measure; a hop, and a trot, and a gallop!

[1] The 'Hexameters' were sent in a letter, written in the winter of 1798–9 from Ratzeburg to the Wordsworths at Goslar. [E.H.C.]
[2] False metre. [S.T.C.]

All my hexameters fly, like stags pursued by the stag-hounds,    10
Breathless and panting, and ready to drop, yet flying still
     onwards.[1]
I would full fain pull in my hard-mouthed runaway hunter;
But our English Spondeans are clumsy yet impotent curb-reins;
And so to make him go slowly, no way have I left but to lame
     him.


William, my head and my heart! dear Poet that feelest and
     thinkest!    15
Dorothy, eager of soul, my most affectionate sister!
Many a mile, O! many a wearisome mile are ye distant,
Long, long, comfortless roads, with no one eye that doth know
     us.
O! it is all too far to send to you mockeries idle:
Yea, and I feel it not right! But O! my friends, my belovéd!    20
Feverish and wakeful I lie, – I am weary of feeling and thinking.
Every thought is worn *down*, – I am weary, yet cannot be
     vacant.
Five long hours have I tossed, rheumatic heats, dry and
     flushing,
Gnawing behind in my head, and wandering and throbbing
     about me,
Busy and tiresome, my friends, as the beat of the boding night-
     spider.[2]    25


*I forget the beginning of the line:*


                           . . . my eyes are a burthen,
Now unwillingly closed, now open and aching with darkness.
O! what a life is the eye! what a fine and inscrutable essence!
Him that is utterly blind, nor glimpses the fire that warms him;
Him that never beheld the swelling breast of his mother;    30
Him that ne'er smiled at the bosom as babe that smiles in its
     slumber;
Even to him it exists, it stirs and moves in its prison;

---

[1] '*Still* flying onwards' were perhaps better. [S.T.C.]
[2] False metre. [S.T.C.]

Lives with a separate life, and 'Is it the spirit?' he murmurs:
Sure, it has thoughts of its own, and to see is only its language.

*There was a great deal more, which I have forgotten . . . The last
line which I wrote, I remember, and write it for the truth of the senti-
ment, scarcely less true in company than in pain and solitude*:

William, my head and my heart! dear William and dear
    Dorothea!
You have all in each other; but I am lonely, and want you!    35
[1798. From MS]


## Catullian Hendecasyllables[1]

Hear, my belovéd, an old Milesian story! —
High, and embosom'd in congregated laurels,
Glimmer'd a temple upon a breezy headland;
In the dim distance amid the skiey billows
Rose a fair island; the god of flocks had blest it.    5
From the far shores of the bleat-resounding island
Oft by the moonlight a little boat came floating,
Came to the sea-cave beneath the breezy headland,
Where amid myrtles a pathway stole in mazes
Up to the groves of the high embosom'd temple.    10
There in a thicket of dedicated roses,
Oft did a priestess, as lovely as a vision,
Pouring her soul to the son of Cytherea,
Pray him to hover around the slight canoe-boat,
And with invisible pilotage to guide it    15
Over the dusk wave, until the nightly sailor
Shivering with ecstasy sank upon her bosom.
[1798]

[1] These lines, which are not 'Hendecasyllables', are a translation of part of Friedrich von Matthisson's *Milesisches Mährchen*. [E.H.C.] D. H. Lawrence may have been influenced by them when he wrote his story 'The Man who Died'.

## The Homeric Hexameter[1]

### DESCRIBED AND EXEMPLIFIED

Strongly it bears us along in swelling and limitless billows,
Nothing before and nothing behind but the sky and the ocean.
[1798]


## The Ovidian Elegiac Metre

### DESCRIBED AND EXEMPLIFIED

In the hexameter rises the fountain's silvery column;
In the pentameter aye falling in melody back.
[1798]


## Something Childish, But Very Natural[2]

### WRITTEN IN GERMANY

If I had but two little wings,
   And were a little feathery bird,
     To you I'd fly, my dear!
But thoughts like these are idle things,
     And I stay here.                    5

But in my sleep to you I fly:
   I'm always with you in my sleep!
     The world is all one's own.
But then one wakes, and where am I?
     All, all alone.                    10

---

[1]An acknowledgement that these 'experiments in metre' are translations from Schiller was first made in a Note to *Poems*, 1844, p. 371. [E.H.C.]

[2]An imitation of the German folk-song *Wenn ich ein Vöglein wär*'. [E.H.C.]

Sleep stays not, though a monarch bids:
   So I love to wake ere break of day:
     For though my sleep be gone,
Yet while 'tis dark, one shuts one's lids,
     And still dreams on.        15
[1798–9]


## The Visit of the Gods

### IMITATED FROM SCHILLER

    Never, believe me,
    Appear the Immortals,
     Never alone:
Scarce had I welcomed the Sorrow-beguiler,
Iacchus! but in came Boy Cupid, the Smiler;     5
Lo! Phoebus the Glorious descends from his throne!
They advance, they float in, the Olympians all!
     With Divinities fills my
      Terrestrial hall!

    How shall I yield you     10
    Due entertainment,
     Celestial quire?
Me rather, bright guests! with your wings of upbuoyance
Bear aloft to your homes, to your banquets of joyance,
That the roofs of Olympus may echo my lyre!     15
Hah! we mount! on their pinions they waft up my soul!
     O give me the nectar!
     O fill me the bowl!

    Give him the nectar!
    Pour out for the poet,     20
     Hebe! pour free!
Quicken his eyes with celestial dew,
That Styx the detested no more he may view,
And like one of us Gods may conceit him to be!

Thanks, Hebe! I quaff it! Io Paean, I cry!        25
          The wine of the Immortals
              Forbids me to die!

[?1799]


## Translation of a Passage in Ottfried's Metrical Paraphrase of the Gospel

[This paraphrase, written about the time of Charlemagne, is by no means deficient in occasional passages of considerable poetic merit. There is a flow, and a tender enthusiasm in the following lines which even in the translation will not, I flatter myself, fail to interest the reader. Ottfried is describing the circumstances immediately following the birth of our Lord. Most interesting is it to consider the effect when the feelings are wrought above the natural pitch by the belief of something mysterious, while all the images are purely natural. Then it is, that religion and poetry strike deepest. *Biographia Literaria*, 1817, i. 203–4.]

          She gave with joy her virgin breast;
          She hid it not, she bared the breast
          Which suckled that divinest babe!
          Blessed, blessed were the breasts
          Which the Saviour infant kiss'd;        5
          And blessed, blessed was the mother
          Who wrapp'd his limbs in swaddling clothes,
          Singing placed him on her lap,
          Hung o'er him with her looks of love,
          And soothed him with a lulling motion.        10
          Blessed! for she shelter'd him
          From the damp and chilling air;
          Blessed, blessed! for she lay
          With such a babe in one blest bed,
          Close as babes and mothers lie!        15
          Blessed, blessed evermore,
          With her virgin lips she kiss'd,
          With her arms, and to her breast,
          She embraced the babe divine,
          Her babe divine the virgin mother!        20
          There lives not on this ring of earth

A mortal, that can sing her praise.
Mighty mother, virgin pure,
In the darkness and the night
For us she *bore* the heavenly Lord!                25
[?1799]

## On an Infant[1]

### WHICH DIED BEFORE BAPTISM

'Be, rather than be called, a child of God,'
Death whispered! With assenting nod,
Its head upon its mother's breast,
    The Baby bowed, without demur —
Of the kingdom of the Blest                5
    Possessor, not Inheritor.
[1799]

## Home-Sick

### WRITTEN IN GERMANY

'Tis sweet to him, who all the week
    Through city-crowds must push his way,
To stroll alone through fields and woods,
    And hallow thus the Sabbath-day.

And sweet it is, in summer bower,                5
    Sincere, affectionate and gay,
One's own dear children feasting round,
    To celebrate one's marriage-day.

But what is all to his delight,
    Who having long been doomed to roam,                10
Throws off the bundle from his back,
    Before the door of his own home?

[1]A few weeks ago an Englishman desired me to write an epitaph on an infant who had died before its Christening. While I wrote it, my heart with a deep misgiving turned my thoughts homeward . . . It refers to the second question in the Church Catechism.' [S.T.C., Letter] The first line echoes Lessing's 'Grabschrift der Tochter eines Freundes'. [K.C.]

Home-sickness is a wasting pang;
   This feel I hourly more and more:
There's healing only in thy wings,                15
   Thou Breeze that play'st on Albion's shore!
[May 1799]


## The Virgin's Cradle-Hymn

### COPIED FROM A PRINT OF THE VIRGIN IN A ROMAN CATHOLIC VILLAGE IN GERMANY

Dormi, Jesu! Mater ridet
Quae tam dulcem somnum videt,
   Dormi, Jesu! blandule!
Si non dormis, Mater plorat,
Inter fila cantans orat,                   5
   Blande, veni, somnule.


### ENGLISH

Sleep, sweet babe! my cares beguiling:
Mother sits beside thee smiling;
   Sleep, my darling, tenderly!
If thou sleep not, mother mourneth,         10
Singing as her wheel she turneth:
   Come, soft slumber, balmily!
[May 1799]

# Lines
## WRITTEN IN THE ALBUM AT ELBINGERODE,
### IN THE HARZ FOREST

I stood on Brocken's[1] sovran height, and saw
Woods crowding upon woods, hills over hills,
A surging scene, and only limited
By the blue distance. Heavily my way
Downward I dragged through fir groves evermore,     5
Where bright green moss heaves in sepulchral forms
Speckled with sunshine; and, but seldom heard,
The sweet bird's song became a hollow sound;
And the breeze, murmuring indivisibly,
Preserved its solemn murmur most distinct     10
From many a note of many a waterfall,
And the brook's chatter; 'mid whose islet-stones
The dingy kidling with its tinkling bell
Leaped frolicsome, or old romantic goat
Sat, his white beard slow waving. I moved on     15
In low and languid mood:[2] for I had found
That outward forms, the loftiest, still receive
Their finer influence from the Life within; –
Fair cyphers else: fair, but of import vague
Or unconcerning, where the heart not finds     20
History or prophecy of friend, or child,
Or gentle maid, our first and early love,
Or father, or the venerable name
Of our adoréd country! O thou Queen,
Thou delegated Deity of Earth,     25
O dear, dear England! how my longing eye

---

[1] The highest Mountain in the Harz, and indeed in North Germany. [S.T.C.]

[2] ————When I have gaz'd
From some high eminence on goodly vales,
And cots and villages embower'd below,
The thought would rise that all to me was strange
Amid the scenes so fair, nor one small spot
Where my tired mind might rest and call it home.
                                    SOUTHEY's *Hymn to the Penates.*
                                                        [S.T.C.]

Turned westward, shaping in the steady clouds
Thy sands and high white cliffs!

                       My native Land!
Filled with the thought of thee this heart was proud,
Yea, mine eye swam with tears: that all the view         30
From sovran Brocken, woods and woody hills,
Floated away, like a departing dream,
Feeble and dim! Stranger, these impulses
Blame thou not lightly; nor will I profane,
With hasty judgment or injurious doubt,         35
That man's sublimer spirit, who can feel
That God is everywhere! the God who framed
Mankind to be one mighty family,
Himself our Father, and the World our Home.
[May 1799]

## The British Stripling's War-Song

### IMITATED FROM STOLBERG

Yes, noble old Warrior! this heart has beat high,
   Since you told of the deeds which our countrymen wrought;
O lend me the sabre that hung by thy thigh,
   And I too will fight as my forefathers fought.

Despise not my youth, for my spirit is steel'd,       5
   And I know there is strength in the grasp of my hand;
Yea, as firm as thyself would I march to the field,
   And as proudly would die for my dear native land.

In the sports of my childhood I mimick'd the fight,
   The sound of a trumpet suspended my breath;      10
And my fancy still wander'd by day and by night,
   Amid battle and tumult, 'mid conquest and death.

My own shout of onset, when the Armies advance,
   How oft it awakes me from visions of glory;
When I meant to have leapt on the Hero of France,     15
   And have dash'd him to earth, pale and breathless and
      gory.

As late thro' the city with banners all streaming
  To the music of trumpets the Warriors flew by,
With helmet and scimitars naked and gleaming,
  On their proud-trampling, thunder-hoof'd steeds did
    they fly;                                                                     20

I sped to yon heath that is lonely and bare,
  For each nerve was unquiet, each pulse in alarm;
And I hurl'd the mock-lance thro' the objectless air,
  And in open-eyed dream proved the strength of my arm.

Yes, noble old Warrior! this heart has beat high,                                  25
  Since you told of the deeds that our countrymen wrought;
O lend me the sabre that hung by thy thigh,
  And I too will fight as my forefathers fought!
[1799]

## The Devil's Thoughts

### I

From his brimstone bed at break of day
   A walking the Devil is gone,
To visit his snug little farm the Earth,
   And see how his stock goes on.

### II

Over the hill and over the dale,
   And he went over the plain,                                      5
And backward and forward he switched his long tail
   As a gentleman switches his cane.

### III

And how then was the Devil drest?
   Oh! he was in his Sunday's best:                                 10
His jacket was red and his breeches were blue,
   And there was a hole where the tail came through.

### IV

He saw a Lawyer killing a Viper
   On a dunghill hard by his own stable;
And the Devil smiled, for it put him in mind                             15
   Of Cain and his brother Abel.

### V

He saw an Apothecary on a white horse
   Ride by on his vocations,
And the Devil thought of his old Friend
   Death in the Revelations.[1]                                     20

### VI

He saw a cottage with a double coach-house,
   A cottage of gentility;

[1] And I looked, and behold a pale horse, and his name that sat on him was Death. – Rev. vi. 8. [S.T.C.]

And the Devil did grin, for his darling sin
Is pride that apes humility.

### VII

He peep'd into a rich bookseller's shop,                    25
    Quoth he! we are both of one college!
For I sate myself, like a cormorant, once
    Hard by the tree of knowledge.[1]

### VIII

Down the river did glide, with wind and tide,
    A pig with vast celerity;                              30
And the Devil look'd wise as he saw how the while,
It cut its own throat. 'There!' quoth he with a smile,
    'Goes "England's commercial prosperity."'

### IX

As he went through Cold-Bath Fields he saw
    A solitary cell;                                       35

[1]"And all amid them stood the TREE OF LIFE
High, eminent, blooming ambrosial fruit
Of vegetable gold (query *paper-money*), and next to Life
*Our* Death, the TREE OF KNOWLEDGE, grew fast by. –

      \*      \*      \*
      \*      \*      \*

So clomb this first grand thief –
Thence up he flew, and on the tree of life
Sat like a cormorant.' – *Par. Lost*, iv.

The allegory here is so apt, that in a catalogue of *various readings* obtained from collating the MSS. one might expect to find it noted, that for 'LIFE' *Cod. quid. habent* ['Some manuscripts read'], 'TRADE'. Though indeed THE TRADE, i.e. the bibliopolic, so called κατ' εξοχήν, ['by way of eminence'], may be regarded as LIFE sensu *eminentiori* ['in a *more eminent* sense']; a suggestion, which I owe to a young retailer in the hosiery line, who on hearing a description of the net profits, dinner parties, country houses, etc., of the trade, exclaimed, 'Ay! that's what I call LIFE now!' – This 'Life, *our* Death,' is thus happily contrasted with the fruits of Authorship. – Sic nos non nobis mellificamus Apes ['So we bees make honey, not for ourselves'].

Of this poem, which with the 'Fire, Famine, and Slaughter' first appeared in the *Morning Post* [6 September 1799], the 1st, 2nd, 3rd, 9th and 16th stanzas were dictated by Mr Southey. See Apologetic Preface [to *Fire, Famine and Slaughter*].

If any one should ask who General —— meant, the Author begs leave to inform him, that he did once see a red-faced person in a dream whom by the dress he took for a General; but he might have been mistaken, and most certainly he did not hear any names mentioned. In simple verity, the author never meant any one, or indeed any thing but to put a concluding stanza to his doggerel. [S.T.C.]

And the Devil was pleased, for it gave him a hint
   For improving his prisons in Hell.


X

He saw a Turnkey in a trice
   Fetter a troublesome blade;
'Nimbly,' quoth he, 'do the fingers move       40
   If a man be but used to his trade.'


XI

He saw the same Turnkey unfetter a man,
   With but little expedition,
Which put him in mind of the long debate
   On the Slave-trade abolition.      45


XII

He saw an old acquaintance
   As he passed by a Methodist meeting; –
She holds a consecrated key,
   And the devil nods her a greeting.


XIII

She turned up her nose, and said,      50
   'Avaunt! my name's Religion,'
And she looked to Mr ——
   And leered like a love-sick pigeon.


XIV

He saw a certain minister
   (A minister to his mind)      55
Go up to a certain House,
   With a majority behind.


XV

The Devil quoted Genesis
   Like a very learnéd clerk,
How 'Noah and his creeping things      60
   Went up into the Ark.'

XVI

He took from the poor,
　　And he gave to the rich,
And he shook hands with a Scotchman,
　　For he was not afraid of the ——　　　　　65

XVII

General ——[1] burning face
　　He saw with consternation,
And back to hell his way did he take,
For the Devil thought by a slight mistake
　　It was general conflagration.　　　　　70
[1799]


## Mahomet[2]

Utter the song, O my soul! the flight and return of Mohammed,
Prophet and priest, who scatter'd abroad both evil and
　　　　blessing,
Huge wasteful empires founded and hallow'd slow persecu-
　　　　tion,
Soul-withering, but crush'd the blasphemous rites of the Pagan
And idolatrous Christians. — For veiling the Gospel of Jesus,　　5
They, the best corrupting, had made it worse than the vilest.
Wherefore Heaven decreed th' enthusiast warrior of Mecca,
Choosing good from iniquity rather than evil from goodness.
　　Loud the tumult in Mecca surrounding the fane of the idol; —
Naked and prostrate the priesthood were laid — the people with
　　　　mad shouts
Thundering now, and now with saddest ululation　　　　　10
Flew, as over the channel of rock-stone the ruinous river
Shatters its waters abreast, and in mazy uproar bewilder'd,
Rushes dividuous all — all rushing impetuous onward.
[1799]

[1] In a MS copy in the B.M. and in some pirated versions the blank is filled up by the word
'Gascoigne's'; but in a MS copy taken at Highgate, in June 1820, by Derwent Coleridge the
line runs, 'General Tarleton's', &c. [E.H.C.]. See previous note also.
[2] These fourteen lines represent Coleridge's contribution to a poem on 'Mahomet' which he
had planned in conjunction with Southey. For Southey's portion, which numbered 109 lines,
see Oliver Newman, by Robert Southey, 1845, pp. 113–15. [E.H.C.]

## On an Insignificant

'Tis Cypher lies beneath this crust —
Whom Death *created* into dust.


## To Mr Pye[1]

On his *Carmen Seculare* (a title which has by various persons who have heard it, been thus translated, 'A Poem *an age long*').

Your Poem must *eternal* be,
    *Eternal!* it can't fail,
For 'tis *incomprehensible*,
    And without head or tail!
[1799, published 1800]


## To a Critic

WHO EXTRACTED A PASSAGE FROM A POEM
WITHOUT ADDING A WORD RESPECTING THE CONTEXT,
AND THEN DERIDED IT AS UNINTELLIGIBLE

Most candid critic, what if I,
By way of joke, pull out your eye,
And holding up the fragment, cry,
'Ha! ha! that men such fools should be!
Behold this shapeless Dab! — and he          5
Who own'd it, fancied it could *see!*'
The joke were mighty analytic,
But should you like it, candid critic?
[1799]

[1] Later reprinted as 'To the Author of the Ancient Mariner'. Cf. Lessing's 'Die Ewigheit gewisser Gedichte'. [K.C.] The much ridiculed Poet Laureate, Henry James Pye, produced his 'Carmen Seculare for the year 1800' to commemorate the turn of the century. In Roman times a 'secular ode' celebrated the end of a 'saeculum' (100 years, or an 'age').

## Names

**FROM LESSING**

I ask'd my fair one happy day,
What I should call her in my lay;
    By what sweet name from Rome or Greece;
Lalage, Neaera, Chloris,
Sappho, Lesbia, or Doris,                              5
    Arethusa or Lucrece.

'Ah!' replied my gentle fair,
'Belovéd, what are names but air?
    Choose thou whatever suits the line;
Call me Sappho, call me Chloris,                       10
Call me Lalage or Doris,
    Only, only call me Thine.'
[1799]

## The Exchange

We pledged our hearts, my love and I, –
    I in my arms the maiden clasping;
I could not guess the reason why,
    But, oh! I trembled like an aspen.

Her father's love she bade me gain;                    5
    I went, but shook like any reed!
I strove to act the man – in vain!
    We had exchanged our hearts indeed.
[1799–1801]

## On a Volunteer Singer

Swans sing before they die – 'twere no bad thing
Should certain persons die before they sing.
[1800]

## Lines Composed in a Concert-Room

Nor cold, nor stern, my soul! yet I detest
   These scented Rooms, where, to a gaudy throng,
Heaves the proud Harlot her distended breast,
   In intricacies of laborious song.

These feel not Music's genuine power, nor deign        5
   To melt at Nature's passion-warbled plaint;
But when the long-breathed singer's uptrilled strain
   Bursts in a squall – they gape for wonderment.

Hark! the deep buzz of Vanity and Hate!
   Scornful, yet envious, with self-torturing sneer       10
My lady eyes some maid of humbler state,
   While the pert Captain, or the primmer Priest,
   Prattles accordant scandal in her ear.

O give me, from this heartless scene released,
   To hear our old Musician, blind and grey,       15
(Whom stretching from my nurse's arms I kissed,)
   His Scottish tunes and warlike marches play,
By moonshine, on the balmy summer-night,
   The while I dance amid the tedded hay
With merry maids, whose ringlets toss in light.       20

Or lies the purple evening on the bay
Of the calm glossy lake, O let me hide
   Unheard, unseen, behind the alder-trees,
For round their roots the fisher's boat is tied,
   On whose trim seat doth Edmund stretch at ease,       25
And while the lazy boat sways to and fro,
   Breathes in his flute sad airs, so wild and slow,
That his own cheek is wet with quiet tears.

But O, dear Anne! when midnight wind careers,
And the gust pelting on the out-house shed       30
   Makes the cock shrilly in the rainstorm crow,
   To hear thee sing some ballad full of woe,

Ballad of ship-wreck'd sailor floating dead,
　　Whom his own true-love buried in the sands!
Thee, gentle woman, for thy voice remeasures                35
Whatever tones and melancholy pleasures
　　The things of Nature utter; birds or trees,
Or moan of ocean-gale in weedy caves,
Or where the stiff grass mid the heath-plant waves,
　　Murmur and music thin of sudden breeze.                  40
[?1799]


# Hexameters

### PARAPHRASE OF PSALM XLVI

Gōd ĭs oŭr Strēngth ănd oŭr Rēfŭge: thērefōre wīll wĕ nŏt
　　trēmblĕ,
Thō' thĕ Eārth bĕ rĕmōvĕd; ănd thō' thĕ pĕrpētŭăl Moūntaĭns
Sink in the Swell of the Ocean! God is our Strength & our
　　Refuge.
There is a River, the Flowing whereof shall gladden the City,
Hallelujah! the City of God! Jehova shall help her.              5

Thē Idōlătĕrs rāgĕd, the Kingdoms were moving in fury –
But He uttered his Voice: Earth melted away from beneath
　　them.
Halleluja! th' Eternal is with us, Almighty Jehova!

Fearful the works of the Lord, yea, fearful his Desolations –
But *He* maketh the Battle to cease, he burneth the Spear & the
　　Chariot.                                                    10
Halleluja! th' Eternal is with us, the God of our Fathers! –
[1799. From MS]

## Ode to Georgiana, Duchess of Devonshire

ON THE TWENTY-FOURTH STANZA IN HER
'PASSAGE OVER MOUNT GOTHARD'

And hail the Chapel! hail the Platform wild!
  Where Tell directed the avenging dart,
With well-strung arm, that first preserv'd his child,
  Then aim'd the arrow at the tyrant's heart.

Splendour's fondly-fostered child!
And did you hail the platform wild,
    Where once the Austrian fell
    Beneath the shaft of Tell?
  O Lady, nursed in pomp and pleasure!          5
  Whence learn'd you that heroic measure?

Light as a dream your days their circlets ran,
From all that teaches brotherhood to Man
Far, far removed! from want, from hope, from fear!
Enchanting music lulled your infant ear,          10
Obeisance, praises soothed your infant heart:
  Emblazonments and old ancestral crests,
With many a bright obtrusive form of art,
  Detained your eye from Nature: stately vests,
That veiling strove to deck your charms divine,          15
Rich viands, and the pleasurable wine,
Were yours unearned by toil; nor could you see
The unenjoying toiler's misery.
And yet, free Nature's uncorrupted child,
You hailed the Chapel and the Platform wild,          20
    Where once the Austrian fell
    Beneath the shaft of Tell!
  O Lady, nursed in pomp and pleasure!
  Whence learn'd you that heroic measure?

There crowd your finely-fibred frame          25
  All living faculties of bliss;
And Genius to your cradle came,
His forehead wreathed with lambent flame,
  And bending low, with godlike kiss
  Breath'd in a more celestial life;          30

But boasts not many a fair compeer
   A heart as sensitive to joy and fear?
And some, perchance, might wage an equal strife,
Some few, to nobler being wrought,
Corrivals in the nobler gift of thought.            35
      Yet these delight to celebrate
      Laurelled War and plumy State;
      Or in verse and music dress
      Tales of rustic happiness –
Pernicious tales! insidious strains!          40
     That steel the rich man's breast,
     And mock the lot unblest,
  The sordid vices and the abject pains,
  Which evermore must be
  The doom of ignorance and penury!       45
But you, free Nature's uncorrupted child,
You hailed the Chapel and the Platform wild,
      Where once the Austrian fell
      Beneath the shaft of Tell!
  O Lady, nursed in pomp and pleasure!     50
  Whence learn'd you that heroic measure?


You were a Mother! That most holy name,
      Which Heaven and Nature bless,
  I may not vilely prostitute to those
      Whose infants owe them less     55
Than the poor caterpillar owes
   Its gaudy parent fly.
You were a mother! at your bosom fed
  The babes that loved you. You, with laughing eye,
Each twilight-thought, each nascent feeling read,   60
  Which you yourself created. Oh! delight!
    A second time to be a mother,
      Without the mother's bitter groans:
    Another thought, and yet another,
      By touch, or taste, by looks or tones,   65
  O'er the growing sense to roll,
  The mother of your infant's soul!
The Angel of the Earth, who, while he guides
  His chariot-planet round the goal of day,
All trembling gazes on the Eye of God     70

A moment turned his awful face away;
And as he viewed you, from his aspect sweet
    New influences in your being rose,
Blest intuitions and communions fleet
    With living Nature, in her joys and woes!          75
    Thenceforth your soul rejoiced to see
    The shrine of social Liberty!
    O beautiful! O Nature's child!
    'Twas thence you hailed the Platform wild,
        Where once the Austrian fell                   80
        Beneath the shaft of Tell!
    O Lady, nursed in pomp and pleasure!
    Thence learn'd you that heroic measure.
[1799]


# Hymn to the Earth

[IMITATED FROM STOLBERG'S 'HYMNE AN DIE ERDE']

### HEXAMETERS

Earth! thou mother of numberless children, the nurse and the
    mother,
Hail! O Goddess, thrice hail! Blest be thou! and, blessing, I
    hymn thee!
Forth, ye sweet sounds! from my harp, and my voice shall float
    on your surges –
Soar thou aloft, O my soul! and bear up my song on thy
    pinions.

Travelling the vale with mine eyes – green meadows and lake
    with green island,                                  5
Dark in its basin of rock, and the bare stream flowing in
    brightness,
Thrilled with thy beauty and love in the wooded slope of the
    mountain,
Here, great mother, I lie, thy child, with his head on thy bosom!
Playful the spirits of noon, that rushing soft through thy tresses,
Green-haired goddess! refresh me; and hark! as they hurry or
    linger,                                             10

Fill the pause of my harp, or sustain it with musical murmurs.
Into my being thou murmurest joy, and tenderest sadness
Shedd'st thou, like dew, on my heart, till the joy and the heavenly
   sadness
Pour themselves forth from my heart in tears, and the hymn of
   thanksgiving.

Earth! thou mother of numberless children, the nurse and the
   mother,                                                          15
Sister thou of the stars, and beloved by the Sun, the rejoicer!
Guardian and friend of the moon, O Earth, whom the comets
   forget not,
Yea, in the measureless distance wheel round and again they
   behold thee!
Fadeless and young (and what if the latest birth of creation?)
Bride and consort of Heaven, that looks down upon thee
   enamoured!                                                       20
Say, mysterious Earth! O say, great mother and goddess,
Was it not well with thee then, when first thy lap was ungirdled,
Thy lap to the genial Heaven, the day that he wooed thee and
   won thee!
Fair was thy blush, the fairest and first of the blushes of morning!
Deep was the shudder, O Earth, the throe of thy self-retention:    25
Inly thou strovest to flee, and didst seek thyself at thy centre!
Mightier far was the joy of thy sudden resilience; and forthwith
Myriad myriads of lives teemed forth from the mighty embrace-
   ment.
Thousand-fold tribes of dwellers, impelled by thousand-fold
   instincts,
Filled, as a dream, the wide waters; the rivers sang on their
   channels;                                                        30
Laughed on their shores the hoarse seas; the yearning ocean
   swelled upward;
Young life lowed through the meadows, the woods, and the
   echoing mountains,
Wandered bleating in valleys, and warbled on blossoming
   branches.
[1799]

## *On a Cataract*[1]

FROM A CAVERN NEAR THE SUMMIT OF
A MOUNTAIN PRECIPICE

STROPHE

Unperishing youth!
Thou leapest from forth
The cell of thy hidden nativity;
Never mortal saw
The cradle of the strong one;                                      5
Never mortal heard
The gathering of his voices;
The deep-murmured charm of the son of the rock,
That is lisp'd evermore at his slumberless fountain.
There's a cloud at the portal, a spray-woven veil              10
At the shrine of his ceaseless renewing;
It embosoms the roses of dawn,
It entangles the shafts of the noon,
And into the bed of its stillness
The moonshine sinks down as in slumber,                         15
That the son of the rock, that the nursling of heaven
May be born in a holy twilight!

ANTISTROPHE

The wild goat in awe
Looks up and beholds
Above thee the cliff inaccessible; —                            20
Thou at once full-born
Madd'nest in thy joyance,
Whirlest, shatter'st, splitt'st,
Life invulnerable.
[?1799]

[1]'Improved from Stolberg'. [E.H.C.]

## Tell's Birth-Place

**IMITATED FROM STOLBERG**

### I

Mark this holy chapel well!
The birth-place, this, of William Tell.
Here, where stands God's altar dread,
Stood his parents' marriage-bed.

### II

Here, first, an infant to her breast,  5
Him his loving mother prest;
And kissed the babe, and blessed the day,
And prayed as mothers use to pray.

### III

'Vouchsafe him health, O God! and give
The child thy servant still to live!'  10
But God had destined to do more
Through him, than through an arméd power.

### IV

God gave him reverence of laws,
Yet stirring blood in Freedom's cause –
A spirit to his rocks akin,  15
The eye of the hawk, and the fire therein!

### V

To Nature and to Holy Writ
Alone did God the boy commit:
Where flashed and roared the torrent, oft
His soul found wings, and soared aloft!  20

### VI

The straining oar and chamois chase
Had formed his limbs to strength and grace:
On wave and wind the boy would toss,
Was great, nor knew how great he was!

### VII

He knew not that his chosen hand,          25
Made strong by God, his native land
Would rescue from the shameful yoke
Of Slavery — the which he broke!
[?1799]

## A Christmas Carol

### I

The shepherds went their hasty way,
    And found the lowly stable-shed
Where the Virgin-Mother lay:
    And now they checked their eager tread,
For to the Babe, that at her bosom clung,          5
A Mother's song the Virgin-Mother sung.

### II

They told her how a glorious light,
    Streaming from a heavenly throng,
Around them shone, suspending night!
    While sweeter than a mother's song,          10
Blest Angels heralded the Saviour's birth,
Glory to God on high! and Peace on Earth.

### III

She listened to the tale divine,
    And closer still the Babe she pressed;
And while she cried, the Babe is mine!          15
    The milk rushed faster to her breast:
Joy rose within her, like a summer's morn;
Peace, Peace on Earth! the Prince of Peace is born.

IV

Thou Mother of the Prince of Peace,
    Poor, simple, and of low estate! 20
That strife should vanish, battle cease,
    O why should this thy soul elate?
Sweet Music's loudest note, the Poet's story, ——
Didst thou ne'er love to hear of fame and glory?

V

And is not War a youthful king, 25
    A stately Hero clad in mail?
Beneath his footsteps laurels spring;
    Him Earth's majestic monarchs hail
Their friend, their playmate! and his bold bright eye
Compels the maiden's love-confessing sigh. 30

VI

'Tell this in some more courtly scene,
    To maids and youths in robes of state!
I am a woman poor and mean,
    And therefore is my soul elate.
War is a ruffian, all with guilt defiled, 35
That from the agéd father tears his child!

VII

'A murderous fiend, by fiends adored,
    He kills the sire and starves the son;
The husband kills, and from her board
    Steals all his widow's toil had won; 40
Plunders God's world of beauty; rends away
All safety from the night, all comfort from the day.

VIII

'Then wisely is my soul elate,
    That strife should vanish, battle cease:
I'm poor and of a low estate,
    The Mother of the Prince of Peace. 45
Joy rises in me, like a summer's morn:
Peace, Peace on Earth! the Prince of Peace is born.'
[1799]

## The Two Round Spaces on the Tombstone

The Devil believes that the Lord will come,
Stealing a march without beat of drum,
About the same time that he came last,
On an Old Christmas-day in a snowy blast:
Till he bids the trump sound neither body nor soul stirs,                    5
For the dead men's heads have slipt under their bolsters.


Oh! ho! brother Bard, in our churchyard,
Both beds and bolsters are soft and green;
Save one alone, and that's of stone,
And under it lies a Counsellor keen.[1]                    10
'Twould be a square tomb, if it were not too long;
And 'tis fenced round with irons sharp, spear-like and strong.


This fellow from Aberdeen hither did skip
With a waxy face and a blubber lip,
And a black tooth in front, to show in part                    15
What was the colour of his whole heart.
    This Counsellor sweet,
    This Scotchman complete,
  (The Devil scotch him for a snake!)
  I trust he lies in his grave awake.                    20


On the sixth of January,
    When all around is white with snow,
    As a Cheshire yeoman's dairy,
        Brother Bard, ho! ho!
        Believe it, or no,                    25
    On that stone tomb to you I'll show
    Two round spaces void of snow.
I swear by our Knight, and his forefathers' souls,
That in size and shape they are just like the holes
            In the house of privity                    30
            Of that ancient family.

[1]Sir James Mackintosh, against whom the poem is directed.

On those two places void of snow,
There have sat in the night for an hour or so,
Before sunrise, and after cock-crow,
  He kicking his heels, she cursing her corns,      35
  All to the tune of the wind in their horns,
      The Devil and his Grannam,
       With a snow-blast to fan 'em;
  Expecting and hoping the trumpet to blow,
  For they are cock-sure of the fellow below!      40
[1800]


## The Mad Monk[1]

I heard a voice from Etna's side;
  Where o'er a cavern's mouth
  That fronted to the south
A chestnut spread its umbrage wide:
A hermit or a monk the man might be;      5
  But him I could not see:
And thus the music flow'd along,
In melody most like to old Sicilian song:

'There was a time when earth, and sea, and skies,[2]
  The bright green vale, and forest's dark recess,      10
With all things, lay before mine eyes
  In steady loveliness:
But now I feel, on earth's uneasy scene,
  Such sorrows as will never cease; –
  I only ask for peace;      15
If I must live to know that such a time has been!'
A silence then ensued:
    Till from the cavern came
    A voice; – it was the same!
And thus, in mournful tone, its dreary plaint renew'd:      20

'Last night, as o'er the sloping turf I trod,
  The smooth green turf, to me a vision gave
Beneath mine eyes, the sod –
  The roof of Rosa's grave!

[1] 'An Ode in Mrs Ratcliff's Manner.' [S.T.C.]
[2] Compare the opening of Wordsworth's Immortality Ode, begun in 1802.

'My heart has need with dreams like these to strive,          25
    For, when I woke, beneath mine eyes I found
        The plot of mossy ground,
On which we oft have sat when Rosa was alive. –
Why must the rock, and margin of the flood,
    Why must the hills so many flow'rets bear,          30
Whose colours to a *murder'd* maiden's blood,
    Such sad resemblance wear? –


'*I struck the wound*, – this hand of mine!
For Oh, thou maid divine,
    I lov'd to agony!
The youth whom thou call'd'st thine          35
    Did never love like me!


'Is it the stormy clouds above
    That flash'd so red a gleam?
    On yonder downward trickling stream? –
'Tis not the blood of her I love. –          40
The sun torments me from his western bed,
    Oh, let him cease for ever to diffuse
    Those crimson spectre hues!
Oh, let me lie in peace, and be for ever dead!'          45


Here ceas'd the voice. In deep dismay,
Down thro' the forest I pursu'd my way.
[1800]


## A Stranger Minstrel

### WRITTEN TO MRS ROBINSON, A FEW WEEKS
### BEFORE HER DEATH

As late on Skiddaw's mount I lay supine,
Midway th' ascent, in that repose divine
When the soul centred in the heart's recess
Hath quaff'd its fill of Nature's loveliness,

Yet still beside the fountain's marge will stay 5
   And fain would thirst again, again to quaff;
Then when the tear, slow travelling on its way,
   Fills up the wrinkles of a silent laugh —
In that sweet mood of sad and humorous thought
A form within me rose, within me wrought 10
With such strong magic, that I cried aloud,
'Thou ancient Skiddaw by thy helm of cloud,
And by thy many-colour'd chasms deep,
And by their shadows that for ever sleep,
By yon small flaky mists that love to creep 15
Along the edges of those spots of light,
Those sunny islands on thy smooth green height,
   And by yon shepherds with their sheep,
   And dogs and boys, a gladsome crowd,
   That rush e'en now with clamour loud 20
   Sudden from forth thy topmost cloud,
   And by this laugh, and by this tear,
   I would, old Skiddaw, she were here!
   A lady of sweet song is she,
   Her soft blue eye was made for thee! 25
   O ancient Skiddaw, by this tear,
   I would, I would that she were here!'

Then ancient Skiddaw, stern and proud,
   In sullen majesty replying,
Thus spake from out his helm of cloud 30
   (His voice was like an echo dying!): —
'She dwells belike in scenes more fair,
And scorns a mount so bleak and bare.'

I only sigh'd when this I heard,
Such mournful thoughts within me stirr'd 35
That all my heart was faint and weak,
   So sorely was I troubled!
No laughter wrinkled on my cheek,
   But O the tears were doubled!
But ancient Skiddaw green and high 40
Heard and understood my sigh;
And now, in tones less stern and rude,
As if he wish'd to end the feud,

Spake he, the proud response renewing
(His voice was like a monarch wooing): – 45
'Nay, but thou dost not know her might,
  The pinions of her soul how strong!
But many a stranger in my height
  Hath sung to me her magic song,
    Sending forth his ecstasy 50
    In her divinest melody,
And hence I know her soul is free,
She is where'er she wills to be,
Unfetter'd by mortality!

Now to the "haunted beach" can fly, 55
  Beside the threshold scourged with waves,
  Now where the maniac wildly raves,
*"Pale moon, thou spectre of the sky!"* [1]
  No wind that hurries o'er my height
  Can travel with so swift a flight. 60
    I too, methinks, might merit
    The presence of her spirit!
    To me too might belong
The honour of her song and witching melody,
    Which most resembles me, 65
    Soft, various, and sublime,
    Exempt from wrongs of Time!'

Thus spake the mighty Mount, and I
Made answer, with a deep-drawn sigh: –
'Thou ancient Skiddaw, by this tear, 70
I would, I would that she were here!'
[November 1800]

## *Drinking* versus *Thinking*

### OR, A SONG AGAINST THE NEW PHILOSOPHY

My Merry men all, that drink with glee
  This fanciful Philosophy,
    Pray tell me what good is it?

[1] Referring to 'The Haunted Beach' and 'Jasper' by Mary Robinson in the *Annual Anthology* for 1800. [E.H.C.]

If *antient Nick* should come and take,
The same across the Stygian Lake,
    I guess we ne'er should miss it.                    5

Away, each pale, self-brooding spark
That goes truth-hunting in the dark,
    Away from our carousing!
To Pallas we resign such fowls –                    10
Grave birds of Wisdom! ye're but owls,
    And all your trade but *mousing*!

My merry men all, here's punch and wine,
And spicy bishop, drink divine!
    Let's live while we are able.                    15
While Mirth and Sense sit, hand in glove,
This Don Philosophy we'll shove
    Dead drunk beneath the table!
[1801]


# The Wills of the Wisp[1]

### A SAPPHIC

*Vix ea nostra voco*[2]

Lunatic Witch-fires! Ghosts of Light and Motion!
Fearless I see you weave your wanton dances
Near me, far off me; you, that tempt the traveller
                    Onward and onward.

Wooing, retreating, till the swamp beneath him                    5
Groans – and 'tis dark! – This woman's wile – I know it!
Learnt it from *thee*, from *thy* perfidious glances!
                    Black-ey'd Rebecca!

[1801]


[1]"Translated *in my way* from Stolberg . . . [S.T.C., Letter, 21 October 1801]
[2]'I scarcely call it mine.'

## Apologia Pro Vita Sua

The poet in his lone yet genial hour
Gives to his eyes a magnifying power:
Or rather he emancipates his eyes
From the black shapeless accidents of size –
In unctuous cones of kindling coal,                           5
Or smoke upwreathing from the pipe's trim bole,
    His gifted ken can see
    Phantoms of sublimity.
[1800]


## The Character of Wallenstein

[*The Death of Wallenstein*, ACT III, SCENE II, LL. 98–110]

A youth who scarce had seen his twentieth year
Was Wallenstein, when he and I were friends:
Yet even then he had a daring soul:
His frame of mind was serious and severe
Beyond his years: his dreams were of great objects.        5
He walked amidst us of a silent spirit,
Communing with himself: yet I have known him
Transported on a sudden into utterance
Of strange conceptions; kindling into splendour
His soul revealed itself, and he spake so                      10
That we looked round perplexed upon each other,
Not knowing whether it were craziness,
Or whether it were a god that spoke in him.
[1800]

## Mythology in an Age of Reason

[*The Piccolomini*, ACT II, SCENE IV, LL. 110–38]

 O never rudely will I blame his faith
In the might of stars and angels! 'Tis not merely
The human being's Pride that peoples space
With life and mystical predominance;
Since likewise for the stricken heart of Love    5
This visible nature, and this common world,
Is all too narrow: yea, a deeper import
Lurks in the legend told my infant years
Than lies upon that truth, we live to learn.
For fable is Love's world, his home, his birth-place:  10
Delightedly dwells he 'mong fays and talismans,
And spirits; and delightedly believes
Divinities, being himself divine.
The intelligible forms of ancient poets,
The fair humanities of old religion,    15
The Power, the Beauty, and the Majesty,
That had their haunts in dale, or piny mountain,
Or forest by slow stream, or pebbly spring,
Or chasms and wat'ry depths; all these have vanished;
They live no longer in the faith of reason!    20
But still the heart doth need a language, still
Doth the old instinct bring back the old names,
And to yon starry world they now are gone,
Spirits or gods, that used to share this earth
With man as with their friend;[1] and to the lover  25
Yonder they move, from yonder visible sky
Shoot influence down: and even at this day
'Tis Jupiter who brings whate'er is great,
And Venus who brings every thing that's fair!
[1800]

---

   [1]No more of talk, where God or Angel Guest
   With Man, as with his friend, familiar used
   To sit indulgent.
       *Paradise Lost*, ix. 1–3. [S.T.C.]

# LOVE AND LOSS

The period of intellectual and poetic experimentation which had followed Coleridge's return from Germany, and his trifling with London life, eventually ended in his yielding to the magnetic force which had been drawing him all the time. In June 1800 he left Nether Stowey with his family and all his possessions and moved to Greta Hall, a house near Keswick with a magnificent view of Skiddaw and Borrowdale. The company of Wordsworth was the chief attraction, but his desire for intellectual stimulation was now reinforced by another motive. Coleridge had fallen in love with Sara Hutchinson, sister of the Mary Hutchinson whom Wordsworth was to marry in 1802. From her he experienced a warmth of affection which he had come to miss in his own marriage; he evidently hoped that continuing faithfulness to his wife could be supplemented by this platonic tenderness.

It is possible that both these attracting forces had a nostalgic implication. It was natural to look back to the period of idyllic happiness with William and Dorothy Wordsworth in Somerset and to hope that the stimulation of Wordsworth's mind, together with Sara Hutchinson's affection, might restore him to the level of creative activity which he had reached during the year before his visit to Germany.

In the event it did not. That Sara Hutchinson would have made a better wife for Coleridge than Sara Fricker is probable but not entirely certain: what is certain is that something more than a platonic attachment would have been necessary if she was to have the chance – and this was forbidden by Coleridge's respect for the sanctity of marriage. Nevertheless, in spite of the unhappiness produced by an impossible situation, he did write good poetry during the following years: and the best of it always owes something to his devotion to Wordsworth, or his affection for Sara – very often to both.

Renewed intercourse with Wordsworth had an important effect upon his handling of symbolism. Wordsworth was not fully at home with poetry of the type of *The Ancient Mariner* or *Christabel* and offered him little encouragement in that field. When *The Ancient Mariner* appeared again in the second edition of *Lyrical Ballads* it was no longer the opening poem but was placed later, with the subtitle 'A Poet's Reverie', while *Christabel*, which was originally to have appeared in the same edition, was reserved for separate publication.

Coleridge now ceased to write poetry with a broad symbolic structure. The method by which a poetry of enchantment could also be read as a visionary poem embodying basic images such as the sun of heat and the moon of light, or the serpent of energy and the wings of love, gave way to a more sober writing. When not writing humorous epigrams, Coleridge now followed Wordsworth's injunction that the poet's eye should be kept firmly on his object.

In this continuing search for the eternal meaning at the heart of man and of nature he could not achieve the completely 'objective' approach of Wordsworth, however. A neat example of the difference between their attitudes occurs in the last lines of two poems: Wordsworth's *Yew-Trees* and Coleridge's *A Sunset*. The first ends:

> or in mute repose
> To lie, and listen to the mountain flood
> Murmuring from Glaramara's inmost caves.

Coleridge's ending has something of the same quality:

> But every leaf through all the forest flutters,
> And deep the cavern of the fountain mutters.

In both a sense of mystery is evoked. In Wordsworth's case, however, the sense is single and direct: the mystery is the mystery of the forces of nature. In Coleridge's poem, on the other hand, the sound of the fountain, unlike the sound of the breeze, has no natural relevance to the sunset. To understand why it appears at this point, we need to return to Coleridge's psychological symbolism, whereby the sun is a symbol of love. Both the stirring of the breeze at sunset and the slightly hostile noise of the fountain are evidently intended to symbolize the disquiet initiated in a human being after the withdrawal of love.

Meanwhile, however, these general symbols had found a new, particular focusing point. Symbols which had been used to suggest a conception of man's relation to the universe could now be supplemented by more personal ones, all related to his love for Sara Hutchinson. As might be expected from the nature of their love, these images tended to be images of peacefulness, indicating times when the passive sensibility had been in full play. The love of firelight in quietness, for example, now became associated with recollection of evenings during which he had sat with Mary and Sara Hutchinson after working at his books all day and of one particular evening which had been filled with a trance-like happiness (*A Day-dream*). He also associated with her a nearby wood and two sounds which appealed particularly to his sensibility – those of a beehive humming and a stock-dove cooing. The lonely bird singing, already a central image of love in *The Ancient Mariner*, is reflected further in the mention of a lark singing (*Recollections of Love*) and of birdsong in general (*A Child's Question*). In particular the dove, already used as a symbol of innocent love in *Christabel*, is developed as an image of the love which is mediated by the passive sensibility.

Most of the images, having been used in short poems, were brought together in his longest treatment of the relationship, the *Letter to Sara Hutchinson*. Apart from this theme, however, the poem has a psychological argument. It stands in part as an argument against Wordsworth's doctrine that exposure to the forces of nature must result in an influx of healing power. Coleridge himself has been making a crucial experiment. He has been standing out of doors on a beautiful evening when he himself is in a state of depression – and the beauty of the scene has not helped him at all. It is grasped rationally but to no emotional effect. The achievement of such an effect, he argues, demands an answering power in the observer, a joy which will respond to the beauty.

The first poem could not be published in its entirety for obvious reasons, but Coleridge discovered that a major part of it, including the psychological argument, could be extracted to form a shorter poem which he entitled *Dejection: an Ode*. His decision to publish it on Wordsworth's wedding-day alluded ruefully to the themes of the longer poem. Wordsworth has found the happiness which will nourish his creative powers: Coleridge can hope only to find a reflection of that happiness in his association with the Wordsworth household.

Each poem has its own peculiar value. *Dejection* stands to its predecessor rather as an engraving may stand in relation to an original painting. Its points are made more sharply and stringently: but in order to hear the full throb of Coleridge's unhappiness the greater length of the earlier version is needed.

Eventually, faced with poor health and an impossible domestic situation, Coleridge decided to spend some time in Malta where, as secretary to the governor, he might be able to earn money in a more beneficial climate. The plan did not succeed as well as he had hoped, for the heat and noise of a sunny climate could not compensate for a loss of tender affection and friendship. His poems of the time include some more strictly symbolic natural pieces: but even when they are introduced into his notebook they are usually introduced hesitantly, with a modesty which may still owe something to Wordsworth's criticisms.

While Coleridge was in Malta, he heard of the death at sea of Captain John Wordsworth, William's brother. The intensity of feeling with which he reacted to this event was partly due, perhaps, to some previous expectation that John would marry Sara Hutchinson. When he returned to England, by way of Italy, his own love for her was in no way diminished. In the sphere of public affairs, meanwhile, he had become increasingly concerned at the conduct of statesmen and others during the current war. His insistence that their constant reliance on expediency ought to be replaced by firmly enunciated principles was the main reason for the launching of another periodical, to be entitled *The Friend*. For this, Sara acted as amanuensis.

Wordsworth, following the death of his brother, had also become preoccupied with public affairs and with the theme of 'Duty'. Coleridge, aware of an occasional 'involuntary jealousy' at the fortune which had given his friend no less than three devoted women while he himself had none, remained for the time being unswerving in public admiration while sometimes critical in private. If *The Barberry Tree* was indeed by him its mixture of parody and delighted pastiche was expressive of that duality. Indeed, his best poem of the period was written after hearing Wordsworth recite passages from *The Prelude*. The difficult state of affairs in the Grasmere household could not last indefinitely, however, and the nervous tension between Coleridge and Sara eventually ended with her removal. Coleridge may have recognized an inevitability in the decision, but found difficulty in forgiving Wordsworth for his attitude: the Latin poem *Ad Vilmum Axiologum* expresses something of his bitterness. For some years to come, in such poetry as he wrote he would return again and again to the one theme of lost love.

# Love

All thoughts, all passions, all delights,
Whatever stirs this mortal frame,
All are but ministers of Love,
    And feed his sacred flame.


Oft in my waking dreams do I           5
Live o'er again that happy hour,
When midway on the mount I lay,
    Beside the ruined tower.


The moonshine, stealing o'er the scene,
Had blended with the lights of eve;        10
And she was there, my hope, my joy,
    My own dear Genevieve!


She leant against the arméd man,
The statue of the arméd knight;[1]
She stood and listened to my lay,        15
    Amid the lingering light.


Few sorrows hath she of her own,
My hope! my joy! my Genevieve!
She loves me best, whene'er I sing
    The songs that make her grieve.        20


I played a soft and doleful air,
I sang an old and moving story —
An old rude song, that suited well
    That ruin wild and hoary.

[1] In the church at Sockburn there is a recumbent statue of an 'armed knight' . . . and in a field near the farm-house there is a 'Grey-Stone' which is said to commemorate the slaying of a monstrous wyverne or 'worme' by the knight who is buried in the church. It is difficult to believe that the 'armed knight' and the 'grey stone' of the first draft were not suggested by the statue in Sockburn Church, and the 'Grey-Stone' in the adjoining field. [E.H.C.]. It was while on a visit to Sockburn in 1799 that Coleridge fell in love with Sara Hutchinson, and E.H.C. no doubt had this in mind.

She listened with a flitting blush,       25
With downcast eyes and modest grace;
For well she knew, I could not choose
     But gaze upon her face.


I told her of the Knight that wore
Upon his shield a burning brand;       30
And that for ten long years he wooed
     The Lady of the Land.


I told her how he pined: and ah!
The deep, the low, the pleading tone
With which I sang another's love,       35
     Interpreted my own.


She listened with a flitting blush,
With downcast eyes, and modest grace;
And she forgave me, that I gazed
     Too fondly on her face!       40


But when I told the cruel scorn
That crazed that bold and lovely Knight,
And that he crossed the mountain-woods,
     Nor rested day nor night;


That sometimes from the savage den,       45
And sometimes from the darksome shade,
And sometimes starting up at once
     In green and sunny glade, –


There came and looked him in the face
An angel beautiful and bright;       50
And that he knew it was a Fiend,
     This miserable Knight!


And that unknowing what he did,
He leaped amid a murderous band,
And saved from outrage worse than death       55
     The Lady of the Land!

And how she wept, and clasped his knees;
And how she tended him in vain –
And ever strove to expiate
    The scorn that crazed his brain; – 60

And that she nursed him in a cave;
And how his madness went away,
When on the yellow forest-leaves
    A dying man he lay; –

His dying words – but when I reached 65
That tenderest strain of all the ditty,
My faultering voice and pausing harp
    Disturbed her soul with pity!

All impulses of soul and sense
Had thrilled my guileless Genevieve; 70
The music and the doleful tale,
    The rich and balmy eve;

And hopes, and fears that kindle hope,
An undistinguishable throng,
And gentle wishes long subdued, 75
    Subdued and cherished long!

She wept with pity and delight,
She blushed with love, and virgin-shame;
And like the murmur of a dream,
    I heard her breathe my name. 80

Her bosom heaved – she stepped aside,
As conscious of my look she stepped –
Then suddenly, with timorous eye
    She fled to me and wept.

She half enclosed me with her arms, 85
She pressed me with a meek embrace;
And bending back her head, looked up,
    And gazed upon my face.

'Twas partly love, and partly fear,
And partly 'twas a bashful art,
That I might rather feel, than see,                    90
    The swelling of her heart.

I calmed her fears, and she was calm,
And told her love with virgin pride;
And so I won my Genevieve,                             95
    My bright and beauteous Bride.
[November–December 1799]

## *The Night-Scene*

A DRAMATIC FRAGMENT

*Sandoval.* You loved the daughter of Don Manrique?
*Earl Henry.*                                             Loved?
*Sand.* Did you not say you wooed her?
*Earl H.*                                      Once I loved
Her whom I dared not woo!
   *Sand.*                    And wooed, perchance,
One whom you loved not!
   *Earl H.*                 Oh! I were most base,
Not loving Oropeza. True, I wooed her,                          5
Hoping to heal a deeper wound; but she
Met my advances with impassioned pride,
That kindled love with love. And when her sire,
Who in his dream of hope already grasped
The golden circlet in his hand, rejected                       10
My suit with insult, and in memory
Of ancient feuds poured curses on my head,
Her blessings overtook and baffled them!
But thou art stern, and with unkindly countenance
Art inly reasoning whilst thou listenest to me.                15
   *Sand.* Anxiously, Henry! reasoning anxiously.
But Oropeza —
   *Earl H.*       Blessings gather round her!
Within this wood there winds a secret passage,
Beneath the walls, which opens out at length
Into the gloomiest covert of the garden. —                     20
The night ere my departure to the army,
She, nothing trembling, led me through that gloom,
And to that covert by a silent stream,
Which, with one star reflected near its marge,
Was the sole object visible around me.                         25
No leaflet stirred; the air was almost sultry;
So deep, so dark, so close, the umbrage o'er us!
No leaflet stirred; — yet pleasure hung upon
The gloom and stillness of the balmy night-air.
A little further on an arbour stood,                           30
Fragrant with flowering trees — I well remember
What an uncertain glimmer in the darkness

Their snow-white blossoms made – thither she led me,
To that sweet bower! Then Oropeza trembled –
I heard her heart beat – if 'twere not my own.                    35
   *Sand.* A rude and scaring note, my friend!
   *Earl H.*                                    Oh! no!
I have small memory of aught but pleasure.
The inquietudes of fear, like lesser streams
Still flowing, still were lost in those of love:
So love grew mightier from the fear, and Nature,                  40
Fleeing from Pain, sheltered herself in Joy.
The stars above our heads were dim and steady,
Like eyes suffused with rapture. Life was in us:
We were all life, each atom of our frames
A living soul – I vowed to die for her:                           45
With the faint voice of one who, having spoken,
Relapses into blessedness, I vowed it:
That solemn vow, a whisper scarcely heard,
A murmur breathed against a lady's ear.
Oh! there is joy above the name of pleasure.                      50
Deep self-possession, an intense repose.
   *Sand.* (*with a sarcastic smile*). No other than as eastern
      sages paint,
The God, who floats upon a Lotos leaf,
Dreams for a thousand ages; then awaking,
Creates a world, and smiling at the bubble,                       55
Relapses into bliss.
   *Earl H.*       Ah! was that bliss
Feared as an alien, and too vast for man?
For suddenly, impatient of its silence,
Did Oropeza, starting, grasp my forehead.
I caught her arms; the veins were swelling on them.               60
Through the dark bower she sent a hollow voice; –
'Oh! what if all betray me? what if thou?'
I swore, and with an inward thought that seemed
The purpose and the substance of my being,
I swore to her, that were she red with guilt,                     65
I would exchange my unblenched state with hers. –
Friend! by that winding passage, to that bower
I now will go – all objects there will teach me
Unwavering love, and singleness of heart.
Go, Sandoval! I am prepared to meet her –                         70

Say nothing of me – I myself will seek her –
Nay, leave me, friend! I cannot bear the torment
And keen inquiry of that scanning eye. –

                [*Earl Henry retires into the wood.*

  *Sand.* (*alone*). O Henry! always striv'st thou to be great
By thine own act – yet art thou never great         75
But by the inspiration of great passion.
The whirl-blast comes, the desert-sands rise up
And shape themselves: from Earth to Heaven they stand,
As though they were the pillars of a temple,
Built by Omnipotence in its own honour!         80
But the blast pauses, and their shaping spirit
Is fled: the mighty columns were but sand,
And lazy snakes trail o'er the level ruins!
[1800–1]

# On Revisiting the Sea-Shore, after Long Absence

## UNDER STRONG MEDICAL RECOMMENDATION
## NOT TO BATHE

God be with thee, gladsome Ocean!
    How gladly greet I thee once more!
Ships and waves, and ceaseless motion,
    And men rejoicing on thy shore.

Dissuading spake the mild Physician,         5
    'Those briny waves for thee are Death!'
But my soul fulfilled her mission,
    And lo! I breathe untroubled breath!

Fashion's pining sons and daughters,
    That seek the crowd they seem to fly,
Trembling they approach thy waters;         10
    And what cares Nature, if they die?

Me a thousand hopes and pleasures,
    A thousand recollections bland,
Thoughts sublime, and stately measures,         15
    Revisit on thy echoing strand:

Dreams (the Soul herself forsaking),
   Tearful raptures, boyish mirth;
Silent adorations, making
   A blessed shadow of this Earth!                    20

O ye hopes, that stir within me,
   Health comes with you from above!
God is with me, God is in me!
   I cannot die, if Life be Love.
[August 1801]

## Inscription for a Fountain on a Heath

This Sycamore, oft musical with bees, –
Such tents the Patriarchs loved! O long unharmed
May all its agéd boughs o'er-canopy
The small round basin, which this jutting stone
Keeps pure from falling leaves! Long may the Spring,                    5
Quietly as a sleeping infant's breath,
Send up cold waters to the traveller
With soft and even pulse! Nor ever cease
Yon tiny cone of sand its soundless dance,
Which at the bottom, like a Fairy's Page,                    10
As merry and no taller, dances still,
Nor wrinkles the smooth surface of the Fount.
Here Twilight is and Coolness: here is moss,
A soft seat, and a deep and ample shade.
Thou may'st toil far and find no second tree.                    15
Drink, Pilgrim, here; Here rest! and if thy heart
Be innocent, here too shalt thou refresh
Thy spirit, listening to some gentle sound,
Or passing gale or hum of murmuring bees!
[? September 1801]

## An Ode to the Rain

COMPOSED BEFORE DAYLIGHT, ON THE MORNING
APPOINTED FOR THE DEPARTURE OF A VERY WORTHY, BUT
NOT VERY PLEASANT, VISITOR WHOM IT WAS FEARED THE
RAIN MIGHT DETAIN

I

I know it is dark; and though I have lain,
Awake, as I guess, an hour or twain,
I have not once opened the lids of my eyes,
But I lie in the dark, as a blind man lies.
O Rain! that I lie listening to,                          5
You're but a doleful sound at best:
I owe you little thanks, 'tis true,
For breaking thus my needful rest!
Yet if, as soon as it is light,
O Rain! you will but take your flight,                    10
I'll neither rail, nor malice keep,
Though sick and sore for want of sleep.
But only now, for this one day,
Do go, dear Rain! do go away!

II

O Rain! with your dull two-fold sound,                    15
The clash hard by, and the murmur all round!
You know, if you know aught, that we,
Both night and day, but ill agree:
For days and months, and almost years,
Have limped on through this vale of tears,                 20
Since body of mine, and rainy weather,
Have lived on easy terms together.
Yet if, as soon as it is light,
O Rain! you will but take your flight,
Though you should come again tomorrow,                     25
And bring with you both pain and sorrow;
Though stomach should sicken, and knees should swell –
I'll nothing speak of you but well.
But only now for this one day,
Do go, dear Rain! do go away!                              30

### III

Dear Rain! I ne'er refused to say
You're a good creature in your way;
Nay, I could write a book myself,
Would fit a parson's lower shelf,
Showing, how very good you are. –          35
What then? sometimes it must be fair!
And if sometimes, why not today?
Do go, dear Rain! do go away!

### IV

Dear Rain! if I've been cold and shy,
Take no offence! I'll tell you why.          40
A dear old Friend e'en now is here,
And with him came my sister dear;
After long absence now first met,
Long months by pain and grief beset –
We three dear friends! in truth, we groan          45
Impatiently to be alone.
We three, you mark! and not one more!
The strong wish makes my spirit sore.
We have so much to talk about,
So many sad things to let out;          50
So many tears in our eye-corners,
Sitting like little Jacky Horners –
In short, as soon as it is day,
Do go, dear Rain! do go away.

### V

And this I'll swear to you, dear Rain!          55
Whenever you shall come again,
Be you as dull as e'er you could
(And by the bye 'tis understood,
You're not so pleasant, as you're good),
Yet, knowing well your worth and place,          60
I'll welcome you with cheerful face;
And though you stayed a week or more,
Were ten times duller than before;
Yet with kind heart, and right good will,
I'll sit and listen to you still;          65

Nor should you go away, dear Rain!
Uninvited to remain.
But only now, for this one day,
Do go, dear Rain! do go away.
[October 1801]


## Ode to Tranquillity

Tranquillity! thou better name
Than all the family of Fame!
Thou ne'er wilt leave my riper age
To low intrigue, or factious rage;
For oh! dear child of thoughtful Truth,                    5
To thee I gave my early youth,
And left the bark, and blest the steadfast shore,
Ere yet the tempest rose and scared me with its roar.


Who late and lingering seeks thy shrine,
On him but seldom, Power divine,                           10
Thy spirit rests! Satiety
And Sloth, poor counterfeits of thee,
Mock the tired worldling. Idle Hope
And dire Remembrance interlope,
To vex the feverish slumbers of the mind:                  15
The bubble floats before, the spectre stalks behind.


But me thy gentle hand will lead
At morning through the accustomed mead;
And in the sultry summer's heat
Will build me up a mossy seat;                             20
And when the gust of Autumn crowds,
And breaks the busy moonlight clouds,
Thou best the thought canst raise, the heart attune,
Light as the busy clouds, calm as the gliding moon.


The feeling heart, the searching soul,                     25
To thee I dedicate the whole!
And while within myself I trace
The greatness of some future race,

Aloof with hermit-eye I scan
   The present works of present man –         30
A wild and dream-like trade of blood and guile,
Too foolish for a tear, too wicked for a smile!
[August–November 1801]


# A Day-Dream

My eyes make pictures, when they are shut:
   I see a fountain, large and fair,
A willow and a ruined hut,
   And thee, and me and Mary there.
O Mary! make thy gentle lap our pillow!         5
Bend o'er us, like a bower, my beautiful green willow!


A wild-rose roofs the ruined shed,
   And that and summer well agree:
And lo! where Mary leans her head,
   Two dear names carved upon the tree!        10
And Mary's tears, they are not tears of sorrow:
Our sister and our friend will both be here tomorrow.


'Twas day! but now few, large, and bright,
   The stars are round the crescent moon!
And now it is a dark warm night,         15
   The balmiest of the month of June!
A glow-worm fall'n, and on the marge remounting
Shines, and its shadow shines, fit stars for our sweet fountain.


O ever – ever be thou blest!
   For dearly, Asra! love I thee!        20
This brooding warmth across my breast,
   This depth of tranquil bliss – ah, me!
Fount, tree and shed are gone, I know not whither,
But in one quiet room we three are still together.


The shadows dance upon the wall,        25
   By the still dancing fire-flames made;
And now they slumber, moveless all!

And now they melt to one deep shade!
But not from me shall this mild darkness steal thee:
I dream thee with mine eyes, and at my heart I feel thee!     30

    Thine eyelash on my cheek doth play —
       'Tis Mary's hand upon my brow!
    But let me check this tender lay
       Which none may hear but she and thou!
Like the still hive at quiet midnight humming,                     35
Murmur it to yourselves, ye two beloved women!
[?27 March 1802]

## *Letter to Sara Hutchinson*[1]

4 APRIL 1802 – SUNDAY EVENING

Well! if the Bard was weatherwise, who made
The grand old Ballad of Sir Patrick Spence,
This Night, so tranquil now, will not go hence
Unrous'd by winds, that ply a busier trade
Than that, which moulds yon clouds in lazy flakes,                5
Or the dull sobbing Draft, that drones & rakes
Upon the Strings of this Eolian Lute,
    Which better far were mute.
For, lo! the New Moon, winter-bright!
And overspread with phantom Light,                                10
(With swimming phantom Light o'erspread
But rimm'd & circled with a silver Thread)
I see the Old Moon in her Lap, foretelling
The coming-on of Rain & squally Blast –
O! Sara! that the Gust ev'n now were swelling,                    15
And the slant Night-shower driving loud & fast!

---

[1]Having written this verse-letter originally to Sara Hutchinson, Coleridge went on to produce several versions from which the private references were removed, including one which he published as *Dejection: An Ode* on 4 October 1802, Wordsworth's wedding day. In the shortened versions the recipient was named variously as 'Wordsworth', 'William' and 'Edmund'; the one for *Sibylline Leaves* (1817), printed on the next few right-hand pages here, is addressed to a 'Lady'. For a study of the various versions see David Pirie, 'A Letter to [Asra]' in *Bicentenary Wordsworth Studies*, ed. J. Wordsworth (1970).

## Dejection: An Ode

> Late, late yestreen I saw the new Moon,
> With the old Moon in her arms;
> And I fear, I fear, my Master dear!
> We shall have a deadly storm.
> *Ballad of Sir Patrick Spence*

### I

Well! If the Bard was weather-wise, who made
  The grand old ballad of Sir Patrick Spence,
  This night, so tranquil now, will not go hence
Unrous'd by winds, that ply a busier trade
Than those which mould yon cloud in lazy flakes,    5
Or the dull sobbing draft, that moans and rakes
Upon the strings of this Æolian lute,
    Which better far were mute.
  For lo! the New-moon winter-bright!
  And overspread with phantom-light,    10
  (With swimming phantom-light o'erspread
  But rimm'd and circled by a silver thread)
I see the old Moon in her lap, foretelling
  The coming on of rain and squally blast.
And oh! that even now the gust were swelling,    15
  And the slant night-shower driving loud and fast!
Those sounds which oft have raised me, whilst they awed,
    And sent my soul abroad,
Might now perhaps their wonted impulse give,
Might startle this dull pain, and make it move and live!    20

A Grief without a pang, void, dark, & drear,
A stifling, drowsy, unimpassion'd Grief
That finds no natural Outlet, no Relief
　　In word, or sigh, or tear –                                    20
This, Sara! well thou know'st,
Is that sore Evil, which I dread the most,
And oft'nest suffer! In this heartless Mood,
To other thoughts by yonder Throstle woo'd,
That pipes within the Larch tree, not unseen,                    25
(The Larch, which pushes out in tassels green
It's bundled Leafits) woo'd to mild Delights
By all the tender Sounds & gentle Sights
Of this sweet Primrose-month – & *vainly* woo'd
O dearest Sara! in this heartless Mood                           30
All this long Eve, so balmy & serene
Have I been gazing on the western Sky
And it's peculiar Tint of Yellow Green –
And still I gaze – & with how blank an eye!
And those thin Clouds above, in flakes & bars,                  35
That give away their Motion to the Stars;
Those Stars, that glide behind them, or between,
Now sparkling, now bedimm'd, but always seen;
Yon crescent Moon, as fix'd as if it grew
In it's own cloudless, starless Lake of Blue –                  40
A boat becalm'd! dear William's Sky Canoe!
– I see them all, so excellently fair!
I see, not feel, how beautiful they are.

　　My genial Spirits fail –
　　And what can these avail
To lift the smoth'ring Weight from off my Breast?               45
　　It were a vain Endeavor,
　　Tho' I should gaze for ever
On that Green Light, which lingers in the West!
I may not hope from outward Forms to win                        50
The Passion & the Life, whose Fountains are within!
These lifeless Shapes, around, below, Above,
　　O what can they impart?
When even the gentle Thought, that thou, my Love!

## II

A grief without a pang, void, dark, and drear,
　　A stifled, drowsy, unimpassion'd grief,
　　Which finds no natural outlet, no relief,
　　　In word, or sigh, or tear –
O Lady! in this wan and heartless mood,                    25
To other thoughts by yonder throstle woo'd,
　　All this long eve, so balmy and serene,
Have I been gazing on the western sky,
　　And its peculiar tint of yellow green:
And still I gaze – and with how blank an eye!              30
And those thin clouds above, in flakes and bars,
That give away their motion to the stars;
Those stars, that glide behind them or between,
Now sparkling, now bedimm'd, but always seen:
Yon crescent Moon, as fix'd as if it grew                  35
In its own cloudless, starless lake of blue;
I see them all so excellently fair,
I see, not feel how beautiful they are!

## III

　　My genial spirits fail;
　　And what can these avail                               40
To lift the smoth'ring weight from off my breast?
　　It were a vain endeavour,
　　Though I should gaze for ever
On that green light that lingers in the west:
I may not hope from outward forms to win                   45
The passion and the life, whose fountains are within.

    Art gazing now, like me,                 55
    And see'st the Heaven, I see –
Sweet Thought it is – yet feebly stirs my Heart!


    Feebly! O feebly! – Yet
    (I well remember it)
In my first Dawn of Youth that Fancy stole    60
With many secret Yearnings on my Soul.
At eve, sky-gazing in 'ecstatic fit'
(Alas! for cloister'd in a city School
The Sky was all, I knew, of Beautiful)
At the barr'd window often did I sit,    65
And oft upon the leaded School-roof lay,
    And to myself would say –
There does not live a Man so stripp'd of good affections
As not to love to see a Maiden's quiet Eyes
Uprais'd, and linking on sweet Dreams by dim
        Connections    70
To moon, or Evening Star, or glorious western Skies –
While yet a Boy, this Thought would so pursue me
That often it became a kind of Vision to me!


    Sweet Thought! and dear of old
    To Hearts of finer Mould!    75
Ten thousand times by Friends & Lovers blest!
    I spake with rash Despair,
    And ere I was aware,
The weight was somewhat lifted from my Breast!
O Sara! in the weather-fended Wood,    80
Thy lov'd haunt! where the Stock-doves coo at Noon,
    I guess, that thou hast stood
And watch'd yon Crescent, & it's ghost-like Moon.
And yet, far rather in my present mood
I would, that thou'dst been sitting all this while    85
Upon the sod-built Seat of Camomile –
And tho' thy Robin may have ceas'd to sing,
Yet needs for *my* sake must thou love to hear
The Bee-hive murmuring near,
That ever-busy & most quiet Thing    90
Which I have heard at Midnight murmuring.

IV¹

O Lady! we receive but what we give,
And in our life alone does Nature live:
Ours is her wedding-garment, ours her shroud!
    And would we aught behold, of higher worth,          50
Than that inanimate cold world allow'd
To the poor loveless ever-anxious crowd,
    Ah! from the soul itself must issue forth
A light, a glory, a fair luminous cloud
        Enveloping the Earth —                             55
And from the soul itself must there be sent
    A sweet and potent voice, of its own birth,
Of all sweet sounds the life and element!

V

O pure of heart! thou need'st not ask of me
What this strong music in the soul may be!               60
What, and wherein it doth exist,
This light, this glory, this fair luminous mist,
This beautiful, and beauty-making power.
    Joy, virtuous Lady! Joy that ne'er was given,
Save to the pure, and in their purest hour,             65
Life, and Life's effluence, cloud at once and shower,
Joy, Lady! is the spirit and the power,
Which wedding Nature to us gives in dow'r
    A new Earth and new Heaven,
Undreamt of by the sensual and the proud —              70
Joy is the sweet voice, Joy the luminous cloud —
        We in ourselves rejoice!
And thence flows all that charms or ear or sight,
    All melodies the echoes of that voice,
All colours a suffusion from that light.                75

VI²

There was a time when, though my path was rough,
    This joy within me dallied with distress,
And all misfortunes were but as the stuff
    Whence Fancy made me dreams of happiness:

¹Lines 47–75 correspond to 296–323 in the *Letter*.
²Lines 76–92 correspond to 231–41 and 265–71 in the *Letter*.

I feel my spirit moved —
And wheresoe'er thou be,
O Sister! O Beloved!
Those dear mild Eyes, that see                                    95
Even now the Heaven, *I* see —
There is a Prayer in them! It is for *me* —
And I, dear Sara — *I* am blessing *thee*!

It was as calm as this, that happy night
When Mary, thou, & I together were,                              100
The low decaying Fire our only light,
And listen'd to the Stillness of the Air!
O that affectionate & blameless Maid,
Dear Mary! on her Lap my head she lay'd —
Her Hand was on my Brow,                                         105
Even as my own is now;
And on my Cheek I felt thy eye-lash play.
Such Joy I had, that I may truly say,
My Spirit was awe-stricken with the Excess
And trance-like Depth of it's brief Happiness.                  110

Ah fair Remembrances, that so revive
The Heart, & fill it with a living Power,
Where were they, Sara? — or did I not strive
To win them to me? — on the fretting Hour
Then when I wrote thee that complaining Scroll                   115
Which even to bodily Sickness bruis'd thy Soul!
And yet thou blam'st thyself alone! And yet
Forbidd'st me all Regret!

And must I not regret, that I distress'd
Thee, best belov'd! who lovest me the best?                      120
My better mind had fled, I know not whither,
For O! was this an Absent Friend's Employ
To send from far both Pain & Sorrow thither
Where still his Blessings should have call'd down Joy!
I read thy guileless Letter o'er again —                         125
I hear thee of thy blameless Self complain —
And only this I learn — & this, alas! I know —
That thou art weak & pale with Sickness, Grief & Pain —
And *I* — *I* made thee so!

For hope grew round me, like the twining vine,               80
And fruits, and foliage, not my own, seemed mine.
But now afflictions bow me down to earth:
Nor care I that they rob me of my mirth,
  But oh! each visitation
Suspends what nature gave me at my birth,                    85
 My shaping spirit of Imagination.
For not to think of what I needs must feel,
 But to be still and patient, all I can;
And haply by abstruse research to steal
  From my own nature all the natural Man –         90
 This was my sole resource, my only plan:
Till that which suits a part infects the whole,
And now is almost grown the habit of my Soul.

VII[1]

Hence, viper thoughts, that coil around my mind,
  Reality's dark dream!                            95
I turn from you, and listen to the wind,
 Which long has rav'd unnotic'd. What a scream
Of agony by torture lengthen'd out
That lute sent forth! Thou Wind, that rav'st without,
 Bare crag, or mountain-tairn,[2] or blasted tree,     100
Or pine-grove whither woodman never clomb,
Or lonely house, long held the witches' home,
 Methinks were fitter instruments for thee,
Mad Lutanist! who in this month of show'rs,
Of dark-brown gardens, and of peeping flow'rs,              105
Mak'st Devils' yule, with worse than wint'ry song,
The blossoms, buds, and tim'rous leaves among.
 Thou Actor, perfect in all tragic sounds!
Thou mighty Poet, e'en to Frenzy bold!
  What tell'st thou now about?                     110
  'Tis of the Rushing of an Host in rout,
 With groans of trampled men, with smarting wounds –
At once they groan with pain, and shudder with the cold!

---

[1]Lines 94–125 correspond to 184–215 in the *Letter*; lines 126–39 to 216–24 and 335–40
there.
 [2]Tairn is a small lake, generally if not always applied to the lakes up in the mountains and
which are the feeders of those in the valleys. This address to the wind will not appear
extravagant to those who have heard it at night and in a mountainous country. [S.T.C.]

O for my own sake I regret perforce                                    130
Whatever turns thee, Sara! from the Course
Of calm Well-being & a Heart at rest!
When thou, & with thee those, whom thou lov'st best,
Shall dwell together in one happy Home,
One House, the dear *abiding* Home of All,                              135
I too will crown me with a Coronal —
Nor shall this Heart in idle Wishes roam
    Morbidly soft!
No! let me trust, that I shall wear away
In no inglorious Toils the manly Day,                                   140
And only now & then, & not too oft,
Some dear & memorable Eve will bless
Dreaming of all your Loves & Quietness.


Be happy, & I need thee not in sight.
Peace in thy Heart, & Quiet in thy Dwelling,                           145
Health in thy Limbs, & in thine Eyes the Light
Of Love, & Hope, & honorable Feeling —
Where e'er I am, I shall be well content!
Not near thee, haply shall be more content!
To all things I prefer the Permanent.                                  150


And better seems it for a heart, like mine,
Always to *know*, than sometimes to behold,
    *Their* Happiness & thine —
For Change doth trouble me with pangs untold!
To see thee, hear thee, feel thee — then to part                       155
    Oh! it weighs down the Heart!
To *visit* those, I love, as I love thee,
Mary, & William, & dear Dorothy,
It is but a temptation to repine —
The transientness is Poison in the Wine,                               160
Eats out the pith of Joy, makes all Joy hollow,
All Pleasure a dim Dream of Pain to follow!
My own peculiar Lot, my house-hold Life
It is, & will remain, Indifference or Strife —
While *ye* are *well & happy*, 'twould but wrong you                    165
If I should fondly yearn to be among you —
Wherefore, O wherefore! should I wish to be
A wither'd branch upon a blossoming Tree?

But hush! there is a pause of deepest silence!
  And all that noise, as of a rushing crowd,                    115
With groans, and tremulous shudderings – all is over –
  It tells another tale, with sounds less deep and loud!
    A tale of less affright,
    And temper'd with delight,
As Otway's self had fram'd the tender lay, –                           120
    'Tis of a little child
    Upon a lonesome wild,
Not far from home, but she hath lost her way:
And now moans low in bitter grief and fear,
And now screams loud, and hopes to make her mother hear.               125

### VIII

'Tis midnight, but small thoughts have I of sleep:
Full seldom may my friend such vigils keep!
Visit her, gentle Sleep! with wings of healing,
  And may this storm be but a mountain-birth,
May all the stars hang bright above her dwelling,                      130
  Silent as though they watch'd the sleeping Earth!
    With light heart may she rise,
      Gay fancy, cheerful eyes,
  Joy lift her spirit, joy attune her voice;
To her may all things live, from Pole to Pole,                         135
Their life the eddying of her living soul!
  O simple spirit, guided from above,
Dear Lady! friend devoutest of my choice,
Thus may'st thou ever, evermore rejoice.
[1817 version]

But (let me say it! for I vainly strive
To beat away the Thought) but if thou pin'd,     170
Whate'er the Cause, in body or in mind,
I were the miserablest Man alive
To know it & be absent! Thy Delights
Far off, or near, alike I may partake —
But O! to mourn for thee, & to forsake     175
All power, all hope of giving comfort to thee —
To know that thou art weak & worn with pain,
And not to hear thee, Sara! not to view thee —
    Not to sit beside thy Bed,
    Not press thy aching Head,     180
    Not bring thee Health again —
    At least to hope, to try —
By this Voice, which thou lov'st, & by this earnest Eye —

Nay, wherefore did I let it haunt my Mind
    The dark distressful Dream!     185
I turn from it, & listen to the Wind
Which long has rav'd unnotic'd! What a Scream
Of agony by Torture lengthen'd out
That Lute sent forth! O thou wild Storm without!
Jagg'd Rock, or mountain Pond, or blasted Tree,     190
Or Pine-Grove, whither Woodman never clomb,
Or lonely House, long held the Witches' Home,
Methinks were fitter Instruments for Thee,
Mad Lutanist! that in this month of Showers,
Of dark brown Gardens, & of peeping Flowers,     195
Mak'st Devil's Yule, with worse than wintry Song
The Blossoms, Buds, and timorous Leaves among!

Thou Actor, perfect in all tragic Sounds!
Thou mighty Poet, even to frenzy bold!
    What tell'st thou now about?     200
'Tis of the Rushing of an Host in Rout —
And many Groans from men with smarting Wounds —
At once they groan with smart, and shudder with the Cold!
'Tis hush'd! there is a Trance of deepest Silence,
Again! but all that Sound, as of a rushing Crowd,     205
And Groans & tremulous Shudderings, all are over —
And it has other Sounds, and all less deep, less loud!

    A Tale of less Affright,
    And temper'd with Delight,
As William's Self had made the tender Lay –          210
    'Tis of a little Child
    Upon a heathy Wild,
Not far from home – but it has lost it's way –
And now moans low in utter grief & fear –
And now screams loud, & hopes to make it's Mother
        hear!          215


'Tis Midnight! and small Thoughts have I of Sleep –
Full seldom may my Friend such Vigils keep –
O breathe She softly in her gentle Sleep!
Cover her, gentle Sleep! with wings of Healing.
And be this Tempest but a Mountain Birth!          220
May all the Stars hang bright about her Dwelling,
Silent, as tho' they *watch'd* the sleeping Earth!
Healthful & light, my Darling! may'st thou rise
    With clear & chearful Eyes –
And of the same good Tidings to me send!          225
    For, oh! beloved Friend!
I am not the buoyant Thing, I was of yore –
When, like an own Child, I to JOY belong'd;
For others mourning oft, myself oft sorely wrong'd,
Yet bearing all things then, as if I nothing bore!          230


    Yes, dearest Sara! Yes!
There *was* a time when tho' my path was rough,
The Joy within me dallied with Distress;
And all Misfortunes were but as the Stuff
Whence Fancy made me Dreams of Happiness:          235
For Hope grew round me, like the climbing Vine,
And Leaves & Fruitage, not my own, seem'd mine!
But now Ill Tidings bow me down to earth –
Nor care I, that they rob me of my Mirth –
    But oh! each Visitation          240
Suspends what Nature gave me at my Birth,
    My shaping Spirit of Imagination!
I speak not now of those habitual Ills
That wear out Life, when two unequal Minds
Meet in one House, & two discordant Wills –          245

This leaves me, where it finds,
Past cure, & past Complaint — a fate austere
Too fix'd & hopeless to partake of Fear!

But thou, dear Sara! (dear indeed thou art,
My Comforter! A Heart within my Heart!)                    250
Thou, & the Few, we love, tho' few ye be,
Make up a world of Hopes & Fears for me.
And if Affliction, or distemp'ring Pain,
Or wayward Chance befall you, I complain
Not that I mourn — O Friends, most dear! most true!        255
    Methinks to weep with you
Were better far than to rejoice alone —
But that my coarse domestic Life has known
No Habits of heart-nursing Sympathy,
No Griefs, but such as dull and deaden me,                 260
No mutual mild Enjoyments of it's own,
No Hopes of its own Vintage. None, O! none —
Whence when I mourn'd for you, my Heart might borrow
Fair forms & living Motions for it's Sorrow.
For not to think of what I needs must feel,                265
But to be still & patient all I can;
And haply by abstruse Research to steal
From my own Nature all the Natural Man —
This was my sole Resource, my wisest plan!
And that, which suits a part, infects the whole,           270
And now is almost grown the Temper of my Soul.

My Little Children are a Joy, a Love,
    A good Gift from above!
But what is Bliss, that still calls up a Woe,
    And makes it doubly keen                               275
Compelling me to *feel*, as well as KNOW,
What a most blessed Lot mine might have been.
Those little Angel Children (woe is me!)
There have been hours, when feeling how they bind
And pluck out the Wing-feathers of my Mind,                280
Turning my Error to Necessity,
I have half-wish'd, they never had been born!
*That* seldom! But sad Thoughts they always bring,
And like the Poet's Philomel, I sing
My Love-song, with my breast against a Thorn.              285

With no unthankful Spirit I confess,
This clinging Grief too, in it's turn, awakes
That Love, and Father's Joy; but O! it makes
The Love the greater, & the Joy far less.
These Mountains too, these Vales, these Woods, these
    Lakes,     290
Scenes full of Beauty & of Loftiness
Where all my Life I fondly hop'd to live –
I were sunk low indeed, did they *no* solace give;
But oft I seem to feel, & evermore I fear,
They are not to me now the Things, which once they were.   295

O Sara! we receive but what we give,
And in *our* Life alone does Nature live.
Our's is her Wedding Garment, our's her Shroud –
And would we aught behold of higher Worth
Than that inanimate cold World allow'd     300
To the poor loveless ever-anxious Crowd,
Ah! from the Soul itself must issue forth
A Light, a Glory, and a luminous Cloud
    Enveloping the Earth!
And from the Soul itself must there be sent     305
A sweet & potent Voice, of it's own Birth,
Of all sweet Sounds the Life & Element.

O pure of Heart! thou need'st not ask of me
What this strong music in the Soul may be,
    What, & wherein it doth exist,     310
This Light, this Glory, this fair luminous Mist,
This beautiful & beauty-making Power!
Joy, innocent Sara! Joy, that ne'er was given
Save to the Pure, & in their purest Hour,
Joy, Sara! is the Spirit & the Power,     315
That wedding Nature to us gives in Dower
    A new Earth & new Heaven
Undreamt of by the Sensual & the Proud!
Joy is that strong Voice, Joy that luminous Cloud –
    We, we ourselves rejoice!     320
And thence flows all that charms or ear or sight,
All melodies the Echoes of that Voice,
All Colors a Suffusion of that Light.

Sister & Friend of my devoutest Choice!
Thou being innocent & full of love,                                325
And nested with the Darlings of thy Love,
And feeling in thy Soul, Heart, Lips, & Arms
Even what the conjugal & mother Dove
That borrows genial Warmth from those, she warms,
Feels in her thrill'd wings, blessedly outspread –                 330
Thou free'd awhile from Cares & human Dread
By the Immenseness of the Good & Fair
    Which thou see'st every where –
Thus, thus should'st thou rejoice!
To thee would all Things live from Pole to Pole,                   335
Their Life the Eddying of thy living Soul. –
O dear! O Innocent! O full of Love!
A very Friend! A Sister of my Choice –
O dear, as Light & Impulse from above,
Thus may'st thou ever, evermore rejoice!                           340

                                        S.T.C.

[From MS]

## A Soliloquy of the full Moon,
### She being in a Mad Passion –

Now as Heaven is my Lot, they're the Pests of the Nation!
Wherever they can come
With clankum and blankum
'Tis all Botheration, & Hell & Damnation,
With fun, jeering                                                        5
Conjuring
Sky-staring,
Loungering,
And still to the tune of Transmogrification –
Those muttering                                                         10
Spluttering
Ventriloquogusty
Poets
With no Hats
Or Hats that are rusty.                                                  15
They're my Torment and Curse
And harass me worse
And bait me and bay me, far sorer I vow
Than the Screech of the Owl
Or the witch-wolf's long howl,                                          20
Or sheep-killing Butcher-dog's inward Bow wow
For me they all spite – an unfortunate Wight.
And the very first moment that I came to Light
A Rascal call'd Voss the more to his scandal,
Turn'd me into a sickle with never a handle.                            25
A Night or two after a worse Rogue there came,
The head of the Gang, one Wordsworth by name –
'Ho! What's in the wind?' 'Tis the voice of a Wizzard!
I saw him look at me most terribly blue!
He was hunting for witch-rhymes from great A to Izzard,                 30
And soon as he'd found them made no more ado
But chang'd me at once to a little Canoe.
From this strange Enchantment uncharm'd by degrees
I began to take courage & hop'd for some Ease,
When one Coleridge, a Raff of the self-same Banditti                    35
Past by – & intending no doubt to be witty,

Because I'd th' ill-fortune his taste to displease,
   He turn'd up his nose,
   And in pitiful Prose
Made me into the half of a small Cheshire Cheese.    40
Well, a night or two past – it was wind, rain & hail –
And I ventur'd abroad in a thick Cloak & veil –
But the very first Evening he saw me again
The last mentioned Ruffian popp'd out of his Den –
I was resting a moment on the bare edge of Naddle    45
I fancy the sight of me turn'd his Brains addle –
   For what was I now?
   A complete Barley-mow
And when I climb'd higher he made a long leg,
And chang'd me at once to an Ostrich's Egg –    50
But now Heaven be praised in contempt of the Loon,
I am I myself I, the jolly full Moon.
   Yet my heart is still fluttering –
   For I heard the Rogue muttering –
He was hulking and skulking at the skirt of a Wood    55
When lightly & brightly on tip-toe I stood
On the long level Line of a motionless Cloud
And ho! what a Skittle-ground! quoth he aloud
And wish'd from his heart nine Nine-pins to see
In brightness & size just proportion'd to me.    60
So I fear'd from my soul,
That he'd make me a Bowl,
But in spite of his spite
This was more than his might
And still Heaven be prais'd! in contempt of the Loon    65
I am I myself I, the jolly full Moon.
[April 1802. From MS]


## Answer to a Child's Question

Do you ask what the birds say? The Sparrow, the Dove,
The Linnet and Thrush say, 'I love and I love!'
In the winter they're silent – the wind is so strong;
What it says, I don't know, but it sings a loud song.
But green leaves, and blossoms, and sunny warm weather,    5
And singing, and loving – all come back together.

But the Lark is so brimful of gladness and love,
The green fields below him, the blue sky above,
That he sings, and he sings; and for ever sings he –
'I love my Love, and my Love loves me!'                    10
[May 1802]

## The Day-Dream

### FROM AN EMIGRANT TO HIS ABSENT WIFE

If thou wert here, these tears were tears of light!
   But from as sweet a vision did I start
As ever made these eyes grow idly bright!
   And though I weep, yet still around my heart
A sweet and playful tenderness doth linger,              5
Touching my heart as with an infant's finger.


My mouth half open, like a witless man,
   I saw our couch, I saw our quiet room,
   Its shadows heaving by the fire-light gloom;
And o'er my lips a subtle feeling ran,                   10
All o'er my lips a soft and breeze-like feeling –
I know not what – but had the same been stealing


Upon a sleeping mother's lips, I guess
   It would have made the loving mother dream
That she was softly bending down to kiss                 15
   Her babe, that something more than babe did seem,
A floating presence of its darling father,
And yet its own dear baby self far rather!


Across my chest there lay a weight, so warm!
   As if some bird had taken shelter there;              20
And lo! I seemed to see a woman's form –
   Thine, Sara, thine? Oh joy, if thine it were!
I gazed with stifled breath, and feared to stir it,
   No deeper trance e'er wrapt a yearning spirit!

And now, when I seemed sure thy face to see, 25
  Thy own dear self in our own quiet home;
There came an elfish laugh, and wakened me:
  'Twas Frederic, who behind my chair had clomb,
And with his bright eyes at my face was peeping.
I blessed him, tried to laugh, and fell a-weeping! 30
[Summer 1802]


## To Asra

Are there two things, of all which men possess
That are so like each other and so near,
As mutual Love seems like to Happiness?
Dear Asra, woman beyond utterance dear!
This Love which ever welling at my heart, 5
Now in its living fount doth heave and fall,
Now overflowing pours thro' every part
Of all my frame, and fills and changes all,
Like vernal waters springing up through snow,
This Love that seeming great beyond the power 10
Of growth, yet seemeth ever more to grow,
Could I transmute the whole to one rich Dower
Of Happy Life, and give it all to Thee,
Thy lot, methinks, were Heaven, thy age, Eternity!
[1801–4. From MS]


## The Happy Husband

### A FRAGMENT

Oft, oft methinks, the while with thee,
  I breathe, as from the heart, thy dear
  And dedicated name, I hear
A promise and a mystery,
  A pledge of more than passing life, 5
  Yea, in that very name of Wife!

A pulse of love, that ne'er can sleep!
  A feeling that upbraids the heart
  With happiness beyond desert,
That gladness half requests to weep!         10
  Nor bless I not the keener sense
  And unalarming turbulence

Of transient joys, that ask no sting
  From jealous fears, or coy denying;
  But born beneath Love's brooding wing,       15
And into tenderness soon dying,
  Wheel out their giddy moment, then
  Resign the soul to love again; —

A more precipitated vein
  Of notes, that eddy in the flow       20
  Of smoothest song, they come, they go,
And leave their sweeter understrain
  Its own sweet self — a love of Thee
  That seems, yet cannot greater be!
[?1802]


# A Thought[1]

### SUGGESTED BY A VIEW OF SADDLEBACK
### IN CUMBERLAND

On stern Blencartha's perilous height
  The winds are tyrannous and strong;
And flashing forth unsteady light
From stern Blencartha's skiey height,
  As loud the torrents throng!       5

[1] A Force is the provincial term in Cumberland for any narrow fall of water from the summit of a mountain precipice. The following stanza (it may not arrogate the name of poem) or versified reflection was composed while the author was gazing on three parallel *Forces* on a moonlight night, at the foot of the Saddleback Fell. [S.T.C.] The first line is an adaptation of a line in a poem of Isaac Ritson, quoted in Hutchinson's *History of Cumberland*, a work which supplied Coleridge with some of the place-names in the Second Part of *Christabel*. [E.H.C.]

Beneath the moon, in gentle weather,
They bind the earth and sky together.
But oh! the sky and all its forms, how quiet! –
The things that seek the earth, how full of noise and riot!
[Summer 1802]


## A Sunset[1]

Upon the mountain's Edge all lightly resting
There a brief while the Globe of splendor sits
And seems a creature of this earth; but soon
   More changeful than the Moon
To wane fantastic his great orb submits,     5
A distant Hill[2] of Fire: till sinking slowly
Even to a Star at length he lessens wholly.

   Abrupt, as Spirits vanish, he is sunk/
A soul-like breeze possesses all the wood;
   The Boughs, the Sprays have stood     10
As motionless, as stands the ancient Trunk,
But every leaf thro' all the forest flutters,
And deep the Cavern of the fountain mutters
[?1802–4. From MS]


## The Keepsake

The tedded hay, the first fruits of the soil,
The tedded hay and corn-sheaves in one field,
Show summer gone, ere come. The foxglove tall
Sheds its loose purple bells, or in the gust,
Or when it bends beneath the up-springing lark,     5
Or mountain-finch alighting. And the rose
(In vain the darling of successful love)
Stands, like some boasted beauty of past years,
The thorns remaining, and the flowers all gone.

[1]These lines I wrote as nonsense verses merely to try a metre; but they are by no means contemptible – at least, on reading them I am surprised at finding them so good. [S.T.C. 1805]
[2]or cone, or mow [S.T.C.]

Nor can I find, amid my lonely walk                    10
By rivulet, or spring, or wet road-side,
That blue and bright-eyed floweret of the brook,
Hope's gentle gem, the sweet Forget-me-not![1]
So will not fade the flowers which Emmeline
With delicate fingers on the snow-white silk            15
Has worked, (the flowers which most she knew I loved),
And, more belov'd than they, her auburn hair.

   In the cool morning twilight, early waked
By her full bosom's joyous restlessness,
Softly she rose, and lightly stole along,               20
Down the slope coppice to the woodbine bower,
Whose rich flowers, swinging in the morning breeze,
Over their dim fast-moving shadows hung,
Making a quiet image of disquiet
In the smooth, scarcely moving river-pool.              25
There, in that bower where first she owned her love,
And let me kiss my own warm tear of joy
From off her glowing cheek, she sate and stretched
The silk upon the frame, and worked her name
Between the Moss-Rose and Forget-me-not –               30
Her own dear name, with her own auburn hair!
That forced to wander till sweet spring return,
I yet might ne'er forget her smile, her look,
Her voice, (that even in her mirthful mood
Has made me wish to steal away and weep),               35
Nor yet the entrancement of that maiden kiss
With which she promised, that when spring returned,
She would resign one half of that dear name,
And own thenceforth no other name but mine!
[1800–2]

[1] One of the names (and meriting to be the only one) of the *Myosotis Scorpioides Palustris*, a flower from six to twelve inches high, with blue blossom and bright yellow eye. It has the same name over the whole Empire of Germany (*Vergissmeinnicht*) and, we believe, in Denmark and Sweden. [S.T.C.]

## *The Picture*[1]

### OR THE LOVER'S RESOLUTION

Through weeds and thorns, and matted underwood
I force my way; now climb, and now descend
O'er rocks, or bare or mossy, with wild foot
Crushing the purple whorts;[2] while oft unseen,
Hurrying along the drifted forest-leaves,                           5
The scared snake rustles. Onward still I toil,
I know not, ask not whither! A new joy,
Lovely as light, sudden as summer gust,
And gladsome as the first-born of the spring,
Beckons me on, or follows from behind,                            10
Playmate, or guide! The master-passion quelled,
I feel that I am free. With dun-red bark
The fir-trees, and the unfrequent slender oak,
Forth from this tangle wild of bush and brake
Soar up, and form a melancholy vault                             15
High o'er me, murmuring like a distant sea.

Here Wisdom might resort, and here Remorse;
Here too the love-lorn man, who, sick in soul,
And of this busy human heart aweary,
Worships the spirit of unconscious life                          20
In tree or wild-flower. – Gentle lunatic!
If so he might not wholly cease to be,
He would far rather not be that, he is;
But would be something, that he knows not of,
In winds or waters, or among the rocks!                          25

But hence, fond wretch! breathe not contagion here!
No myrtle-walks are these: these are no groves
Where Love dare loiter! If in sullen mood
He should stray hither, the low stumps shall gore
His dainty feet, the briar and the thorn                         30
Make his plumes haggard. Like a wounded bird

---

[1] Some parts are adapted from Gessner's 'Der Feste Vorsatz'. [E.H.C.]
[2] *Vaccinium Myrtillus*, known by the different names of Whorts, Whortleberries, Bilberries; and in the North of England, Blea-berries and Bloom-berries. [S.T.C.]

Easily caught, ensnare him, O ye Nymphs,
Ye Oreads chaste, ye dusky Dryades!
And you, ye Earth-winds! you that make at morn
The dew-drops quiver on the spiders' webs!                    35
You, O ye wingless Airs! that creep between
The rigid stems of heath and bitten furze,
Within whose scanty shade, at summer-noon,
The mother-sheep hath worn a hollow bed –
Ye, that now cool her fleece with dropless damp,              40
Now pant and murmur with her feeding lamb.
Chase, chase him, all ye Fays, and elfin Gnomes!
With prickles sharper than his darts bemock
His little Godship, making him perforce
Creep through a thorn-bush on yon hedgehog's back.           45

This is my hour of triumph! I can now
With my own fancies play the merry fool,
And laugh away worse folly, being free.
Here will I seat myself, beside this old,
Hollow, and weedy oak, which ivy-twine                        50
Clothes as with net-work: here will I couch my limbs,
Close by this river, in this silent shade,
As safe and sacred from the step of man
As an invisible world – unheard, unseen,
And listening only to the pebbly brook                        55
That murmurs with a dead, yet tinkling sound;
Or to the bees, that in the neighbouring trunk
Make honey-hoards. The breeze, that visits me,
Was never Love's accomplice, never raised
The tendril ringlets from the maiden's brow,                  60
And the blue, delicate veins above her cheek;
Ne'er played the wanton – never half disclosed
The maiden's snowy bosom, scattering thence
Eye-poisons for some love-distempered youth,
Who ne'er henceforth may see an aspen-grove                   65
Shiver in sunshine, but his feeble heart
Shall flow away like a dissolving thing.

Sweet breeze! thou only, if I guess aright,
Liftest the feathers of the robin's breast,
That swells its little breast, so full of song,               70

Singing above me, on the mountain-ash.
And thou too, desert stream! no pool of thine,
Though clear as lake in latest summer-eve,
Did e'er reflect the stately virgin's robe,
The face, the form divine, the downcast look          75
Contemplative! Behold! her open palm
Presses her cheek and brow! her elbow rests
On the bare branch of half-uprooted tree,
That leans towards its mirror! Who erewhile
Had from her countenance turned, or looked by stealth,          80
(For Fear is true-love's cruel nurse), he now
With steadfast gaze and unoffending eye,
Worships the watery idol, dreaming hopes
Delicious to the soul, but fleeting, vain,
E'en as that phantom-world on which he gazed,          85
But not unheeded gazed: for see, ah! see,
The sportive tyrant with her left hand plucks
The heads of tall flowers that behind her grow,
Lychnis, and willow-herb, and fox-glove bells:
And suddenly, as one that toys with time,          90
Scatters them on the pool! Then all the charm
Is broken – all that phantom-world so fair
Vanishes, and a thousand circlets spread,
And each mis-shape the other. Stay awhile,
Poor youth, who scarcely dar'st lift up thine eyes!          95
The stream will soon renew its smoothness, soon
The visions will return! And lo! he stays:
And soon the fragments dim of lovely forms
Come trembling back, unite, and now once more
The pool becomes a mirror; and behold          100
Each wildflower on the marge inverted there,
And there the half-uprooted tree – but where,
O where the virgin's snowy arm, that leaned
On its bare branch? He turns, and she is gone!
Homeward she steals through many a woodland maze          105
Which he shall seek in vain. Ill-fated youth!
Go, day by day, and waste thy manly prime
In mad love-yearning by the vacant brook,
Till sickly thoughts bewitch thine eyes, and thou
Behold'st her shadow still abiding there,          110
The Naiad of the mirror!

Not to thee,
O wild and desert stream! belongs this tale:
Gloomy and dark art thou – the crowded firs
Spire from thy shores, and stretch across thy bed,
Making thee doleful as a cavern-well:                    115
Save when the shy king-fishers build their nest
On thy steep banks, no loves hast thou, wild stream!

    This be my chosen haunt – emancipate
From Passion's dreams, a freeman, and alone,
I rise and trace its devious course. O lead,             120
Lead me to deeper shades and lonelier glooms.
Lo! stealing through the canopy of firs,
How fair the sunshine spots that mossy rock,
Isle of the river, whose disparted waves
Dart off asunder with an angry sound,                    125
How soon to re-unite! And see! they meet,
Each in the other lost and found: and see
Placeless, as spirits, one soft water-sun
Throbbing within them, heart at once and eye!
With its soft neighbourhood of filmy clouds,             130
The stains and shadings of forgotten tears,
Dimness o'erswum with lustre! Such the hour
Of deep enjoyment, following love's brief feuds;
And hark, the noise of a near waterfall!
I pass forth into light – I find myself                  135
Beneath a weeping birch (most beautiful
Of forest trees, the Lady of the Woods),
Hard by the brink of a tall weedy rock
That overbrows the cataract. How bursts
The landscape on my sight! Two crescent hills            140
Fold in behind each other, and so make
A circular vale, and land-locked, as might seem,
With brook and bridge, and grey stone cottages,
Half hid by rocks and fruit-trees. At my feet,
The whortle-berries are bedewed with spray,              145
Dashed upwards by the furious waterfall.
How solemnly the pendent ivy-mass
Swings in its winnow! All the air is calm.
The smoke from cottage-chimneys, tinged with light,
Rises in columns; from this house alone,                 150

Close by the water-fall, the column slants,
And feels its ceaseless breeze. But what is this?
That cottage, with its slanting chimney-smoke,
And close beside its porch a sleeping child,
His dear head pillowed on a sleeping dog –                155
One arm between its fore-legs, and the hand
Holds loosely its small handful of wild-flowers,
Unfilletted, and of unequal lengths.
A curious picture, with a master's haste
Sketched on a strip of pinky-silver skin,                160
Peeled from the birchen bark! Divinest maid!
Yon bark her canvas, and those purple berries
Her pencil! See, the juice is scarcely dried
On the fine skin! She has been newly here;
And lo! yon patch of heath has been her couch –          165
The pressure still remains! O blessèd couch!
For this may'st thou flower early, and the sun,
Slanting at eve, rest bright, and linger long
Upon thy purple bells! O Isabel!
Daughter of genius! stateliest of our maids!             170
More beautiful than whom Alcaeus wooed,
The Lesbian woman of immortal song!
O child of genius! stately, beautiful,
And full of love to all, save only me,
And not ungentle e'en to me! My heart,                   175
Why beats it thus? Through yonder coppice-wood
Needs must the pathway turn, that leads straightway
On to her father's house. She is alone!
The night draws on – such ways are hard to hit –
And fit it is I should restore this sketch,              180
Dropt unawares, no doubt. Why should I yearn
To keep the relique? 'twill but idly feed
The passion that consumes me. Let me haste!
The picture in my hand which she has left;
She cannot blame me that I followed her:                 185
And I may be her guide the long wood through.
[August 1802]

## Hymn Before Sun-Rise, in the Vale of Chamouni

### AFTER THE GERMAN OF FRIEDERIKE BRUN[1]

Besides the Rivers, Arve and Arveiron, which have their sources in the foot of Mont Blanc, five conspicuous torrents rush down its sides; and within a few paces of the Glaciers, the Gentiana Major grows in immense numbers, with its 'flowers of loveliest blue'.

Hast thou a charm to stay the morning-star
In his steep course? So long he seems to pause
On thy bald awful head, O sovran BLANC,
The Arve and Arveiron at thy base
Rave ceaselessly; but thou, most awful Form!                        5
Risest from forth thy silent sea of pines,
How silently! Around thee and above
Deep is the air and dark, substantial, black,
An ebon mass: methinks thou piercest it,
As with a wedge! But when I look again,                             10
It is thine own calm home, thy crystal shrine,
Thy habitation from eternity!
O dread and silent Mount! I gazed upon thee,
Till thou, still present to the bodily sense,
Didst vanish from my thought: entranced in prayer                   15
I worshipped the Invisible alone.

    Yet, like some sweet beguiling melody,
So sweet, we know not we are listening to it,
Thou, the meanwhile, wast blending with my Thought,
Yea, with my Life and Life's own secret joy:                        20
Till the dilating Soul, enrapt, transfused,
Into the mighty vision passing – there
As in her natural form, swelled vast to Heaven!

    Awake, my soul! not only passive praise
Thou owest! not alone these swelling tears,                         25
Mute thanks and secret ecstasy! Awake,
Voice of sweet song! Awake, my Heart, awake!
Green vales and icy cliffs, all join my Hymn.

[1] Friederike Brun's 'Chamouny beym Sonnenaufgange' runs to no more than twenty lines, but in Coleridge's original printing he also used her notes without acknowledgement for a long prose preface.

Thou first and chief, sole sovereign of the Vale!
O struggling with the darkness all the night, 30
And visited all night by troops of stars,
Or when they climb the sky or when they sink:
Companion of the morning-star at dawn,
Thyself Earth's rosy star, and of the dawn
Co-herald: wake, O wake, and utter praise! 35
Who sank thy sunless pillars deep in Earth?
Who filled thy countenance with rosy light?
Who made thee parent of perpetual streams?

And you, ye five wild torrents fiercely glad!
Who called you forth from night and utter death, 40
From dark and icy caverns called you forth,
Down those precipitous, black, jaggéd rocks,
For ever shattered and the same for ever?
Who gave you your invulnerable life,
Your strength, your speed, your fury, and your joy, 45
Unceasing thunder and eternal foam?
And who commanded (and the silence came),
Here let the billows stiffen, and have rest?

Ye Ice-falls! ye that from the mountain's brow
Adown enormous ravines slope amain – 50
Torrents, methinks, that heard a mighty voice,
And stopped at once amid their maddest plunge!
Motionless torrents! silent cataracts!
Who made you glorious as the Gates of Heaven
Beneath the keen full moon? Who bade the sun 55
Clothe you with rainbows? Who, with living flowers
Of loveliest blue, spread garlands at your feet? –
GOD! let the torrents, like a shout of nations,
Answer! and let the ice-plains echo, GOD!
GOD! sing ye meadow-streams with gladsome voice! 60
Ye pine-groves, with your soft and soul-like sounds!
And they too have a voice, yon piles of snow,
And in their perilous fall shall thunder, GOD!

Ye living flowers that skirt the eternal frost!
Ye wild goats sporting round the eagle's nest! 65
Ye eagles, play-mates of the mountain-storm!

Ye lightnings, the dread arrows of the clouds!
Ye signs and wonders of the element!
Utter forth God, and fill the hills with praise!

Thou too, hoar Mount! with thy sky-pointing peaks,      70
Oft from whose feet the avalanche, unheard,
Shoots downward, glittering through the pure serene
Into the depth of clouds, that veil thy breast –
Thou too again, stupendous Mountain! thou
That as I raise my head, awhile bowed low      75
In adoration, upward from thy base
Slow travelling with dim eyes suffused with tears,
Solemnly seemest, like a vapoury cloud,
To rise before me – Rise, O ever rise,
Rise like a cloud of incense, from the Earth!      80
Thou kingly Spirit throned among the hills,
Thou dread ambassador from Earth to Heaven,
Great Hierarch! tell thou the silent sky,
And tell the stars, and tell yon rising sun
Earth, with her thousand voices, praises GOD.      85
[August–September 1802]

## The Good Great Man

'How seldom, friend! a good great man inherits
    Honour or wealth with all his worth and pains!
It sounds like stories from the land of spirits
If any man obtain that which he merits
    Or any merit that which he obtains.'      5

### REPLY TO THE ABOVE

For shame, dear friend, renounce this canting strain!
What would'st thou have a good great man obtain?
Place? titles? salary? a gilded chain?
Or throne of corses which his sword had slain?
Greatness and goodness are not *means*, but *ends*!      10
Hath he not always treasures, always friends,
The good great man? *three* treasures, LOVE, and LIGHT,
    And CALM THOUGHTS, regular as infant's breath:
And three firm friends, more sure than day and night,
    HIMSELF, his MAKER and the ANGEL DEATH!      15
[1802]

## The Knight's Tomb

### AN EXPERIMENT FOR A METRE

Where is the grave of Sir Arthur O'Kellyn?
Where may the grave of that good man be?—
By the side of a spring, on the breast of Helvellyn,
Under the twigs of a young birch tree!
The oak that in summer was sweet to hear,                5
And rustled its leaves in the fall of the year,
And whistled and roared in the winter alone,
Is gone, – and the birch in its stead is grown. –
The Knight's bones are dust,
And his good sword rust; –                               10
His soul is with the saints, I trust.
[?1802]

## To Matilda Betham from a Stranger

Matilda! I have heard a sweet tune played
On a sweet instrument – thy Poesie –
Sent to my soul by Boughton's pleading voice,
Where friendship's zealous wish inspirited,
Deepened and filled the subtle tones of *taste*:        5
(So have I heard a Nightingale's fine notes
Blend with the murmur of a hidden stream!)
And now the fair, wild offspring of thy genius,
Those wanderers whom thy fancy had sent forth
To seek their fortune in this motley world,             10
Have found a little home within *my* heart,
And brought me, as the quit-rent of their lodging,
Rose-buds, and fruit-blossoms, and pretty weeds,
And timorous laurel leaflets half-disclosed,
Engarlanded with gadding woodbine tendrils!             15
A coronal, which, with undoubting hand,
I twine around the brows of patriot HOPE!

The Almighty, having first composed a Man,
Set him to music, framing Woman for him,
And fitted each to each, and made them one!                    20
And 'tis my faith, that there's a natural bond
Between the female mind and measured sounds,
Nor do I know a sweeter Hope than this,
That this sweet Hope, by judgment unreproved,
That our own Britain, our dear mother Isle,                     25
May boast one Maid, a poetess *indeed*,
Great as th' impassioned Lesbian, in sweet song,
And O! of holier mind, and happier fate.


Matilda! I dare twine *thy* vernal wreath
Around the brows of patriot Hope! But thou                     30
Be wise! be bold! fulfil my auspices!
Tho' sweet thy measures, stern must be thy thought,
Patient thy study, watchful thy mild eye!
Poetic feelings, like the stretching boughs
Of mighty oaks, pay homage to the gales,                       35
Toss in the strong winds, drive before the gust,
Themselves one giddy storm of fluttering leaves;
Yet, all the while self-limited, remain
Equally near the fixed and solid trunk
Of Truth and Nature in the howling storm,                      40
As in the calm that stills the aspen grove.
Be bold, meek Woman! but be wisely bold!
Fly, ostrich-like, firm land beneath thy feet,
Yet hurried onward by thy wings of fancy
Swift as the whirlwind, singing in their quills.               45
Look round thee! look within thee! think and feel!
What nobler meed, Matilda! canst thou win,
Than tears of gladness in a BOUGHTON's[1] eyes,
And exultation even in strangers' hearts?
[September 1802. From MS]


[1] Catherine Rose, wife of Sir Charles William Rouse-Boughton, Bart. Sir Charles and Lady
Boughton visited Greta Hall in September 1802. [E.H.C.]

## *To One Who Published in Print*[1]

WHAT HAD BEEN ENTRUSTED TO HIM BY MY FIRESIDE

Two things hast thou made known to half the nation,
My secrets and my want of penetration:
For O! far more than all which thou hast penn'd
It shames me to have call'd a wretch, like thee, my friend!


## *Westphalian Song*

[The following is an almost literal translation of a very old and very favourite song among the Westphalian Boors. The turn at the end is the same with one of Mr Dibdin's excellent songs, and the air to which it is sung by the Boors is remarkably sweet and lively.]

> When thou to my true-love com'st
>     Greet her from me kindly;
> When she asks thee how I fare?
>     Say, folks in Heaven fare finely.
>
> When she asks, 'What! Is he sick?'                    5
>     Say, dead! – and when for sorrow
> She begins to sob and cry,
>     Say, I come tomorrow.
> [1799–1802]


## [*Life in Death*]

Such love as mourning Husbands have./
To her whose spirit has been newly given/
To be his guardian Saint in Heaven/
Whose Beauty lieth in the Grave Unconquered/

---

[1] Adapted from Wernicke's *Epigrams* I, xii, and prompted perhaps by Charles Lloyd's novel *Edmund Oliver* (1798).

as if the Soul could find no *purer* Tabernacle, nor place of Sojourn, than the virgin Body it had before dwelt in, & wished to stay there till the Resurrection – Far liker to a Flower now than when alive – Cold to the Touch & blooming to the eye –
[September 1803. From MS]

## *The Pains of Sleep*

Ere on my bed my limbs I lay,
It hath not been my use to pray
With moving lips or bended knees;
But silently, by slow degrees,
My spirit I to Love compose,                          5
In humble trust mine eye-lids close,
With reverential resignation,
No wish conceived, no thought exprest,
Only a sense of supplication;
A sense o'er all my soul imprest                     10
That I am weak, yet not unblest,
Since in me, round me, every where
Eternal Strength and Wisdom are.

But yester-night I prayed aloud
In anguish and in agony,                              15
Up-starting from the fiendish crowd
Of shapes and thoughts that tortured me:
A lurid light, a trampling throng,
Sense of intolerable wrong,
And whom I scorned, those only strong!               20
Thirst of revenge, the powerless will
Still baffled, and yet burning still!
Desire with loathing strangely mixed
On wild or hateful objects fixed.
Fantastic passions! maddening brawl!                 25
And shame and terror over all!
Deeds to be hid which were not hid,
Which all confused I could not know,
Whether I suffered, or I did:
For all seemed guilt, remorse or woe,                30
My own or others still the same
Life-stifling fear, soul-stifling shame.

So two nights passed: the night's dismay
Saddened and stunned the coming day.
Sleep, the wide blessing, seemed to me                    35
Distemper's worst calamity.
The third night, when my own loud scream
Had waked me from the fiendish dream,
O'ercome with sufferings strange and wild,
I wept as I had been a child;                             40
And having thus by tears subdued
My anguish to a milder mood,
Such punishments, I said, were due
To natures deepliest stained with sin, –
For aye entempesting anew                                 45
The unfathomable hell within,
The horror of their deeds to view,
To know and loathe, yet wish and do!
Such griefs with such men well agree,
But wherefore, wherefore fall on me?                      50
To be beloved is all I need,
And whom I love, I love indeed.
[September 1803]


## [*Her Thoughts*][1]

Sole Maid, associate sole, to me beyond
Compare, above all living Creatures Dear –

———————————

Thoughts which how found they harbour in thy Breast,
Sara, misthoughts of him to thee so dear.
[February–March 1804. From MS]

[1]Closely adapted from *Paradise Lost*, ix, 227–8, 288–9. See *Notebooks* II, 1945–7 and nn.

## Phantom

All Look or Likeness caught from Earth,
All accident of Kin or Birth,
Had pass'd Away: there seem'd no Trace
Of Aught upon her brighten'd Face
Uprais'd beneath the rifted Stone,                    5
Save of one Spirit, all her own/
She, she herself, and only she
Shone in her body visibly.
[Early 1804. From MS]


## What is Life?

Resembles Life what once was deem'd of Light,
Too simple in itself for human Sight?
An absolute Self – an Element ungrounded?
All, that we see, all colors of all shade
        By incroach of Darkness made? –                    5
Is Life itself by consciousness unbounded?
And all the Thoughts, Pains, Joys of mortal Breath,
A War-embrace of wrestling Life and Death?
[October 1804]


## An Angel Visitant[1]

Within these circling Hollies Woodbine-clad
Beneath this small blue Roof of vernal Sky
How warm, how still! tho' Tears should dim mine eye,
Yet will my Heart for days continue glad –
For here, my Love! thou art! and here am I!                    5
[1804. From MS]

[1]Adapted from *Die Vögel*, by Friedrich von Hagedorn. [K.C.]

## Love's Sanctuary

This yearning heart (Love! witness what I say)
Enshrines thy form as purely as it may,
Round which, as to some spirit uttering bliss,
My thoughts all stand ministrant night and day
Like saintly Priests, that dare not think amiss.     5
[?1804]


## Reason for Love's Blindness

I have heard of reasons manifold
   Why Love must needs be blind,
But this the best of all I hold –
   His eyes are in his mind.

What outward form and feature are     5
   He guesseth but in part;
But that within is good and fair
   He seeth with the heart.
[February 1805]


## [Uncertainty in Love]

O th' oppressive, irksome weight
Felt in an uncertain State:
Comfort, peace, and rest adieu,
Should I prove at last untrue!
Self-confiding Wretch, I thought     5
I could love thee as I ought,
Win thee and deserve to feel
All the love, thou can'st reveal
And still I chuse thee, follow still
Every notice [. . .]
[1805. From MS]

## [*The Veil of Spirit*]

O Beauty, in a beauteous Body dight!
Body! that veiling Brightness becom'st bright/
Fair Cloud which less we see, than by thee see the Light!
[May–June 1805. From MS]

## *An Exile*

Friend, Lover, Husband, Sister, Brother!
Dear names! close in upon each other!
Alas! poor Fancy's Bitter-sweet!
Our names, and *but* our names, can meet.
[Oct 1805. From MS]

## [*The Night-Mare Death in Life*]

I know 'tis but a Dream, yet feel more anguish
Than if 'twere Truth. It has been often so:
Must I die under it? Is no one near?
Will no one hear these stifled groans, & wake me?
[February–March 1806. From MS]

## *Constancy to an Ideal Object*[1]

Since all that beat about in Nature's range,
Or veer or vanish; why should'st thou remain
The only constant in a world of change,
O yearning Thought! that liv'st but in the brain?

---

[1]The date is unusually uncertain, the main clue being in a letter by Coleridge of June 1825 referring to part at least of it as '. . . those lines which a long time ago I sent to Mrs Green'. His interest in the 'Glory' dated back to the 1790s: see J. L. Lowes, *The Road to Xanadu* (1927), pp. 29, 470–1.

Call to the Hours, that in the distance play, 5
The faery people of the future day —
Fond Thought! not one of all that shining swarm
Will breathe on thee with life-enkindling breath,
Till when, like strangers shelt'ring from a storm,
Hope and Despair meet in the porch of Death! 10
Yet still thou haunt'st me; and though well I see,
She is not thou, and only thou art she,
Still, still as though some dear embodied Good,
Some living Love before my eyes there stood
With answering look a ready ear to lend, 15
I mourn to thee and say — 'Ah! loveliest friend!
That this the meed of all my toils might be,
To have a home, an English home, and thee!'
Vain repetition! Home and Thou are one.
The peacefull'st cot, the moon shall shine upon, 20
Lulled by the thrush and wakened by the lark,
Without thee were but a becalméd bark,
Whose Helmsman on an ocean waste and wide
Sits mute and pale his mouldering helm beside.

And art thou nothing? Such thou art, as when 25
The woodman winding westward up the glen
At wintry dawn, where o'er the sheep-track's maze
The viewless snow-mist weaves a glist'ning haze,
Sees full before him, gliding without tread,
An image[1] with a glory round its head; 30
The enamoured rustic worships its fair hues,
Nor knows he makes the shadow, he pursues!

[1] This phenomenon, which the Author has himself experienced, and of which the reader may find a description in one of the earlier volumes of the *Manchester Philosophical Transactions*, is applied figuratively in the following passage of the *Aids to Reflection*: –
'Pindar's fine remark respecting the different effects of Music, on different characters, holds equally true of Genius – as many as are not delighted by it are disturbed, perplexed, irritated. The beholder either recognizes it as a projected form of his own Being, that moves before him with a Glory round its head, or recoils from it as a Spectre.' – *Aids to Reflection* [1825], p. 220. [S.T.C.]

## [A Death Wish][1]

Come, come, thou bleak December Wind,
    And blow the dry Leaves from the Tree!
Flash, like a Love-thought, thro' me, Death
    And take a Life, that wearies me.
[June 1806. From MS]

## Farewell to Love[2]

Farewell, sweet Love! yet blame you not my truth;
    More fondly ne'er did mother eye her child
Than I your form: *yours* were my hopes of youth,
    And as *you* shaped my thoughts I sighed or smiled.

While most were wooing wealth, or gaily swerving      5
    To pleasure's secret haunts, and some apart
Stood strong in pride, self-conscious of deserving,
    To you I gave my whole weak wishing heart.

And when I met the maid that realized
    Your fair creations, and had won her kindness,    10
Say, but for her if aught on earth I prized!
    *Your* dreams alone I dreamt, and caught your blindness.

O grief! – but farewell, Love! I will go play me
With thoughts that please me less, and less betray me.
[August–September 1806]

[1] Adapted from Percy's version of 'Waly, Waly, Love be bonny', st. 3.

> Marti'mas wind when wilt thou blaw,
>     And shake the green leaves aff the tree?
> O gentle death, when wilt thou cum?
>     For of my life I am wearie.
>
>                   [E.H.C.]

[2] This sonnet is modelled upon and in part borrowed from Lord Brooke's (Fulke Greville's) Sonnet LXXXIV of *Caelica*. [E.H.C.]

## Hope and Time[1]

In the great City rear'd, my fancy rude
By natural Forms unnurs'd & unsubdued
An Alien from the Rivers & the Fields
And all the Charms, that Hill or Woodland yields,
It was the pride & passion of my Youth                    5
T' impersonate & color moral Truth[:]
Rare Allegories in those Days I spun,
That oft had mystic senses oft'ner none.
Of all Resemblances however faint,
So dear a Lover was I, that with quaint                  10
Figures fantastically grouped I made
Of commonest Thoughts a moving Masquerade.
'Twas then I fram'd this obscure uncouth Rhyme,
A sort of Emblem 'tis of HOPE & TIME.

In ancient Days, but when I have not read,               15
Nor know I, where – but 'twas some elfish Place
Their pennons, ostrich-like for Sails outspread,
Two wingéd Children run an endless Race –
    A Sister & a Brother
    But HOPE outruns the other –                          20
Yet ever flies she with reverted Face,
And looks & listens for the Boy behind
Time is his Name – & he, alas! is blind,
With regular Step o'er rough & smooth he past,
And knows not whether he is first or last.               25
[1802–7. From MS]

[1]Part of this poem was reworked and published under the title, *Time, Real and Imaginary*.

## [*The Veil of Light*][1]

Bright clouds of reverence, sufferably bright
That intercept the dazzle not the Light
That veil the finite form, the boundless power reveal
Itself an earthly sun, of pure intensest White . . .
[1806. From MS]

## [*Inward Light*][2]

His own fair countenance, his kingly forehead
His tender smiles, Love's day-dawn on his Lips
That put on such heavenly spiritual light
At the same moment in his steadfast eyes/
Were virtue's native crest, the innocent Soul's          5
Unconscious meek Self-heraldry – to man
Genial, and pleasant to his guardian angel –
He suffered, nor complain'd; tho' oft, with tears,
He mourn'd the oppression of his helpless Brethren, –
And sometimes with a deeper, holier grief          10
Mourn'd for the oppressor: but that in Sabbath Hours –
a solemn grief,
That like a Cloud at Sunset,
Was but the veil of inward meditation,
Pierc'd thro'
And saturate with the intellectual rays, it soften'd.          15
[October–November 1806. From MS]

## [*The Eagle and the Tortoise*]

Let Eagle bid the Tortoise sunward soar –
As vainly Strength speaks to a broken Mind.
[1806. From MS]

[1]This and the next two fragments were inspired by Coleridge's reading of Fulke Greville's
*Alaham*: see *Notebooks* II 2921. [K.C., J.C.C.M.]
[2]Compare Teresa's speech to Valdez, *Remorse*, Act IV, Scene II, lines 52–63. [E.H.C.]

## *Metrical Feet*

### LESSON FOR A BOY

Trōchĕe trīps frŏm lōng tŏ shōrt;
From long to long in solemn sort
Slōw Spōndēe stālks; strōng fōot! yet ill able
Ēvĕr tŏ cōme ŭp wĭth Dāctȳl trĭsȳllăblĕ.
Ĭāmbĭcs mārch frŏm shōrt tŏ lōng; —                           5
Wĭth ă leāp ănd ă boūnd thĕ swĭft Ănăpæsts thrōng;
One syllable long, with one short at each side,
Ămphībrăchȳs hāstes wĭth ă stātelȳ stride; —
Fīrst ănd lāst beĭng lōng, mĭddlĕ shōrt, Ămphĭmācer
Strīkes hĭs thūndērĭng hōofs līke ă proūd hīgh-brĕd Rācer.   10
If Derwent be innocent, steady and wise,
And delight in the things of earth, water, and skies;
Tender warmth at his heart, with these metres to show it,
With sound sense in his brains, may make Derwent a poet, —
May crown him with fame, and must win him the love        15
Of his father on earth and his Father above.
             My dear, dear child!
Could you stand upon Skiddaw, you would not from its
             whole ridge
See a man who so loves you as your fond S. T. COLERIDGE.
[December 1806–March 1807]


## [*The Timorous Hind*]

As the shy Hind, the soft-eyed gentle Brute,
Now moves, now stops, approaching by degrees
At length emerges from the shelt'ring Trees,
Lur'd by her Hunter with the shepherd's Flute
Whose music travelling on the twilight Breeze,                5
    When all beside was mute,
She oft had heard unharm'd and ever loves to hear,
She, fearful Beast! but that no sound of Fear.
[November–December 1806. From MS]

## Psyche

The butterfly the ancient Grecians made
The soul's fair emblem, and its only name – [1]
But of the soul, escaped the slavish trade
Of mortal life! – For in this earthly frame
Ours is the reptile's lot, much toil, much blame,          5
Manifold motions making little speed,
And to deform and kill the things whereon we feed.
[?Winter 1806–7 to 1817]

[1] Psyche means both Butterfly and Soul. [S.T.C.]

# To W. Wordsworth[1]

LINES COMPOSED, FOR THE GREATER PART ON THE NIGHT,
ON WHICH HE FINISHED THE RECITATION OF HIS POEM
(IN THIRTEEN BOOKS) CONCERNING THE GROWTH
AND HISTORY OF HIS OWN MIND

January 1807. Cole-orton, near Ashby de la Zouch.

O Friend! O Teacher! God's great Gift to me!
Into my heart have I receiv'd that Lay,
More than historic, that prophetic Lay,
Wherein (high theme by Thee first sung aright)
Of the Foundations and the Building-up                          5
Of thy own Spirit, thou hast lov'd to tell
What may be told, to th' understanding mind
Revealable; and what within the mind
May rise enkindled. Theme as hard as high!
Of Smiles spontaneous, and mysterious Fears;                   10
(The First-born they of Reason, and Twin-birth)
Of Tides obedient to external Force,
And *currents* self-determin'd, as might seem,
Or by interior Power: of Moments aweful,
Now in thy hidden Life; and now abroad,                         15
Mid festive Crowds, *thy* Brows too garlanded,
A Brother of the Feast: of *Fancies* fair,
Hyblæan Murmurs of poetic Thought,
Industrious in its Joy, by lilied Streams
Native or outland, Lakes and famous Hills!                     20

Of more than Fancy, of the Hope of Man
Amid the tremor of a Realm aglow –

---

[1] The version on the left-hand pages is from a MS in the Wordsworth family, that on right-hand pages from *Sibylline Leaves* (1817). They display the changes Coleridge felt to be appropriate not only in revising for publication, but in offering to the public a document originally written as a private tribute. In 1817 *The Prelude* was still unpublished, and would remain so for the next thirty-three years; Coleridge respected this decision by addressing his own poem to an anonymous 'Gentleman', but may have hoped that its publication would encourage Wordsworth to put *The Prelude* into print.

## *To a Gentleman*

**COMPOSED ON THE NIGHT AFTER HIS RECITATION
OF A POEM ON THE GROWTH OF
AN INDIVIDUAL MIND**

Friend of the Wise! and Teacher of the Good!
Into my heart have I received that Lay
More than historic, that prophetic Lay
Wherein (high theme by thee first sung aright)
Of the foundations and the building up                          5
Of the Human Spirit, thou hast dared to tell
What may be told, to th' understanding mind
Revealable; and what within the mind
By vital Breathings, like the secret soul
Of vernal growth, oft quickens in the Heart          10
Thoughts all too deep for words! –

                        Theme hard as high!
Of smiles spontaneous, and mysterious fears
(The first-born they of Reason and twin-birth)
Of tides obedient to external force,                            15
And currents self-determined, as might seem,
Or by some inner Power; of moments awful,
Now in thy inner life, and now abroad,
When Power stream'd from thee, and thy soul received
The light reflected, as a light bestow'd –          20
Of Fancies fair, and milder hours of youth,
Hyblean murmurs of Poetic Thought
Industrious in its Joy, in Vales and Glens
Native or outland, Lakes and famous Hills!
Or on the lonely High-road, when the Stars          25
Were rising; or by secret Mountain-streams,
The Guides and the Companions of thy way!

  Of more than Fancy, of the Social Sense
Distending wide, and Man belov'd as Man,

Where France in all her Towns lay vibrating,
Ev'n as a Bark becalm'd on sultry seas
Beneath the voice from Heaven, the bursting Crash    25
Of Heaven's immediate thunder! when no Cloud
Is visible, or Shadow on the Main!
Ah! soon night roll'd on night, and every Cloud
Open'd its eye of Fire: and Hope aloft
Now flutter'd, and now toss'd upon the Storm    30
Floating! Of Hope afflicted, and struck down,
Thence summon'd homeward – homeward to thy
        Heart,
Oft from the Watch-tower of Man's absolute Self,
With Light unwaning on her eyes, to look
Far on – herself a Glory to behold,    35
The Angel of the Vision! Then (last strain!)
Of *Duty*, chosen Laws controlling choice,
Virtue and Love! An Orphic Tale indeed,
A Tale divine of high and passionate Thoughts
To their own music chaunted!

                                    Ah great Bard!    40
Ere yet that last Swell dying aw'd the Air,
With stedfast ken I view'd thee in the Choir
Of ever-enduring Men. The truly Great
Have all one Age, and from one visible space
Shed influence: for they, both power and act,    45
Are permanent, and Time is not with them,
Save as it worketh for them, they in it.
Nor less a sacred Roll, than those of old,
And to be plac'd as they, with gradual fame
Among the Archives of mankind, thy Work    50
Makes audible a linked Song of Truth,
Of Truth profound a sweet continuous Song
Not learnt, but native, her own natural Notes!
Dear shall it be to every human Heart,
To me how more than dearest! Me, on whom    55
Comfort from Thee and utterance of thy Love
Came with such heights and depths of Harmony
Such sense of Wings uplifting, that the Storm
Scatter'd and whirl'd me, till my Thoughts became
A bodily Tumult! and thy faithful Hopes,    60

Where France in all her Towns lay vibrating                              30
Even as a Bark becalm'd beneath the Burst
Of Heaven's immediate Thunder, when no cloud
Is visible, or shadow on the Main.
For thou wert there, thine own brows garlanded,
Amid the tremor of a realm aglow,                                        35
Amid a mighty nation jubilant,
When from the general Heart of Human kind
Hope sprang forth like a full-born Deity!
— Of that dear Hope afflicted and struck down,
So summon'd homeward, thenceforth calm and sure                         40
From the dread Watch-Tower of man's absolute Self,
With light unwaning on her eyes, to look
Far on — herself a glory to behold,
The Angel of the vision! Then (last strain)
Of Duty, chosen Laws controlling choice,                                45
Action and Joy! — An orphic song indeed,
A song divine of high and passionate thoughts,
To their own Music chaunted!

                              O great Bard!
Ere yet that last strain dying awed the air,
With stedfast eye I view'd thee in the choir                            50
Of ever-enduring men. The truly Great
Have all one age, and from one visible space
Shed influence! They, both in power and act,
Are permanent, and Time is not with *them*,
Save as it worketh *for* them, they *in* it.                            55
Nor less a sacred Roll, than those of old,
And to be placed, as they, with gradual fame
Among the Archives of Mankind, thy work
Makes audible a linkéd lay of Truth,
Of Truth profound a sweet continuous lay,                               60
Not learnt, but native, her own natural notes!

Thy Hopes of me, dear Friend! by me unfelt
Were troublous to me, almost as a Voice
Familiar once and more than musical
To one cast forth, whose hope had seem'd to die,
A Wanderer with a worn-out heart,                                    65
Mid Strangers pining with untended Wounds!

O Friend! too well thou know'st, of what sad years
The long suppression had benumb'd my soul,
That even as Life returns upon the Drown'd,
Th' unusual Joy awoke a throng of Pains —                            70
Keen Pangs of LOVE, awakening, as a Babe,
Turbulent, with an outcry in the Heart:
And Fears self-will'd, that shunn'd the eye of Hope,
And Hope, that would not know itself from Fear:
Sense of pass'd Youth, and Manhood come in vain;                     75
And Genius given, and knowledge won in vain;
And all, which I had cull'd in Wood-walks wild,
And all, which patient Toil had rear'd, and all,
Commune with Thee had open'd out, but Flowers
Strew'd on my Corse, and borne upon my Bier,                         80
In the same Coffin, for the self-same Grave!

    That way no more! and ill beseems it me,
Who came a Welcomer in Herald's guise
Singing of Glory and Futurity,
To wander back on such unhealthful Roads                             85
Plucking the Poisons of Self-harm! and ill
Such Intertwine beseems triumphal wreaths
Strew'd before thy Advancing! Thou too, Friend!
O injure not the memory of that Hour
Of thy communion with my nobler mind                                90
By pity or grief, already felt too long!
Nor let my words import more blame than needs.
The Tumult rose and ceas'd: for Peace is nigh
Where Wisdom's Voice has found a list'ning Heart.
Amid the howl of more than wintry Storms                             95
The Halcyon hears the voice of vernal Hours,
Already on the wing!

Ah! as I listen'd with a heart forlorn
The pulses of my Being beat anew:
And even as Life returns upon the Drown'd,
Life's joy rekindling rous'd a throng of Pains —                    65
Keen Pangs of Love, awakening as a babe
Turbulent, with an outcry in the heart;
And Fears self-will'd, that shunn'd the eye of Hope;
And Hope that scarce would know itself from Fear;
Sense of past Youth, and Manhood come in vain,                    70
And Genius given, and Knowledge won in vain;
And all which I had cull'd in Wood-walks wild,
And all which patient toil had rear'd, and all,
Commune with *thee* had open'd out – but Flowers
Strew'd on my corse, and borne upon my Bier,                    75
In the same Coffin, for the self-same Grave!

That way no more! and ill beseems it me,
Who came a welcomer in Herald's Guise,
Singing of Glory, and Futurity,
To wander back on such unhealthful road,                    80
Plucking the poisons of self-harm! And ill
Such Intertwine beseems triumphal wreaths
Strew'd before *thy* advancing!

                         Nor do thou,
Sage Bard! impair the memory of that hour                    85
Of thy communion with my nobler mind
By Pity or Grief, already felt too long!
Nor let my words import more blame than needs.
The tumult rose and ceas'd: for Peace is nigh
Where wisdom's voice has found a listening heart.                    90
Amid the howl of more than wintry storms,
The Halcyon hears the voice of vernal Hours
Already on the wing!

                              Eve following eve,
Dear tranquil Time, when the sweet sense of Home
Becomes most sweet! hours for their own sake hail'd,
And more desir'd, more precious, for thy song!          100
In silence list'ning, like a devout Child,
My soul lay passive; by thy various strain
Driven as in surges now, beneath the stars,
With momentary Stars of my own Birth,
Fair constellated Foam still darting off                105
Into the darkness! now a tranquil Sea
Outspread and bright, yet swelling to the Moon!

And when O Friend! my Comforter! my Guide!
Strong in thyself and powerful to give strength!
Thy long sustained Lay finally clos'd,                  110
And thy deep Voice had ceas'd (yet thou thyself
Wert still before mine eyes, and round us both
That happy Vision of beloved Faces!
All, whom I deepliest love, in one room all!),
Scarce conscious and yet conscious of it's Close,       115
I sate, my Being blended in one Thought,
(Thought was it? or aspiration? or Resolve?)
Absorb'd, yet hanging still upon the sound:
And when I rose, I found myself in Prayer!
[January 1807]

Eve following Eve,
Dear tranquil time, when the sweet sense of Home
Is sweetest! moments for their own sake hail'd
And more desired, more precious for thy song,                    95
In silence listening, like a devout child,
My soul lay passive, by thy various strain
Driven, as in surges now beneath the stars,
With momentary Stars of my own birth,
Fair constellated[1] Foam, still darting off                    100
Into the darkness; now a tranquil sea,
Outspread and bright, yet swelling to the Moon.

And when – O Friend! my comforter and guide!
Strong in thy self, and powerful to give strength! –
Thy long sustainéd Song finally closed,                         105
And thy deep voice had ceased – yet thou thyself
Wert still before my eyes, and round us both
That happy vision of beloved Faces –
Scarce conscious, and yet conscious of its close
I sate, my being blended in one thought                         110
(Thought was it? or Aspiration? or Resolve?)
Absorb'd, yet hanging still upon the sound –
And when I rose, I found myself in prayer.
[1817]

[1] 'A beautiful white cloud of Foam at momentary intervals coursed by the side of the Vessel with a Roar, and little stars of flame danced and sparkled and went out in it: and every now and then light detachments of this white cloud-like foam darted off from the vessel's side, each with its own small constellation, over the Sea, and scoured out of sight like a Tartar Troop over a Wilderness.' – THE FRIEND, p. 220.

## [*The Tree of Mystery*]

As some vast tropic Tree, itself a Wood,
That crests its Head with clouds, beneath the flood
Feeds its deep roots, and with the bulging flank
Of its wide Base controlls the fronting bank,
(By the slant current's pressure scoop'd away       5
The fronting Bank becomes a foam-piled Bay)
High in its Fork the uncouth Idol knits
His channel'd Brows: low murmurs stir by fits:
And dark below the horrid Faquir sits;
An Horror from its broad Head's branching Wreath     10
Broods o'er the rude Idolatry beneath —
[February 1807. From MS]


## [*Lunar Entrancement*]

The moon — how definite its orb!
Yet gaze again & with a steady gaze
'Tis there indeed — but where is it not —
It is suffused o'er all the sapphire Heaven,
Trees, herbage, snake-like Stream, unwrinkled Lake,     5
Whose very murmur does of it partake/
And low & close the broad smooth mountain
Is more a thing of Heaven than when
Distinct by one dim shade
yet undivided from the universal cloud
In which it towers, infinite in height/ —           10
[1807–8. From MS]

## [*Unity with Nature*][1]

Life wakeful over all knew no gradation
That Bliss in its excess became a Dream;
For every sense, each thought, & each sensation
Lived in my eye, transfigured not supprest.
And Time drew out his subtle threads so quick,    5
And with such Spirit-speed & silentness,
That only in the web, of space like Time,
On the still spreading web I still diffused
Lay still commensurate –
For Memory & all undoubting Hope    10
Sang the same note & in the selfsame Voice,
with each sweet *now* of my Felicity,
and blended momently,
Like Milk that coming comes & in its easy stream
Flows ever in, upon the mingling milk    15
in the Babe's murmuring Mouth/
or mirrors each reflecting each/–

## [*The Indifference of the Heavens*]

What never is but only is to be
This is not Life –
O Hopeless Hope, and Death's Hypocrisy!
And with perpetual Promise, breaks its Promises. –

The Stars that wont to start, as on a chase,[2]    5
And twinkling insult on Heaven's darkened Face,
Like a conven'd Conspiracy of Spies
Wink at each other with confiding eyes,

[1]This fragmentary draft and the next piece appear together in a notebook of 1807 (*Notebooks* II 3107) and express contrary moods in nature. At the end of the second Coleridge noted, 'I wrote these Lines, as an imitation of Du Bartas, as translated by our Sylvester.'

[2]The last 11 lines were extracted and published separately by E.H.C. under the title 'Coeli Enarrant' ['The heavens are telling': see Psalm xix]. They are based by Coleridge on a childhood memory of an occasion when he was punished so hard by his father in the schoolroom that instead of the required lesson he could only cry 'O!'

Turn from the portent, all is blank on high,
No constellations alphabet the Sky —                          10
The Heavens one large black Letter only shews,
And as a Child beneath its master's Blows
Shrills out at once its Task and its Affright,
The groaning world now learns to read aright,
And with its Voice of Voices cries out, O!                     15


## [*The Presence of Love*]

And in Life's noisiest hour,
There whispers still the ceaseless Love of Thee,
The heart's *Self-solace*, and soliloquy.

You mould my Hopes, you fashion me within;
    And to the leading Love-throb in the Heart
Thro' all my Being all my pulses beat.
You lie in all my many Thoughts, like Light
Like the fair Light of Dawn, or summer-Eve                    5
On rippling Stream, or cloud-reflecting Lake.

And looking to the Heaven, that bends above you
How oft I bless the Lot, that made me love you.
[1807. From MS]


## *Recollections of Love*

### I

How warm this woodland wild Recess!
    Love surely hath been breathing here;
    And this sweet bed of heath, my dear!
Swells up, then sinks with fair caress,
    As if to have you yet more near.                          5

II

Eight springs have flown, since last I lay
     On sea-ward Quantock's heathy hills,
     Where quiet sounds from hidden rills
Float here and there, like things astray,
     And high o'er head the sky-lark shrills.                    10

III

No voice as yet had made the air
     Be music with your name; yet why
     That asking look? that yearning sigh?
That sense of promise every where?
     Belovéd! flew your spirit by?                               15

IV

As when a mother doth explore
     The rose-mark on her long-lost child,
     I met, I loved you, maiden mild!
As whom I long had loved before –
     So deeply had I been beguiled.                              20

V

You stood before me like a thought,
     A dream remembered in a dream.
     But when those meek eyes first did seem
To tell me, Love within you wrought –
     O Greta, dear domestic stream!                             25

VI

Has not, since then, Love's prompture deep,
     Has not Love's whisper evermore
     Been ceaseless, as thy gentle roar?
Sole voice, when other voices sleep,
     Dear under-song in Clamor's hour.                          30
[1807–17]

# The Blossoming of the Solitary Date-Tree[1]

### A LAMENT

I seem to have an indistinct recollection of having read either in
one of the ponderous tomes of George of Venice, or in some
other compilation from the uninspired Hebrew writers, an
apologue or Rabbinical tradition to the following purpose:

5   While our first parents stood before their offended Maker,
and the last words of the sentence were yet sounding in Adam's
ear, the guileful false serpent, a counterfeit and a usurper from
the beginning, presumptuously took on himself the character of
advocate or mediator, and pretending to intercede for Adam,
10  exclaimed: 'Nay, Lord, in thy justice, not so! for the Man was the
least in fault. Rather let the Woman return at once to the dust,
and let Adam remain in this thy Paradise.' And the word of the
Most High answered Satan: '*The tender mercies of the wicked
are cruel.* Treacherous Fiend! if with guilt like thine, it had been
15  possible for thee to have the heart of a Man, and to feel the
yearning of a human soul for its counterpart, the sentence, which
thou now counsellest, should have been inflicted on thyself.'

The title of the following poem was suggested by a fact
mentioned by Linnaeus, of a date-tree in a nobleman's garden
20  which year after year had put forth a full show of blossoms, but
never produced fruit, till a branch from another date-tree had
been conveyed from a distance of some hundred leagues. The
first leaf of the MS from which the poem has been transcribed,
and which contained the two or three introductory stanzas, is
25  wanting: and the author has in vain taxed his memory to repair
the loss. But a rude draught of the poem contains the substance
of the stanzas, and the reader is requested to receive it as the
substitute. It is not impossible, that some congenial spirit,
whose years do not exceed those of the Author at the time the
30  poem was written, may find a pleasure in restoring the Lament
to its original integrity by a reduction of the thoughts to the
requisite metre.

                                                      S.T.C.

[1]The date of this poem is uncertain, but a letter of 1822 (V 216) recalling that lines 76–8
were addressed to Sara Hutchinson suggests that the verse part of the poem belongs to the time
of his love for her. The prologue, which in diction resembles that of the introduction to *Kubla
Khan* and some of the glosses for *The Ancient Mariner*, may well have been added later on
similar lines to such framing devices.

I

Beneath the blaze of a tropical sun the mountain peaks are the
Thrones of Frost, through the absence of objects to reflect the
rays. 'What no one with us shares, seems scarce our own.' The          35
presence of a ONE,

> The best belov'd, who loveth me the best,

is for the heart, what the supporting air from within is for the
hollow globe with its suspended car. Deprive it of this, and all
without, that would have buoyed it aloft even to the seat of the       40
gods, becomes a burthen and crushes it into flatness.


II

The finer the sense for the beautiful and the lovely, and the
fairer and lovelier the object presented to the sense; the more
exquisite the individual's capacity of joy, and the more ample
his means and opportunities of enjoyment, the more heavily            45
will he feel the ache of solitariness, the more unsubstantial
becomes the feast spread around him. What matters it, whether
in fact the viands and the ministering graces are shadowy or
real, to him who has not hand to grasp nor arms to embrace
them?                                                                  50


III

Imagination; honourable aims;
Free commune with the choir that cannot die;
Science and song; delight in little things,
The buoyant child surviving in the man;
Fields, forests, ancient mountains, ocean, sky,
With all their voices – O dare I accuse
My earthly lot as guilty of my spleen,
Or call my destiny niggard! O no! no!
It is her largeness, and her overflow,
Which being incomplete, disquieteth me so!


IV

For never touch of gladness stirs my heart,
But tim'rously beginning to rejoice

Like a blind Arab, that from sleep doth start
In lonesome tent, I listen for thy voice.
Belovéd! 'tis not thine; thou art not there!
Then melts the bubble into idle air,
And wishing without hope I restlessly despair.

### V

The mother with anticipated glee
Smiles o'er the child, that, standing by her chair
And flatt'ning its round cheek upon her knee,
Looks up, and doth its rosy lips prepare
To mock the coming sounds. At that sweet sight
She hears her own voice with a new delight;
And if the babe perchance should lisp the notes aright,

### VI

Then is she tenfold gladder than before!
But should disease or chance the darling take,
What then avail those songs, which sweet of yore
Were only sweet for their sweet echo's sake?
Dear maid! no prattler at a mother's knee
Was e'er so dearly prized as I prize thee:
Why was I made for Love and Love denied to me?

## The Barberry-Tree[1]

AN ATTEMPT AT *GENUINE POETRY*,
*After the manner of the* NEW SCHOOL.

Late on a breezy vernal eve
  When breezes wheel'd their whirling flight;
I wander'd forth; and I believe
  I never saw so sweet a sight:
    It nodded in the breeze,            5
      It rustled in mine ear;
    Fairest of blossom'd trees
      In hill or valley, far or near;
No tree that grew in hill or vale
  Such blithesome blossoms e'er display'd;     10
They LAUGH'D and DANC'D upon the gale. –
  They seem'd as they could never fade:
As they could never fade they seem'd,
  And still they danc'd, now high, now low;
In VERY JOY their colours gleam'd;         15
  But whether it be thus or no;
That while they danc'd upon the wind
They felt a joy like human-kind:
That this blithe breeze which cheerly sung
While the merry boughs he swung:        20
Did in that moment; while the bough
 ,  Whisper'd to his gladsome singing:
Feel the pleasures that ev'n now
  In my breast are springing:
And whether, *as I said before*,        25
    These golden blossoms dancing high,
    These breezes piping thro' the sky,

---

[1]The authorship of this poem is unknown, but Coleridge is one strong candidate: it was published in *Felix Farley's Bristol Journal* in 1807, at a time when he was spending some time in the West Country; its parodic mode has points of contact with that of the Higginbottom sonnets above; the rhythm of the couplet 'And dance to and fro to the loud-singing breeze,/The blithest of gales, and the maddest of trees' is close to that of the then unpublished *Christabel*; while some reminiscences of Wordsworth, such as the associating of a statue with a trance, are from poems of his not yet published, but which Coleridge would have known. The verse is also surprisingly uneven, sometimes rising to high quality in a way that a simple parodist would normally avoid, but which would be characteristic of a poet writing a parody of a friend whom he also admired.

Have in themselves of joy a store:
And mingling breath and murmur'd motion
Like eddies of the gusty ocean,                          30
Do in their leafy morris bear
Mirth and gladness thro' the air:
As up and down the branches toss,
And above and beneath and across
The breezes brush on lusty pinion                        35
Sportive struggling for dominion;
If living sympathy be theirs,
    And leaves and airs,
The piping breeze and dancing tree,
Are all ALIVE and glad as we;                            40
Whether this be truth or no
I cannot tell, I do not know;
Nay – whether now I reason well,
I do not know, I cannot tell! –
But this I know, and will declare,                       45
  Rightly and surely *this* I know;
That never *here*; that never *there*;
    Around me, aloft, or alow;
Nor here, nor there, nor *any*-where,
Saw I a scene so very fair.                              50
And on this FOOD of THOUGHT I fed
Till moments, minutes, hours had fled:
And had not sudden the church-chimes
  Rung out the well-known peal I love;
I had forgotten *Peter Grimes*;                          55
  His nuts and cyder in the apple-grove:
I say, and I aver it true,
  That had I not the warning heard
    Which told how late it grew;
  (And I to *Grimes* had pledg'd my word;)             60
In that most happy mood of mind
  There like a statue I had stood *till now*:
    And when my trance was ended
    And on my way I tended,
  Still, so it was, I knew not how,                    65
But pass'd it not away; that piping wind!
For as I went, in sober sooth
  It seem'd to go along with me;

I tell you now the very truth,
   It seem'd part of MYSELF to be:       70
That in my inner self I had
Those whisp'ring sounds that made me glad. —
Now if you feel a wish dear *Jones*,
   To see these branches dancing so;
Lest you in vain should stir your bones       75
   I will advise you where to go.
That is if you should wish to see
This piping, skipping *Barberry*,
(For so they call the shrub I mean
Whose blossom'd branches thus are seen       80
   Uptossing their leafy shrouds,
   As if they were fain to spring
   On the whirl-zephyr's wing
      Up to the clouds.)
If *Jacob Jones*, you have at heart       85
   To hear this sound, and see this sight:
Then this advice I do impart
   That *Jacob*, you don't go by night.
For then 'tis possible the shrub so green
And yellow, may not *well* be *seen*.       90
Nor *Jacob*, would I have you go
When the blithe winds forbear to blow;
I think it may be safely then averr'd
The piping leaves will not be *heard*.
   But when the wind rushes       95
   Thro' brakes and thro' bushes;
And around and within and without
   Makes a roar and a rout;
     Then may you see
     The *Barberry-tree*,       100
   With all its yellow flow'rs
   And interwoven bow'rs,
   Toss in merry madness
   Ev'ry bough of gladness:
And dance to and fro to the loud-singing breeze —   105
The blithest of gales, and the maddest of trees!
     And then like me
  Ev'n from the blossoms of the *Barberry*,
   May'st thou a STORE of THOUGHT lay by

For present time and long futurity:                    110
And teach to fellow-men a lore
*They never learn'd before,*
The *manly* strain of *nat'ral* poesy!


## To Two Sisters

### [MARY MORGAN AND CHARLOTTE BRENT]

#### A WANDERER'S FAREWELL

To know, to esteem, to love, – and then to part –
Makes up life's tale to many a feeling heart;
Alas for some abiding-place of love,
O'er which my spirit, like the mother dove,
Might brood with warming wings!

                      O fair! O kind!          5
Sisters in blood, yet each with each intwined
More close by sisterhood of heart and mind!
Me disinherited in form and face
By nature, and mishap of outward grace;
Who, soul and body, through one guiltless fault      10
Waste daily with the poison of sad thought,
Me did you soothe, when solace hoped I none!
And as on unthaw'd ice the winter sun,
Though stern the frost, though brief the genial day,
You bless my heart with many a cheerful ray;         15
For gratitude suspends the heart's despair,
Reflecting bright though cold your image there.
Nay more! its music by some sweeter strain
Makes us live o'er our happiest hours again,
Hope re-appearing dim in memory's guise –            20
Even thus did you call up before mine eyes
Two dear, dear Sisters, prized all price above,
Sisters, like you, with more than sisters' love;
*So* like you *they*, and so in *you* were seen
Their relative statures, tempers, looks, and mien,   25
That oft, dear ladies! you have been to me
At once a vision and reality.
Sight seem'd a sort of memory, and amaze
Mingled a trouble with affection's gaze.

Oft to my eager soul I whisper blame,                                    30
A Stranger bid it feel the Stranger's shame –
My eager soul, impatient of the name,
No strangeness owns, no Stranger's form descries:
The chidden heart spreads trembling on the eyes.

First-seen I gazed, as I would look you thro'!                           35
My best-beloved regain'd their youth in you, –
And still I ask, though now familiar grown,
Are you for *their* sakes dear, or for your own?
O doubly dear! may Quiet with you dwell!

In Grief I love you, yet I love you well!                                40
Hope long is dead to me! an orphan's tear
Love wept despairing o'er his nurse's bier.
Yet she flutters o'er her grave's green slope:
For Love's despair is but the ghost of Hope!

Sweet Sisters! were you placed around one hearth                         45
With those, your other selves in shape and worth,
Far rather would I sit in solitude,
Fond recollections all my fond heart's food,
And dream of *you*, sweet Sisters! (ah! not mine!)
And only *dream* of you (ah! dream and pine!)                            50
Than boast the presence and partake the pride,
And shine in the eye, of all the world beside.
[November–December 1807]

## A Child's Evening Prayer

Ere on my bed my limbs I lay,
God grant me grace my prayers to say:
O God! preserve my mother dear
In strength and health for many a year;
And, O! preserve my father too,                                          5
And may I pay him reverence due;
And may I my best thoughts employ
To be my parents' hope and joy;
And O! preserve my brothers both

From evil doings and from sloth,                                    10
And may we always love each other
Our friends, our father, and our mother:
And still, O Lord, to me impart
An innocent and grateful heart,
That after my great sleep I may                                     15
Awake to thy eternal day! *Amen*.
[?1808. From MS]


## Ad Vilmum Axiologum[1]

Me n' Asræ perferre jubes oblivia? et Asræ
    Me aversos oculos posse videre meæ?
Scire et eam falsam, crudelem, quæ mihi semper
    Cara fuit, semper cara futura mihi?
Meque pati lucem, cui vanam perdite amanti,                          5
    Quicquid Naturæ est, omne tremit, titubat?
Cur non ut patiarque fodi mea viscera ferro,
    Dissimulato etiam, Vilme, dolore jubes?
Quin Cor, quin Oculosque meos, quin erue vel quod
    Carius est, si quid carius esse potest!                          10
Deficientem animam, quod vis, tolerare jubebo,
    Asræ dum superet, me moriente, fides.
At Fidis Inferias vidi! et morior! – Ratione
    Victum iri facili, me *Ratione*, putas?
Ah pereat, qui in Amore potest rationibus uti!                       15
    Ah pereat, qui, ni perdite, amare potest!
Quid deceat, quid non, videant quibus integra mens est!
    Vixi! vivit adhuc immemor ASRA mei.
[?1808. From MS]

[1][*Translation*: Do you command me to endure Asra's neglect? and to be able to see the eyes of my Asra averted? And to know her as false and cruel who always was, always will be dear to me? And me to suffer the daylight when, since I desperately love one who is false, the whole of Nature trembles and shudders? Why do you not also command me, William, to suffer my bowels to be pierced with a sword and then to pretend that it does not hurt? Nay, why not pluck out my heart and eyes or whatever is dearer, if anything can be dearer? I shall command my failing spirit to tolerate anything as long as Asra's faith remains, even if I die. But I have seen the last rites of her faithfulness! and I die! Do you think that I am to be overcome by mere Reason? by *Reason*? Ah, perish the man who can make use of reasons in matters of love – perish he who can love except desperately! What may be fitting, what not, let them consider who are whole of mind! My life is done! Yet Asra still lives, unmindful of me.]

## Tribute to Wordsworth[1]

### 'AD VILMUM AXIOLOGUM'

This be the meed, that thy Song creates a thousandfold Echo!
Sweet as the warble of woods that awake at the gale of the
      Morning!
List! the Hearts of the Pure, like Caves in the ancient
      Mountains
Deep, deep *in* the Bosom, and *from* the Bosom resound it,
Each with a different Tone, complete or in musical fragments,    5
All have welcom'd thy Voice, and receive and retain and
      prolong it!
This is the word of the Lord! it is spoken, and Beings Eternal
Live and are born, as an Infant – the Eternal begets the
      Immortal!
– Love is the Spirit of Life, and Music the Life of the Spirit. –
[1807–8. From MS]

## [The Happy Home]

    The singing Kettle & the purring Cat,
    The gentle Breathing of the cradled Babe,
    The silence of the Mother's love-bright Eye,
    And tender Smile answ'ring its smile of Sleep.
    [January 1808]

## Alla Sua Amica[2]

### [TRANSLATED FROM MARINO]

    Lady, to Death we're doom'd, our crime the same!
    Thou, that in me thou kindledst such fierce Heat;
    I, that my Heart did of a Sun so sweet
    The Rays concenter to so hot a flame.

[1] In the notebook where it appears this poem immediately follows a draft for the preceding one and is evidently meant as a countering tribute after its bitterness.
[2] 'To his Beloved Lady'.

I, fascinated by an Adder's Eye,　　　　　　　　　　5
Deaf as an Adder thou to all my Pain;
Thou obstinate in Scorn, in Passion I –
I lov'd too much, too much didst thou disdain.
Hear then our doom in Hell as just as stern,
Our sentence equal as our crimes conspire　　　　　10
Who living basked at Beauty's earthly Fire
In living flames eternal there must burn/–
Hell for us both fit places too supplies –
In *my* Heart thou wilt burn, I roast before thine Eyes –
[September 1808. From MS]


# [*Wedded Love*]

Two wedded Hearts, if e'er were such,
Imprison'd in adjoining cells
Across whose thin partition wall
The Builder left one narrow rent,
And there most content in discontent　　　　　　5
A Joy with itself at strife,
Die into an intenser Life/

### ANOTHER VERSION

The Builder left one narrow rent,
Two wedded Hearts, if e'er were such,
Contented most in discontent　　　　　　　　　10
There cling, and try in vain to touch!
O Joy with thy own Joy at Strife,
That yearning for the Realm above
Would'st die into intenser Life,
And union absolute of Love.　　　　　　　　　15
[September 1808. From MS]

## Epitaph on an Infant

Its balmy lips the infant blest
Relaxing from its Mother's breast,
How sweet it heaves the happy sigh
Of innocent satiety!

And such my Infant's latest sigh!                    5
Oh tell, rude stone! the passer by,
That here the pretty babe doth lie,
Death sang to sleep with Lullaby.
[1809]

## For a Market-Clock

### (IMPROMPTU)

What now, O Man! thou dost, or mean'st to do,
Will help to give thee Peace or make thee rue,
When hovering o'er the Dot this Hand shall tell
The moment that secures thee HEAVEN or HELL!
[1809. From MS]

## Separation from Asra¹

Made worthy by excess of Love
A wretch thro' power of Happiness,
    And poor from wealth, I dare not use.

    This separation is, alas!
Too great a punishment to bear:                      5
O take my Life, or let me pass
    That Life, that happy Life, with her!

¹The later stanzas are adapted from some in Cotton's *Chlorinda*. The poem was later re-modelled as 'Separation', beginning with a different narrator:
    A sworded man whose trade is blood,
        In grief, in anger, and in fear,
    Thro' jungle, swamp, and torrent flood,
        I seek the wealth you hold so dear!

The dazzling charm of outward Form,
The power of Gold, the pride of Birth,                    10
Have taken Woman's heart by storm,
   Supplied the place of inward worth.

Is not true Love of higher price,
Than outward Form, tho' fair to see,
Wealth's glitt'ring fairy-dome of Ice,                    15
   Or echo of proud Ancestry?

O ASRA! ASRA! could'st thou see
Into the bottom of my Heart!
There's such a Mine of Love for Thee—
   That Treasure would supply desert!           20

Death, erst contemn'd, O ASRA! why
Now terror-stricken do I see?
Oh! I have heart enough to die,
   Not half enough to part from Thee!
[?1809–10]

## [*Hope and Tranquillity*]

When Hope but made Tranquillity be felt –
A Flight of Hopes for ever on the wing
But made Tranquillity a conscious Thing –
And wheeling round and round in sportive Coil,
Fann'd the calm Air upon the brow of Toil –            5
[March 1810. From MS]

## [*Body Imaging Soul*]

The body
   Eternal Shadow of the finite Soul/
   The Soul's self-symbol/its image of itself,
   Its own yet not itself –
   [April–June 1810. From MS]

## [Despair]

I have experienc'd
The worst, the World can wreak on me; the worst
That can make Life indifferent, yet disturb
With whisper'd Discontents the dying prayer.
I have beheld the whole of all, wherein                      5
My Heart had any interest in this Life,
To be disrent and torn from off my Hopes
That nothing now is left. Why then live on?
That Hostage, which the world had in it's keeping
Given by me as a Pledge that I would live,                   10
That Hope of Her, say rather, that pure Faith
In her fix'd Love, which held me to keep truce
With the Tyranny of Life – is gone ah whither?
What boots it to reply? – 'tis gone! and now
Well may I break this Pact, this League of Blood             15
That ties me to myself – and break I shall! –
[May 1810. From MS]

## The Visionary Hope

Sad lot, to have no Hope! Though lowly kneeling
He fain would frame a prayer within his breast,
Would fain entreat for some sweet breath of healing,
That his sick body might have ease and rest;
He strove in vain! the dull sighs from his chest             5
Against his will the stifling load revealing,
Though Nature forced; though like some captive guest,
Some royal prisoner at his conqueror's feast,
An alien's restless mood but half concealing,
The sternness of his gentle brow confessed                   10
Sickness within and miserable feeling:
Though obscure pangs made curses of his dreams,
And dreaded sleep, each night repelled in vain,
Each night was scattered by its own loud screams:

Yet never could his heart command, though fain,          15
One deep full wish to be no more in pain.


    That Hope, which was his inward bliss and boast,
Which waned and died, yet ever near him stood,
Though changed in nature, wander where he would —
For Love's Despair is but Hope's pining Ghost!          20
For this one hope he makes his hourly moan,
He wishes and can wish for this alone!
Pierced, as with light from Heaven, before its gleams
(So the love-stricken visionary deems)
Disease would vanish, like a summer shower,          25
Whose dews fling sunshine from the noon-tide bower!
Or let it stay! yet this one Hope should give
Such strength that he would bless his pains and live.
[?1810]


# [The Moon and the Waves]

As when the new or full moon urges
The high, long, large, unbreaking surges
Of the pacific Main.
[1811. From MS]


# [A Mighty Fountain]

## FRAGMENT OF AN ODE ON NAPOLEON

O'erhung with yew, midway the Muses mount
  From thy sweet murmurs far, O Hippocrene!
Turbid and black upboils an angry fount
  Tossing its shatter'd foam in vengeful spleen —
Phlegethon's rage Cocytus' wailings hoarse
Alternate now, now mixt, made known its headlong course:          5
  Thither with terror stricken and surprise,
(For sure such haunts were ne'er to Muse's choice)
  Euterpe led me. Mute with asking eyes

I stood expectant of her heavenly voice.                    10
Her voice entranc'd my terror and made flow
In a rude understrain the maniac fount below.
'Whene'er (the Goddess said) abhorr'd of Jove
Usurping Power his hands in blood imbrues —'
[?1811. From MS]


# [*Loss*][1]

I stand alone, nor tho' my Heart should break
Have I, to whom I may complain or speak.
Here I stand, a hopeless man and sad
Who hoped to have seen my Love, my Life.
And strange it were indeed, could I be glad
Remembring her, my Soul's betrothed Wife/
For in this World no creature, that has life,
Was e'er to me so gracious & so good/
Her Love was to my Heart, like the Heart-blood.
[?1811. From MS]


# [*A Bitter Reflection*]

O mercy, O me miserable man!
Slowly my wisdom, & how slowly comes
My Virtue! and how rapidly pass off
My Joys, my Hopes, my Friendships, & my Love!
[1811. From MS]


# [*A Wish for Dreamful Sleep*][2]

A low dead Thunder muttered thro' the Night,
As twere a Giant angry in his Sleep —

———————————————

[1] Inscribed by Coleridge in a copy of Menzini's *Poesie*.
[2] After J. P. F. Richter. [K.C.]

Nature! sweet Nurse! O take me in thy Lap –
And tell me of my Father yet unseen
Sweet Tales & True, that lull me into Sleep,          5
& leave me dreaming. –
[1811. From MS]

## The Suicide's Argument

Ere the birth of my life, if I wished it or no
No question was asked me – it could not be so!
If the life was the question, a thing sent to try
And to live on be YES; what can No be? to die.

### NATURE'S ANSWER

Is't returned, as 'twas sent? Is't no worse for the wear?          5
Think first, what you ARE! Call to mind what you WERE!
I gave you innocence, I gave you hope,
Gave health, and genius, and an ample scope,
Return you me guilt, lethargy, despair?
Make out the Invent'ry; inspect, compare!          10
Then die – if die you dare!
[1811]

## A Tombless Epitaph[1]

'Tis true, Idoloclastes Satyrane!
(So call him, for so mingling blame with praise,
And smiles with anxious looks, his earliest friends,
Masking his birth-name, wont to character
His wild-wood fancy and impetuous zeal,)          5
'Tis true that, passionate for ancient truths,
And honouring with religious love the Great
Of elder times, he hated to excess,

[1] Imitated, though in the movements rather than the thoughts, from the vii[th] of *Gli Epitafi* of Chiabrera. [S.T.C.]

With an unquiet and intolerant scorn,
The hollow Puppets of a hollow Age,                         10
Ever idolatrous, and changing ever
Its worthless Idols! Learning, Power, and Time,
(Too much of all) thus wasting in vain war
Of fervid colloquy. Sickness, 'tis true,
Whole years of weary days, besieged him close,             15
Even to the gates and inlets of his life!
But it is true, no less, that strenuous, firm,
And with a natural gladness, he maintained
The citadel unconquered, and in joy
Was strong to follow the delightful Muse.                  20
For not a hidden path, that to the shades
Of the beloved Parnassian forest leads,
Lurked undiscovered by him; not a rill
There issues from the fount of Hippocrene,
But he had traced it upward to its source,                 25
Through open glade, dark glen, and secret dell,
Knew the gay wild flowers on its banks, and culled
Its med'cinable herbs. Yea, oft alone,
Piercing the long-neglected holy cave,
The haunt obscure of old Philosophy,                       30
He bade with lifted torch its starry walls
Sparkle, as erst they sparkled to the flame
Of odorous lamps tended by Saint and Sage.
O framed for calmer times and nobler hearts!
O studious Poet, eloquent for truth!                       35
Philosopher! contemning wealth and death,
Yet docile, childlike, full of Life and Love!
Here, rather than on monumental stone,
This record of thy worth thy Friend inscribes,
Thoughtful, with quiet tears upon his cheek.               40
[?1809]

# THE CRITIC AS POET

The period immediately following the break with Sara Hutchinson was the darkest of Coleridge's life. His disappointment with Wordsworth, hitherto expressed only in occasional notebook entries, now emerged more openly to be followed by anguish when a wounding remark of Wordsworth's was carelessly repeated to him. For some time he remained in London, nursing his grievances and producing little. Opium retained its powerful hold, and the writings which survive from this period are redolent of a general unhappiness.

Self-dramatization, veering towards self-pity, is a dominant trait in writings of the following years. On the one hand thinly veiled accounts of himself, such as *A Tombless Epitaph* and *A Character*, portray a neglected, misunderstood seeker after truth and wisdom. On the other, the anguish of his unsatisfied craving for love is constantly present in verses which show a recurrent eddying of the same thoughts, the same nagging sorrows.

In spite of this, however, there also appear signs of a slow revival. This was aided by a new spirit in the London of the day. From 1811 onwards the Regency stimulated a new interest in the arts which was to flourish still more strongly when the Napoleonic wars ended. For the first time Coleridge knew what it was to be a fashionable figure. A course of lectures delivered during the winter of 1811–12 attracted a large audience, which included Samuel Rogers and Lord Byron. Shortly afterwards his early play *Osorio* was accepted by the proprietors of Drury Lane and produced, with the title *Remorse*, in January 1812.

The success of this and other productions of *Remorse*, accompanied by further demands for his services as lecturer, stimulated Coleridge to set about a new collection of his poems and to begin an autobiography as a prelude to his projected great philosophical work. As in Wordsworth's case, the 'prelude' assumed an importance of its own and, published with the title *Biographia Literaria*, proved to be his best and most sustained prose work.

Several poems of the period, such as *Fancy in Nubibus* or *On*

*Donne's First Poem*, can be regarded as by-products of his pre-occupation with literary criticism during these years. The emergence from the latter of two further poems, *Limbo* and *Ne Plus Ultra*, demonstrates how intensely the critical impulse was inhabiting his embittered spirit. And while he did not produce much original poetry for a time, his lectures, and the publication of *Christabel* and *Kubla Khan* in 1816, followed by the long collection of his poems entitled *Sibylline Leaves* in 1817, were prime stimulants to the extraordinary flowering of poetry among his contemporaries during the same period.

In a further attempt to free himself from the opium habit, Coleridge put himself under the care of James Gillman, a surgeon living at Highgate, and lived with his family from 1816 until his death. During the years following the conclusion of the Napoleonic wars, he became greatly preoccupied by the political problems of the post-war scene. While England's victory had broken the French bid for supremacy, it had not solved the more basic problems posed by the French Revolution. Coleridge stated his own views in two *Lay Sermons* and in a refashioned version of *The Friend*. Since his solution involved a return to religious principles, he found his attention turning more and more to theological topics. (His most important work in this field, *Aids to Reflection* (1825), was to be followed by a final attempt to relate the theological and political issues of the day in *On the Constitution of the Church and State* (1829).) At the same time, scattered poems, including the songs in his poetic drama *Zapolya*, showed that the lyrical impulse was by no means dead.

# On Donne's First Poem[1]

Be proud, as Spaniards! and Leap for Pride, ye Fleas
Henceforth in Nature's *Minim* World Grandees,
In Phœbus' Archives registered are ye –
And this your Patent of Nobility.
No Skip-Jacks now, nor civiller Skip-Johns,                    5
Dread Anthropophagi! Specks of living Bronze,
I hail you one & all, sans Pros or Cons,
Descendants from a noble Race of *Dons*.

What tho' that great ancestral Flea be gone
Immortal with immortalizing Donne –                          10
His earthly Spots bleach'd off as Papists gloze,
In purgatory fire on Bardolph's Nose,
Or else starved out, his aery tread defied
By the dry Potticary's bladdery Hide,
Which cross'd unchang'd and still keeps in ghost-Light        15
Of lank Half-nothings his, the thinnest Sprite
The sole true *Something* this in Limbo Den
It frightens Ghosts as Ghosts here frighten men –
For skimming in the wake, it mock'd the care
Of the Old Boat-God for his Farthing Fare,                   20
Tho' Irus' Ghost itself he neer frown'd blacker on,
The skin and skin-pent Druggist crost the Acheron,
Styx and with Puriphlegethon Cocytus:
The very names, methinks, might thither fright us –
Unchang'd it cross'd & shall, some fated Hour,               25
Be pulverized by Demogorgon's Power
And given as poison, to annilate Souls –
Even now it shrinks them! they shrink in, as Moles
(Nature's mute Monks, live Mandrakes of the ground)
Creep back from Light, then listen for its Sound –           30
See but to dread, and dread they know not why
The natural Alien of their negative Eye.

[1]This and the next two poems were originally written in continuous sequence in a notebook of 1811 (III 4073–4), and evidently grew out of each other. This one was in turn sparked off partly by some previous verses on different kinds of insect-like wit and by Donne's *The Flea*.

## *Limbo*[1]

Tis a strange Place, this Limbo! not a Place,
Yet name it so – where Time & weary Space
Fetter'd from flight, with night-mair sense of Fleeing
Strive for their last crepuscular Half-being –
Lank Space, and scytheless Time with branny Hands          5
Barren and soundless as the measuring Sands,
Mark'd but by Flit of Shades – unmeaning they
As Moonlight on the Dial of the Day –
But that is lovely – looks like Human Time,
An old Man with a steady Look sublime          10
That stops his earthly Task to watch the Skies –
But he is blind – a statue hath such Eyes –
Yet having moon-ward turn'd his face by chance –
Gazes the orb with moon-like Countenance
With scant white hairs, with fore-top bald & high          15
He gazes still, his eyeless Face all Eye –
As twere an Organ full of silent Sight
His whole Face seemeth to rejoice in Light/
Lip touching Lip, all moveless, Bust and Limb,
He seems to gaze at that which seems to gaze on Him!          20

No such sweet Sights doth Limbo Den immure,
Wall'd round and made a Spirit-jail secure
By the mere Horror of blank Nought at all –
Whose circumambience doth these Ghosts enthrall.
A lurid Thought is growthless dull Privation,          25
But the Hag, Madness, scalds the Fiends of Hell
With frenzy-dreams, all incompassible
Of aye-unepithetable Negation

A lurid thought is growthless dull Privation
Yet that is but a Purgatory Curse
Hell knows a fear far worse,          30
A fear, a future fate. Tis *positive Negation!*[2]

---

[1] There seem to be further echoes of Donne here: 'Hell is but privation/ Of him' in 'To Mr
T. W.' [K.C.] and the 'dull privations' of the 'Nocturnall upon St Lucies Day' [Ed.].

[2] 'A Specimen of the Sublime dashed to pieces by cutting too close with her fiery Four in
Hand round the corner of Nonsense': MS note by S.T.C. in a printed copy.

## *Ne Plus Ultra*[1]

Sole Positive of Night!
Antipathist of Light!
Fate's only Essence! Primal Scorpion Rod!
The one permitted Opposite of God!
Condensed Blackness, and Abysmal Storm     5
Compacted to one Sceptre
Arms the Grasp enorm,
The Intercepter!
The Substance, that still casts the Shadow, Death!
The Dragon foul and fell!     10
The unrevealable
And hidden one, whose Breath
Gives Wind and Fuel to the fires of Hell!
Ah sole Despair
Of both th' Eternities in Heaven!     15
Sole Interdict of all-bedewing Prayer,
The All-compassionate!
Save to the Lampads seven
Reveal'd to none of all th' Angelic State,
Save to the Lampads seven     20
That watch the Throne of Heaven!
[1811. From MS]

## *Human Life*

### ON THE DENIAL OF IMMORTALITY

If dead, we cease to be; if total gloom
  Swallow up life's brief flash for aye, we fare
As summer-gusts, of sudden birth and doom,
  Whose sound and motion not alone declare,
But *are* their whole of being! If the breath     5
  Be Life itself, and not its task and tent,
If even a soul like Milton's can know death;

''No Further'.

O Man! thou vessel purposeless, unmeant,
Yet drone-hive strange of phantom purposes!
   Surplus of Nature's dread activity,                    10
Which, as she gazed on some nigh-finished vase,
Retreating slow, with meditative pause,
   She formed with restless hands unconsciously.
Blank accident! nothing's anomaly!
   If rootless thus, thus substanceless thy state,    15
Go, weigh thy dreams, and be thy hopes, thy fears,
The counter-weights! – Thy laughter and thy tears
   Mean but themselves, each fittest to create
And to repay the other! Why rejoices
   Thy heart with hollow joy for hollow good?        20
   Why cowl thy face beneath the mourner's hood?
Why waste thy sighs, and thy lamenting voices,
   Image of Image, Ghost of Ghostly Elf,
That such a thing as thou feel'st warm or cold?
Yet what and whence thy gain, if thou withhold        25
   These costless shadows of thy shadowy self?
Be sad! be glad! be neither! seek, or shun!
Thou hast no reason why! Thou canst have none;
Thy being's being is contradiction.
[?1811–15]


## To a Lady

### OFFENDED BY A SPORTIVE OBSERVATION
### THAT WOMEN HAVE NO SOULS

Nay, dearest Anna! why so grave?
   I said, you had no soul, 'tis true!
For what you are, you cannot have:
   'Tis I, that have one since I first had you!
[1811–12]

## *Faith, Hope, and Charity*

FROM THE ITALIAN OF GUARINI

### FAITH

Let those whose low delights to Earth are given
    Chaunt forth their earthly Loves! but we
    Must make an holier minstrelsy,
And, heavenly-born, will sing the Things of Heaven.

### CHARITY

But who for us the listening Heart shall gain?        5
    Inaudible as of the sphere
    Our music dies upon the ear,
Enchanted with the mortal Syren's strain.

### HOPE

Yet let our choral songs abound!
    Th' inspiring Power, its living Source,        10
    May flow with them and give them force,
If, elsewhere all unheard, in Heaven they sound.

### ALL

Aid thou our voice, Great Spirit! thou whose flame
    Kindled the Songster sweet of Israel,
    Who made so high to swell        15
Beyond a mortal strain thy glorious Name.

### CHARITY AND FAITH

Though rapt to Heaven, our mission and our care
    Is still to sojourn on the Earth,
    To shape, to soothe, Man's second Birth,
And re-ascend to Heaven, Heaven's prodigal Heir!    20

### CHARITY

What is Man's soul of Love deprived?

### HOPE. FAITH

It like a Harp untunéd is,
That sounds, indeed, but sounds amiss.

### CHARITY. HOPE

From holy Love all good gifts are derived.

### FAITH

But 'tis time that every nation                    25
Should hear how loftily we sing.

### FAITH. HOPE. CHARITY

See, O World, see thy salvation!
Let the Heavens with praises ring.
Who would have a Throne above,
Let him hope, believe and love;                    30
And whoso loves no earthly song,
But does for heavenly music long,
Faith, Hope, and Charity for him,
Shall sing like wingéd Cherubim.

[?1812 ?1815]


## An Invocation

FROM *Remorse*, ACT III, SCENE I, LL. 69–82

Hear, sweet spirit, hear the spell,
Lest a blacker charm compel!
So shall the midnight breezes swell
With thy deep long-lingering knell.

And at evening evermore,                           5
In a Chapel on the shore,

Shall the Chaunters sad and saintly,
Yellow tapers burning faintly,
Doleful Masses chaunt for thee,
    Miserere Domine!               10

Hush! the cadence dies away
   On the quiet moonlight sea:
The boatmen rest their oars and say,
    Miserere Domine!
[1797–1812]


# [*Looking Seaward*]

Sea-ward, white-gleaming thro' the busy Scud
With arching Wings the Sea-mew o'er my head
Posts on, as bent on speed; now passaging
Edges the stiffer Breeze, now yielding *drifts*,
Now floats upon the Air, and sends from far     5
A wildly-wailing Note.
[?May 1814]


# *To a Lady*

### WITH FALCONER'S 'SHIPWRECK'

Ah! not by Cam or Isis, famous streams,
  In archéd groves, the youthful poet's choice;
Nor while half-listening, 'mid delicious dreams,
  To harp and song from lady's hand and voice;

Nor yet while gazing in sublimer mood     5
  On cliff, or cataract, in Alpine dell;
Nor in dim cave with bladdery sea-weed strewed,
  Framing wild fancies to the ocean's swell;

Our sea-bard sang this song! which still he sings,
  And sings for thee, sweet friend! Hark, Pity, hark!    10

Now mounts, now totters on the tempest's wings,
   Now groans, and shivers, the replunging bark!

'Cling to the shrouds!' In vain! The breakers roar –
   Death shrieks! With two alone of all his clan
Forlorn the poet paced the Grecian shore,                    15
   No classic roamer, but a shipwrecked man!

Say then, what muse inspired these genial strains,
   And lit his spirit to so bright a flame?
The elevating thought of suffered pains,
   Which gentle hearts shall mourn; but chief, the name   20

Of gratitude! remembrances of friend,
   Or absent or no more! shades of the Past,
Which Love makes substance! Hence to thee I send,
   O dear as long as life and memory last!

I send with deep regards of heart and head,                 25
   Sweet maid, for friendship formed! this work to thee:
And thou, the while thou canst not choose but shed
   A tear for Falconer, wilt remember me.
[June 1814]


# *Song*[1]

### FROM *Zapolya*, ACT II, SCENE I, LL. 65–80

A sunny shaft did I behold,
   From sky to earth it slanted:
And poised therein a bird so bold –
   Sweet bird, thou wert enchanted!

He sank, he rose, he twinkled, he trolled               5
   Within that shaft of sunny mist;
His eyes of fire, his beak of gold,
   All else of amethyst!

[1]Adapted from Tieck's *Herbstlied*. [Ed.]

And thus he sang: 'Adieu! adieu!
Love's dreams prove seldom true.                                    10
The blossoms they make no delay:
The sparkling dew-drops will not stay.
    Sweet month of May,
        We must away;
            Far, far away!                                          15
                Today! today!'
[?April 1815–Feb 1816]


## Hunting Song

FROM *Zapolya*, ACT IV, SCENE II, LL. 56–71

Up, up! ye dames, ye lasses gay!
To the meadows trip away.
'Tis you must tend the flocks this morn,
And scare the small birds from the corn.
    Not a soul at home may stay:                                    5
        For the shepherds must go
            With lance and bow
    To hunt the wolf in the woods today.

Leave the hearth and leave the house
To the cricket and the mouse:                                       10
Find grannam out a sunny seat
With babe and lambkin at her feet.
    Not a soul at home may stay:
        For the shepherds must go
            With lance and bow                                      15
    To hunt the wolf in the woods today.
[April 1815–February 1816]

## [*Superstition*]

O! Superstition is the Giant Shadow
Which the Solicitude of weak Mortality
Its Back toward Religion's rising Sun,
Casts on the thin mist of the uncertain Future.
[1815–16]


## [*The Traveller through Infinity*][1]

Let klumps of Earth however glorified
Roll round & round & still renew their cycle/
Man rushes like a wingéd Cherub thro'
The infinite Space, and that which has been
Can therefore never be again —                                    5
[1815–16]


## *Fancy in Nubibus*[2]

### OR THE POET IN THE CLOUDS

O! it is pleasant, with a heart at ease,
   Just after sunset, or by moonlight skies,
To make the shifting clouds be what you please,
   Or let the easily persuaded eyes
Own each quaint likeness issuing from the mould          5
   Of a friend's fancy; or with head bent low
And cheek aslant see rivers flow of gold
   'Twixt crimson banks; and then, a traveller, go
From mount to mount through Cloudland, gorgeous land!
   Or list'ning to the tide, with closéd sight,          10

[1]After J. P. F. Richter. [K.C.]
[2]'Fancy in the Clouds'. The ending draws on Stolberg's *An das Mer*.

Be that blind bard, who on the Chian strand
  By those deep sounds possessed with inward light,
Beheld the Iliad and the Odyssee
  Rise to the swelling of the voiceful sea.
[October 1817]


## Israel's Lament

'A Hebrew Dirge, chaunted in the Great Synagogue, St James's Place, Aldgate, on the day of the Funeral of her Royal Highness the Princess Charlotte. By Hyman Hurwitz, Master of the Hebrew Academy, Highgate: with a Translation in English Verse, by S. T. Coleridge, Esq., 1817.'

Mourn, Israel! Sons of Israel, mourn!
  Give utterance to the inward throe!
As wails, of her first love forlorn,
  The Virgin clad in robes of woe.

Mourn the young Mother, snatch'd away           5
  From Light and Life's ascending Sun!
Mourn for the Babe, Death's voiceless prey,
  Earn'd by long pangs and lost ere won.

Mourn the bright Rose that bloom'd and went,
  Ere half disclosed its vernal hue!           10
Mourn the green Bud, so rudely rent,
  It brake the stem on which it grew.

Mourn for the universal woe
  With solemn dirge and fault'ring tongue:
For England's Lady is laid low,           15
  So dear, so lovely, and so young!

The blossoms on her Tree of Life
  Shone with the dews of recent bliss:
Transplanted in that deadly strife,
  She plucks its fruits in Paradise.           20

Mourn for the widow'd Lord in chief,
  Who wails and will not solaced be!
Mourn for the childless Father's grief,
  The wedded LOVER's agony!

Mourn for the Prince, who rose at morn                         25
  To seek and bless the firstling bud
Of his own Rose, and found the thorn,
  Its point bedew'd with tears of blood.


O press again that murmuring string!
  Again bewail that princely Sire!                             30
A destined Queen, a future King,
  He mourns on one funereal pyre.


Mourn for Britannia's hopes decay'd,
  Her daughters wail their dear defence;
Their fair example, prostrate laid,                            35
  Chaste Love and fervid Innocence.


While Grief in song shall seek repose,
  We will take up a Mourning yearly:
To wail the blow that crush'd the Rose,
  So dearly priz'd and lov'd so dearly.                        40


Long as the fount of Song o'erflows
  Will I the yearly dirge renew:
Mourn for the firstling of the Rose,
  That snapt the stem on which it grew.


The proud shall pass, forgot; the chill,                       45
  Damp, trickling Vault their only mourner!
Not so the regal Rose, that still
  Clung to the breast which first had worn her!


O thou, who mark'st the Mourner's path
  To sad Jeshurun's Sons attend!                               50
Amid the Light'nings of thy Wrath
  The showers of Consolation send!


Jehovah frowns! the Islands bow!
  And Prince and People kiss the Rod! –
Their dread chastising Judge wert thou!                        55
  Be thou their Comforter, O God!
[November 1817]

# A Character[1]

A bird, who for his other sins
Had liv'd amongst the Jacobins;
Though like a kitten amid rats,
Or callow tit in nest of bats,
He much abhorr'd all democrats;   5
Yet nathless stood in ill report
Of wishing ill to Church and Court,
Tho' he'd nor claw, nor tooth, nor sting,
And learnt to pipe God save the King;
Tho' each day did new feathers bring,   10
All swore he had a leathern wing;
Nor polish'd wing, nor feather'd tail,
Nor down-clad thigh would aught avail;
And tho' – his tongue devoid of gall –
He civilly assur'd them all: –   15
'A bird am I of Phoebus' breed,
And on the sunflower cling and feed;
My name, good Sirs, is Thomas Tit!'
The bats would hail him Brother Cit,
Or, at the furthest, cousin-german.   20
At length the matter to determine,
He publicly denounced the vermin;
He spared the mouse, he praised the owl;
But bats were neither flesh nor fowl.
Blood-sucker, vampire, harpy, goul,   25
Came in full clatter from his throat,
Till his old nest-mates chang'd their note
To hireling, traitor, and turncoat, –
A base apostate who had sold
His very teeth and claws for gold; –   30
And then his feathers! – sharp the jest –
No doubt he feather'd well his nest!
'A Tit indeed! aye, tit for tat –
With place and title, brother Bat,

---

[1] It is probable that the immediate provocation of these lines was the publication of Hazlitt's attacks on Coleridge.

We soon shall see how well he'll play                    35
Count Goldfinch, or Sir Joseph Jay!'
    Alas, poor Bird! and ill-bestarr'd –
Or rather let us say, poor Bard!
And henceforth quit the allegoric
With metaphor and simile,                                40
For simple facts and style historic: –
Alas, poor Bard! no gold had he;
Behind another's team he stept,
And plough'd and sow'd, while others reapt;
The work was his, but theirs the glory,                  45
*Sic vos non vobis*,[1] his whole story.
Besides, whate'er he wrote or said
Came from his heart as well as head;
And though he never left in lurch
His king, his country, or his church,                    50
'Twas but to humour his own cynical
Contempt of doctrines Jacobinical;
To his own conscience only hearty,
'Twas but by chance he serv'd the party; –
The self-same things had said and writ,                  55
Had Pitt been Fox, and Fox been Pitt;
Content his own applause to win,
Would never dash thro' thick and thin,
And he can make, so say the wise,
No claim who makes no sacrifice; –                       60
And bard still less: – what claim had he,
Who swore it vex'd his soul to see
So grand a cause, so proud a realm
With Goose and Goody at the helm;
Who long ago had fall'n asunder                          65
But for their rivals' baser blunder,
The coward whine and Frenchified
Slaver and slang of the other side? –


    Thus, his own whim his only bribe,
Our Bard pursued his old A. B. C.                        70
Contented if he could subscribe
In fullest sense his name Ἔστησε;

---

[1]'*Sic vos non vobis mellificatis apes*' ['So you bees make honey, not for yourselves'].
Attributed to Virgil: cf. p. 307 above.

('Tis Punic Greek for 'He hath stood!')
Whate'er the men, the cause was good;
And therefore with a right good will,                    75
Poor fool, he fights their battles still.
Tush! squeak'd the Bats; – a mere bravado
To whitewash that base renegado;
'Tis plain unless you're blind or mad,
His conscience for the bays he barters; –               80
And true it is – as true as sad –
These circlets of green baize he had –
But then, alas! they were his garters!
   Ah! silly Bard, unfed, untended,
His lamp but glimmer'd in its socket;                   85
He lived unhonour'd and unfriended
With scarce a penny in his pocket; –
Nay – tho' he hid it from the many –
With scarce a pocket for his penny!
[?November 1819]


## Lines

### TO A COMIC AUTHOR, ON AN ABUSIVE REVIEW

What though the chilly wide-mouth'd quacking chorus
From the rank swamps of murk Review-land croak:
So was it, neighbour, in the times before us,
When Momus, throwing on his Attic cloak,
Romp'd with the Graces; and each tickled Muse           5
(That Turk, Dan Phœbus, whom bards call divine,
Was married to – at least, he kept – all nine)
Fled, but still with reverted faces ran;
Yet, somewhat the broad freedoms to excuse,
They had allured the audacious Greek to use,            10
Swore they mistook him for their own good man.
This Momus – Aristophanes on earth
Men call'd him – maugre all his wit and worth,
Was croak'd and gabbled at. How, then, should you,
Or I, friend, hope to 'scape the skulking crew?        15
No! laugh, and say aloud, in tones of glee,
'I hate the quacking tribe, and they hate me!'
[?November 1819]

## To Nature

It may indeed be phantasy, when I
   Essay to draw from all created things
   Deep, heartfelt, inward joy that closely clings;
And trace in leaves and flowers that round me lie
Lessons of love and earnest piety.         5
   So let it be; and if the wide world rings
   In mock of this belief, it brings
Nor fear, nor grief, nor vain perplexity.
So will I build my altar in the fields,
   And the blue sky my fretted dome shall be,   10
And the sweet fragrance that the wild flower yields
   Shall be the incense I will yield to Thee,
Thee only God! and thou shalt not despise
Even me, the priest of this poor sacrifice.
[?1820. From MS]

## Reason

['Finally, what is Reason? You have often asked me: and this is my answer': –]

Whene'er the mist, that stands 'twixt God and thee,
Defecates to a pure transparency,
That intercepts no light and adds no stain –
There Reason is, and then begins her reign!

But alas!         5

   — 'tu stesso, ti fai grosso
Col falso immaginar, sì che non vedi
Ciò che vedresti, se l'avessi scosso.'[1]
             Dante, *Paradiso*, Canto i.
[1821–2 and 1829]

[1]Tr. Cary (1814):
        With false imagination thou thyself
        Makest dull; so that thou seest not the thing
        Which thou hadst seen, had that been shaken off.

## [*The Philosophical Trinity*]

Where'er I find the Good, the True, the Fair,
I ask no names – God's spirit dwelleth there!
The unconfounded, undivided Three,
Each for itself, and all in each, to see
In man and Nature, is Philosophy.          5
[1822. From MS]

## *First Advent of Love*

O fair is Love's first hope to gentle mind!
As Eve's first star thro' fleecy cloudlet peeping;
And sweeter than the gentle south-west wind,
O'er willowy meads and shadow'd waters creeping,
And Ceres' golden fields;[1] – the sultry hind          5
Meets it with brow uplift, and stays his reaping.
[1821–7]

## *Mignon's Song*

### FROM THE GERMAN OF GOETHE

Know'st thou the land where the pale citrons grow,
The golden fruits in darker foliage glow?
Soft blows the wind that breathes from that blue sky!
Still stands the myrtle and the laurel high!
Know'st thou it well, that land, belovéd Friend?          5
Thither with thee, O, thither would I wend!
[?1823–4]

[1]Compare Sidney's *Arcadia*: 'Her breath is more sweet than a gentle south-west wind, which comes creeping over flowering fields and shadowed waters in the heat of summer' and see *Notebooks* IV, 4810 and n. [E.H.C. and Ed.]

## The Reproof and Reply

Or, The Flower-Thief's Apology, for a robbery committed in Mr and Mrs —'s garden, on Sunday morning, 25th of May, 1823, between the hours of eleven and twelve.

'Fie, Mr Coleridge! – and can this be you?
Break two commandments? and in church-time too!
Have you not heard, or have you heard in vain,
The birth-and-parentage-recording strain? –
Confessions shrill, that out-shrill'd mack'rel drown          5
Fresh from the drop – the youth not yet cut down –
Letter to sweet-heart – the last dying speech –
And didn't all this begin in Sabbath-breach?
You, that knew better! In broad open day,
Steal in, steal out, and steal our flowers away?          10
What could possess you? Ah! sweet youth, I fear
The chap with horns and tail was at your ear!'

Such sounds of late, accusing fancy brought
From fair Chisholm to the Poet's thought.
Now hear the meek Parnassian youth's reply: –          15
A bow – a pleading look – a downcast eye, –
And then:
        'Fair dame! a visionary wight,
Hard by your hill-side mansion sparkling white,
His thoughts all hovering round the Muses' home,
Long hath it been your Poet's wont to roam,          20
And many a morn, on his becharméd sense
So rich a stream of music issued thence,
He deem'd himself, as it flowed warbling on,
Beside the vocal fount of Helicon!
But when, as if to settle the concern,          25
A Nymph too he beheld, in many a turn,
Guiding the sweet rill from its fontal urn, –
Say, can you blame? – No! none that saw and heard
Could blame a bard, that he thus inly stirr'd;
A muse beholding in each fervent trait,          30
Took Mary H — for Polly Hymnia!
Or haply as there stood beside the maid

One loftier form in sable stole array'd,
If with regretful thought he hail'd in *thee*
Chisholm, his long-lost friend, Mol Pomene!                    35
But most of *you*, soft warblings, I complain!
'Twas ye that from the bee-hive of my brain
Did lure the fancies forth, a freakish rout,
And witch'd the air with dreams turn'd inside out.

'Thus all conspir'd — each power of eye and ear,                    40
And this gay month, th' enchantress of the year,
To cheat poor me (no conjuror, God wot!)
And Chisholm's self accomplice in the plot.
Can you then wonder if I went astray?
Not bards alone, nor lovers mad as they; —                    45
All Nature *day-dreams* in the month of May.
And if I pluck'd "each flower that *sweetest* blows," —
Who walks in sleep, needs follow must his *nose*.

Thus, long accustom'd on the twy-fork'd hill,[1]
To pluck both flower and floweret at my will;                    50
The garden's maze, like No-man's-land, I tread,
Nor common law, nor statute in my head;
For my own proper smell, sight, fancy, feeling,
With autocratic hand at once repealing
Five Acts of Parliament 'gainst private stealing!                    55
But yet from Chisholm who despairs of grace?
There's no spring-gun or man-trap in *that* face!
Let Moses then look black, and Aaron blue,
That look as if they had little else to do:
For Chisholm speaks, "Poor youth! he's but a waif!                    60
The spoons all right? the hen and chickens safe?
Well, well, he shall not forfeit our regards —
The Eighth Commandment was not made for Bards!"'
[May 1823]

---

[1]The English Parnassus is remarkable for its two summits of unequal height, the lower denominated Hampstead, the higher Highgate. [S.T.C.]

# LAST POEMS

From 1823, Coleridge's versatile genius found another outlet. In December of that year, the Gillmans removed to The Grove, Highgate, and their house became an object of pilgrimage for all who wished to hear Coleridge's conversation. Simultaneously his poetic powers began to revive. The theme of self-dramatization persisted, but the note of querulousness was less marked. In poems such as *Youth and Age* and *Work without Hope* recognition of his infirmity is accompanied by acceptance: the quality of the poetry is correspondingly higher. In *The Pang More Sharp than All*, which may have been composed as late as 1826, wistfulness plays its full part, but the pain has been distanced. The indications are that, as E. K. Chambers suggested, his powers were enjoying an Indian summer.

In the remaining years of his life, meanwhile, his beliefs came full circle. The death of love and even of hope is now taken for granted and in a series of poems he writes of other qualities which he now relies on to take their place. In *Duty Surviving Self-Love*, for example, he deals with the duty of continued love, even if the love is not returned; in *The Improvisatore* the death of Love and Hope leaves Contentment; in *Love, Hope and Patience*, Patience is the sole survivor. But the continued necessity of returning to this theme shows that even now the problem has not been finally solved. In the last year of his life Coleridge can still write a poem entitled *Love's Apparition and Evanishment* in which a vision of the love he never quite found comes to trouble him again for a brief period. The glimpse of love now does little more than remind him of his own dead state:

> Alas! 'twas but a chilling breath
> Woke just enough of life in death
> To make Hope die anew.

This acceptance, however wistfully, of the loss of hope is accompanied by a growing orthodoxy in religion. The poet who had in his youth written:

> For all that meets the bodily sense I deem
> Symbolical, one mighty alphabet
> For infant minds . . .
> > (*The Destiny of Nations*)

has since written:

> . . . all is blank on high,
> No constellations alphabet the Sky –
> The Heavens one large black Letter only shew . . .
> > (*Coeli Enarrant*)

Similarly, the philosopher who had, in *Biographia Literaria*, written in praise of the Greek maxim 'Know Thyself', now crosses out those words and writes instead the poem *Self-Knowledge*. Charity and humility, the traditional Christian virtues, are his final theme, and he spends some time during his last year in revising and polishing his *Epitaph*:

> Mercy for praise – to be forgiven for fame
> He ask'd, and hop'd, through Christ. Do thou the same!

(He explains in a letter that 'for' here means 'instead of'.)

In this last self-dramatization he recognizes by ironic reference that the curse of the seamen in *The Ancient Mariner* has been his own fate through life, and prays that the curse of the Mariner may now be his own blessing:

> That he who many a year with toil of breath
> Found death in life, may here find life in death!

The first line of the *Epitaph*, however, is an unconscious testimony that the vision of the Mariner has remained with him: by lighting on the phrase 'child of God' he shows a continuing faith in his old ideal of 'keeping alive the child in the man'.

There are many ways of achieving this end, for children have many different qualities. But in the sense which meant most to Coleridge he had been successful. Despite the extraordinary intricacy of his thinking – not to mention his capacity at times for prevarication and self-deception – he had retained under it all an innocent sensibility. His sense of the wonderful, also a childlike characteristic, continues to emerge; while all his poetry displays a sensitive response to the minute and delicate beauties of nature which provides the most distinctively 'Coleridgean' note in his work and thinking as a whole.

# Youth and Age

10 September 1823. Wednesday Morning. 10 o'clock[1]

> On the tenth day of September,
> Eighteen Hundred Twenty Three,
> Wednesday Morn, as I remember,
> Ten on the Clock the Hour to be.

An *Air* that whizzed δία ἐγκεφάλον (right across the diameter of my Brain) exactly like a Hummel Bee, alias Dombeldore, the gentleman with Rappee Spenser,[2] with bands of Red, and Orange Plush Breeches, close by my ear, at once sharp and *burry*, right over the Summit of Quantock, [item of Skiddaw (*erased*)] at earliest Dawn, just between the Nightingale that I had stopt to hear in the Copse at the Foot of Quantock, and the first Sky-Lark that was a Song-Fountain, dashing up and sparkling to the Ear's Eye, in full Column, or ornamented Shaft of Sound in the Order of Gothic Extravaganza, out of Sight, over the Cornfields on the Descent of the Mountain on the other side out of sight, tho' twice I beheld its *mute* shoot downward in the sunshine like a falling Star of melted Silver: –

> Verse, a breeze mid blossoms straying,
> Where Hope clung feeding, like a bee –
> Both were mine! Life went a maying
> > With Nature, Hope, and Poesy,
> > > When I was young!                     5

> When I was young? – Ah, woful When!
> Ah! for the change 'twixt Now and Then!
> This breathing house not built with hands,
> This body that does me grievous wrong,
> O'er aery cliffs and glittering sands,          10
> How lightly then it flashed along: –
> Like those trim skiffs, unknown of yore,
> On winding lakes and rivers wide,
> That ask no aid of sail or oar,
> That fear no spite of wind or tide!          15

[1]This introduction was written in a notebook before the first draft for the poem, which, beginning at lines 18–22, embodied the rhythm of the first stanza here: see above p. xl.

[2]Rappee is a snuff, a spencer, a jacket, named after the earl.

Nought cared this body for wind or weather
When Youth and I lived in't together.

Flowers are lovely; Love is flower-like;
Friendship is a sheltering tree;
O! the joys, that came down shower-like,                    20
Of Friendship, Love, and Liberty,
                 Ere I was old!

Ere I was old? Ah woful Ere,
Which tells me, Youth's no longer here!
O Youth! for years so many and sweet,                       25
'Tis known, that Thou and I were one,
I'll think it but a fond conceit —
It cannot be that Thou art gone!
Thy vesper-bell hath not yet toll'd: —
And thou wert aye a masker bold!                            30
What strange disguise hast now put on,
To make believe, that thou art gone?
I see these locks in silvery slips,
This drooping gait, this altered size:
But Spring-tide blossoms on thy lips,                       35
And tears take sunshine from thine eyes!
Life is but thought: so think I will
That Youth and I are house-mates still.

Dew-drops are the gems of morning,
But the tears of mournful eve!                              40
Where no hope is, life's a warning
That only serves to make us grieve,
                When we are old:

That only serves to make us grieve
With oft and tedious taking-leave,                          45
Like some poor nigh-related guest,
That may not rudely be dismist;
Yet hath outstay'd his welcome while,
And tells the jest without the smile.
[September–October 1823]

## *Desire*[1]

Where true Love burns Desire is Love's pure flame;
It is the reflex of our earthly frame,
That takes its meaning from the nobler part,
And but translates the language of the heart.
[April 1824]

[1] The language of the original notebook version (IV, 5146) is more physiological:
    Desire, of pure Love born, itself's the same:
    A Pulse, that animates the outer frame,
    It but repeats the life-throb of the Heart –
    And takes the impress of the nobler part

## The Delinquent Travellers

Some are home-sick – some two or three,
Their third year on the Arctic Sea –
Brave Captain Lyon tells us so[1] –
Spite of those charming Esquimaux.
But O, what scores are sick of Home,                              5
Agog for Paris or for Rome!
Nay! tho' contented to abide,
You should prefer your own fireside;
Yet since grim War has ceas'd its madding,
And Peace has set John Bull agadding,                           10
'Twould such a vulgar taste betray,
For very shame you must away!
'What? not yet seen the coast of France!
The folks will swear, for lack of bail,
You've spent your last five years in jail!'                      15

Keep moving! Steam, or Gas, or Stage,
Hold, cabin, steerage, hencoop's cage –
Tour, Journey, Voyage, Lounge, Ride, Walk,
Skim, Sketch, Excursion, Travel-talk –
For move you must! 'Tis now the rage,                           20
The law and fashion of the Age.
If you but perch, where Dover tallies,
So strangely with the coast of Calais,
With a good glass and knowing look,
You'll soon get matter for a book!                              25
Or else, in Gas-car, take your chance
Like that adventurous king of France,
Who, once, with twenty thousand men
Went up – and then came down again;
At least, he moved if nothing more:                             30
And if there's nought left to explore,
Yet while your well-greased wheels keep spinning,
The traveller's honoured name you're winning,
And, snug as Jonas in the Whale,

[1] *The Private Journal of Captain G. F. Lyon of the Mt Hecla, during the recent voyage of discovery under Captain Parry*, was published by John Murray in 1824. [E.H.C.]

You may loll back and dream a tale.                                35
Move, or be moved – there's no protection,
Our Mother Earth has ta'en the infection –
(That rogue Copernicus, 'tis said
First put the whirring in her head,)
A planet She, and can't endure                                     40
T'exist without her annual Tour:
The *name* were else a mere misnomer,
Since Planet is but Greek for *Roamer*.
The atmosphere, too, can do no less
Than ventilate her emptiness,                                      45
Bilks turn-pike gates, for no one cares,
And gives herself a thousand airs –
While streams and shopkeepers, we see,
Will have their run toward the sea –
And if, meantime, like old King Log,                               50
Or ass with tether and a clog,
Must graze at home! to yawn and bray
'I guess we shall have rain to-day!
Nor clog nor tether can be worse
Than the dead palsy of the purse.                                  55
Money, I've heard a wise man say,
Makes herself wings and flys away:
Ah! would She take it in her head
To make a pair for me instead!
At all events, the Fancy's free,                                   60
No traveller so bold as she.
From Fear and Poverty released
I'll saddle Pegasus, at least,
And when she's seated to her mind,
I within I can mount behind:                                       65
And since this outward I, you know,
Must stay because he cannot go,
My fellow-travellers shall be they
Who go because they cannot stay –
Rogues, rascals, sharpers, blanks and prizes,                      70
Delinquents of all sorts and sizes,
Fraudulent bankrupts, Knights burglarious,
And demireps of means precarious –
All whom Law thwarted, Arms or Arts,
Compel to visit foreign parts,                                     75

All hail! No compliments, I pray,
I'll follow where you lead the way!
But ere we cross the main once more,
Methinks, along my native shore,
Dismounting from my steed I'll stray,                    80
Beneath the cliffs of Dumpton Bay,[1]
Where, Ramsgate and Broadstairs between,
Rude caves and grated doors are seen:
And here I'll watch till break of day,
(For Fancy in her magic might                            85
Can turn broad noon to starless night!)
When lo! methinks a sudden band
Of smock-clad smugglers round me stand.
Denials, oaths, in vain I try,
At once they gag me for a spy,                           90
And stow me in the boat hard by.
Suppose us fairly now afloat,
Till Boulogne mouth receives our Boat.
But, bless us! what a numerous band
Of cockneys anglicise the strand!                        95
Delinquent bankrupts, leg-bail'd debtors,
Some for the news, and some for letters –
With hungry look and tarnished dress,
French shrugs and British surliness.
Sick of the country for their sake                       100
Of them and France *French leave* I take –
And lo! a transport comes in view
I hear the merry motley crew,
Well skill'd in pocket to make entry,
Of Dieman's Land the elected Gentry,                     105
And founders of Australian Races. –
The Rogues! I see it in their faces!
Receive me, Lads! I'll go with you,
Hunt the black swan and kangaroo,
And that New Holland we'll presume                       110
Old England with some elbow-room.
Across the mountains we will roam,
And each man make himself a home:

[1] A coast village near Ramsgate. In several years, including 1824, Coleridge passed some weeks at Ramsgate during the late autumn.

Or, if old habits ne'er forsaking,
Like clock-work of the Devil's making,                    115
Ourselves inveterate rogues should be,
We'll have a virtuous progeny;
And on the dunghill of our vices
Raise human pine-apples and spices.
Of all the children of John Bull                          120
With empty heads and bellies full,
Who ramble East, West, North and South,
With leaky purse and open mouth,
In search of varieties exotic
The usefullest and most patriotic,                        125
And merriest, too, believe me, Sirs!
Are your Delinquent Travellers!
[1824]


# Work Without Hope

### LINES COMPOSED 21ST FEBRUARY 1825

All Nature seems at work. Slugs leave their lair –
The bees are stirring – birds are on the wing –
And Winter slumbering in the open air,
Wears on his smiling face a dream of Spring!
And I the while, the sole unbusy thing,                    5
Nor honey make, nor pair, nor build, nor sing.

   Yet well I ken the banks where amaranths blow,
Have traced the fount whence streams of nectar flow.
Bloom, O ye amaranths! bloom for whom ye may,
For me ye bloom not! Glide, rich streams, away!           10
With lips unbrightened, wreathless brow, I stroll:
And would you learn the spells that drowse my soul?
Work without Hope draws nectar in a sieve,
And Hope without an object cannot live.
[February 1825]

## The Two Founts

STANZAS ADDRESSED TO A LADY ON HER RECOVERY, WITH
UNBLEMISHED LOOKS, FROM A SEVERE ATTACK OF PAIN

'Twas my last waking thought, how it could be,
That thou, sweet friend, such anguish should'st endure;
When straight from Dreamland came a Dwarf, and he
Could tell the cause, forsooth, and knew the cure.

Methought he fronted me with peering look                    5
Fix'd on my heart; and read aloud in game
The loves and griefs therein, as from a book:
And uttered praise like one who wished to blame.

In every heart (quoth he) since Adam's sin
Two Founts there are, of Suffering and of Cheer!            10
That to let forth, and this to keep within!
But she, whose aspect I find imaged here,

Of Pleasure only will to all dispense,
That Fount alone unlock, by no distress
Choked or turned inward, but still issue thence             15
Unconquered cheer, persistent loveliness.

As on the driving cloud the shiny bow,
That gracious thing made up of tears and light,
Mid the wild rack and rain that slants below
Stands smiling forth, unmoved and freshly bright;           20

As though the spirits of all lovely flowers,
Inweaving each its wreath and dewy crown,
Or ere they sank to earth in vernal showers,
Had built a bridge to tempt the angels down.

Even so, Eliza! on that face of thine,                      25
On that benignant face, whose look alone
(The soul's translucence thro' her crystal shrine!)
Has power to soothe all anguish but thine own,

A beauty hovers still, and ne'er takes wing,
But with a silent charm compels the stern          30
And tort'ring Genius of the bitter spring,
To shrink aback, and cower upon his urn.

Who then needs wonder, if (no outlet found
In passion, spleen, or strife,) the Fount of Pain
O'erflowing beats against its lovely mound,        35
And in wild flashes shoots from heart to brain?

Sleep, and the Dwarf with that unsteady gleam
On his raised lip, that aped a critic smile,
Had passed: yet I, my sad thoughts to beguile,
Lay weaving on the tissue of my dream;             40

Till audibly at length I cried, as though
Thou hadst indeed been present to my eyes,
O sweet, sweet sufferer; if the case be so,
I pray thee, be less good, less sweet, less wise!

In every look a barbéd arrow send,                 45
On those soft lips let scorn and anger live!
Do any thing, rather than thus, sweet friend!
Hoard for thyself the pain, thou wilt not give!
[May–June 1826]


## The Pang More Sharp Than All

### AN ALLEGORY

I

He too has flitted from his secret nest,
Hope's last and dearest child without a name! –
Has flitted from me, like the warmthless flame,
That makes false promise of a place of rest
To the tired Pilgrim's still believing mind; –     5
Or like some Elfin Knight in kingly court,
Who having won all guerdons in his sport,
Glides out of view, and whither none can find!

### II

Yes! he hath flitted from me — with what aim,
Or why, I know not! 'Twas a home of bliss,                    10
And he was innocent, as the pretty shame
Of babe, that tempts and shuns the menaced kiss,
From its twy-cluster'd hiding place of snow!
Pure as the babe, I ween, and all aglow
As the dear hopes, that swell the mother's breast —          15
Her eyes down gazing o'er her claspéd charge; —
Yet gay as that twice happy father's kiss,
That well might glance aside, yet never miss,
Where the sweet mark emboss'd so sweet a targe —
Twice wretched he who hath been doubly blest!                20

### III

Like a loose blossom on a gusty night
He flitted from me — and has left behind
(As if to them his faith he ne'er did plight)
Of either sex and answerable mind
Two playmates, twin-births of his foster-dame: —            25
The one a steady lad (Esteem he hight)
And Kindness is the gentler sister's name.
Dim likeness now, though fair she be and good,
Of that bright Boy who hath us all forsook; —
But in his full-eyed aspect when she stood,                  30
And while her face reflected every look,
And in reflection kindled — she became
So like Him, that almost she seem'd the same!

### IV

Ah! he is gone, and yet will not depart! —
Is with me still, yet I from him exiled!                     35
For still there lives within my secret heart
The magic image of the magic Child,
Which there he made up-grow by his strong art,
As in that crystal[1] orb — wise Merlin's feat, —
The wondrous 'World of Glass', wherein inisled               40
All long'd for things their beings did repeat; —

[1] *Faerie Queene*, b. III, c. 2, s. 19. [S.T.C.]

And there he left it, like a Sylph beguiled,
To live and yearn and languish incomplete!

V

Can wit of man a heavier grief reveal?
Can sharper pang from hate or scorn arise? –          45
Yes! one more sharp there is that deeper lies,
Which fond Esteem but mocks when he would heal.
Yet neither scorn nor hate did it devise,
But sad compassion and atoning zeal!
One pang more blighting-keen than hope betray'd!          50
And this it is my woful hap to feel,
When, at her Brother's hest, the twin-born Maid
With face averted and unsteady eyes,
Her truant playmate's faded robe puts on;
And inly shrinking from her own disguise          55
Enacts the faery Boy that's lost and gone.
O worse than all! O pang all pangs above
Is Kindness counterfeiting absent Love!
[Date uncertain. 1807 onwards? 1823–5 onwards?]

## Sancti Dominici Pallium[1]

### A DIALOGUE BETWEEN POET AND FRIEND

#### FOUND WRITTEN ON THE BLANK LEAF AT THE BEGINNING OF BUTLER'S 'BOOK OF THE CHURCH' (1825)

##### POET

I note the moods and feelings men betray,
And heed them more than aught they do or say;
The lingering ghosts of many a secret deed
Still-born or haply strangled in its birth;

[1] 'The Robe of St Dominic'. The poem reflects the heat of religious debate in the mid 1820s, when the question of Roman Catholic emancipation was being discussed, along with that of the Church of England and its authority. Southey's *Book of the Church* (1825) had been answered by Charles Butler's *Book of the Roman Catholic Church* and an anonymous pamphlet written by John Milner entitled *Merlin's Strictures*; Southey had then returned to the fray with *Vindiciae Ecclesiae Anglicanae* (1826). The title of the poem refers obliquely to the part played by St Dominic and his black-robed order in such things as the Inquisition and the persecution of the Albigenses.

*These* best reveal the smooth man's inward creed!                    5
*These* mark the spot where lies the treasure – Worth!


   Milner made up of impudence and trick,
With cloven tongue prepared to hiss and lick,
Rome's Brazen Serpent – boldly dares discuss
The roasting of thy heart, O brave John Huss!                         10
And with grim triumph and a truculent glee
Absolves anew the Pope-wrought perfidy,
That made an empire's plighted faith a lie,
And fix'd a broad stare on the Devil's eye –
(Pleas'd with the guilt, yet envy-stung at heart                      15
To stand outmaster'd in his own black art!)
Yet Milner –


### FRIEND

      Enough of Milner! we're agreed,
Who now defends would then have done the deed.
But who not feels persuasion's gentle sway,
Who but must meet the proffered hand half way                         20
When courteous Butler –


### POET (*aside*)

      (Rome's smooth go-between!)


### FRIEND

   Laments the advice that soured a milky queen –
(For 'bloody' all enlightened men confess
An antiquated error of the press:)
Who rapt by zeal beyond her sex's bounds,                             25
With actual cautery staunched the Church's wounds!
And tho' he deems, that with too broad a blur
We damn the French and Irish massacre,
Yet *blames* them both – and thinks the Pope *might* err!
What think you now? Boots it with spear and shield                    30
Against such gentle foes to take the field
Whose beckoning hands the mild Caduceus wield?

### POET

What think I now? Even what I thought before; —
What Milner boasts though Butler may deplore,
Still I repeat, words lead me not astray                          35
When the *shown* feeling points a different way.
Smooth Butler can say grace at slander's feast,[1]
And bless each haut-gout cook'd by monk or priest;
Leaves the full lie on Milner's gong to swell,
Content with half-truths that do just as well;                   40
But duly decks his mitred comrade's flanks,
And with him shares the Irish nation's thanks!


So much for you, my friend! who own a Church,
And would not leave your mother in the lurch!
But when a Liberal asks me what I think —                        45
Scared by the blood and soot of Cobbett's ink,
And Jeffrey's glairy phlegm and Connor's foam,
In search of some safe parable I roam —
An emblem sometimes may comprise a tome!


Disclaimant of his uncaught grandsire's mood,                    50
I see a tiger lapping kitten's food:
And who shall blame him that he purs applause,
When brother Brindle pleads the good old cause;
And frisks his pretty tail, and half unsheathes his claws!
Yet not the less, for modern lights unapt,                       55
I trust the bolts and cross-bars of the laws
More than the Protestant milk all newly lapt,
Impearling a tame wild-cat's whisker'd jaws!
[c. 1826]            —

---

[1] 'Smooth Butler.' See the Rev. Blanco White's Letter to C. Butler, Esq. [MS note by S.T.C.,
1827.]

# The Improvisatore

## OR, 'JOHN ANDERSON, MY JO, JOHN'

*Scene – A spacious drawing-room, with music-room adjoining.*

*Katharine.* What are the words?

*Eliza.* Ask our friend, the Improvisatore; here he comes. Kate has a favour to ask of you, Sir; it is that you will repeat the ballad that Mr — sang so sweetly.

*Friend.* It is in Moore's Irish Melodies; but I do not recollect the words distinctly. The moral of them, however, I take to be this: –

> Love would remain the same if true,
> When we were neither young nor new;
> Yea, and in all within the will that came,
> By the same proofs would show itself the same.

*Eliz.* What are the lines you repeated from Beaumont and Fletcher, which my mother admired so much? It begins with something about two vines so close that their tendrils intermingle.

*Fri.* You mean Charles' speech to Angelina, in *The Elder Brother.*

> We'll live together, like two neighbour vines,
> Circling our souls and loves in one another!
> We'll spring together, and we'll bear one fruit;
> One joy shall make us smile, and one grief mourn;
> One age go with us, and one hour of death
> Shall close our eyes, and one grave make us happy.

*Kath.* A precious boon, that would go far to reconcile one to old age – *if* true! But is there any such true love?

*Fri.* I hope so.

*Kath.* But do you believe it?

*Eliz.* (*eagerly*). I am sure he does.

*Fri.* From a man turned of fifty, Katharine, I imagine, expects a less confident answer.

*Kath.* A more sincere one, perhaps.

*Fri.* Even though he should have obtained the nick-name of Improvisatore, by perpetrating charades and extempore verses at Christmas times?

*Eliz.* Nay, but be serious.

*Fri.* Serious! Doubtless. A grave personage of my years giving a

Love-lecture to two young ladies, cannot well be otherwise. The difficulty, I suspect, would be for them to remain so. It will be asked whether I am not the 'elderly gentleman' who sate 'despairing beside a clear stream', with a willow for his wig-block.

*Eliz.* Say another word, and we will call it downright affectation.

*Kath.* No! we will be affronted, drop a courtesy, and ask pardon for our presumption in expecting that Mr — would waste his sense on two insignificant girls.

*Fri.* Well, well, I will be serious. Hem! Now then commences the discourse; Mr Moore's song being the text. Love, as distinguished from Friendship, on the one hand, and from the passion that too often usurps its name, on the other –

*Lucius (Eliza's brother, who had just joined the trio, in a whisper to the Friend).* But is not Love the union of both?

*Fri. (aside to Lucius).* He never loved who thinks so.

*Eliz.* Brother, we don't want *you.* There! Mrs H. cannot arrange the flower vase without you. Thank you, Mrs Hartman.

*Luc.* I'll have my revenge! I know what I will say!

*Eliz.* Off! Off! Now, dear Sir, – Love, you were saying –

*Fri.* Hush! *Preaching,* you mean, Eliza.

*Eliz. (impatiently).* Pshaw!

*Fri.* Well then, I was *saying* that Love, truly such, is itself not the most common thing in the world: and mutual love still less so. But that enduring personal attachment, so beautifully delineated by Erin's sweet melodist, and still more touchingly, perhaps, in the well-known ballad, 'John Anderson, my Jo, John,' in addition to a depth and constancy of character of no every-day occurrence, supposes a peculiar sensibility and tenderness of nature; a constitutional communicativeness and *utterancy* of heart and soul; a delight in the detail of sympathy, in the outward and visible signs of the sacrament within – to count, as it were, the pulses of the life of love. But above all, it supposes a soul which, even in the pride and summer-tide of life – even in the lustihood of health and strength, had felt oftenest and prized highest that which age cannot take away and which, in all our lovings, is *the* Love; —

*Eliz.* There is something *here (pointing to her heart)* that *seems* to understand you, but wants the *word* that would make it understand itself.

*Kath.* I, too, seem to *feel* what you mean. Interpret the feeling for us.

*Fri.* — I mean that *willing* sense of the insufficingness of the *self* for itself, which predisposes a generous nature to see, in the total being of another, the supplement and completion of its own; — that quiet perpetual *seeking* which the presence of the beloved object modulates, not suspends, where the heart momently finds, and, finding, again seeks on; — lastly, when 'life's changeful orb has pass'd the full', a confirmed faith in the nobleness of humanity, thus brought home and pressed, as it were, to the very bosom of hourly experience; it supposes, I say, a heartfelt reverence for worth, not the less deep because divested of its solemnity by habit, by familiarity, by mutual infirmities, and even by a feeling of modesty which will arise in delicate minds, when they are conscious of possessing the same or the correspondent excellence in their own characters. In short, there must be a mind, which, while it feels the beautiful and the excellent in the beloved as its own, and by right of love appropriates it, can call Goodness its Playfellow; and dares make sport of time and infirmity, while, in the person of a thousand-foldly endeared partner, we feel for aged Virtue the caressing fondness that belongs to the Innocence of childhood, and repeat the same attentions and tender courtesies which had been dictated by the same affection to the same object when attired in feminine loveliness or in manly beauty.

*Eliz.* What a soothing — what an elevating idea!

*Kath.* If it be not only an *idea.*

*Fri.* At all events, these qualities which I have enumerated, are rarely found united in a single individual. How much more rare must it be, that two such individuals should meet together in this wide world under circumstances that admit of their union as Husband and Wife. A person may be highly estimable on the whole, nay, amiable as neighbour, friend, housemate — in short, in all the concentric circles of attachment save only the last and inmost; and yet from how many causes be estranged from the highest perfection in this! Pride, coldness, or fastidiousness of nature, worldly cares, an anxious or ambitious disposition, a passion for display, a sullen temper, — one or the other — too often proves 'the dead fly in the compost of spices', and any one is enough to unfit it for the precious balm of unction. For some mighty good sort of people, too, there is not seldom a sort of solemn saturnine, or, if you will, *ursine* vanity, that keeps itself alive by sucking the paws of its own self-importance. And as this high sense, or rather sensation of their own value is, for the most part, grounded on negative qualities, so they have no better means of preserving the same but by *negatives* — that is, by *not* doing or saying any thing, that might be put down for fond, silly, or nonsensical; — or (to use their own phrase) by *never forgetting themselves*, which some of their acquaintance are uncharitable enough to think the most worthless object they could be employed in remembering.

*Eliz.* (*in answer to a whisper from Katharine*). To a hair! He must have sate for it himself. Save me from such folks! But they are out of the question.

*Fri.* True! but the same effect is produced in thousands by the too general insensibility to a very important truth; this, namely, that the MISERY of human life is made up of large masses, each separated from the other by certain intervals. One year, the death of a child; years after, a failure in trade; after another longer or shorter interval, a daughter may have married unhappily; – in all but the singularly unfortunate, the integral parts that compose the sum total of the unhappiness of a man's life, are easily counted, and distinctly remembered. The HAPPINESS of life, on the contrary, is made up of minute fractions – the little, soon-forgotten charities of a kiss, a smile, a kind look, a heartfelt compliment in the disguise of playful raillery, and the countless other infinitesimals of pleasurable thought and genial feeling.

*Kath.* Well, Sir; you have said quite enough to make me despair of finding a 'John Anderson, my Jo, John', with whom to totter down the hill of life.

*Fri.* Not so! Good men are not, I trust, so much scarcer than good women, but that what another would find in you, you may hope to find in another. But well, however, may that boon be rare, the possession of which would be more than an adequate reward for the rarest virtue.

*Eliz.* Surely, he, who has described it so well, must have possessed it?

*Fri.* If he were worthy to have possessed it, and had believingly anticipated and not found it, how bitter the disappointment!

(*Then, after a pause of a few minutes*)

ANSWER, *ex improviso*

Yes, yes! that boon, life's richest treat,
He had, or fancied that he had;
Say, 'twas but in his own conceit –
    The fancy made him glad!
Crown of his cup, and garnish of his dish,
The boon, prefigured in his earliest wish,                    5

The fair fulfilment of his poesy,
When his young heart first yearn'd for sympathy!
But e'en the meteor offspring of the brain
　　　　　Unnourished wane;　　　　　　　　　10
Faith asks her daily bread,
And Fancy must be fed.
Now so it chanced — from wet or dry,
It boots not how — I know not why —
She missed her wonted food; and quickly　　　15
Poor Fancy stagger'd and grew sickly.
Then came a restless state, 'twixt yea and nay,
His faith was fix'd, his heart all ebb and flow;
Or like a bark, in some half-shelter'd bay,
Above its anchor driving to and fro.　　　　　20

That boon, which but to have possess'd
In a *belief*, gave life a zest —
Uncertain both what it *had* been,
And if by error lost, or luck;
And what it *was*; — an evergreen　　　　　　25
Which some insidious blight had struck,
Or annual flower, which, past its blow,
No vernal spell shall e'er revive;
Uncertain, and afraid to know,
　　Doubts toss'd him to and fro:　　　　　　30
Hope keeping Love, Love Hope alive,
Like babes bewildered in the snow,
That cling and huddle from the cold
In hollow tree or ruin'd fold.

Those sparkling colours, once his boast,　　　35
　　Fading, one by one away,
Thin and hueless as a ghost,
　　Poor Fancy on her sick bed lay;
Ill at distance, worse when near,
Telling her dreams to jealous Fear!　　　　　40
Where was it then, the sociable sprite
That crown'd the Poet's cup and deck'd his dish!
Poor shadow cast from an unsteady wish,
Itself a substance by no other right,
But that it intercepted Reason's light;　　　45

It dimm'd his eye, it darken'd on his brow,
A peevish mood, a tedious time, I trow!
    Thank Heaven! 'tis not so now.

O bliss of blissful hours!
The boon of Heaven's decreeing,                    50
While yet in Eden's bowers
Dwelt the first husband and his sinless mate!
The one sweet plant, which, piteous Heaven agreeing,
They bore with them thro' Eden's closing gate!
Of life's gay summer tide the sovran Rose!          55
Late autumn's Amaranth, that more fragrant blows
When Passion's flowers all fall or fade;
If this were ever his, in outward being,
Or but his own true love's projected shade,
Now that at length by certain proof he knows,       60
That whether real or a magic show,
Whate'er it *was*, it *is* no longer so;
Though heart be lonesome, Hope laid low,
Yet, Lady! deem him not unblest:
The certainty that struck Hope dead,                65
Hath left Contentment in her stead:
    And that is next to Best!
[?Summer 1826]


## Love's Burial-Place

*Lady.* If Love be dead —
    *Poet.* And I aver it!
*Lady.* Tell me, Bard! where Love lies buried?
    *Poet.* Love lies buried where 'twas born:
Oh, gentle dame! think it no scorn                   5
If, in my fancy, I presume
To call thy bosom poor Love's Tomb.
And on that tomb to read the line: —
'Here lies a Love that once seem'd mine,
But caught a chill, as I divine,                    10
And died at length of a Decline.'
[?1826]

## Lines

### SUGGESTED BY THE LAST WORDS OF BERENGARIUS
### (OB. ANNO DOM. 1088)

No more 'twixt conscience staggering and the Pope,
Soon shall I now before my God appear/
By him to be acquitted, as I hope:
By him to be condemnéd, as I fear.

#### REFLECTION ON THE ABOVE

Lynx amid moles! had I stood by thy Bed,                    5
Be of good cheer, meek Soul! I would have said:
I see a Hope spring from that humble Fear.
All are not strong alike thro' storms to steer
Right onward. What? tho' dread of threaten'd death
And dungeon torture made thy Hand and Breath        10
Inconstant to the truth within thy Heart?
That truth, from which thro' fear thou twice didst start,
FEAR haply told thee, was a *learnéd* strife,
Or not so vital as to claim thy life:
And Myriads had reached Heaven, who never knew   15
Where lay the difference 'twixt the false and true!

Ye, who secure mid trophies not your own
Judge him who won them when he stood alone,
And proudly talk of *recreant* BERENGARE —
O first the Age, and then the Man compare!            20
That Age how dark! congenial minds how rare!
No Host of Friends with kindred zeal did burn!
No throbbing Hearts awaited *his* return!
Prostrate alike when Prince and Peasant fell,
He only disenchanted from the Spell,                        25
Like the weak Worm that gems the starless night,
Mov'd in the scanty circlet of his Light:
And was it strange if he withdrew the ray
That did but guide the Night-birds to their Prey?

The ascending Day-star with a bolder eye               30
Hath lit each Dew-drop on our trimmer Lawn!

Yet not for this, if wise, shall we decry
The Spots and Struggles of the timid DAWN;
Lest so we tempt th' approaching NOON to scorn
The Mists and painted Vapours of our MORN.                    35
[?1826. From MS]


## Epitaphium Testamentarium[1]

Τὸ τοῦ ῬΕΣΤΗΣΕ τοῦ ἐπιθανοῦς
epitaphium testamentarium αὐτόγραφον.


Quae linquam, aut nihil, aut nihili, aut vix sunt mea. Sordes
Do MORTI: reddo caetera, Christe! tibi.
[1826. From MS]


## Duty Surviving Self-Love

### THE ONLY SURE FRIEND OF DECLINING LIFE

#### A SOLILOQUY

Unchanged within, to see all changed without,
Is a blank lot and hard to bear, no doubt.
Yet why at others' wanings should'st thou fret?
Then only might'st thou feel a just regret,
Hadst thou withheld thy love or hid thy light          5
In selfish forethought of neglect and slight.
O wiselier then, from feeble yearnings freed,
While, and on whom, thou may'st – shine on! nor heed
Whether the object by reflected light
Return thy radiance or absorb it quite:                10
And though thou notest from thy safe recess
Old Friends burn dim, like lamps in noisome air,
Love them for what they are; nor love them less,
Because to thee they are not what they were.
[September 1826]


[1]"*Testamentary Epitaph*. The epitaph of S.T.C., written by himself on the point of death.
The things I shall leave are either nothing, or of no value, or scarce my own. The dregs I give to
Death: I restore the rest, O Christ! to thee.'
    These lines were first published in the *Literary Souvenir* for 1827 as a footnote to the title of
the preceding poem. [E.H.C.]

## Homeless

'O! Christmas Day, Oh! happy day!
    A foretaste from above,
To him who hath a happy home,
    And love returned from love!'

O! Christmas Day, O gloomy day,                    5
    The barb in Memory's dart,
To him who walks alone through Life,
    The desolate in heart.
[?December 1826]

## Ἔρως ἀεὶ λάληθρος ἑταῖρος[1]

In many ways does the full heart reveal
The presence of the love it would conceal;
But in far more th' estrangéd heart lets know
The absence of the love, which yet it fain would shew.
[before May 1827]

## Song

Though veiled in spires of myrtle wreath,
Love is a sword that cuts its sheath,
And through the clefts, itself has made,
We spy the flashes of the blade!

But through the clefts, itself has made,            5
We likewise see Love's flashing blade
By rust consumed or snapt in twain:
And only hilt and stump remain.
[before May 1827]

[1]'Love, always a talkative companion.'

## Song, ex improviso

### ON HEARING A SONG IN PRAISE OF A LADY'S BEAUTY

'Tis not the lily-brow I prize,
   Nor roseate cheeks, nor sunny eyes,
   Enough of lilies and of roses!
A thousand-fold more dear to me
The gentle look that Love discloses, –       5
   The look that Love alone can see!
[1820s]


## To Mary Pridham

### [AFTERWARDS MRS DERWENT COLERIDGE]

Dear tho' unseen! tho' I have left behind
Life's gayer views and all that stirs the mind,
Now I revive, Hope making a new start,
Since I have heard with most believing heart,
That all my glad eyes would grow bright to see,     5
My Derwent hath found realiz'd in thee,
The boon prefigur'd in his earliest wish
Crown of his cup and garnish of his dish!
The fair fulfilment of his poesy,
When his young heart first yearn'd for sympathy!    10
Dear tho' unseen! unseen, yet long portray'd!
A Father's blessing on thee, gentle Maid!
                        S. T. COLERIDGE

[16 October 1827]

## Verses Trivocular

Of one scrap of science I've evidence ocular.
A heart of one chamber they call unilocular,
And in a sharp frost, or when snow-flakes fall floccular,
Your wise man of old wrapp'd himself in a Roquelaure,
Which was called a Wrap-rascal when folks would be jocular.    5
And shell-fish, the small, Periwinkle and Cockle are,
So with them will I finish these verses trivocular.
[January 1828. From MS]

## Water Ballad

### FROM THE FRENCH

'Come hither, gently rowing,
    Come, bear me quickly o'er
This stream so brightly flowing
    To yonder woodland shore.
But vain were my endeavour                    5
    To pay thee, courteous guide;
Row on, row on, for ever
    I'd have thee by my side.

'Good boatman, prithee haste thee,
    I seek my father-land.' —                 10
'Say, when I there have placed thee,
    Dare I demand thy hand?'
'A maiden's head can never
    So hard a point decide;
Row on, row on, for ever                      15
    I'd have thee by my side.'

The happy bridal over
    The wanderer ceased to roam,
For, seated by her lover,
    The boat became her home.                 20

And still they sang together
  As steering o'er the tide:
'Row on through wind and weather
  For ever by my side.'
[June–July 1828]

## Cologne

In Köhln, a town of monks and bones,
And pavements fang'd with murderous stones,
And rags, and hags, and hideous wenches;
I counted two and seventy stenches,
All well defined, and several stinks!     5
Ye Nymphs that reign o'er sewers and sinks,
The river Rhine, it is well known,
Doth wash your city of Cologne;
But tell me, Nymphs, what power divine
Shall henceforth wash the river Rhine?     10
[July 1828]

## On My Joyful Departure

### FROM THE SAME CITY

  As I am a Rhymer,
And now at least a merry one,
Mr Mum's Rudesheimer[1]
And the church of St Geryon
Are the two things alone     5
That deserve to be known
In the body-and-soul-stinking town of Cologne.
[July 1828]

[1] The *apotheosis* of Rhenish wine. [S.T.C.]

## The Netherlands

Water and windmills, greenness, Islets green; —
Willows whose Trunks beside the shadows stood
Of their own higher half, and willowy swamp: —
Farmhouses that at anchor seem'd — in the inland sky
The fog-transfixing Spires —                                    5
Water, wide water, greenness and green banks,
And water seen —
[August 1828. From MS]

## The Garden of Boccaccio

Of late, in one of those most weary hours,
When life seems emptied of all genial powers,
A dreary mood, which he who ne'er has known
May bless his happy lot, I sate alone;
And, from the numbing spell to win relief,                    5
Call'd on the Past for thought of glee or grief.
In vain! bereft alike of grief and glee,
I sate and cow'r'd o'er my own vacancy!
And as I watch'd the dull continuous ache,
Which, all else slumb'ring, seem'd alone to wake;            10
O Friend! long wont to notice yet conceal,
And soothe by silence what words cannot heal,
I but half saw that quiet hand of thine
Place on my desk this exquisite design,
Boccaccio's Garden and its faery,                            15
The love, the joyaunce, and the gallantry!
An Idyll, with Boccaccio's spirit warm,
Framed in the silent poesy of form.

Like flocks adown a newly-bathéd steep
    Emerging from a mist; or like a stream                   20
Of music soft that not dispels the sleep,
    But casts in happier moulds the slumberer's dream,
Gazed by an idle eye with silent might
The picture stole upon my inward sight.
A tremulous warmth crept gradual o'er my chest,             25
As though an infant's finger touch'd my breast.
And one by one (I know not whence) were brought
All spirits of power that most had stirr'd my thought
In selfless boyhood, on a new world tost
Of wonder, and in its own fancies lost;                     30
Or charm'd my youth, that, kindled from above,
Loved ere it loved, and sought a form for love;
Or lent a lustre to the earnest scan
Of manhood, musing what and whence is man!
Wild strain of Scalds, that in the sea-worn caves          35
Rehearsed their war-spell to the winds and waves;
Or fateful hymn of those prophetic maids,

That call'd on Hertha in deep forest glades;
Or minstrel lay, that cheer'd the baron's feast;
Or rhyme of city pomp, of monk and priest,                    40
Judge, mayor, and many a guild in long array,
To high-church pacing on the great saint's day.
And many a verse which to myself I sang,
That woke the tear, yet stole away the pang,
Of hopes which in lamenting I renew'd.                        45
And last, a matron now, of sober mien,
Yet radiant still and with no earthly sheen,
Whom as a faery child my childhood woo'd
Even in my dawn of thought – Philosophy;
Though then unconscious of herself, pardie,                   50
She bore no other name than Poesy;
And, like a gift from heaven, in lifeful glee,
That had but newly left a mother's knee,
Prattled and play'd with bird and flower, and stone,
As if with elfin playfellows well known,                      55
And life reveal'd to innocence alone.

Thanks, gentle artist! now I can descry
Thy fair creation with a mastering eye,
And all awake! And now in fix'd gaze stand,
Now wander through the Eden of thy hand;                      60
Praise the green arches, on the fountain clear
See fragment shadows of the crossing deer;
And with that serviceable nymph I stoop,
The crystal from its restless pool to scoop.
I see no longer! I myself am there,                           65
Sit on the ground-sward, and the banquet share.
'Tis I, that sweep that lute's love-echoing strings,
And gaze upon the maid who gazing sings:
Or pause and listen to the tinkling bells
From the high tower, and think that there she dwells.         70
With old Boccaccio's soul I stand possest,
And breathe an air like life, that swells my chest.

The brightness of the world, O thou once free,
And always fair, rare land of courtesy!
O Florence! with the Tuscan fields and hills,                75
And famous Arno, fed with all their rills;

Thou brightest star of star-bright Italy!
Rich, ornate, populous, – all treasures thine,
The golden corn, the olive, and the vine.
Fair cities, gallant mansions, castles old, 80
And forests, where beside his leafy hold
The sullen boar hath heard the distant horn,
And whets his tusks against the gnarléd thorn;
Palladian palace with its storied halls;
Fountains, where Love lies listening to their falls; 85
Gardens, where flings the bridge its airy span,
And Nature makes her happy home with man;
Where many a gorgeous flower is duly fed
With its own rill, on its own spangled bed,
And wreathes the marble urn, or leans its head, 90
A mimic mourner, that with veil withdrawn
Weeps liquid gems, the presents of the dawn; –
Thine all delights, and every muse is thine;
And more than all, the embrace and intertwine
Of all with all in gay and twinkling dance! 95
Mid gods of Greece and warriors of romance,
See! Boccace sits, unfolding on his knees
The new-found roll of old Maeonides;[1]
But from his mantle's fold, and near the heart,
Peers Ovid's Holy Book of Love's sweet smart![2] 100
O all-enjoying and all-blending sage,
Long be it mine to con thy mazy page,
Where, half conceal'd, the eye of fancy views
Fauns, nymphs, and wingéd saints, all gracious to thy muse!

[1]Boccaccio claimed for himself the glory of having first introduced the works of Homer to his countrymen. [S.T.C.]

[2]I know few more striking or more interesting proofs of the overwhelming influence which the study of the Greek and Roman classics exercised on the judgments, feelings, and imaginations of the literati of Europe at the commencement of the restoration of literature, than the passage in the *Filocopo* of Boccaccio: where the sage instructor, Racheo, as soon as the young prince and the beautiful girl Biancofiore had learned their letters, sets them to study the Holy Book, Ovid's Art of Love. 'Incominciò Racheo a mettere il suo officio in esecuzione con intera sollecitudine. E loro, in breve tempo, insegnato a conoscer le lettere, fece leggere il santo libro d'Ovvidio, nel quale il sommo poeta mostra, come i santi fuochi di Venere si debbano ne' freddi cuori consol lecitudine accendere.' [S.T.C.] ['Deeply interesting – but observe, p. 63, ll. 33–5 (*loc. cit.*), The *holy* Book – Ovid's Art of Love!! This is not the result of mere Immorality:

> Multum, Multum
> Hic jacet sepultum.'

– MS. note on the fly-leaf of S.T.C.'s copy of vol. i of Boccaccio's *Opera*, 1723.]

Still in thy garden let me watch their pranks,
And see in Dian's vest between the ranks
Of the trim vines, some maid that half believes
The vestal fires, of which her lover grieves,
With that sly satyr peeping through the leaves!
[?June–August 1828]

# *Alice Du Clos*

### OR THE FORKED TONGUE

### A BALLAD

'One word with two meanings is the traitor's shield and shaft: and a slit tongue be his blazon!' *Caucasian Proverb*.

'The Sun is not yet risen,
But the dawn lies red on the dew:
Lord Julian has stolen from the hunters away,
Is seeking, Lady! for you.
Put on your dress of green,                                     5
  Your buskins and your quiver;
Lord Julian is a hasty man,
  Long waiting brook'd he never.
I dare not doubt him, that he means
  To wed you on a day,                                    10
Your lord and master for to be,
  And you his lady gay.
O Lady! throw your book aside!
I would not that my Lord should chide.'

Thus spake Sir Hugh the vassal knight                            15
  To Alice, child of old Du Clos,
As spotless fair, as airy light
  As that moon-shiny doe,
The gold star on its brow, her sire's ancestral crest!
For ere the lark had left his nest,                              20
  She in the garden bower below
Sate loosely wrapt in maiden white,
Her face half drooping from the sight,
  A snow-drop on a tuft of snow!

O close your eyes, and strive to see                             25
The studious maid, with book on knee, —
  Ah! earliest-open'd flower;
While yet with keen unblunted light
The morning star shone opposite
  The lattice of her bower —                             30

Alone of all the starry host,
　　As if in prideful scorn
Of flight and fear he stay'd behind,
　　To brave th' advancing morn.

O! Alice could read passing well,　　　　　　35
　　And she was conning then
Dan Ovid's mazy tale of loves,
　　And gods, and beasts, and men.

The vassal's speech, his taunting vein,
It thrill'd like venom thro' her brain;　　　40
　　Yet never from the book
She rais'd her head, nor did she deign
　　The knight a single look.

'Off, traitor friend! how dar'st thou fix
　　Thy wanton gaze on me?　　　　　　45
And why, against my earnest suit,
　　Does Julian send by thee?

'Go, tell thy Lord, that slow is sure:
　　Fair speed his shafts today!
I follow here a stronger lure,　　　　　　50
　　And chase a gentler prey.'

She said: and with a baleful smile
　　The vassal knight reel'd off –
Like a huge billow from a bark
　　Toil'd in the deep sea-trough,　　　　　55
That shouldering sideways in mid plunge,
　　Is travers'd by a flash.
And staggering onward, leaves the ear
　　With dull and distant crash.

And Alice sate with troubled mien　　　　60
A moment; for the scoff was keen,
　　And thro' her veins did shiver!
Then rose and donn'd her dress of green,
　　Her buskins and her quiver.

There stands the flow'ring may-thorn tree!                    65
From thro' the veiling mist you see
    The black and shadowy stem; —
Smit by the sun the mist in glee
Dissolves to lightsome jewelry —
    Each blossom hath its gem!                                70


With tear-drop glittering to a smile,
The gay maid on the garden-stile
    Mimics the hunter's shout.
'Hip! Florian, hip! To horse, to horse!
    Go, bring the palfrey out.                                75


'My Julian's out with all his clan,
    And, bonny boy, you wis,
Lord Julian is a hasty man,
    Who comes late, comes amiss.'


Now Florian was a stripling squire,                           80
    A gallant boy of Spain,
That toss'd his head in joy and pride,
Behind his Lady fair to ride,
    But blush'd to hold her train.


The huntress is in her dress of green, —                      85
And forth they go; she with her bow,
    Her buskins and her quiver! —
The squire — no younger e'er was seen —
With restless arm and laughing een,
    He makes his javelin quiver.                              90


And had not Ellen[1] stay'd the race,
And stopp'd to see, a moment's space,
    The whole great globe of light
Give the last parting kiss-like touch
To the eastern ridge, it lack'd not much,                     95
    They had o'erta'en the knight.

[1]'Ellen' is no doubt a slip of the pen for 'Alice'. [E.H.C.]

It chanced that up the covert lane,
    Where Julian waiting stood,
A neighbour knight prick'd on to join
    The huntsmen in the wood. 100


And with him must Lord Julian go,
    Tho' with an anger'd mind:
Betroth'd not wedded to his bride,
    In vain he sought, 'twixt shame and pride,
    Excuse to stay behind. 105


He bit his lip, he wrung his glove,
He look'd around, he look'd above,
    But pretext none could find or frame!
Alas! alas! and well-a-day!
It grieves me sore to think, to say, 110
That names so seldom meet with Love,
    Yet Love wants courage without a name!


Straight from the forest's skirt the trees
    O'er-branching, made an aisle,
Where hermit old might pace and chaunt 115
    As in a minster's pile.


From underneath its leafy screen,
    And from the twilight shade,
You pass at once into a green,
    A green and lightsome glade. 120


And there Lord Julian sate on steed;
    Behind him, in a round,
Stood knight and squire, and menial train;
Against the leash the greyhounds strain;
    The horses paw'd the ground. 125


When up the alley green, Sir Hugh
    Spurr'd in upon the sward,
And mute, without a word, did he
    Fall in behind his lord.

Lord Julian turn'd his steed half round. – 130
  'What! doth not Alice deign
To accept your loving convoy, knight?
Or doth she fear our woodland sleight,
  And joins us on the plain?'

With stifled tones the knight replied, 135
And look'd askance on either side, –
  'Nay, let the hunt proceed! –
The Lady's message that I bear,
I guess would scantly please your ear,
  And less deserves your heed. 140

'You sent betimes. Not yet unbarr'd
  I found the middle door; –
Two sitters only met my eyes,
  Fair Alice, and one more.

'I came unlook'd for: and, it seem'd, 145
  In an unwelcome hour;
And found the daughter of Du Clos
  Within the lattic'd bower.

'But hush! the rest may wait. If lost,
  No great loss, I divine; 150
And idle words will better suit
  A fair maid's lips than mine.'

'God's wrath! speak out, man,' Julian cried,
  O'ermaster'd by the sudden smart; –
And feigning wrath, sharp, blunt, and rude, 155
The knight his subtle shift pursued. –
'Scowl not at me; command my skill,
To lure your hawk back, if you will,
  But not a woman's heart.

' "Go! (said she) tell him, – slow is sure; 160
  Fair speed his shafts today!
I follow here a stronger lure,
  And chase a gentler prey." '

'The game, pardie, was full in sight,
That then did, if I saw aright,                                165
    The fair dame's eyes engage;
For turning, as I took my ways,
I saw them fix'd with steadfast gaze
    Full on her wanton page.'

The last word of the traitor knight
    It had but entered Julian's ear, —                        170
From two o'erarching oaks between,
With glist'ning helm-like cap is seen,
    Borne on in giddy cheer,

A youth, that ill his steed can guide;                        175
Yet with reverted face doth ride,
    As answering to a voice,
That seems at once to laugh and chide —
'Not mine, dear mistress,' still he cried,
    ''Tis this mad filly's choice.'                           180

With sudden bound, beyond the boy,
See! see! that face of hope and joy,
    That regal front! those cheeks aglow!
Thou needed'st but the crescent sheen,
A quiver'd Dian to have been,                                 185
    Thou lovely child of old Du Clos!

Dark as a dream Lord Julian stood,
Swift as a dream, from forth the wood,
    Sprang on the plighted Maid!
With fatal aim, and frantic force,                            190
The shaft was hurl'd! — a lifeless corse,
Fair Alice from her vaulting horse,
    Lies bleeding on the glade.
[?1828–9]

## Love, Hope, and Patience in Education

O'er wayward childhood would'st thou hold firm rule,
And sun thee in the light of happy faces;
Love, Hope, and Patience, these must be thy graces,
And in thine own heart let them first keep school.
For as old Atlas on his broad neck places                    5
Heaven's starry globe, and there sustains it; – so
Do these upbear the little world below
Of Education, – Patience, Love, and Hope.
Methinks, I see them group'd in seemly show,
The straiten'd arms upraised, the palms aslope,             10
And robes that touching as adown they flow,
Distinctly blend, like snow emboss'd in snow.

O part them never! If Hope prostrate lie,
                    Love too will sink and die.
But Love is subtle, and doth proof derive                    15
From her own life that Hope is yet alive;
And bending o'er, with soul-transfusing eyes,
And the soft murmurs of the mother dove,
Woos back the fleeting spirit, and half supplies; –
Thus Love repays to Hope what Hope first gave to Love.       20

Yet haply there will come a weary day,
                    When overtask'd at length
Both Love and Hope beneath the load give way.
Then with a statue's smile, a statue's strength,
Stands the mute sister, Patience, nothing loth,              25
And both supporting does the work of both.
[?June 1829]

## Love and Friendship Opposite

Her attachment may differ from yours in degree,
    Provided they are both of one kind;
But Friendship, how tender so ever it be,
    Gives no accord to Love, however refined.

Love, that meets not with Love, its true nature revealing,          5
    Grows ashamed of itself, and demurs:
If you cannot lift hers up to your state of feeling,
    You must lower down your state to hers.
[?1830]

## Not at Home

That Jealousy may rule a mind
    Where Love could never be
I know; but ne'er expect to find
    Love without Jealousy.

She has a strange cast in her ee,                          5
    A swart sour-visaged maid –
But yet Love's own twin-sister she
    His house-mate and his shade.

Ask for her and she'll be denied: –
    What then? they only mean                              10
Their mistress has lain down to sleep,
    And can't just then be seen.
[?1830]

*OBIIT* Saturday, 10 September 1830

## *W. H. Eheu!*[1]

Beneath this stone does William Hazlitt lie,
  Thankless of all that God or man could give,
He lived like one who never thought to die,
  He died like one who dared not hope to live.
[From MS]

## *Phantom or Fact?*

### A DIALOGUE IN VERSE

#### AUTHOR

A lovely form there sate beside my bed,
And such a feeding calm its presence shed,
A tender love so pure from earthly leaven,
That I unnethe the fancy might control,
'Twas my own spirit newly come from heaven,                5
Wooing its gentle way into my soul!
But ah! the change – It had not stirr'd, and yet –
Alas! that change how fain would I forget!
That shrinking back, like one that had mistook!
That weary, wandering, disavowing look!                   10
'Twas all another, feature, look, and frame,
And still, methought, I knew, it was the same!

#### FRIEND

This riddling tale, to what does it belong?
Is't history? vision? or an idle song?

[1]'W. H. *Alas!*' In 1801 Coleridge had published a different version of this poem as 'Epitaph on a Bad Man'. The present one, naming Hazlitt, he did not publish; to it he added a note: 'With a sadness at heart, and an earnest hope grounded on his misanthropic sadness, when I first knew him in his twentieth or twenty-first year, that a something existed in his bodily organism that in the sight of the All-Merciful lessened his responsibility, and the moral imputation of his acts and feelings.'

Or rather say at once, within what space                              15
Of time this wild disastrous change took place?

### AUTHOR

Call it a moment's work (and such it seems)
This tale's a fragment from the life of dreams;
But say, that years matur'd the silent strife,
And 'tis a record from the dream of life.                             20
[?1830]


## Charity in Thought

To praise men as good, and take them for such,
　　Is a grace which no soul can mete out to a tittle; –
Of which he who has not a little too much,
　　Will by Charity's gauge surely have much too little.
[?1830]


## Humility the Mother of Charity

Frail creatures are we all! To be the best,
　　Is but the fewest faults to have: –
Look thou then to thyself, and leave the rest
　　To God, thy conscience and the grave.
[?1830]

## Forbearance

Beareth all things. – I COR. xiii. 7

Gently I took that which ungently came,[1]
And without scorn forgave: – Do thou the same.
A wrong done to thee think a cat's-eye spark
Thou wouldst not see, were not thine own heart dark.
Thine own keen sense of wrong that thirsts for sin,                 5
Fear that – the spark self-kindled from within,
Which blown upon will blind thee with its glare,
Or smother'd stifle thee with noisome air.
Clap on the extinguisher, pull up the blinds,
And soon the ventilated spirit finds                               10
Its natural daylight. If a foe have kenn'd,
Or worse than foe, an alienated friend,
A rib of dry rot in thy ship's stout side,
Think it God's message, and in humble pride
With heart of oak replace it; – thine the gains –                  15
Give him the rotten timber for his pains!
[?1819 ?1832]

## Love's Apparition and Evanishment

### AN ALLEGORIC ROMANCE

Like a lone Arab, old and blind,
    Some caravan had left behind,
Who sits beside a ruin'd well,
    Where the shy sand-asps bask and swell;
And now he hangs his agéd head aslant,                             5
And listens for a human sound – in vain!
And now the aid, which Heaven alone can grant,

---

[1]Compare Spenser's *Shepherd's Calendar* (Februarie):

> 'Ne ever was to Fortune foeman,
> But gently tooke, that ungently came.'
>                     [E.H.C.]

Upturns his eyeless face from Heaven to gain;—
Even thus, in vacant mood, one sultry hour,
Resting my eye upon a drooping plant,                       10
With brow low-bent, within my garden-bower,
I sate upon the couch of camomile;[1]
And – whether 'twas a transient sleep, perchance,
Flitted across the idle brain, the while
I watch'd the sickly calm with aimless scope,              15
In my own heart; or that, indeed a trance,
Turn'd my eye inward – thee, O genial Hope,
Love's elder sister! thee did I behold,
Drest as a bridesmaid, but all pale and cold,
With roseless cheek, all pale and cold and dim,            20
   Lie lifeless at my feet!
And then came Love, a sylph in bridal trim,
   And stood beside my seat;
She bent, and kiss'd her sister's lips,
   As she was wont to do; –
Alas! 'twas but a chilling breath                          25
Woke just enough of life in death
   To make Hope die anew.


### L'ENVOY

In vain we supplicate the Powers above;
There is no resurrection for the Love                      30
That, nursed in tenderest care, yet fades away
In the chill'd heart by gradual self-decay.
[1833]

---

[1] A 'Seat of Camomile' had long before been associated with Sara Hutchinson: see above, p. 352.

## To the Young Artist[1]

### KAYSER OF KAYSERWERTH

Kayser! to whom, as to a second self,
Nature, or Nature's next-of-kin, the Elf,
Hight Genius, hath dispensed the happy skill
To cheer or soothe the parting friend's 'Alas!'
Turning the blank scroll to a magic glass,                    5
That makes the absent present at our will;
And to the shadowing of thy pencil gives
Such seeming substance, that it almost lives.

Well hast thou given the thoughtful Poet's face!
Yet hast thou on the tablet of his mind                    10
A more delightful portrait left behind –
Even thy own youthful beauty, and artless grace,
Thy natural gladness and eyes bright with glee!
        Kayser! farewell!
Be wise! be happy! and forget not me.
[August–October 1833]

## Self-Knowledge

– E coelo descendit γνῶθι σεαυτόν. – JUVENAL, xi. 27

Γνῶθι σεαυτόν! – and is this the prime
And heaven-sprung adage of the olden time! –
Say, canst thou make thyself? – Learn first that trade; –
Haply thou mayst know what thyself had made.
What hast thou, Man, that thou dar'st call thine own? –                    5
What is there in thee, Man, that can be known? –

---

[1] J. Kayser made a pencil-sketch of Coleridge in 1833. Coleridge was more pleased with the artist than with the result: 'a Likeness, certainly; but with such unhappy Density of the Nose & ideotic Drooping of the Lip, with a certain pervading Woodenness of the whole Countenance, that it has not been thought guilty of any great Flattery by Mr Coleridge's Friends'. See *Letters* VI 974, where the sketch is also reproduced.

Dark fluxion, all unfixable by thought,
A phantom dim of past and future wrought,
Vain sister of the worm, – life, death, soul, clod –
Ignore thyself, and strive to know thy God!                    10
[?January 1834]


## My Baptismal Birth-Day

God's child in Christ adopted, – Christ my all, –
What that earth boasts were not lost cheaply, rather
Than forfeit that blest name, by which I call
The Holy One, the Almighty God, my Father? –
Father! in Christ we live, and Christ in Thee –                    5
Eternal Thou, and everlasting we.
The heir of heaven, henceforth I fear not death:
In Christ I live! in Christ I draw the breath
Of the true life! – Let then earth, sea, and sky
Make war against me! On my heart I show                    10
Their mighty master's seal. In vain they try
To end my life, that can but end its woe. –
Is that a death-bed where a Christian lies? –
Yes! but not his – 'tis Death itself there dies.
[October–November 1833]


## Epitaph

Stop, Christian passer-by! – Stop, child of God,
And read with gentle breast. Beneath this sod
A poet lies, or that which once seem'd he. –
O, lift one thought in prayer for S.T.C.;
That he who many a year with toil of breath                    5
Found death in life, may here find life in death!
Mercy for praise – to be forgiven for fame
He ask'd, and hoped, through Christ. Do thou the same!
[October–November 1833]

# APPENDIX

## The 1798 and 1817 Versions of
## The Rime of the Ancient Mariner

### COLERIDGE'S CHANGES TO THE ORIGINAL VERSION

The revised text of *The Ancient Mariner* appearing on pp. 215–55 corresponds largely to that which Coleridge approved for printings of the poem after 1817, when he collected the poem in the volume entitled *Sibylline Leaves*. It marked the second of two major revisions which he carried out during his career. When *Lyrical Ballads* was first being reprinted in 1800 he made a number of small changes, some to do with natural imagery: it was then that the lavrock was changed to a skylark and the 'morning frosts y-spread' to 'April hoar-frost spread'. 'The strong wind reached the ship' in 1798 (line 319); in 1800, more sinisterly, 'The loud wind never reached the ship/Yet still the ship moved on!' Most of the changes at this time, however, were changes of diction and tone, smoothing obtrusive archaisms, deleting some extravagant Gothic details, such as the 'rust/Of mouldy damps and charnel crust' that had discoloured the bones of Death, and removing an awkwardly phrased reference to animal magnetisim (lines 363–5). The vague 'Argument' at the beginning of the 1798 version was changed to include a more explicit account of what had happened: 'how the Ancient Mariner cruelly and in contempt of the laws of hospitality killed a Sea-bird and how he was followed by many and strange Judgements . . . ' The only long passage to be cut was the episode at the end of the poem when, against the calm moonlight of the harbour bay, the Mariner saw the dead men standing up, the right arm of each burning like a torch, their stony eye-balls glittering. This vision (drawn perhaps, as Lowes points out, from the tradition known as the 'Hand of Glory') may have been removed on artistic grounds, Coleridge feeling that the final scene did not

need yet another infusion of horror, yet it can be seen to add to a
pattern of interplay between forms and energies that has run
through the whole poem, bringing out the subtle relationship
between the powers of life and death throughout nature.

When Coleridge revised the poem again for *Sibylline Leaves*
(where it appeared for the first time under his own authorship) the
'Argument' disappeared altogether, to be replaced by the passage
adapted from Thomas Burnet's *Archaeologiae Philosophicae*. Its
interpretative function was now taken up by the marginal glosses,
written apparently in the person of an ancient scribe, who
develops the theme of hospitality both directly, in the account of
the Mariner's crime, and indirectly, in the beautiful description of
the ceremonious movements of the stars above – moving up the
blue sky as 'their native country and their natural homes, which
they enter unannounced, as lords that are certainly expected . . .'

There are some fine additions to the 1817 version. The
description of the Storm-blast (lines 41–50) is vivid and arresting,
even if it forfeits the direct address of the original ('Listen Stranger!
Storm and Wind . . . !'). In the scene on shipboard after the
departure of the spectre-ship, the fearfulness of the scene is brought
out directly in the vivid imagery of the steersman's face in the
lamplight and the dew dripping from the sails. These lines were first
written down in 1806, after Coleridge had undertaken a long sea-
voyage for the first time. The experience of actually travelling on
board a ship also produced a less happy alteration, from 'The
furrow followed free' (line 100) to 'The furrow streamed off free' –
a line which might be more accurate but broke the run of
assonance. Coleridge evidently recognized the fact, since after
having introduced it in the 1817 edition he dropped it in the next.

The main effect of the glosses is ambiguous. At a first reading
they give the poem a more overtly Christian appearance: the
water-snakes become 'God's creatures of the great calm' and the
Mariner's invocation of his guardian saint and belief in the power
of Mary, which might otherwise be read as endearing supersti-
tions, are reinforced by being endorsed in the commentary as
well. The Mariner's belief in the existence of spirits, meanwhile, is
supported by the scribe's long note referring the reader to
authorities such as Josephus and Michael Psellus.

Coleridge's decision to add such points may well have sprung
from a recognition that the story of the poem as it stood was
puzzling. As some later critics have pointed out, the moral point

of the poem in its original form is by no means clear. The separate fates whereby the Mariner who actually killed the albatross is permitted to live, whereas his shipmates, whose only crime was to approve the deed once it was performed, die in fearful torments do not readily accord with our notions of just deserts. The means by which these fates are determined, Death winning the shipmates and Life-in-Death the Mariner purely on a turn of the dice, adds to the sense that a cruel wantonness is at work. And the 'supernatural machinery' of the tale, as a whole, in which events occur in an apparently random manner, gives little evidence that a moral design is being worked out.

Although the marginal glosses play down the effects of such uncertainties by emphasizing the benevolence of the power behind them, it does not cause them to disappear. One or two indications of cosmic wantonness had been removed in the earlier revision (in the original description of the Storm and Wind, 'For days and weeks it play'd us freaks' and the final vision of the dead men added to the sense of arbitrariness) but no real reason is offered, even now, as to why the killing of a single albatross should have resulted in such excessive suffering on the part of so many human beings, nor why such an experience should seem an appropriate occasion for the teaching of the necessity to love 'all things both great and small'. In that sense the introduction of the glosses only serves to obscure the issues, since an inquiring reader may be tempted to conclude that the scribe whom we figure as having written them was even more deluded than the Mariner. On such a reading, indeed, the poem may seem to be the vehicle of a savage irony.

Coleridge himself was aware of the problem. Late in life he told how his contemporary Mrs Barbauld had once objected that the poem had no moral, to which he had rejoined that in his opinion it had too much, and that it ought to have had no more moral than that of the *Arabian Nights*' tale in which a merchant sits down to eat and throws a date-stone over his shoulder — whereupon a genie rises up and tells him that he must die because the date-stone has killed his son. I have suggested in the commentary above (pp. 209–13) the kind of interpretative pattern that was probably in Coleridge's mind when he originally wrote the poem, a pattern which drew on Coleridge's sense at the time that the energies of the universe, which made up the 'one life' in all things, were a key to understanding the true relationship between human beings and the natural universe on the one hand, and between them and the God who created them on the other. On those terms the Catholicism in the poem was merely being used to indicate the powers that were concealed by – and misunderstood in – superstitious beliefs. If read so, the poem was intended not as a straightforward moral allegory but as a shock-tactic to awaken readers to the true nature of the universe in which they lived and the need to live by that union of heart and imagination which was awakened in the Mariner only by his sufferings. In 1817, on the other hand, Coleridge was aware that few, if any, of his readers had discovered any such point in the poem; nor would he have been altogether happy by then if they had done so, since such a view would have seemed to him dangerously pantheistic and even arrogant. The introduction of the marginal glosses allowed the Christian reader to be less puzzled by the poem, since it encouraged a reading in more conventional terms. A more perceptive reader, on the other hand, might still see that the poem remained a puzzle. The possibility of finding an interpretation in more esoteric terms was thus retained: the distancing of the glosses into a past which belonged to much the same period as the poem's events could work to either end. The device enabled Coleridge to emphasize his main injunction that human beings ought to learn to cultivate the virtues of love and imaginative sympathy, while not altogether forfeiting the larger possibilities of human enlightenment, which continued to haunt him.

The printing of the poem in its 1798 version enables the reader to sense more fully both the urgency of the original form and the strange contradictions which the poem embodied, dating from a time when Coleridge was particularly fascinated by the ambiguous and vivid energies of nature, and the ancient mythologies that seemed to reflect them.


### COLERIDGE'S USE OF OLDER WORDS

The stock of words, out of date in his own time, which Coleridge occasionally draws on in his poems (and particularly *The Ancient Mariner*) seems to have derived more from memory of his accumulated reading than from any investigation undertaken especially for the purpose.

Few, indeed, would have been unfamiliar to a reader well acquainted with previous English poetry. Several, including 'eftsoons' (soon afterwards), 'clomb' (climbed) and 'swound' (swoon), had been used by Spenser (by whose time they were already becoming, or had become, out of date); some had then passed into the work of later poets such as Thomson. 'Eldritch', a more uncommon Scottish word meaning 'hideous', which had appeared in the ballads and in Burns, was used only in the first edition of *The Ancient Mariner*, after which it was dropped.

In some cases, Coleridge's usages would seem to be imprecise. His use of 'gramercy' meaning 'God have mercy!' may well rest upon Johnson's apparent misunderstanding of certain texts, where the term really means 'thank you'; when used in the sense taken up by Coleridge it had normally appeared in the form 'gramercies'. The form 'shrieve' (for shrive) is regarded by the editors of the *Oxford English Dictionary* as 'pseudo-archaic'. Nor is it clear what Coleridge had in mind when he used the phrase 'Broad as a weft' in the 1798 edition to describe the sun's going down into the sea. It is conceivable that some image from weaving was in his mind (even that he might have thought of a kind of bobbin, which would at least fit the visual image) or that he was simply thinking of a weft of cloud stretched across the sky. J. L. Lowes, on the other hand, pointed out that a weft was also the name for a rolled ensign, flown at sea in times of distress.

In general, the sweeping pace of the poem carries such usages in its stride, and modern readers are likely to have little difficulty in following the sense. Nor should they, in their search for exact meanings, miss Coleridge's evident enjoyment of simple quaintnesses of sound, as in 'eftsoons'. Occasionally, however, further investigation proves useful: it is clear, for example, that the Spenserian word 'ivy-tod' must refer to some formation of ivy, but only resort to a good dictionary will establish that it is an ivy-*bush* that is in question.

# COLERIDGE AND HIS CRITICS[1]

Some of the best criticism Coleridge received during his lifetime came as early as 1796–7, from his friend Charles Lamb, whose injunction to 'cultivate simplicity' was quoted in the Introduction. In spite of having given such advice Lamb was much attracted to Coleridge's conceptions of the sublime. *Religious Musings*, he wrote, was 'the noblest poem in the language, next after the Paradise lost, & even that was not made the vehicle of such grand truths'. In the same way he much admired the *Ode on the Departing Year*, though his criticisms were interlaced with subtle points of detail.

The opening, he wrote,

> is in the spirit of sublimest allegory. The idea of the 'Skirts of the departing year, seen far onwards, waving on the wind' is one of those noble Hints at which the Reader's imagination is apt to kindle into grand conceptions. – Do the words 'impetuous' & 'solemnize' harmonize well in the same line? Think & judge.

Later, similarly, he devoted some attention to the 'Antistrophe' (i.e. ll. 62–73):

> The Antistrophe that follows is not inferior in grandeur or original: but is I think not faultless v: g: How is Memory *alone*, when all the etherial multitude are there. Reflect. – Again 'storiedst thy sad hours' is harsh, I need not tell you, but you have gained your point in expressing much meaning in few words. 'Purple locks & snow white Glories', 'mild Arcadians, ever blooming', 'seas of milk & ships of amber' – these are things the muse talks about, when to borrow H. Walpole's witty phrase, she is not finely-phrenzied, only a little light headed, that's all –. 'Purple locks'? – they may manage things differently in fairy land, but your 'golden tresses' are to my fancy. The spirit of the Earth is a most happy conceit: and the last line is one of the luckiest I ever heard – '*& stood up beautiful* before the cloudy seat' – I cannot enough admire it. 'Tis somehow picturesque in the very sound.

[1]For most of my nineteenth-century examples I am deeply indebted to the volumes *Coleridge: The Critical Heritage*, edited by J. R. de J. Jackson (1970, 1991), to which readers are referred for further details.

When Coleridge, collaborating with Southey on *Joan of Arc*, tried to introduce some realistic detail in the poem, in a passage (*The Destiny of Nations*, ll. 162–78) that was not unlike Wordsworth's writing at that time, by describing how as a child she had ministered to passing travellers, Lamb was not sympathetic:

> You cannot surely mean to degrade the Joan of Arc into a pot girl; you are not going, I hope, to annex to that most splendid ornament of Southey's poem all this cock & a bull story of Joan the Publican's daughter of Neufchatel, with the lamentable episode of a waggoner, his wife & six children, the texture will be most lamentably disproportionate. The first 40 or 50 lines of these addenda are no doubt in their way admirable too, but many would prefer the Joan of Southey, 'on mightiest deeds to brood Of shadowy vastness, such as made my heart throb fast. Anon I paus'd & in a state of half expectance listen'd to the wind.'

Lamb offered many more criticisms during this period; he also encouraged Coleridge in his plan to write a poem on the Origin of Evil – a plan which may have found oblique fulfilment in *The Ancient Mariner*. Coleridge was never again to receive sustained criticism of so careful and acute a kind. Although he profited from his intercourse with Wordsworth, the benefits were less direct; and indeed his friend's decision to give *The Ancient Mariner* a subordinate position in the second edition of *Lyrical Ballads*, subtitling it 'A Poet's Reverie', must have been positively discouraging.

The fact that the form of that poem owed a great deal not to the English ballads but to the more regular form of the contemporary German ballad, with its use of strong internal rhymes (compare the lines 'The steed is wight, the spur is bright,/The flashing pebbles flee', in Scott's translation of Bürger with Coleridge's 'The fair breeze blew, the white foam flew,/The furrow followed free', for example) was to be missed by most critics writing afterwards, while those contemporaries who noticed such an influence disliked it: an anonymous critic wrote, 'In our opinion it has more of the extravagance of a mad german poet, than of the simplicity of our ancient ballad writers', while Southey called it 'a Dutch attempt at german sublimity'. In response Lamb countered that it was 'a right English attempt, and a successful one, to dethrone german sublimity'. *Lyrical Ballads* as a whole found little approval among the reviewers, contemporaries responding more favourably to the concurrently published *Fears in Solitude* and

*Frost at Midnight*. Young writers such as Hazlitt and De Quincey, on the other hand, found the volume exciting – 'the ray of a new morning'.

During the next fifteen years Coleridge confined his poetic output largely to individual poems, published usually in newspapers, with the result that there was no opportunity to judge his work on a large scale. In 1816, encouraged by Lord Byron, he published *Kubla Khan*, along with *The Pains of Sleep* (which could be regarded as a companion piece, warning against the results of opium) and *Christabel*. Unfortunately, he was in favour neither with the conservatives (who still recalled his early radicalism) nor with the radicals, who were coming to see him as a renegade. This fact, combined with the fact that two of the poems were presented in fragmentary form, boded ill for the poem. The fact that Byron had described *Christabel* as a 'wild and singularly original and beautiful poem' did not help matters: 'That the poem of "Christabel" is wild and singular cannot be denied,' wrote William Roberts, 'and if this be not eulogy sufficient let it be allowed to be original'; nevertheless it remained a 'weak and singularly nonsensical and affected performance'. Thomas Moore, writing in the *Edinburgh Review*, described the volume as 'one of the most notable pieces of impertinence of which the press has lately been guilty', and as 'utterly destitute of value', defying any man to point out a passage of poetical merit – apart, perhaps, from the passage beginning 'Alas! they had been friends in youth,' in *Christabel*. He continued by attacking Coleridge from a political point of view:

> Must we then be doomed to hear such a mixture of raving and driv'ling, extolled as the work of a '*wild and original*' genius, simply because Mr Coleridge has now and then written fine verses, and a brother poet chooses, in his milder mood, to laud him from courtesy or from interest? And are such panegyrics to be echoed by the mean tools of a political faction, because they relate to one whose daily prose is understood to be dedicated to the support of all that courtiers think should be supported? If it be true that the author has thus earned the patronage of those liberal dispensers of bounty, we can have no objection that they should give him proper proofs of their gratitude; but we cannot help wishing, for his sake, as well as our own, that they would pay in solid pudding instead of empty praise.

Hazlitt trickled similar criticisms on the poem, accompanied by a darker innuendo:

There is something disgusting at the bottom of his subject, which is but ill glossed over by a veil of Della Cruscan sentiment and fine writing – like moon-beams playing on a charnel-house, or flowers strewn on a dead body.

A tale had been spread abroad, it seems, that Geraldine was a man in disguise. Hazlitt then went on to praise the very same passage as Moore, asking,

Why does not Mr Coleridge always write in this manner, that we might always read him? *Kubla Khan*, we think, only shews that Mr Coleridge can write better *nonsense* verses than any man in England. It is not a poem but a musical composition.

Yet his final comment, 'We could repeat these lines to ourselves not the less often for not knowing the meaning of them', suggests that he was more responsive than some other critics to this poem (which he may well have heard Coleridge read aloud in person). He was not alone. A reviewer in the *Literary Panorama* commented on Coleridge's 'strong powers of thought, with a command of original and striking images, united to those softer touches of nature which speak at once to the heart'. Others, again, dwelt on the poet's current state as one of weakness, expressing a hope that he would 'yet awake in his strength', as one of them put it.

Even while some reviewers were attacking Coleridge's writing, a new generation was coming to the fore which found it deeply inspiring. The enthusiasm of Byron and Keats was surpassed by that of Shelley, who much admired Coleridge both for the imaginative radicalism of a poem such as *France: An Ode* and for his visionary metaphysics, seeing him, in the context of the contemporary literary world, as 'a hooded eagle among blinking owls'.

Hazlitt's description of *Kubla Khan* as 'not a poem, but a musical composition' pointed a way forward for some subsequent critics, who saw that poetry of this kind might need to be read in a new way. The tide could be said to have turned in 1819 with an article by J. G. Lockhart in *Blackwood's Edinburgh Magazine*. For once there was hardly a word of criticism; Lockhart claimed that *The Ancient Mariner* 'is a poem to be felt, cherished, mused upon, not to be talked about, not capable of being described, analyzed, or criticized. It is the wildest of all the creations of genius, it is not like a thing of the living, listening, moving world. . .' If Coleridge would finish *Christabel*, likewise, he would probably make it 'the finest exemplification to be found in the English, or perhaps in any language since Homer's, of an idea which may be traced in most popular superstitions'.

In 1821 Coleridge's nephew H. N. Coleridge wrote a piece for *The Etonian* in which he praised Coleridge as a poet of feeling: 'The purity of his feelings is unequalled; yet with seeming contradiction, they are ardent, impatient, and contemplative. It is Petrarch and Shakespeare transfused into each other. It is, if I may be allowed so fanciful an illustration, the Midsummer Moonlight of Love Poetry.' In the same year Leigh Hunt wrote a long piece in which he was able to draw on a long familiarity with Coleridge's reputation, having been at Christ's Hospital just after he left. Among other things this had made him aware of Coleridge's longstanding taste for imaginative metaphysical speculations:

> Mr Coleridge began with metaphysics when at school; and what the boy begins with, the man will end with, come what will between. He does not turn metaphysical upon the strength of his poetry, like Spenser and Tasso; but poet upon the strength of his metaphysics.

Hunt could also see that the best way of appraising a poem such as *Kubla Khan* might be to write a poetic prose of one's own:

> *Kubla Khan* is a voice and a vision, an everlasting tune in our mouths, a dream fit for Cambuscan and all his poets, a dance of pictures such as Giotto or Cimabue, revived and re-inspired, would have made for a Storie of Old Tartarie, a piece of the invisible world made visible by a sun at midnight and sliding before our eyes.

From this time forward the balance of opinion in the reviews was in Coleridge's favour. In 1830 an essay appeared in the *Westminster Review* (founded a few years previously) from the pen of John Bowring, a friend of Jeremy Bentham's. Bowring made a connection (which he admitted his readers might find unexpected, though it was to be traced in more detail some years later by J. S. Mill) between Coleridge's mind and Bentham's. He was particularly drawn to Coleridge's habit of meditating in verse, which led him to poems other than the three 'supernatural' ones:

> They are exhibitions of the writer's mind under certain circumstances or influences. They shew what at least appear to be its involuntary trains of thought and feeling. Few minds could be so exposed with any very pleasurable results to writer or reader. The process is a test of the

strength or weakness, the wealth or poverty of the intellect, and of its poetical and moral qualities. It is a sort of Algebraic equation (this article is an attempt to work it), in which the circumstances and the result, are known or given quantities, and the author's intellectual rank, the unknown quantity, to be discovered by their means. The solution scarcely leaves Mr Coleridge an equal amongst the philosophical poets of our country.

Bowring's article was swiftly countered by the writer of an unsigned article in the *Athenaeum* who took exception to the idea that Coleridge's mind was best exhibited in his poetry, arguing on the contrary that Coleridge's intellectual achievements, for all their difficulty, were best to be appreciated by those who were willing to wrestle with the prose of one who, 'more successfully than all other Englishmen, has laboured to reconcile the speculative understanding with the instinctive consciousness'.

By 1834, the year of Coleridge's death, the bearings of his nineteenth-century reputation had been set. The popularity of his poem *Genevieve* (printed in the present collection as *Love*) was foreshadowed by an anonymous reviewer who asked ' . . . where has what may be called the metaphysics of the heart – that subtle music of "all impulses of soul and sense" – been so charmingly developed, or set to such exquisite music, as in "Genevieve"?' In the same year a long and thoughtful piece on Coleridge as poet greeted the appearance of the last edition published in his lifetime. The author was almost certainly the editor of that collection, Henry Nelson Coleridge, who was evidently taking the opportunity to draw on the work that he had carried out on it in conjunction with Coleridge in such a way as to bring out what he regarded as most important in his achievement. Once again he dwelt on the musical element in Coleridge's verse, supplementing what he was saying by an account of Coleridge's manner of reading a poem such as *Kubla Khan* aloud:

> It is not rhetorical, but musical: so very near recitative, that for any one else to attempt it would be ridiculous; and yet it is perfectly miraculous with what exquisite searching he elicits and makes sensible every particle of the meaning, not leaving a shadow of a shade of the feeling, the mood, the degree, untouched.

After H. N. Coleridge's essay there was to be no major critical essay devoted to Coleridge's poetry alone for a quarter of a century. In his excellent essay of 1855 on Coleridge's thought, however, F. J. A. Hort devoted a few pages to this aspect of his achievement. He was particularly interested in the poems of the supernatural and their relationship to the 'actual spiritual powers':

> For the purposes of poetry, which can only deal in the concrete, they must needs assume a separate existence, and become extranatural as well as supernatural. This is in truth the secret of Coleridge's success in what is incorrectly called his skill in treating the supernatural. The human fancy has always a tendency to conjure up beings in which the imagination sees symbols of the truly supernatural; and then, when a man or nation or age has lost its imagination, superstition steps in, and the creatures of fancy become *substitutes* for the true unseen world, and men believe in ghosts because they have ceased to believe in anything above nature in themselves or higher than themselves. But Coleridge never cuts off his 'spirits' from the rest of creation; they are not ghosts haunting an alien earth, but have their appropriate homes in some region of land, or air, or water. If it be answered that in this he is but following popular dreams, so let it be: the dreams of ignorant childhood are, it is true, no more than dreams (whatever that may be), but they differ widely from the dreams of remorse or madness. Coleridge takes pains to let us see the mere stuff of which they are made: he dissolves them into the common sights and sounds of nature; and, when they have passed quite away, the mystery of their power is thenceforth transferred to nature herself, and eye and ear bear messages to and fro in a language not their own.

Hort was also highly appreciative of the way in which Coleridge had achieved a poetic revolution against writers of the eighteenth century, with their constantly held balance between rhyme and rhyme:

> In the hands of that polished school, the art of versification consisted in cutting down the pleasant hilly road into a level or decorously inclined railway, along which the voice slid with gathering momentum to the grand shock at the final goal. One great mechanical change made by Coleridge was of itself a thorough revolution, that is to say, what he called reckoning by accents instead of syllables; in other words, the occasional and temperate use of feet unequal in length, at least in numerical length. By introducing at the same time new forms of metre, he became indirectly the fashioner of the best known poetry of the present century, from *The Lay of the Last Minstrel* onwards. Yet these, after all, are only modes of composition: their greatest value is, that they were able to furnish an appropriate body to that deep and spiritual music which heaves and plays through so many of Coleridge's

poems, and which has flowed from him into the great master of our own generation.

In those years writers on Coleridge were usually dwelling on his religious writings, particularly his emphasis on spirituality. Even in the 1880s, when Matthew Arnold was producing the studies of major poets which were to form his second series of *Essays in Criticism*, he produced essays on four of the five Romantic poets who were best known in his time – Wordsworth, Keats, Shelley and Byron – but none on Coleridge, the expression of his opinions being limited to a few remarks in his 1865 essay on Joubert. One reason must have been the ambiguous reputation of Coleridge as a thinker in the years after his death – a reputation which combined a sense of his importance as an important spiritual teacher with reservations concerning his moral failings.

By the 1860s, nevertheless, the moral certitude that had characterized writing such as Arnold's had been affected by the impact of Darwin's ideas, with the result that critics began to be aware of the importance of thinking in relativist terms. In these circumstances, Coleridge's 'music' seemed more relevant to the times. Walter Pater, choosing Coleridge as the subject of his first major published essay, wrote of the age:

Forms of intellectual and spiritual culture often exercise their subtlest and most artful charm when life is already passing from them. Searching and irresistible as are the changes of the human spirit on its way to perfection, there is yet so much elasticity of temper that what must pass away sooner or later is not disengaged all at once even from the highest order of minds. Nature, which by one law of development evolves ideas, moralities, modes of inward life, and represses them in turn, has in this way provided that the earlier growth should propel its fibres into the later, and so transmit the whole of its forces in an unbroken continuity of life. Then comes the spectacle of the reserve of the elder generation exquisitely refined by the antagonism of the new. That current of new life chastens them as they contend against it. Weaker minds do not perceive the change, clearer minds abandon themselves to it. To feel the change everywhere, yet not to abandon oneself to it, is a situation of difficulty and contention. Communicating in this way to the passing stage of culture the charm of what is chastened, high-strung, athletic, they yet detach the highest minds from the past by pressing home its difficulties and finally proving it impossible. Such is the charm of Julian, of St Louis, perhaps of Luther; in the narrower compass of modern times, of Dr Newman and Lacordaire; it is also the peculiar charm of Coleridge.

Pater did not altogether approve of Coleridge's temperament, writing of a 'faintness and obscure dejection which cling like some contagious damp to all his writings' – as against the *élan* which he found everywhere in Wordsworth. Wordsworth, he believed knew how to limit his conviction of a latent intelligence in nature, whereas in Coleridge it stiffened into a formula. Pater saw Coleridge, nevertheless, as 'the perfect flower of the Romantic type', representing 'that inexhaustible discontent, languor, and home-sickness, the chords of which ring all through our modern literature'. Although he identified himself rather with the Greek spirit, 'with its engaging naturalness, simple, chastened, debonair', Coleridge, 'with his passion for the absolute, for something fixed where all is moving', remained for him 'among the interpreters of one of the constituent elements of our life'.

A decade later Swinburne wrote in more exalted terms. Again he was held back by a sense of valetudinarianism in the poet:

Some poems, touched with exquisite grace, with clear and pure harmony, are tainted with somewhat of feeble and sickly which impairs our relish; 'Lewti', for instance, an early sample of his admirable melody, of tender colour and dim grace as of clouds, but effeminate in build, loose hung, weak of eye and foot. Yet nothing of more precious and rare sweetness exists in verse than that stanza of the swans disturbed [ll. 57–75]. His style indeed was a plant of strangely slow growth, but perfect and wonderful in its final flower. Even in the famous verses called 'Love', he has not attained to that strength and solidity of beauty which was his special gift at last. For melody rather than for harmony it is perfect; but in this œnomel there is as yet more of honey than of wine.

His account of *The Ancient Mariner* echoed a number of previous critics in praising its vividnesses, but also drew a notable distinction concerning Coleridge's 'feminine' qualities and firmly emphasized the 'organic' nature of his artistry:

The 'Ancient Mariner' has doubtless more of breadth and space, more of material force and motion, than anything else of the poet's. And the tenderness of sentiment which touches with significant colour the pure white imagination is here no longer morbid or languid, as in the earlier poems of feeling and emotion. It is soft and piteous enough, but womanly rather than effeminate; and thus serves indeed to set off the strange splendours and boundless beauties of the story. For the execution, I presume no human eye is too dull to see how perfect it is, and how high in kind of perfection. Here is not the speckless and elaborate finish which shows everywhere the fresh rasp of file or chisel on its smooth and spruce excellence; this is faultless after the fashion of a flower or a tree. Thus it has grown: not thus has it been carved.

As might be expected, the idea of *Kubla Khan* as a 'musical' poem appealed particularly to Swinburne, who called it

perhaps the most wonderful of all poems. In reading it we seem rapt into that paradise revealed to Swedenborg, where music and colour and perfume were one, where you could hear the hues and see the harmonies of heaven. For absolute melody and splendour it were hardly rash to call it the first poem in the language. An exquisite instinct married to a subtle science of verse has made it the supreme model of music in our language, a model unapproachable except by Shelley.

In an aside Swinburne also pointed to a feature of Coleridge's writing which linked him to contemporary conceptions of orientalism: 'All through this brilliant course we may discern the power of the Asiatic temperament, of that voluptuousness which is perhaps connected with his appreciation of the intimacy, the almost mystical *rapport* between man and nature.' He also gave time to Coleridge's other writings, praising *France: An Ode* for its 'noble and loyal love of freedom, though less fiery at once and less firm than Shelley's, as it proved in the end less durable and deep'. *Remorse* he found more notable for its lyrical or reflective interludes than for the dramatic writing; in the case of *Zapolya*, similarly, there was 'little enough indeed of high dramatic quality, but a native grace and ease which give it something of the charm of life'. His admiration for some of the later poems, on the other hand, was unqualified:

Of such later work as the divine verses on 'Youth and Age', 'The Garden of Boccaccio', sun-bright and honey-sweet, 'Work without Hope', (what more could be left to hope for when the man could already do such work?) – of these, and of how many more! what can be said but that they are perfect, flawless, priceless?

With the growth in popularity of an 'impressionist' Coleridge, critics responded more readily to the subtlety of his mind. Writing in 1889, Edward Dowden avowed that 'it would need Coleridge the critic to discover the secret of Coleridge the poet' and worked on from a memorable image in *The Picture* (ll. 92–4):

> All that phantom-world so fair
> Vanishes, and a thousand circlets spread,
> And each mis-shape the other

The description might stand for that of Coleridge's own poetry personified, with its visionary beauty and its harmony of exquisite colours; and what shall be said of the critic who flings his heavy stone of formula and scatters the loveliness?

Dowden also continued the Victorian tradition by finding Coleridge's greatest qualities as a poet in his ability to depict human love and in the strange co-existence of this with imaginative powers that seemed at times almost unearthly:

> If we would express the whole truth about Coleridge as a poet, we must find some mode of reconciling the conception of him as the footless bird of paradise with our knowledge of his affluent and sweet humanity.

Even while Coleridge was being praised for his humanity, however, the collecting and publishing of his correspondence and the discovery of other biographically relevant material, as in the notebooks, was drawing attention to his contradictions as a human being. Leslie Stephen, who had been given access to some of these materials, was sardonic about Coleridge's career – and indeed about some aspects of *The Ancient Mariner*, commenting that 'the moral, which would apparently be that people who sympathize with a man who shoots an albatross will die in prolonged torture of thirst, is open to obvious objections'. Yet he also perceived, like Hort, the subtlety of Coleridge's mind, the intricacy of which emerged most fully in that poem. Although not able to read all its riddles in full, he paid tribute to their power:

> The germ of all Coleridge's utterances may be found – by a little ingenuity – in the 'Ancient Mariner'. For what is the secret of the strange charm of that unique achievement? I do not speak of what may be called its purely literary merits – the melody of versification, the command of language, the vividness of the descriptive passages, and so forth – I leave such points to critics of finer perception and a greater command of superlatives. But part, at least, of the secret is the ease with which Coleridge moves in a world of which the machinery (as the old critics called it) is supplied by the mystic philosopher . . . It is a world in which both animated things, and stones, and brooks, and clouds, and plants are moved by spiritual agency; in which, as he would put it, the veil of the senses is nothing but a symbolism

everywhere telling of unseen and supernatural forces. What we call the solid and the substantial becomes a dream; and the dream is the true underlying reality.

With the brief triumph of liberalism in the first decade of the twentieth century, Coleridge was read enthusiastically by rising members of the new generation such as D. H. Lawrence and his friends. One of the most attractive accounts came from Sir Arthur Quiller-Couch in the introduction to his 1907 edition of the *Poems*. On the question whether Coleridge's influence on Wordsworth was greater than that of Wordsworth on him he drew attention to the fact that Coleridge had been producing a 'Wordsworthian' note in some of his meditative poems before Wordsworth himself did so. Praise of a special kind was reserved for one poem in particular: 'Still, after more than a hundred years, *The Ancient Mariner* is the wild thing of wonder, the captured star, which Coleridge brought in his hands to Alfoxden and showed to Dorothy and William Wordsworth.'

To Coleridge's thought Quiller-Couch paid relatively little attention, being more concerned with the effects on him of his opium-taking and his partly successful struggle to wean himself of the habit. His tendency to follow the description which Coleridge himself had given of *The Ancient Mariner* as 'a poem of the pure imagination', and so to believe that it contained very little thought, was not uncommon at the time, receiving powerful support with the advent of Amy Lowell and the Imagist movement. In 1927 John Livingston Lowes, who worked, like her, in Boston, produced *The Road to Xanadu*, which had as its subtitle 'A Study in the Ways of the Imagination'. Lowes's approach was constructed around the belief that *The Ancient Mariner* and *Kubla Khan* owed their value as poems to their imaginative quality, which was independent of any meanings they might contain, and that the work of the imagination could be traced by careful study to travel books that Coleridge was known to have read, where the source of a vivid phrase was often to be found. When he turns to Coleridge's thought, accordingly, we find him writing contemptuously of 'a mist of Godwinian and Berkeleyian speculations' and declaring of Neoplatonism, 'With the nebulous and grandiose speculations which resulted, we have nothing whatever to do.' While his book is a splendid example of what can be done by simply attending to the work of the poetic imagination, the two poems he is discussing are gradually set apart in an enclave of their own, while the fact that the poetic imagination might actually work more effectively in some contexts when dealing with metaphysical issues could find no place in his Imagist scheme of things.

In the case of *Kubla Khan*, moreover, some of Lowes's conclusions diminish in power once it is recognized that in some instances the particular sources he has found can be supplemented by many others, so that their presence comes to be seen as over-determined rather than fortuitous. Studied in their contexts, also, they may be seen to link with trains of symbolism in which Coleridge was interested.

Critics were not likely to ignore the latter range of possibilities forever, particularly as the advent of more and more of Coleridge's writings such as letters and notebooks gave further evidence of his tendency to think in symbolic terms. The possibility of a different kind of reading from Lowes's came to the fore in 1946, with Robert Penn Warren's essay 'A Poem of the Pure Imagination'. Warren took issue with those who held that it was wrong to look for ideas in the poem, commenting,

> I trust that I am not more insensitive than most to the 'magical lines', but at the same time I cannot admit that our experience, even our aesthetic experience, is ineluctably and vindictively divided into the 'magical' and the rational, with an abyss between. If poetry does anything for us, it reconciles, by its symbolical reading of experience (for by its very nature it is in itself a myth of the unity of being), the self-divisive internecine malices which arise at the superficial level on which we conduct most of our living.

He further maintained not only that Coleridge's use of images such as the sun and moon contained strong symbolic implications, but that these were fairly straightforward, the moon being identifiable with the imagination and the sun with the understanding, the 'reflective faculty that partakes of death'. 'Good' events, he maintained, took place under the aegis of the moon, 'bad' under that of the sun, and the whole poem could be read in terms of a 'sacramental vision', that of the 'one Life', which the Mariner violated and to which he must be restored.

Once such possibilities began to be explored, Warren's scheme, for all its attractiveness and initial plausibility, was seen as not fitting squarely with the detailed events of the poem. In my 1959 study *Coleridge the Visionary* I agreed that there was indeed symbolism in the poem but argued that it was more intricate than in Warren's account, answering to a much more complex skein of symbolic thinking by Coleridge as he tried to elaborate a new mythology for his age and to find evidences for its existence in earlier myths and images. The newly fashionable Swedenborgianism, which had recently been influencing Blake in a similar fashion, read certain elements in nature such as the sun as symbolic of spiritual truths. If taken in conjunction with the myth of Isis and Osiris, the destructive heat and largely powerless light of sun and moon respectively might be viewed as a fallen dialectic which yet shadowed out the true tempering of heat and light of the spiritual sun. On such a reading it followed that in *The Ancient Mariner* both sun and moon were ambiguous symbols, which in different circumstances could indicate either benevolence or cruelty, the central point of benevolence being traceable in the dawn vision when the spirits of the dead men are seen flying back and forth between the ship and the sun in a harmony combining both light and sound.

The implications for Coleridge of such an esoteric knowledge have been discussed further in the Introduction (page xxi). The fragility of Warren's assertion that the poem was about a sacramental vision of the universe was emphasized further when E. E. Bostetter wrote his 1962 essay 'The Nightmare World of *The Ancient Mariner*'. Bostetter pointed out that any large interpretation on symbolic lines ran the risk of suggesting that the world of *The Ancient Mariner* was to be conceived basically as benevolent, in spite of the fact that an intelligent reader coming to that world directly was more likely to see it as nightmarish. The fact that the fates both of the Mariner and of his shipmates were initiated in the poem by a pair of people casting dice seemed far removed from a benevolent and sacramental order; and it was (as Leslie Stephen had pointed out) not easy to make sense of those fates in simple moral terms.

The question of the poem's moral has continued, and will continue, to be argued; it may be that the poem is best approached as a dramatization of problems that Coleridge himself had not solved – problems set up by the imaginatively convincing quality of his own myth-making and the power of the vision of nature he was sharing with the Wordsworths in 1798, in contrast with his brutal awareness of human obtuseness and the arbitrary wantonness of events in the natural world.

In an essay of 1946, 'The Mariner and the Albatross', George Whalley demonstrated the extraordinary degree to which it is also possible to read *The Ancient Mariner* as a personal allegory of Coleridge's own career, with its constant weight of guilt over actions that might have seemed of little importance at the time he undertook them. There is something fascinating in the idea of a poet setting out an allegory which he then proceeds to live out almost against his will; it is certainly the case that in later life Coleridge sometimes used lines from the poem to describe his own condition. He often saw himself as one passing through human life in the form of an alienated stranger; in Malta (reached after a voyage which, as I pointed out in the Introduction, reminded him at times of the one projected in his poem) he wrote on one occasion, 'I raise my limbs "like lifeless *Tools*".'

Lowes refrained from commenting on *Christabel*, stating that the tracts of the imagination from which they arose were off the road that led to the two poems with which he had concerned himself, and that the 'elusive clue' was 'still to capture'. A few years later, A. H. Nethercot published *The Road to Tryermaine*, in which he claimed to have found the requisite clues, primarily in Hutchinson's *History of Cumberland* and in works on witch-craft. Nethercot's approach did not prove as effective as Lowes's, however, one reason being that the sources he found, while sometimes persuasive, were more likely to have been from books to which Coleridge had turned for local colour or in-formation during the actual writing of his poem.

Swinburne thought *Christabel* the best of all Coleridge's poems. In the twentieth century it has not always received such high valuation, the somewhat child-like quality of its rhythms at times causing some to rate it below the other two. Discussion has focused on what Coleridge might have thought himself to be doing, and how he might have expected to end the poem. In particular, critics divide as to whether Geraldine is to be seen as basically good or evil, and it is possible that Coleridge himself was not sure. The idea of the poem was, on his own confession, 'a very difficult one', and that 'difficulty' may well have been an important factor in his failure to complete the poem; evaluating Geraldine is perhaps rather like evaluating energy. Charles Tomlinson's 1955 account examines the poem against both its context in the contemporary tale of terror and some considerations raised by twentieth-century surrealism. My own view is presented above in this volume.

The nature of the experience that gave rise to *Kubla Khan* also continues to provide matter for debate. Coleridge's own assertion that it was composed in a reverie is backed by the Crewe manuscript, and by the fact that other cases of composition in a less-than-conscious state are known to have occurred – as in that of Coleridge's friend Mary Robinson. We do not need to accept every detail in the 1816 account to believe that the poem was composed in an unusual state of consciousness. Lowes's view, concerning the conclusion, that 'nobody in his waking senses could have fabricated those amazing eighteen lines', and his account of the manner in which they display 'the vivid incoherence, and the illusion of natural and expected sequence, and the sense of an identity that is yet not identity, which are the distinctive attributes of dreams', still deserve to be taken seriously. Those who consider that the poem was composed in full consciousness include Elisabeth Schneider, who dates the poem later (on rather shaky grounds) and believes it to have been constructed out of the Oriental works of Southey (rather than the other way round), and George Watson, who believes it to be a poem about poetry, with the first stanza representing Augustan verse while the second is the embodiment of Romantic.

Recent interests in historical and cultural context which have left their mark on criticism at the end of the twentieth century have directed attention back to the poems of the 1790s. Ian Wylie has drawn out the range of interests, linking contemporary scientific thinking of the kind associated with Joseph Priestley to older traditions in Neoplatonism and mythology, that can be found to underlie *Religious Musings*, while Kelvin Everest has examined his writing more largely against the radical thinking of that decade. George Dekker has thought about the poetry in relation to the literature of sensibility and Reeve Parker has looked at the traditions that lie behind its meditative elements. The various strands of psychological thinking, rooted in a distinctive philosophy of being, that run through much of the writing have been examined by Richard Haven and Edward Kessler and in my own *Coleridge's Poetic Intelligence*.

Yet on returning to the poetry after considering all these approaches, one will still be struck by qualities – more apparent to critics in the nineteenth century – which, though difficult to analyze, are likely to be picked up by any readers with a feeling for 'verbal music'. They remind us that Coleridge will always find readers who might be at a loss to explain exactly why they are so attracted so deeply to his work.

# SUGGESTIONS FOR FURTHER READING

## Collections of Poems

*Poems on Various Subjects* (1796; enlarged edition, 1797; new edition, 1803).
*Fears in Solitude, France: an Ode* and *Frost at Midnight* (1798).
*Lyrical Ballads* (with W. Wordsworth; 1798).
*Christabel, Kubla Khan, The Pains of Sleep* (1816).
*Sibylline Leaves* (1817).
*Poetical Works* (1828 and 1829).
*Poetical Works* (1834).
*Poetical Works*, ed. J. D. Campbell (1893).
*Complete Poetical Works*, ed. E. H. Coleridge (Oxford Standard Authors, 1912).

## Biographies

J. D. CAMPBELL, *Samuel Taylor Coleridge, A Narrative of the Events of his Life* (1894).
E. K. CHAMBERS, *Coleridge* (1938).
LAWRENCE HANSON, *The Life of S. T. Coleridge: The Early Years* (1938).
JOHN CORNWELL, *Coleridge: Poet and Revolutionary, 1772–1804* (1973).
ALETHEA HAYTER, *A Voyage in Vain* (1973; on the Malta years).
RICHARD HOLMES, *Coleridge, I: Early Visions* (1989).

## Studies of Coleridge the Poet

### I GENERAL

(a) *Nineteenth Century*
A. C. SWINBURNE, *Essays and Studies* (1875).
WALTER PATER, *Appreciations* (1889).
LESLIE STEPHEN, *Hours in a Library*, III (1892).

(b) *Twentieth Century*

J. L. LOWES, *The Road to Xanadu* (1927; second edition, 1930).

A. H. HOUSE, *Coleridge* (Clark Lectures; 1953).

J. B. BEER, *Coleridge the Visionary* (1959).

E. E. BOSTETTER, *The Romantic Ventriloquists* (1963).

M. F. SCHULZ, *The Poetic Voices of Coleridge* (1963).

G. G. WATSON, *Coleridge the Poet* (1966).

PATRICIA ADAIR, *The Waking Dream* (1967).

S. PRICKETT, *Coleridge and Wordsworth: The Poetry of Growth* (1970).

WILLIAM EMPSON, Introduction to *Coleridge's Verse: A Selection*, ed. with D. Pirie (1972).

REEVE PARKER, *Coleridge's Meditative Art* (1975).

J. B. BEER, *Coleridge's Poetic Intelligence* (1977).

G. DEKKER, *Coleridge and the Literature of Sensibility* (1978).

K. M. WHEELER, *The Creative Mind in Coleridge's Poetry* (1980).

THOMAS MCFARLAND, *Romanticism and the Forms of Ruin* (1981; particularly on Coleridge and Wordsworth and on Coleridge's anxiety).

J. S. HILL, *A Coleridge Companion* (1983).

## (c) Shorter Studies

KATHLEEN RAINE, *Coleridge*, Writers and their Work Series (1953).

R. WATTERS, *Coleridge*, Literature in Perspective Series (1971).

W. STEVENSON, *Nimbus of Glory: A Study of Coleridge's Three Great Poems* (1983).

## 2 SPECIAL TOPICS

### (a) The Ancient Mariner

M. BODKIN, *Archetypal Patterns in Poetry: Psychological Studies of Imagination* (1934).

G. WHALLEY, 'The Mariner and the Albatross', *UTQ* xvi (1946–7).

E. E. STOLL, 'Symbolism in Coleridge', *PMLA* lxiii (1948).

ELDER OLSON, 'A Symbolic Reading of "The Ancient Mariner"', *Critics and Criticism*, ed. R. S. Crane (1952).

R. L. BRETT, *Reason and Imagination: A Study of Form and Meaning in Four Poems* (1960).

E. E. BOSTETTER, 'The Nightmare World of "The Ancient Mariner"', *Studies in Romanticism*, I (1962).

R. PENN WARREN, 'A Poem of Pure Imagination' (1946), *Selected Essays* (1964).

M. GARDNER, ed., *The Annotated 'Ancient Mariner'*, with illustrations by Gustav Doré (1966).

J. B. BEER, 'Poems of the Supernatural' in *S. T. Coleridge*, ed. R. L. Brett (1971).

WILLIAM EMPSON, *Introduction to Coleridge's Verse: a Selection*, ed. Empson and Pirie (1972).

(b) *Christabel*

C. TOMLINSON, 'Christabel', *Interpretations*, ed. J. B. Wain (1955).

R. H. FOGLE, in *The Idea of Coleridge's Criticism* (1962).

A. H. NETHERCOT, *The Road to Tryermaine* (1962).

S. M. LUTHER, *'Christabel' as Dream-reverie* (1976).

A. J. HARDING, 'Mythopoesis: the unity of *Christabel*' in *Coleridge's Imagination*, ed. Gravil, Newlyn and Roe (1985).

(c) *Kubla Khan*

Discussed in books by Lowes, House, Beer and Watson (Section 1 (b) above). See also Elinor Shaffer, *'Kubla Khan' and The Fall of Jerusalem* (1975), and J. B. Beer, 'The Languages of *Kubla Khan*', in *Coleridge's Imagination*, ed. Gravil, Newlyn and Roe (1985).

(d) *Conversation Poems*

W. WALSH, *Coleridge: The Work and the Relevance* (1967), Ch. iii.

A. GÉRARD, *English Romantic Poetry: Ethos, Structure and Symbol in Coleridge, Wordsworth, Shelley and Keats* (1968).

D. PIRIE, 'A Letter to [Asra]', *Bicentenary Wordsworth Studies*, ed. J. Wordsworth (1970).

A. R. JONES, 'The Conversational and other Poems' in *S. T. Coleridge*, ed. R. L. Brett (1971).

REEVE PARKER, *Coleridge's Meditative Art* (1975).

KELVIN EVEREST, *Coleridge's Secret Ministry* (1979).

J. R. BARTH, 'Coleridge's *Dejection*' in *Coleridge's Imagination*, ed. Gravil, Newlyn and Roe (1985).

(e) *Other Topics*

G. WHALLEY, *Coleridge and Sara Hutchinson and the Asra Poems* (1955).

G. WHALLEY, 'Coleridge's debt to Charles Lamb', *Essays and Studies by Members of the English Association* (1958, NS. XI).

G. WILSON KNIGHT, *The Starlit Dome* (second edition, 1959).

H. W. PIPER, *The Active Universe* (1962; on scientific and philosophical themes).

STEPHEN PRICKETT, *Coleridge and Wordsworth: The Poetry of Growth* (1970).

N. FRUMAN, *Coleridge the Damaged Archangel* (1971; for details of Coleridge's poetic borrowings).

E. KESSLER, *Coleridge's Metaphors of Being* (1979).

LUCY NEWLYN, *Coleridge, Wordsworth and the Language of Allusion* (1986).

IAN WYLIE, *Young Coleridge and the Philosophers of Nature* (1989; on 'Religious Musings').

Collected studies of Coleridge's poetry (including some of those mentioned above) will be found in:

K. COBURN, ed., *Coleridge*, Twentieth Century Views Series (1967).

J. D. BOULGER, ed., *Twentieth Century Interpretations of 'The Rime of the Ancient Mariner'* (1969).

A. R. JONES and W. TYDEMAN, eds., *Coleridge: 'The Ancient Mariner' and other Poems; a Casebook* (1973).

For further studies of Coleridge's poetry and for a complete bibliography of his other works in prose, *The Cambridge Bibliography of English Literature* (revised edition, 1969) should be consulted; the fullest biography of all is *Samuel Taylor Coleridge: An Annotated Biography of Criticism and Scholarship* (Vol. I, 1793–1899, ed. Haven, Haven and Adams; Vol. II, 1900 to present, ed. Crawford and Lauterbacht, 1976, 1983).

The Bollingen Edition of Coleridge's writings (*The Collected Coleridge*) published under the general editorship of Kathleen Coburn will, together with her edition of the *Notebooks* (1957–, four volumes so far published), and the *Collected Letters*, ed. E. L. Griggs (six volumes, 1956–71), constitute the standard edition of Coleridge's works.

# INDEX OF TITLES AND FIRST LINES

First titles are shown in bold italic type

# POETRY
# IN EVERYMAN

## A SELECTION

### Silver Poets of the Sixteenth Century

EDITED BY
DOUGLAS BROOKS-DAVIES
A new edition of this famous
Everyman collection **£6.99**

### Complete Poems

JOHN DONNE
The father of metaphysical verse in
this highly-acclaimed edition **£4.99**

### Complete English Poems, Of Education, Areopagitica

JOHN MILTON
An excellent introduction to
Milton's poetry and prose **£6.99**

### Selected Poems

JOHN DRYDEN
A poet's portrait of Restoration
England **£4.99**

### Selected Poems

PERCY BYSSHE SHELLEY
'The essential Shelley' in one
volume **£3.50**

### Women Romantic Poets 1780-1830: An Anthology

Hidden talent from the Romantic era,
rediscovered for the first time. **£5.99**

### Poems in Scots and English

ROBERT BURNS
The best of Scotland's greatest lyric
poet **£4.99**

### Selected Poems

D. H. LAWRENCE
A newly-edited selection spanning
the whole of Lawrence's literary
career **£4.99**

### The Poems

W. B. YEATS
Ireland's greatest lyric poet
surveyed in this ground-breaking
edition **£6.50**

**£5.99**

**£4.99**

**£3.50**

---

## AVAILABILITY

All books are available from your local bookshop or direct from
**Littlehampton Book Services Cash Sales, 14 Eldon Way, LinesideEstate,
Littlehampton, West Sussex BN17 7HE.** PRICES ARE SUBJECT TO CHANGE.

To order any of the books, please enclose a cheque (in £ sterling) made payable to
Littlehampton Book Services, or phone your order through with credit card details (Access,
Visa or Mastercard) on 0903 721596 (24 hour answering service) stating card number and
expiry date. Please add £1.25 for package and postage to the total value of your order.

# PHILOSOPHY AND RELIGIOUS
# WRITING IN EVERYMAN

## A SELECTION

### An Essay Concerning Human Understanding
JOHN LOCKE
A central work in the development of modern philosophy **£4.99**

### Philosophical Writings
GOTTFRIED WILHELM LEIBNIZ
The only paperback edition available **£3.99**

### Critique of Pure Reason
IMMANUEL KANT
The capacity of the human intellect examined **£6.99**

### A Discourse on Method, Meditations, and Principles
RENE DESCARTES
Takes the theory of mind over matter into a new dimension **£4.99**

### Philosophical Works including the Works on Vision
GEORGE BERKELEY
An eloquent defence of the power of the spirit in the physical world **£4.99**

### The Social Contract and Discourses
JEAN-JAQUES ROUSSEAU
Rousseau's most influential works in one volume **£3.99**

### Utilitarianism/OnLiberty/Considerations on Representative Government
J. S. MILL
Three radical works which transformed political science **£4.99**

### Utopia
THOMAS MORE
A critique of contemporary ills allied with a visionary ideal for society **£2.99**

### Ethics
SPINOZA
Spinoza's famous discourse on the power of understanding **£4.99**

### The Buddha's Philosophy of Man
Ten dialogues representing the cornerstone of early Buddhist thought **£4.99**

### Hindu Scriptures
The most important ancient Hindu writings in one volume **£6.99**

### Apologia Pro Vita Sua
JOHN HENRY NEWMAN
A moving and inspiring account of a Christian's spiritual journey **£5.99**

---

## AVAILABILITY

All books are available from your local bookshop or direct from
**Littlehampton Book Services Cash Sales, 14 Eldon Way, LinesideEstate, Littlehampton, West Sussex BN17 7HE.** PRICES ARE SUBJECT TO CHANGE.

To order any of the books, please enclose a cheque (in £ sterling) made payable to Littlehampton Book Services, or phone your order through with credit card details (Access, Visa or Mastercard) on 0903 721596 (24 hour answering service) stating card number and expiry date. Please add £1.25 for package and postage to the total value of your order.

# ESSAYS, CRITICISM AND HISTORY IN EVERYMAN

## A SELECTION

### The Embassy to Constantinople and Other Writings
LIUDPRAND OF CREMONA
An insider's view of political machinations in medieval Europe
**£5.99**

### The Rights of Man
THOMAS PAINE
One of the great masterpieces of English radicalism **£4.99**

### Speeches and Letters
ABRAHAM LINCOLN
A key document of the American Civil War **£4.99**

### Essays
FRANCIS BACON
An excellent introduction to Bacon's incisive wit and moral outlook **£3.99**

### Puritanism and Liberty: Being the Army Debates (1647-49) from the Clarke Manuscripts
A fascinating revelation of Puritan minds in action **£7.99**

### History of His Own Time
BISHOP GILBERT BURNET
A highly readable contemporary account of the Glorious Revolution of 1688 **£7.99**

### Biographia Literaria
SAMUEL TAYLOR COLERIDGE
A masterpiece of criticism, marrying the study of literature with philosophy **£4.99**

### Essays on Literature and Art
WALTER PATER
Insights on culture and literature from a major voice of the 1890s **£3.99**

### Chesterton on Dickens: Criticisms and Appreciations
A landmark in Dickens criticism, rarely surpassed **£4.99**

### Essays and Poems
R. L. STEVENSON
Stevenson's hidden treasures in a new selection **£4.99**

**£3.99**

**£4.99**

---

## AVAILABILITY

All books are available from your local bookshop or direct from
**Littlehampton Book Services Cash Sales, 14 Eldon Way, LinesideEstate, Littlehampton, West Sussex BN17 7HE.** PRICES ARE SUBJECT TO CHANGE.

To order any of the books, please enclose a cheque (in £ sterling) made payable to Littlehampton Book Services, or phone your order through with credit card details (Access, Visa or Mastercard) on 0903 721596 (24 hour answering service) stating card number and expiry date. Please add £1.25 for package and postage to the total value of your order.

# CLASSIC NOVELS
# IN EVERYMAN

## A SELECTION

### The Way of All Flesh
SAMUEL BUTLER
A savagely funny odyssey from joyless duty to unbridled liberalism **£4.99**

### Born in Exile
GEORGE GISSING
A rationalist's progress towards love and compromise in class-ridden Victorian England **£4.99**

### David Copperfield
CHARLES DICKENS
One of Dickens' best-loved novels, brimming with humour **£3.99**

### The Last Chronicle of Barset
ANTHONY TROLLOPE
Trollope's magnificent conclusion to his Barsetshire novels **£4.99**

### He Knew He Was Right
ANTHONY TROLLOPE
Sexual jealousy, money and women's rights within marriage – a novel ahead of its time **£6.99**

### Tess of the D'Urbervilles
THOMAS HARDY
The powerful, poetic classic of wronged innocence **£3.99**

### Wuthering Heights and Poems
EMILY BRONTE
A powerful work of genius – one of the great masterpieces of literature **£3.50**

### Tom Jones
HENRY FIELDING
The wayward adventures of one of literatures most likable heroes **£5.99**

### The Master of Ballantrae and Weir of Hermiston
R. L. STEVENSON
Together in one volume, two great novels of high adventure and family conflict **£4.99**

£3.99

£2.99

£3.99

---

## AVAILABILITY

All books are available from your local bookshop or direct from
**Littlehampton Book Services Cash Sales, 14 Eldon Way, LinesideEstate, Littlehampton, West Sussex BN17 7HE.** PRICES ARE SUBJECT TO CHANGE.

To order any of the books, please enclose a cheque (in £ sterling) made payable to Littlehampton Book Services, or phone your order through with credit card details (Access, Visa or Mastercard) on 0903 721596 (24 hour answering service) stating card number and expiry date. Please add £1.25 for package and postage to the total value of your order.

# MEDIEVAL LITERATURE
# IN EVERYMAN

## A SELECTION

### Canterbury Tales
GEOFFREY CHAUCER
EDITED BY A. C. CAWLEY
The complete medieval text with translations **£3.99**

### Arthurian Romances
CHRÉTIEN DE TROYES
TRANSLATED BY D. D. R. OWEN
Classic tales from the father of Arthurian romance **£5.99**

### Everyman and Medieval Miracle Plays
EDITED BY A. C. CAWLEY
A fully representative selection from the major play cycles **£3.99**

### Fergus of Galloway: Knight of King Arthur
TRANSLATED BY D. D. R. OWEN
Scotland's own Arthurian romance **£3.99**

### The Vision of Piers Plowman
WILLIAM LANGLAND
EDITED BY A. V. C. SCHMIDT
The only complete edition of the B-version available **£4.99**

### Sir Gawain and the Green Knight, Pearl, Cleanness, Patience
EDITED BY A. C. CAWLEY
AND J. J. ANDERSON
Four major English medieval poems in one volume **£3.99**

### Six Middle English Romances
EDITED BY MALDWYN MILLS
Tales of heroism and piety **£4.99**

### Ywain and Gawain, Sir Percyvell of Gales, The Anturs of Arther
EDITED BY MALDWYN MILLS
Three Middle English romances portraying the adventures of Gawain **£5.99**

### The Birth of Romance: An Anthology
TRANSLATED BY JUDITH WEISS
The first-ever English translation of these fascinating Anglo-Norman romances **£4.99**

### Brut
LAWMAN
TRANSLATED BY ROSAMUND ALLEN
A major new translation of the earliest myths and history of Britain **£7.99**

### The Piers Plowman Tradition
EDITED BY HELEN BARR
Four medieval poems of political and religious dissent – widely available for the first time **£5.99**

### Love and Chivalry: An Anthology of Middle English Romance
EDITED BY JENNIFER FELLOWS
A unique collection of tales of courtly love and heroic deeds **£5.99**

---

## AVAILABILITY

All books are available from your local bookshop or direct from
**Littlehampton Book Services Cash Sales, 14 Eldon Way, LinesideEstate,
Littlehampton, West Sussex BN17 7HE.** PRICES ARE SUBJECT TO CHANGE.

To order any of the books, please enclose a cheque (in £ sterling) made payable to
Littlehampton Book Services, or phone your order through with credit card details (Access,
Visa or Mastercard) on 0903 721596 (24 hour answering service) stating card number and
expiry date. Please add £1.25 for package and postage to the total value of your order.